Blue & Gray NAVIES

Blue & Gray

THE CIVIL WAR AFLOAT

NAVIES

Spencer C. Tucker

NAVAL INSTITUTE PRESS
Annapolis, Maryland

The latest edition of this book has been brought to publication with the generous assistance of Marguerite and Gerry Lenfest.

Naval Institute Press
291 Wood Road
Annapolis, MD 21402

First Naval Institute Press paperback edition published 2022.

ISBN 978-1-68247-899-8 (paperback)

The Library of Congress has cataloged the hardcover edition as follows:
Tucker, Spencer, 1937–
Blue and gray navies : the Civil War afloat / Spencer C. Tucker.
    p. cm.
Includes bibliographical references and index.
ISBN 1-59114-882-0 (alk. paper)
1. United States—History—Civil War, 1861–1865—Naval operations. 2. United States. Navy—History—Civil War, 1861–1865. 3. Confederate States of America. Navy—History. I. Title.

2006016646

E591.T825 2006
973.7'5—dc22

All maps in the text are the work of the author.

Printed in the United States of America on acid-free paper

9 8 7 6 5 4 3 2 1

For my brother, John R. Tucker,
with love and great appreciation

Contents

Preface

UNTIL RECENT YEARS, books on the naval aspects of the Civil War were few and far between. Studies treating the war at sea were completely overshadowed by those on the land war. The public has been fed a steady diet of biographies of land commanders, studies of campaigns and battles, and unit histories. The result has been a decidedly unbalanced treatment of the war, and the view that the naval war mattered little. If the general public has any knowledge of the war at sea it tends to be about such events as the battle between the *Monitor* and *Virginia* or the activities of the Confederate commerce raider *Alabama* on the high seas. This is unfortunate, for the U.S. Navy played a vital role in the Union victory by isolating the Confederacy through an extensive coastal blockade and in conducting combined arms operations, especially along the great western rivers.

The last major broad treatment of the naval Civil War has been Ivan Musicant's *Divided Waters* (1995). While Musicant covers all major campaigns and chief battles, his book largely ignores logistics and amphibious operations along the Atlantic seaboard. Increasing numbers of books have appeared on specialized topics, however. Robert Browning's *Success Is All That Was Expected* provides important insight into the workings of the South Atlantic Blockading Squadron and is a worthy addition to his earlier study of the South Atlantic Blockading Squadron. Other wider studies worthy of note include the complementary William N. Still's *The Confederate Navy: The Ships, Men and Organization, 1861–65* and Donald Canney's *Lincoln's Navy: The Ships, Men and Organization, 1861–65*. There has been a spate of important biographies of naval commanders, such as David G. Farragut, Franklin Buchanan, Andrew Foote, David D. Porter, and Samuel F. Du Pont. Recent biographies of lesser figures include works on William Cushing and Charles W. Read. There are important new social histories, such as Dennis J. Ringle's *Life in Mr. Lincoln's Navy*, Steven J. Ramold's *Slaves, Sailors, Citizens: African Americans in the Union Navy*, and Michael Bennett's *Union Jacks: Yankee Sailors in the Civil War*, an important study of the sailors of the Union Navy. James Conrad's new book, *Rebel Reefers*, treats the organization and midshipmen of the Confederate Naval Academy.

New ship studies include William N. Roberts's *USS New Ironsides in the Civil War* and David A. Mindell's *War, Technology, and Experience Aboard the USS* Monitor. Thanks to its recent salvaging, there are also a number of books treating the Confederate submarine *H. L. Hunley*.

Diaries and recollections by participants in the war have also been published, including George M. Brooke's *Ironclads and Big Guns of the Confederacy: The Journal and Letters of John M. Brooke*, John W. Grattan's *Under the Blue Pennant, or Notes of a Naval Officer, 1863–1865*, and James and Patricia McPherson's *Lamson of the* Gettysburg: *The Civil War Letters of Lieutenant Roswell H. Lamson*. And there are interesting new books on specialized topics, such as Chester G. Hearn's *Ellet's Brigade* and David Surdam's *Northern Naval Superiority and the Economics of the American Civil War*. I have made use of these here as well as relying on many standard earlier works, especially the *Official Records of the War of the Rebellion*, still a highly useful source for official reports and correspondence.

I am especially grateful to Dr. Paul Wilderson, former executive director of the Naval Institute Press, for suggesting that I undertake this study. This is my fourth book with the Naval Institute Press, and it has always been a pleasurable process. Even with 145,000 words, however, it is impossible to treat all aspects of the naval Civil War. I have tried to provide a full discussion of the strategies North and South, a lively narrative of the war at sea and on the inland waters to include the key battles, and a discussion of the changing technologies. I have endeavored to include short sketches of the leading players as well as some eyewitness accounts.

It is rare in history for one service to win a war on its own, and the Civil War is no exception. I have sought to emphasize joint army-navy operations, and how the fighting on land and sea either complemented or worked against one another.

In presenting the story of the naval Civil War I have chosen to move more in large chronological blocks by chapter. This, rather than a straight chronological treatment, seems to provide the best flow, and I hope it makes it easier for the reader to follow events.

I am very appreciative of those individuals who read and commented on parts of the manuscript, including naval historian Mr. Jack Greene, my brother, Mr. John R. Tucker, and Civil War specialist Dr. Steven E. Woodworth. Ms. Beth Queman drew the excellent maps from material I provided to her. As always, I am especially grateful to my wife, Dr. Beverly Tucker, for her forbearance and patience regarding my writing projects, her judicious editing, her many helpful suggestions, and her encouragement.

Spencer C. Tucker

Introduction

UNTIL THE CIVIL WAR, the United States was largely an inconsequential naval power, this despite the fact that it was one of the world's leading trading nations. At sea during wartime the young nation had pursued what is known as the *guerre de course*. There are two basic strategies at sea: the *guerre d'escadre* and the *guerre de course*. The *guerre d'escadre* refers to squadrons or battle fleets of the largest ships fighting major engagements with enemy fleets to secure command of the sea. In the eighteenth century, the largest warships were the three-masted ships of the line. Such ships usually mounted sixty to one hundred guns, with the workhorse of the period in the Royal Navy being the third-rate seventy-four. Ships of the line were so named because they were sufficiently powerful in construction and armament to stand in the line of battle that characterized naval warfare of the time. This tactic took advantage of the fact that almost all heavy ship guns were mounted in broadsides. Opposing battle fleets usually sailed in stately, line-ahead formation with the ships banging away at the counterpart enemy battle line, often at dueling pistol range. The first American ships of the line to be commissioned in U.S. service were not authorized until during the War of 1812, but did not get to sea until after the end of that conflict.

The second strategy, the *guerre de course*, implied a concentration on the destruction of enemy seaborne trade, carried out by smaller warships operating either in concert or independently. Such ships included fast frigates and the smaller sloops and brigs, as well as privately-owned ships known as privateers. The latter sailed under special commissions issued by their governments in time of war, authorizing them to capture enemy ships, be they warships or merchant ships. Although the attendant risks were great, sizable fortunes could be made in such activity, and a great many American privateers took to the seas in the Revolutionary War and the War of 1812.

Until 1775 the American colonies enjoyed the protection of the Royal Navy. In that year, when the War for American Independence began, the rebellious colonies found themselves confronting the world's most powerful navy. The new nation had extensive shipbuilding experience, ample supplies of naval stores, and limited amounts of ordnance with which to arm warships, but a fleet would have to be created from scratch, and meanwhile the powerful Royal Navy had control of the American coasts. The Patriot side created and sent to sea at least three separate naval forces during the war: the Continental Navy, the state navies, and privateers.

At the beginning of the war, and without authorization from the Congress, Continental Army commander Gen. George Washington commissioned armed ships to attack British supply ships in the Atlantic. He hoped thereby to deny supplies to the British Army in North America, while securing them for his own army, which was chronically short of virtually everything of military value. In October 1775, meanwhile, Congress took the first steps toward a navy with the creation of a "Naval Committee" to draw up regulations and to secure and equip ships for sea. In November the Continental Navy acquired its first warships: two ships and two brigs.

Other merchant ships were also purchased and converted to warships, but the Continental Navy remained small. The largest American ships in commission during the conflict were thirteen Continental Navy frigates. Authorized by Congress at the end of 1775, they mounted eighteen, twenty-four, or thirty-two guns each. The Americans built only one ship of the line, but the seventy-four-gun *America* was never commissioned in Continental service; in 1782 the government presented it as a gift to France.

During the war, the Continental Navy enjoyed little success at sea, although there were commanders of note and a few spectacular engagements. The best known occurred in September 1779 when Capt. John Paul Jones, commanding the converted ex-Indiaman *Bonhomme Richard*, defeated the British frigate *Serapis* in one of the most sanguinary single-ship engagements in the Age of Fighting Sail.

All thirteen colonies, save Delaware and New Jersey, also created their own navies. These forces were quite small, being limited almost entirely to coastal craft engaged in defensive operations. They accomplished little during the war.

In contrast, a large number of American privateers took to the sea. During 1776–83 the Continental Congress issued letters of marque for 1,697 privateers mounting 14,872 guns and manned by 58,400 crewmen. The state governments added many additional ships. Massachusetts alone may have authorized as many as 1,000. Although a number of these were probably duplications, the United States sent to sea during the war at least 2,000 privateers carrying some 18,000 guns and manned by 70,000 men. Indeed, the draw of privateering was such that it became difficult to secure seamen for the regular navy.[1]

Privateers carried the bulk of the naval war for the infant republic. Along with Continental Navy ships, privateers attempted to capture British military transports and cargo ships but also to take as prizes British civilian ships wherever they could be found. The overall national goals were to disrupt British trade and drive up insurance rates in order to create powerful opposition to the war from the merchant classes. These were precisely the aims of the Confederacy during the Civil War when it sent out commerce raiders to attack Union merchant ships.

Just how effective were the American privateers against Britain during the War for Independence? During the conflict, they captured some 3,087 British ships. A number of these were retaken, leaving 2,208 in American hands. The Americans also took 89 British privateers, of which 75 remained in American hands. (British privateers captured 1,135 American merchantmen of which 27 were retaken or ransomed. The British also captured 216 American privateers.) These figures compare with a total of 196 ships captured by the Continental Navy. In addition to the important arms and stores taken, American privateers and Continental Navy ships may have taken prisoner as many as 16,000 British seamen, compared to 22,000 British soldiers taken by the Continental Army during the war. Estimates vary widely as to the monetary value of the prizes taken, from a low of $18 million to as much as $66 million. British insurance rates soared as much as 30 percent, and the premium for merchant ships sailing without convoy was 50 percent.[2]

The most important force at sea for the United States during the war was not American at all, but the French Navy. France entered the contest in early 1778. Its navy, second in the world only to that of Britain, not only posed the threat of invasion of Britain but transported essential military supplies and French troops to America. The French also won the war's most important strategic sea victory, the September 1781 Battle of the Chesapeake that made possible the October land victory of Yorktown, in which one-third of the British Army in North America surrendered to American and French forces. Although the war continued another two years, the Battle of Yorktown led London to adopt a strategy of cutting its losses.

Following the end of the war in 1783, Congress sold off the entire navy. In order to practice their profession, naval officers such as John Paul Jones were obliged to join the service of other nations, such as France or Russia. The United States limped along without a regular naval establishment until 1794. In that year under the twin pressures of merchant shipping losses to the North African (Barbary) states of Algiers, Tunis, and Tripoli and being caught in a naval war between France and Britain, Congress passed an act calling for the construction of six frigates.

This act of 1794 effectively marked the birth of the U.S. Navy. The new frigates included some of the most famous ships in American history, among them the *Constitution, President*, and *United States*. They entered service beginning in 1797 and were the most powerful of their class in the world. They and converted merchant ships of the new U.S. Navy enjoyed success not only in a brief undeclared naval war with France (the Quasi-War of 1798–1801) but also, after some fits and starts, in fighting against Tripoli during 1801–5.

Following victory over Tripoli, Congress reverted to the now-established U.S. practice of downsizing the military establishment. President Thomas Jefferson (1801–9), ironically the only U.S. president to spend more money on the navy than the army, cut the size of the navy dramatically. In April 1806 Congress authorized the president to maintain in service such frigates and other warships as he considered necessary but also restricted to only 928 the total number of seamen and boys to man them. This came at a time of increasing tension with Great Britain over maritime matters, but Jefferson and Secretary of the Treasury Albert Gallatin shrank from the expense of a larger navy and feared that such a force would actually encourage hostilities with Britain or France.

Jefferson chose to rely on a defensive system of seacoast fortifications and flotillas of small gunboats to protect the nation's harbors and coastal communications. Ultimately Congress authorized up to 160 of these gunboats, mounting only one to two guns each. Even in the best of circumstances, the gunboats would not be able to contest an enemy naval force employing a loose blockade, and they suffered from numerous drawbacks from a tactical point of view as well. Although the gunboats did prove useful in shoal waters along the Gulf and Atlantic coasts during the War of 1812, against large warships even a number of them operating together were all but useless.[3]

In June 1812 the United States declared war on Britain. The issues were chiefly maritime: the impressment of U.S. seamen into the Royal Navy and the British government's orders in council that restricted U.S. trade and led to the confiscation of American merchant ships. Other issues included the American desire to annex Upper Canada and British support for the Indians of the Old Northwest. Despite at least a decade of acrimony with the British leading up to the war, the U.S. Navy on the eve of the "second war of independence" was, by any standard, minuscule. Jefferson's successor, President James Madison (1809–17), planned to contest Britain not on the high seas but rather in a land invasion of Canada.

In many ways, the War of 1812 was a repeat of the War for Independence, only this time there was no direct assistance from France. On the seas the Royal Navy enjoyed even greater domination than in 1775. It could put to sea 130 ships of the line and 600 frigates and smaller ships. But in the eleven years before the war, the United States had not added a single frigate (let alone a ship of the line) to its navy, while several frigates had been allowed to decay into uselessness. For all practical purposes, the navy numbered but nine frigates, six of which were in commission; three sloops; three brigs; four schooners; and sixty-two gunboats. Many ships listed in service actually needed extensive repairs, and few were ready for sea. Another three frigates (two of which were unseaworthy), four bomb vessels, and some one hundred gunboats were in ordinary (reserve status).[4]

Fortunately for the United States, Britain was then waging war against France, and it was 1813 before the Royal Navy could shift substantial naval assets to North America. In the meantime, much to the surprise and chagrin of the British, the U.S. Navy won a series of single-ship engagements. In dramatic encounters, the *Constitution* defeated the frigate *Guerriere* and pounded the frigate *Java* into a useless hulk; the sloop-of-war *Wasp* defeated the *Frolic*; the *Hornet* sank the *Peacock*; and the frigate *United States* took the frigate *Macedonian*. Too late Congress passed appropriations to increase the size of the navy by four ships of the line and seven heavy frigates. Unfortunately for the republic, this construction would not be completed until after the conclusion of hostilities.

In 1813, when sufficient British warships had arrived on station to impose an effective coastal blockade, the U.S. Navy was for all practical purposes confined to port. Only occasionally did a warship escape the blockade, as with the *Constitution* near the end of the conflict. Thus the situation at sea for the United States in 1813–14 was much as it had been during the War for Independence, with the British able to move land forces virtually at will. The navy did experience success on inland waters, however. In September 1813 the Americans won the Battle of Lake Erie, securing control of that important lake, and in September 1814 the navy was also victorious at Plattsburg on Lake Champlain, turning back a powerful British land invasion from Canada. These two inland victories fortified the backdoor of the United States.

Once again the Americans waged a *guerre de course* on the high seas, utilizing both naval ships and privateers to prey on British shipping. Of 22 U.S. Navy ships, 18 were engaged in commerce warfare, and these took 165 prizes. Of 526 registered privateers, only some 200 engaged in extended operations on the high seas, taking 1,344 prizes. This effort grew in intensity during the conflict, for 1,054 of the prizes were taken in the last eighteen months of the war, an average of 2 per day. Again, British insurance rates soared. Although the commerce raiding activities could not win the war for the United States, they did produce a strong financial incentive for Britain to conclude peace.[5]

Immediately after the ratification of the December 1814 Treaty of Ghent that ended the war, Commo. Stephen Decatur sailed with a nine-ship U.S. Navy squadron to the Mediterranean to punish Algiers for having seized American merchant ships. Decatur captured two enemy warships before Algiers even knew of American intentions, and he dictated peace in a matter of weeks. After Decatur threatened the other Barbary states of Tunis and Tripoli, they also agreed to respect U.S. merchant trade in the Mediterranean.

The navy's performance during the War of 1812 and Algerine conflict endeared it to the American public, and in April 1816 Congress passed the Gradual Increase Act. The first real naval construction act in the nation's peacetime history, it came at a time when there was no major foreign threat to the United States. The act called for the creation of a permanent naval force of nine 74-gun ships of the line, twelve 44-gun frigates, and three steam-powered coast defense batteries. This would have meant a navy of some consequence. The first ships of the line in the U.S. Navy were the 74-gun *Independence, Washington,* and *Franklin.* Authorized during the War of 1812, these three *Independence*-class ships entered service in the second half of 1815.[6]

Economic reality soon forced retrenchment, however. The postwar boom that had helped fuel the Gradual Increase Act gave way to an economic recession, and Congress cut military programs and slashed naval building appropriations in half. Heavier ships that had been completed were soon placed in ordinary, with available funding to be used only for securing timber, and actual construction deferred until the need for the ships arose. Another ship of the line, the *Colombus*, was commissioned in 1819. Others authorized in April 1816 and completed were the *North Carolina* (1825), *Delaware* (1828), and *Ohio* (1838). The *Pennsylvania* (1841) was, at 120 guns, the largest sailing ship ever in the U.S. Navy; when launched, it was the most powerful warship in the world. The *Alabama, New York, Vermont,* and *Virginia* were completed ready for launch but were kept in reserve until they might be needed. The *Vermont* and *New Hampshire* were launched and commissioned during the Civil War, but as store/receiving ships.[7]

The U.S. Navy, although it remained small, was formed into semi-permanent squadrons and regularly dispatched to various parts of the world, with its chief duty the protection of commerce. The most important of these remained the Mediterranean Squadron, maintained until the Civil War. A West Indies Squadron also came into being in the early 1820s to end the piracy in the Caribbean that followed the collapse of Spanish authority in Latin America. Having accomplished its mission, it was absorbed into the new Home Squadron.

U.S. warships also sailed into the Pacific to help protect U.S. trade in that ocean. The East India Squadron secured "most-favored nation" status for the United States in China. Other U.S. squadrons protected American interests off both Brazil and West Africa. In the latter case they worked with the Royal Navy in enforcing a ban against the international trade in African slaves. In July 1853 Commo. Matthew Perry arrived in Tokyo Bay, Japan, with four "black ships." He returned the next February with an even more powerful squadron, this time to Yokohama. Following elaborate negotiations, Perry concluded a treaty that led to the opening of two treaty ports and Japanese assurances of fair treatment for shipwrecked American sailors.

The navy also carried out important voyages of exploration, survey, and scientific discovery. These included Lt. Charles Wilkes's six-ship Exploring Expedition in the Pacific during 1838–42. Lt. Matthew Fontaine Maury made significant contributions to the study of oceanography. His system of charts and records of currents greatly reduced sailing times on the world's oceans.

There were few wars involving the navy between the War of 1812 and the Mexican War of 1846–48, but during 1836–42 the U.S. Navy and Marine Corps participated in the fighting against both the Seminole and Creek Indians. The navy did play a critical role in the Mexican War. It blockaded the Mexican coasts, maintained the long water supply and communication lines between the United States and Mexico, made possible army amphibious operations on both coasts, and conducted riverine operations. The Mexican Navy posed no threat; it had only two warships of consequence, the steamers *Guadaloupe* and *Montezuma*, both of which Britain repossessed at the start of the war.

Commo. David Conner's Home Squadron quickly secured control of the Gulf of Mexico. As was the case in the Barbary Wars and would be for the U.S. Navy early in the Civil War, operations were initially handicapped by a shortage of shallow-draft ships capable of working in coastal waters and in rivers. Nonetheless, the U.S. naval blockade was an important source of political and economic pressure on the Mexican government. The navy also protected U.S. commerce against Mexican privateers and ensured that no large quantities of war supplies reached Mexico during the war.

The U.S. Navy's most dramatic role in the war, however, occurred in supporting the army's landing at Veracruz. In March 1847 in the largest U.S. amphibious operation before World War II, sixty-five "surf boats" shipped in transports put ashore in twenty-four hours Maj. Gen. Winfield Scott's entire army of twelve thousand men with artillery, horses, vehicles, and supplies. Once Veracruz had been secured, Scott struck out for the interior and Mexico City. In a brilliant campaign in which his forces in large part lived off the land, he took the Mexico capital in September. Peace was concluded five months later.

The U.S. Navy had reason to be proud of its accomplishment. As with the U.S. Army, the war provided valuable training in blockade and amphibious operations for its junior officers, many of whom held senior command positions during the Civil War. The Mexican conflict also conclusively proved the reliability and efficiency of steamships over those of sail.

No major conflicts occupied the United States in the period between the Mexican War and the Civil War. U.S. naval forces did participate in fighting in China in concert with the British. Acting to protect U.S. interests, in

November 1856 Capt. Andrew H. Foote of the sloop *Portsmouth* led an attack on the Chinese barrier forts below Canton. The United States also mounted a punitive expedition against Paraguay, Washington dispatching a powerful squadron to the La Plata River in 1859. And the navy continued its involvement in scientific work and exploration.

The half century before the Civil War saw considerable administrative and educational changes in the navy. Although at first the navy was headed by the secretary of war, in 1798 a civilian secretary of the navy, appointed by the president, took charge. In 1815, on the recommendation of Secretary of the Navy William Jones, Congress authorized the creation of a Board of Navy Commissioners, the result of a recommendation from senior naval officers even before the war for an entity to advise the secretary on the performance of his duties. The board consisted of three post-captains appointed by the president and confirmed by the Senate; it was entirely subordinate to the secretary of the navy and roughly analogous to the British Lords of the Admiralty.

With the greater complexities that came with steam propulsion and iron ships, in 1842 the navy instituted a system of five bureaus, each headed by a serving officer: Yards and Docks; Construction, Equipment, and Repairs; Provisions and Clothing; Ordnance and Hydrography; and Medicine and Surgery. The bureau chiefs oversaw the day-to-day running of the navy, with no single officer charged with advising the secretary on the conduct of naval operations. The rise of steam power also led in 1837 to the introduction of a new category of officer, the engineer. In contrast to British Navy practice, the engineer was from the beginning a commissioned officer, although he fulfilled staff duties.

The quest for professionalism in the officer corps that marked this period also led to changes in officer education. Training of midshipmen had often been haphazard, with this usually aboard the ships to which they were assigned. The quality varied dramatically, according to the degree of attention paid to it by individual captains. Midshipmen thus trained then prepared for their examinations, after which they became "passed midshipmen," eligible when vacancies occurred for promotion to lieutenant. In order to train naval officers to basic standards with a common body of knowledge, in 1845 Secretary of the Navy George Bancroft, a historian and educator, secured establishment of the Naval Academy at Annapolis. It was a considerable improvement.

The half century before the Civil War also saw rapid change in naval technology, and although it was small, the U.S. Navy was one of the world's leaders in this process. Steam power, shell guns, and ironclad ships all transformed naval warfare. Steam engines had been introduced in ships early in the nineteenth century, but at first they were highly inefficient and broke down frequently. Despite these shortcomings, the importance of steam power, especially in riverine warfare and for maneuvering during battle, was undeniable. But warships mounted their heaviest guns in broadside, and the large paddle wheels of the early steamers masked up to a third of these weapons. Also the half of the paddle wheel out of the water at any time was extraordinarily vulnerable to enemy fire. Despite these shortcomings, even traditionalists among the naval officers came to appreciate the ability of steam as an auxiliary power source for maneuvering in conditions of contrary wind or no wind at all.

The U.S. Navy was the first in the world with a steam-powered warship. Robert Fulton's *Demologus* (later the *Fulton*) of 1815 was a catamaran with a central paddle wheel located between thick twin hulls to protect it from enemy fire. Fulton designed his steam warship as essentially a floating battery that mounted powerful guns behind thick bulwarks. Specifically intended to defend New York harbor, under steam power it could move at about five and a half knots. In 1837, with other navies experimenting with steam, the U.S. Navy launched a second steam warship, the *Fulton II*.

Because early steam engines were so inefficient and because relatively little fuel could be carried, steam warships retained sail rigs, a practice continued well past the Civil War, indeed to the end of the nineteenth century. The *Fulton II* was schooner rigged with four funnels in pairs. An unsuccessful design, it was too small for its guns and not sufficiently powerful for ocean operation. Eventually the *Fulton II* became a gunnery training ship.

In 1842, largely thanks to the ability of the *Fulton II*'s captain, Matthew C. Perry, to promote steam warships, the U.S. Navy took a temporary lead over other navies with its side-wheelers *Mississippi* and *Missouri*. At 3,220 tons displacement, these were the largest U.S. warships to that time. Although the *Missouri* succumbed to fire in 1843, the *Mississippi* had an exceptional service record, proving the value of steam propulsion in warships during the Mexican War and serving as the flagship of Perry's squadron in the opening of Japan. The *Mississippi* remained in service well into the Civil War, when it was destroyed in

U.S. Navy sidewheel frigate Mississippi. Naval Historical Center (NH 60656)

March 1863 by Confederate shore batteries at Port Hudson, Louisiana, ironically in the very river for which it was named.

The screw propeller, credited both to Francis Petit Smith of England and John Ericsson of Sweden, helped overcome many of the objections to steam propulsion for warships. More efficient than the paddle wheel because the entire propeller remained underwater, it was also protected from enemy fire. The U.S. Navy steam sloop *Princeton* was the world's first propeller-driven warship. It incorporated a number of other firsts, including being the first warship with its machinery below the waterline (where it would be protected from enemy shot) and the first to have a telescoping funnel. The *Princeton* entered service in 1843. Ericsson designed its power plant and propeller, and Capt. Robert F. Stockton was responsible for the hull and sail rig. The *Princeton* incorporated the change to an armament of fewer and more powerful guns capable of firing both spherical shot and explosive shell.[8]

In the 1830s explosive shell came into general use at sea. Solid shot had been the principal projectile at sea for centuries. It was used to hole an enemy ship, wound and destroy spars and masts, and inflict personnel casualties. But wooden warships with thick oak sides could absorb a tremendous number of hits. Even if it penetrated, shot tended to leave regular rounded holes easily plugged by a ship's carpenter, especially as wooden fibers tended to close after shot had passed through. In any case, it required many such holes at the waterline to sink a wooden warship, and such losses were rare unless a wounded ship succumbed to weather conditions. Occasionally, ships were lost through the explosion of their magazines. Ships also might be captured as a consequence of heavy personnel casualties that made them vulnerable to boarding, or from damage to masts, spars, and rigging that rendered them immobile and subject to be being raked by an enemy ship (whereby the opposing warship could position itself perpendicular to its opponent and bring all of its broadside guns to bear on the length of the enemy ship, whereas the latter could reply only with the few guns at its bow or stern). The antipersonnel effects of solid shot occurred when it struck wood and produced showers of splinters. This was greatest when the force of the shot was only slightly more than that required to pass through the wood. Not infrequently, however, round shot penetrated one side of a ship and exited the other without inflicting serious damage.

Shell was designed not to penetrate the hull of a wooden ship but to move at a relatively slow velocity in order to lodge and then explode in the side of a ship, causing an irregular hole that would be both difficult to patch and large enough that it might even sink the ship. Shot had greater accuracy and range, but shell was much more destructive. Shell was slow to gain acceptance, in part because early fuses were not reliable and often exploded their charges too soon.

Indeed, most early shell at sea was fired from special warships, known as bombards or "bombs." In British and American sea service, the most common "bombs" mounted 10-inch or 13-inch mortars (meaning that they fired a shell of that diameter) and were used to lob shells in a high arc against strong points ashore. Such firing was often accomplished with the gun crews behind protective barriers. That shells often exploded too early is seen in the British bombardment of Fort McHenry in 1814, when Francis Scott Key observed "the bombs bursting in air."

Despite its shortcomings, shell was undeniably effective at sea against wooden ships, as was definitively demonstrated during the Battle of Sinope (Sinop) in November 1853, when a Russian squadron destroyed a Turkish fleet at anchor. The Russians fired both shot and shell, but shell inflicted the greatest damage. Sinope led both to interest in shell and to protecting wooden ships from its effects by applying iron armor plate.

The United States might have had the world's first ironclad warship in John Stevens's ironclad steam battery, funded by Congress in 1842. When John Ericsson emigrated to the United States, he brought with him a powerful new gun of his design, the "Oregon," the shot of which could penetrate the projected armor of the Stevens battery. This necessitated the ship's redesign to take heavier iron plate, but the ship was never completed, not even during the Civil War, and was finally broken up for scrap.[9]

Ultimately, the French and British navies led in ironclad development. The French were the first to commission an ironclad warship. During the Crimean War (1854–56) French Emperor Napoleon III ordered construction of ironclad steam-powered batteries. In October 1855 three of these *batteries flottantes cuirassées* (armored floating batteries), protected by a 4-inch iron plate over wood, carried out an attack on Russia's Kinburn forts in an estuary at the mouth of the Dnieper and Bug rivers. Although sustaining little damage themselves, the *Dévastation, Lave,* and *Tonnante* effectively destroyed the five Russian forts. Some observers concluded that the engagement marked the passing of the old wooden ships of the line.

The world's first ironclad seagoing warship was the French *La Gloire* of 1859, but it was basically a wooden ship protected by 4.5-inch iron plate and was not capable of sustained operations at sea. Designer Dupuy de Lôme later admitted as much. Spurred by this French move, however, the British used their advanced metallurgical technology to produce a far superior ship, the armored frigate *Warrior*. It entered service in 1861. Essentially of iron construction, the *Warrior*'s vitals were protected by 4.5-inch plate and, unlike the *La Gloire*, the British ship was designed for sustained sea service. The *Warrior* began a new era in warship construction, and other navies eventually followed its example.[10]

Ship armament also underwent substantial change. The many smaller broadside guns gave way to fewer but larger guns, usually mounted in pivot to increase their arc of fire. At the same time, some guns were developed exclusively to fire shell. The French took the lead in this with the experiments conducted by Gen. Henri Paixhans at Cherbourg in the 1820s. Because shell was fired with reduced charges, these guns could be made considerably lighter than shot guns, which meant that guns of the same weight could fire a much larger shell. In effect, the weight of metal fired by a warship in broadside might actually be increased at the same time that the weight of its ordnance was reduced, a revolutionary development.

To provide a wide firing arc, the new heavy guns tended to be located along the ship centerline in more exposed positions. To protect the crews, British Capt. Cowper Coles developed the naval gun turret. In 1855 during the Crimean War, Coles devised an armored raft, the *Lady Nancy*, for inshore operations against the Russians in the shallow Sea of Azov. After the war Coles developed his gunhouse design, which featured angled sides, but the breakthrough resulted from a suggestion by his friend I. K. Brunel that he place a railway turntable under the gunhouse. By 1858 the Coles turret, now a plain cylinder mounted on a roller path (Ericsson's Civil War *Monitor* employed a central pivot in its turret), was ready for trials. The Royal Navy found that the turret had real advantages, especially for the new, heavier guns, and adopted it for the coast assault ships *Royal Sovereign* and *Prince Albert*, ordered in April 1862. The first use of a turret in actual warfare, however, occurred in Hampton Roads the previous month when the USS *Monitor* fought the CSS *Virginia*.

Danger always lurked aboard ship in the form of an explosion of a gun because of the era's relatively primitive metallurgical knowledge. On 28 February 1844, one of the *Princeton*'s two great 12-inch guns, the wrought-iron "Peacemaker," ordered by Captain Stockton and manufactured in the United States, exploded when it was fired during a demonstration cruise in the Potomac River. President John Tyler was aboard the ship at the time but was spared injury as he was below during the blast. Among the eight dead were Secretary of the Navy Thomas W. Gilmer and Abel P. Upshur, former secretary of the navy and now secretary of state. The event led to a Navy Department decree sharply reducing powder charges for guns, a regulation still in effect during the Civil War engagement between the *Virginia* and the *Monitor* that probably affected the battle's outcome.[11]

The positive side to the "Peacemaker" explosion was that it led to the production of stronger and more reliable ordnance. Lt. John Dahlgren of the U.S. Navy was one of the world leaders in this. He developed an entire system of highly reliable heavy smoothbore guns about which much more will be said later. It is ironic, however, that the Dahlgren smoothbores, developed to project shell against wooden ships, were often employed during the Civil War to fire solid shot against Confederate ironclads.

The world's navies also experimented with rifled guns. The greater accuracy of these was obvious. Rifling had been in use in individual firearms for several centuries. The technique involved cutting spiraled lands and grooves into the inside of the barrel, which imparted spin to the projectile when it was fired, producing both greater range and accuracy than with a smoothbore weapon. The projectile had to fit very tightly in the bore and thus rifles took much longer to load than smoothbores, so they were not the mainstay of eighteenth-century infantry tactics that stressed maximum firepower at short distances. Nonetheless, rifled small arms had great value, and the Continental Army employed specialized units of riflemen with great effectiveness during the War of Independence, as in the Saratoga Campaign.

Applying the rifling technique to large-bore weapons with their considerably larger charges was much more difficult, especially as the strain on the metal was far greater for rifled guns than for smoothbores. Rifled guns fired an elongated projectile that had to fit very tightly in the bore. Because this projectile was heavier than round shot of comparable diameter and was in greater contact with the barrel, it developed more friction. Under the strain of the reduced windage (the distance between the projectile and the bore), any bore imperfections could burst the gun. For all these reasons, serious efforts to apply rifling to cannon had to await improvements in metallurgy in the 1820s.

The advantages of longer range, greater projectile penetration, and more accurate fire were nonetheless tempting. These advantages were, however, in large part offset by the effects of the blowing up of a gun, which could be especially disastrous in the close confines of a ship. An example of this came during the siege of Island No. 10 during the Civil War in 1862, when an old army 42-pounder converted to a rifle burst on board the U.S. ironclad *St. Louis*, killing or wounding fifteen officers and men.

Rifled guns were also hard to aim accurately on the heaving deck of a ship under way and could not fire in ricochet. The latter was important at sea because gunners were routinely instructed to fire low for fear that shot would go high and miss the target ship entirely. Ricochet fire also greatly increased the range of shot; on hitting the water, the round ball from a smoothbore gun would continue on line to the target, whereas a rifle projectile might take off at any angle. Early rifle projectiles also tended to tumble in flight. Finally, rifled guns were very expensive.

Pioneering rifled guns included the Swedish Wahrendorff, the Sardinian Cavalli, and the British Lancaster. The first two were unsatisfactory breechloaders, but the muzzle-loading Lancaster offered promise. The British and Americans expressed the weight of guns at sea in three sets of numbers: hundred weights (cwt) of 112 pounds, quarters of 28 pounds, and individual pounds, and the Lancaster weighed some 95 cwt (10,640 pounds). It had an elliptical eight-inch bore with spiraled one-quarter rotation rifling and a range of some 5,600 yards. The British employed Lancaster guns to shell the Russian port of Sebastopol during the Crimean War. Demonstrating the danger inherent in early rifles, two Lancasters burst during an attack on the Russian Kinburn forts. Other British rifled guns included the Armstrong, Whitworth, and Blakely, all of which were purchased and employed by the Confederacy during the Civil War. In part because of the Crimean War experience, there was renewed interest in large rifled guns at sea, but these were not part of U.S. Navy ordnance until the Civil War.

In many ways, the Civil War proved to be both a testing ground for, and the culmination of, a host of new technologies. This was certainly true at sea. As will be seen, both the Union and Confederate navies, especially the latter as the weaker naval power, embraced technological change in the hopes that it might turn the tide of war.

Blue & Gray NAVIES

CHAPTER ONE

The Union and Confederate Navies

———~∿∿~———

Organization, Personnel, and Shipboard Life

THE U.S. NAVY

The U.S. Navy underwent dramatic expansion during the Civil War, from 42 ships in commission in March 1861 to 671 ships by 1865. Personnel underwent similar growth. Between 1861 and 1865 the number of officers increased from 1,300 to 6,700, while seamen went from 7,500 to 51,500. In the same period, annual naval expenditures leapt tenfold, from $12 million to $123 million.[1]

President Abraham Lincoln headed the Union war effort on land and sea. Largely self-educated, his military experience was sharply limited, consisting of service as a militia captain in the 1832 Black Hawk War; even then he had not seen combat. Although he made a spate of poor military appointments, Lincoln had the capacity to learn from his mistakes and, from the very beginning, a firm grasp of what would be required to win the war. He was interested in all branches of the government, but for the most part his military attention was centered on the army.

Lincoln and his secretary of the navy, Gideon Welles, enjoyed an excellent relationship. Assuming his post on 7 March 1861, Welles had the final decision on ship construction, purchases, and conversions. He also determined the broad outlines of naval policy, and he oversaw the conduct of actual operations. Born in Connecticut in 1802, Welles had been a newspaper editor, lawyer, and Connecticut legislator. For three years during 1846–49 he had been chief of the Naval Bureau of Provisions and Clothing. Welles took an active role in the effort to elect Lincoln to the presidency in 1860 and was rewarded by being named the New England representative in the new president's cabinet.

Although his naval experience was limited, Welles was certainly one of Lincoln's best appointments. Hardworking, fair-minded, honest, and generous in his praise of others, he easily overcame his lack of specialist knowledge. A strong proponent of a naval blockade of the Confederate coasts, Welles also became an advocate of ironclad construction. Welles was an avid diarist, and his recollections, published in 1911 well after his death, provide important insight on key strategic decisions and person- alities of the war. For the most part, Welles had a free hand in running the Navy Department, although Lincoln occasionally intervened, as when the president secured the appointment of Rear Adm. John Dahlgren to replace Rear Adm. Samuel Du Pont in command of the South Atlantic Blockading Squadron.[2]

In administering the Navy Department, Welles had the able assistance of the energetic Gustavus Vasa Fox. Hailing from Massachusetts, Fox had entered the navy in 1838 as a midshipman. Rising to lieutenant in 1852, he had resigned that same year to command mail steamers, and in 1856 he had entered private business. Having developed Republican connec- tions (his brother-in-law was the politically powerful Montgomery Blair of Maryland, who became postmaster general in the Lincoln cabinet), Fox joined the Navy Department in May 1861 as chief clerk; that August he moved up to the new post of assistant secretary. Fox worked well with Welles, handling much of the day-to-day department administration and leaving the secretary free to set policy.

Regarding subjects he himself was not knowledgeable about, Welles often established boards to study the problem. Such was the case with the Blockade Strategy Board and the Ironclad Board, with the former becom- ing a strategic planning staff. Welles also overhauled and reorganized the Navy Department administration. He established the post of assistant sec- retary and pushed for an increase in the number of staff bureaus to eight, which Congress approved in July 1862. The bureaus were Yards and Docks; Equipment and Recruiting; Navigation; Ordnance; Construction and Repair; Steam Engineering; Provisions and Clothing; and Medicine and Surgery. Under Welles, the department was also largely free of corruption and graft.[3]

Examining boards met during the war and forced into retirement ineffective officers and advanced the notion of promotion on merit alone. The navy also systematized officer ranks. Most of these administrative changes remained in place long after Welles's departure in 1869.

U.S. Secretary of the Navy Gideon Welles. U.S. NAVAL INSTITUTE PHOTO ARCHIVE

Given its vast expansion in a short span of time and the enormous pressures of the war, the Navy Department functioned remarkably well. Nonetheless, there were problems, chiefly the result of the bureau system. Each bureau operated as a virtually independent entity, irrespective of the needs of other bureaus or the overall interests of the navy. The most notable failure of the department in the war could be laid to this system. This was Fox's championing of monitors in the creation of a Monitor Bureau, despite the obvious advantage of more effective ship types. The worst example of the fixation on monitors was the light-draft monitor program debacle late in the war.

Welles's first task on becoming secretary was to call home overseas ships. He promptly dissolved the Mediterranean, Brazil, Pacific, East Indian, and African squadrons. In the beginning of the war, Welles dispatched most of his available ships to begin the blockade of the long Confederate coastline from northern Virginia to Brownsville, Texas. The ships were organized into three squadrons: the Home Squadron, based at Fortress Monroe; the Coast Blockading Squadron (soon redesignated the Atlantic Blockading Squadron), with the Potomac Flotilla (centered on the Potomac and Rappahannock rivers and charged with the defense of Washington); and the Gulf Coast Blockading Squadron. The Atlantic Blockading Squadron was responsible for enforcing the blockade all the way from Alexandria, Virginia, to Key West, Florida, a distance of some one thousand miles. The Gulf Coast Squadron covered the even greater distance from Key West to Brownsville.

Given the vast distances involved, in October 1861 Welles further divided the squadrons. He separated the Atlantic blockaders into two: a North Atlantic Blockading Squadron, responsible for the Virginia and North Carolina coasts, and a South Atlantic Blockading Squadron for the Southern coastline from South Carolina to Key West. In February 1862 Welles also divided the Gulf Coast Blockading Squadron, making four Federal blockading squadrons in all. The East Gulf Coast Blockading Squadron patrolled from Cape Canaveral on the Atlantic coast of Florida to St. Andrews Bay on the Florida Gulf Coast. The West Gulf Coast Blockading Squadron was responsible for the Southern coast from St. Andrews Bay to Brownsville.

There was also an important Union flotilla in the Western Theater, operating in conjunction with army forces on the Tennessee, Cumberland,

and Mississippi rivers. The fact that this was conceived as basically an army show is shown in the fact that the flotilla initially was under the army, which purchased its vessels. Navy officers, however, commanded its ships. The western flotilla was transferred to navy control in October 1862.

Concern over the proximity of the U.S. Naval Academy at Annapolis, Maryland, led Welles in late April 1861 to order it relocated to Newport, Rhode Island. On 9 May 1861 the old sailing frigate *Constitution* and the steamer *Baltic* arrived at Newport with the academy's officers and midshipmen. The *Constitution* remained at Newport as a training ship, and the midshipmen were lodged both on it and in the hotel Atlantic House for the duration of the war. The academy's former buildings at Annapolis became an army post and hospital. At Newport, Naval Academy Superintendent Capt. George D. Blake introduced changes in the curriculum to include the study of analytical geometry, calculus, mechanical drawing, and chemistry. Although these changes remained in place, not a few officers in the navy looked askance at them, believing they sacrificed practical education. The academy relocated to Annapolis in May 1865.

There is disagreement among sources regarding the number of personnel in the Union Navy. Historian Raimondo Luraghi gives a figure of 11,412 officers, sailors, and marines at the beginning of the war, with 6,759 officers, 51,357 sailors, and 3,850 marines at its end. He also notes more than 84,000 Union enlistments in the navy in the course of the war, but historian Michael Bennett, who has done a thorough study of Union sailors in the war, places wartime enlistments at 118,044 men.[4]

The naval officer corps included not only deck officers, but also engineers, paymasters, and surgeons. The latter three categories were limited to the rank of lieutenant commander. In July 1861, as part of the expansion of the navy, Congress authorized creation of a naval volunteer officer corps. Toward the end of the war, it included 2,060 line officers, 1,805 engineers, 370 paymasters, and 245 surgeons.

In July 1862 Congress approved two formal ranks above captain for the first time in U.S. Navy history: commodore (one star) and rear admiral (two stars). Two new lower officer ranks were also authorized, those of ensign (for graduates of the Naval Academy) and lieutenant commander. This made the ranks, in descending order, rear admiral, commodore, captain, commander, lieutenant commander, lieutenant, master, ensign, and cadet. In 1864 yet another rank was instituted, that of vice admiral, with

David G. Farragut the first to hold it. (Three years later, in 1867, Farragut also became the nation's first full admiral.) In all, the U.S. Navy had 82 officers of flag rank (commodore and above) during the war.[5]

For the most part, both Union naval officers and their Southern counterparts performed capably during the war. Foreign service had provided many with a broader outlook and polish than their army counterparts. The officer corps also boasted strong ties of heredity. Rodgers and Porter were family names extending back to the very beginnings of the navy, and a number of family members enjoyed positions of influence in the Civil War.

One dramatic change during the war flowed from the sharp increase in steamships: a sharp increase in the number of engineering corps officers. Fortunately for the Union Navy, only 22 engineer officers elected to join the Confederacy (a much smaller percentage than deck officers who went South). By the end of 1861 there were 404 engineer officers in the navy, but by the end of the war this had risen to 2,277 (474 regulars and 1,803 volunteers).[6]

Although the total of 118,044 sailors pales next to the 2.2 million men who served in the Union armies, it is nonetheless a daunting number to study. In an important recent work, Michael Bennett analyzed information on every 25th "blue jacket" or "jack," as the seamen were known, in each U.S. Navy rendezvous or ship enlistment between April 1861 and April 1865. Bennett studied a total of 4,570 men, most of whom were in the blockading squadrons. His conclusions are startling. For one thing, Union sailors were older than their army counterparts. Their average age was twenty-six. Although no age statistics are available for the armies of the war, most scholars agree that the majority of soldiers on both sides in the war were under twenty-one. The Union Army alone reportedly had some 100,000 soldiers who were not yet fifteen.

Most Union sailors were easterners. New York State and New York City provided the largest number (35,164), followed by Massachusetts (19,983) and Pennsylvania (14,037). The western states produced but 12,375 enlistments. The sailors also differed significantly from their army counterparts in that they tended to be from the poor, working urban classes. In Bennett's sample, only 3 percent had made their living on farms before the war, whereas half of Union soldiers were from farms.[7]

Sailors also tended to be a rougher group of individuals and not as idealistic or as committed to the war effort as the soldiers. Whereas soldiers tended to join the service for patriotic, idealistic reasons, most native-born Americans who enlisted as seamen did so (after 1862) for the prosaic reasons of avoiding the draft and receiving regular pay, better food, and shelter. A U.S. Navy recruiting poster on the Ohio River proclaimed, "On board the Gunboats you have your meals regularly and are always at home."[8]

The navy also had larger percentages of foreign born personnel and African-Americans, including ex-slaves, most of whom joined for reasons of security. Whereas an estimated 75 percent of Union soldiers were native born, this was true of only 55 percent of sailors. Of the foreign born who enlisted in the navy, the largest number (20 percent) came from Ireland, whereas Irish immigrants formed just 7 percent of the Union Army. Ten percent came from Britain (only 2 percent of the Union Army).

Despite an 1813 law prohibiting noncitizens from joining the navy, a great many foreigners joined both Union and Confederate service. It is impossible to tell from the enlistment information just how many were naturalized American citizens. For some recent immigrants, enlistment was prompted by a sense of adventure, but for most it was simply financial security for men who were essentially unskilled. As Irish Seaman Patrick Meade put it: "Being without any trade, I had to work at anything that came up. I soon found out that there was nothing to be had by such occupation but hard knocks and abuse."[9]

Certainly, some were attracted by the fact that they could fulfill their patriotic duty by being less likely to see combat than in the army. While the Union Army lost roughly one in every fifteen recruits dead to disease, the Navy lost only one in forty. Death rates in combat were one in nine for the army but only one in sixty-five for the navy. In raw numbers, the Union Army lost some 380,000 soldiers, while the navy sustained about 2,110 killed.[10]

African-Americans constituted about 16 percent of U.S. Navy total strength during the war, or roughly nineteen thousand men. The navy attracted a number of African-Americans away from the army both because of higher wages and because of the expectation of more meaningful employment than the construction work performed by African-Americans in the Union Army. Also, unlike army units, ship crews were integrated. The navy offered equality in pay and such benefits as prize distributions, promotion, and better conditions. It did, however, restrict the African-Americans' tasks aboard ship. Perhaps surprisingly, in contrast to the army there were remarkably few racial incidents between white and African-American sailors.[11]

The most famous African-American of the war at sea was undoubtedly Robert Smalls. A South Carolina slave in 1861, Smalls worked as a wheelman on the two-gun 313-ton Confederate steamer *Planter* that functioned both as a dispatch boat and a transport. Smalls took the lead in a daring plan, executed on 13 May 1862, in which he, his family, and a crew of slaves (seventeen people in all) escaped Charleston in the *Planter*, delivering it and its cargo to the South Atlantic Blockading Squadron. Appointed a pilot in the U.S. Navy, Smalls became the captain of the now U.S. Navy *Planter* in 1863 and took part in the Union attack on Charleston. After the war he served first in the South Carolina legislature and then in the U.S. Congress.[12]

THE CONFEDERATE STATES NAVY

The Confederate Congress created the Confederate States Navy Department on 20 February 1861. The next day President Jefferson Davis appointed Stephen R. Mallory secretary of the navy. The Confederate Navy thus came into existence less than two months before the start of the war. Although the tasks facing the Confederacy at sea were formidable, Southern leaders envisioned only a small naval force. Davis's interest remained the army and, for the most part, he gave Mallory a free hand. The president attended Transylvania College but graduated from the U.S. Military Academy at West Point in 1828. Following seven years of frontier duty, Davis left the army as a first lieutenant to become a planter in Mississippi. Elected to Congress in 1845, he resigned his seat to serve as a colonel of volunteers in the Mexican War, distinguishing himself as a regimental commander in the Battle of Buena Vista. Davis was a highly effective secretary of war in the Franklin Pierce administration during 1853–57. Elected to the Senate in 1857, he resigned his seat on the secession of Mississippi and was elected provisional president of the Confederacy on 9 February 1861.

As commander in chief, Davis was handicapped both by his dogmatic, prickly personality and by his poor decisions regarding personnel appointments. Certainly, he did not understand the role a navy might play in securing a Southern victory and was in no rush to build and secure ships.

Confederate States of America Secretary of the Navy Stephen R. Mallory.
U.S. NAVAL INSTITUTE PHOTO ARCHIVE

Whereas the Union naval budget for 1861–62 represented about 9 percent of the total Federal budget, the budget for the South's navy was only about 4 percent of the total. In consequence, Mallory planned for a force of only about 3,000 officers and men. The top strength of the Confederate States Navy occurred in the spring of 1864, with 753 officers and 4,450 enlisted men. Marine Corps strength the same year totaled 749 officers and men. These figures represent about one-tenth of the U.S. Navy.[13]

Mallory may have been President Davis's best cabinet appointment. Born on the island of Trinidad in the West Indies in 1811, the son of a construction engineer from Connecticut, Mallory grew up in Key West, Florida. He began his professional career as a lawyer specializing in maritime cases and had served as a volunteer aboard a gunboat during the Second Seminole War of 1836–40. He then became collector of customs at Key West. Elected to the U.S. Senate from Florida in 1851, Mallory served on the Naval Affairs Committee, and in 1857 became its chairman. A staunch advocate of American naval power, he worked hard to improve the quality of the officer corps and to modernize its ships.

Mallory opposed secession but resigned his Senate seat in January 1861 when Florida left the Union. Davis knew Mallory from the Senate and, although Mallory brought the great political advantage of being from Florida, Davis appointed him primarily for his expertise in naval matters. The Confederate Congress approved the appointment on 4 March 1861.

In part because he got on so well with Davis, Mallory was one of only two Confederate cabinet officers to keep the same position throughout the war. The chain of command extended directly from Mallory to area naval officers. Only on rare occasion did Davis bypass Mallory and issue direct orders to commanders, as in April 1862 when he ordered obstruction of the Elizabeth River to prevent Union forces from retaking the Norfolk Navy Yard.[14]

The tasks facing Mallory were daunting. He had to figure out how to thwart the Union blockade both by combating the Union ships off the Confederate coasts and in running supplies through the blockade itself. Mallory also had to develop the means to defend the Confederate coasts, ports, and great interior rivers against a Union assault from the sea.

In the several months before the outbreak of fighting, Mallory dispatched individuals to purchase supplies in the North, as well as in Canada and Europe. He was a staunch advocate of commerce raiding, which he hoped would disrupt the North financially, divert Union warships from the blockade of Southern ports, and help bring an end to the war. With Southern shipbuilding facilities lacking, Mallory ordered his naval agents to Europe both to purchase cruisers and to contract for the construction of others.

Mallory's other chief goal was to acquire sufficient numbers of ironclad ships to break the Union blockade and to allow the Confederacy to take the offensive in attacking Northern ports. A strong advocate of technological innovation, Mallory established a Torpedo Bureau, which experimented with torpedoes (naval mines) and the means to deliver them against Union warships.

Mallory had his critics, both in the Confederate Navy and in Congress, including opponents of Davis who saw in his friend a way to attack the president. This criticism sharply increased following Confederate military reverses, including the loss to the Union of such key ports as New Orleans, Memphis, and Norfolk, as well as the scuttling of the ironclads *Virginia* and *Mississippi*. In fact, critics brought forward a bill to abolish the Confederate Navy and transfer its functions to the Army Department, and in August 1862 they also engineered a vote to censure Mallory personally. Both failed. A five-man committee of the Congress, although not from the Committee on Naval Affairs, did investigate the department's "inadequacy." Mallory did not have to testify and was cleared of any wrongdoing, but the proceedings both deeply hurt him and took a considerable amount of his time. In retrospect, given the situation and resources available, it is hard to see how anyone else could have performed more effectively in the post, and the chairman of the Congressional Committee on Naval Affairs, Albert Gallatin Brown, remained his strong supporter throughout the war.[15]

It says much about Davis as a leader that he criticized his loyal supporter. Chief of the Confederate Army Ordnance Bureau Josiah Gorgas noted in his diary that Davis "sneers continually at Mr. Mallory and his Navy and is at no pains to conceal his opinions before the secretary." Nonetheless, Mallory retained his post until his resignation on 2 May 1865. Briefly imprisoned by Federal authorities after the war, Mallory was released in March 1866 and returned to Florida to practice law.[16]

Unlike his Union counterpart, Mallory was always hard-pressed for cash, as was the case of course with the Confederate government generally. Unable, or unwilling, to finance the war through taxation, the Confederate Congress resorted to borrowing, which brought chronic and even ruinous inflation. As a result Mallory was never able to fund any program at the approved amount, and naval purchases abroad became increasingly problematic.

Mallory's task was also more difficult than that facing Welles in that Mallory had to establish all the Confederate naval institutions from scratch. It was natural that Southern authorities look to the U.S. Navy for inspiration, and Confederate naval organization was similar, and naval practices virtually identical, to those of the Union. The Confederate Navy *Ordnance Instructions*, for example, is a word-for-word copy of its Union counterpart.

Chief Clerk Edward M. Tidball assisted in handling the department's administration. Before the war, Tidball had been a clerk in the U.S. Navy Bureau of Ordnance and Hydrography. He turned out to be an excellent administrator. With the increase in responsibilities that flowed from Confederate naval activity, he was later joined by Second Clerk Z. P. Moses. The Confederate Navy did suffer from the lack of a counterpart to Fox in the Union Navy. Establishing the post of assistant secretary of the navy would have taken some of the day-to-day decision making from Mallory and rendered the department more efficient.

In March 1861 the Confederate Congress created four naval bureaus, known as offices. The Office of Orders and Detail, the most important of these, handled all personnel issues, including assignments. Its first chief was Capt. Franklin Buchanan, and at war's end it was headed by Capt. Sidney Smith Lee, older brother of Gen. Robert E. Lee. This bureau also had charge of the details of equipping ships. The Office of Ordnance and Hydrography, first headed by Capt. Duncan N. Ingraham, originally also oversaw the construction and repair of ships. The last two bureaus were the Office of Provisions and Clothing and the Office of Medicine and Surgery. John L. Porter was the South's naval constructor, although he did not receive formal appointment to the post until January 1864. He and his two assistants reported not to the bureaus but rather directly to Mallory.[17]

Originally, the Bureau of Ordnance and Hydrography had charge of naval mine warfare, but in October 1862 Mallory created the Torpedo Bureau specifically for this purpose, and largely under pressure from Matthew Fontaine Maury, who had charge of mine development at first for the state of Virginia. Mallory's initial skepticism, fueled by animosity between him and Maury, gave way to support when he saw the promise of this new weapon. When Maury traveled to Europe on special service in late 1862, Lt. Hunter Davidson proved to be a highly effective replacement, and by the end of the war the Confederacy had developed a number of successful types of naval mines.

The Confederate Navy operated as many as fourteen naval stations during the war. Included in its naval structure was an operational European command. In the summer of 1863, Mallory assigned Flag Officer Samuel Barron command of the newly formed European

Squadron. Operating from Paris, Barron had charge of Confederate commerce raiders in the Atlantic, then consisting of the *Florida* and *Georgia*. Unsuccessful in securing additional cruisers in Europe, Barron shifted his focus to the supervision of Confederate naval officers awaiting assignment to the few cruisers that were in operation.[18]

In early 1861 many U.S. Navy officers (although few of its sailors) were from the South. Some 43 percent of the 1,563 officers of the U.S. Navy (1,338) and Marine Corps (225) were Southerners. By June 1861 about one-fifth of these had resigned, including 16 captains, 34 commanders, 76 lieutenants, 5 midshipmen, and 106 acting midshipmen. The total of resigned officers, 321 (299 navy and 22 marines), is less, however, than the number of native-born Southerners, 350 (283 navy and 67 marines), who remained loyal to the Union cause. Also, no Southern officer ever managed to deliver his ship to the Confederacy.[19]

Because the Confederate Navy remained relatively small, Mallory did not have Welles's problem of having to secure a great many additional officers. Indeed, almost all Confederate Navy line officers had served in the U.S. Navy. Mallory's major officer problems were that he had too many senior officers and too few engineer officers. Despite efforts, Mallory never was able to end squabbling among his senior officers regarding command responsibilities.[20]

In officer ranks, the Confederacy continued the prewar U.S. Navy policy of conferring the courtesy title of commodore to those captains in command squadrons; but unlike the U.S. Navy during the war, commodore never became a formal rank. In April 1862 the Confederates made allowance for nine admirals and six commodores. In the course of the war, however, the Confederate States Navy commissioned just two admirals: Franklin Buchanan in August 1862 and Raphael Semmes in February 1865. Confederate ranks in descending order were rear admiral, commodore, captain, commander, first lieutenant, second lieutenant, master, and passed midshipman.[21]

As with the Union Navy, the Confederates distinguished between line and staff officers. Staff officers included naval surgeons, naval constructors, paymasters, and chief engineers. Such officers were not permitted to command afloat, save with special authority.[22]

In April 1862 the Confederate Congress voted to establish a naval academy with 106 acting midshipmen, traditionally known as "reefers." The project had Mallory's enthusiastic backing. On 15 May he detached the CSS *Patrick Henry* from the James River Squadron and ordered it converted into a school ship and stationed in the James at Drewry's Bluff, the largest and most important Confederate defensive works guarding the water approach to Richmond, Virginia. Placing the school there would provide additional man-power for the defenses should that prove necessary, and cabins erected ashore housed the overflow of midshipmen. Because the academy came under the Bureau of Ordnance and Hydrography, Cdr. John M. Brooke organized it. Lt. William H. Parker, former instructor in seamanship at the U.S. Naval Academy, was its first superintendent.

Faculty worked with the midshipmen both aboard the *Patrick Henry* and ashore in a curriculum closely modeled on that of the U.S. Naval Academy. The midshipmen ranged in age from fourteen to eighteen. Conditions at Drewry's Bluff were spartan, and Mallory was never able to secure adequate funding, but he rigorously defended the school against those who sought to utilize its resources in actual fighting. Yet budget shortfalls led to half the navy's midshipmen receiving their naval education aboard ship. Confederate midshipmen also saw extensive military service, participating in the February 1864 attack and capture of the U.S. gunboat *Underwriter* in the Neuse River, North Carolina, and of the U.S. sloop *Water Witch* in Ossabow Sound, Georgia, that June. At the end of the war the midshipmen served in the defense of the capital and then acted as a guard for $777,000 in gold and silver of the Confederate and Virginia treasuries that Confederate leaders hoped to prevent from falling into Union hands.[23]

Mallory had far more difficulty securing seamen than officers. Like much else in the prewar United States, shipbuilding and seafaring were principally located in the North, with relatively few Southerners attracted to the sea. Also, as the South had but a small percentage of the North's population, manpower was always in short supply, and army needs always took priority.

A large number of foreigners served in the navy. Historian William Still puts seamen of Irish birth or origin at nearly 17 percent. Many of English birth also signed on, especially on the commerce raiders. Thus, whereas its officers were native Southerners, the crew of the *Alabama* was essentially foreigners, chiefly British citizens. The crew ultimately included Dutch, French, Italian, and Spanish sailors. Captain Semmes recalled how, following the new cruiser's commissioning ceremony at Terceira in the Azores on

24 August 1862, he and his officers donned dress uniforms and mustered the British crews of the *Alabama* and the British ship *Bahama* that had brought out Semmes and the other officers. The *Alabama* had sailed with about sixty men and the *Bahama* with thirty. In a rousing speech to the assembled men, Semmes stressed not Southern nationalism but economic benefits, including double standard wages in gold and prize money from the Confederate Congress for any ships they destroyed. Semmes recalled, "I got eighty of these ninety men, and felt very much relieved in consequence."[24]

The Confederate cruisers recruited some men from among seamen on the prizes they captured. The *Florida* and other cruisers that were able to access Confederate ports had many more Southerners in their crews. Lt. John Maffitt, captain of the *Florida*, risked the Union blockade off Mobile, Alabama, in September 1862 in order to secure desperately needed crewmen and supplies, but the one hundred or so men he secured before sailing again in January 1863 were a mixed lot. Maffitt noted, "many rated as seamen who in the old service would merely pass as very ordinary O.S. [ordinary seamen]."[25]

Perhaps not surprisingly, free African-Americans served in the Confederate Navy. Slaves could do so, but only at the pleasure of their masters. The number of African-Americans was strictly regulated not to exceed 5 percent of a particular unit.

The best-known African-American in the Confederate Navy was Moses Dallas of Duval County, Florida. An elusive figure, Dallas was evidently a pilot in the Union Navy in 1863 who deserted to join the Confederates and earned both high praise and pay for his services as a pilot for the Savannah Squadron. One report had Dallas killed on the night of 2–3 June 1864 during the Confederate capture of the U.S. Navy sidewheeler sloop *Water Witch* and accorded a funeral at Confederate expense. But several months later a Moses Dallas from Duval County turned up in the 128th U.S. Colored Infantry, and after the war he returned to Duval County.[26]

LIFE ABOARD SHIP, NORTH AND SOUTH

Circumstances of service were remarkably the same in both navies, although more is known about Union sailors, in large part because more of their journals survive. To serve in the U.S. Navy a recruit had to be at least four feet, eight inches tall and be eighteen years old. No inexperienced men over age thirty-five were accepted, but men with naval experience were accepted to age thirty-eight. By regulation of 1863, boys could be enlisted at age thirteen, but strictly with parental consent.

Although some U.S. Navy enlisted personnel came from the U.S. Army, most notably in the case of the gunboats on the western waters, the vast majority of seamen enlisted at regularly recruiting stations, known as "rendezvous," and located at the naval yards and in seaport cities where recruits were likely to be found. Shortages of seamen led both sides to offer bounties for long-term enlistment. In the Union Navy, this could be as much as $300, or two years' pay, for a three-year enlistment. Bonuses were also paid for reenlistments. Early in 1862 the Confederate Navy offered a $50 bonus to any recruit enlisting for three years or for the duration of the war. The draft law passed by the Confederate Congress in April 1862 provided that any trained seaman in the army could apply for transfer to the navy; however, with the army refusing to release recruits and the demand high for trained seamen, in May 1863 the Congress passed a bill that required the army to release any seaman requested by the Navy Department who desired a transfer.

Enlistment times varied from as little as a month in critical need to as long as the duration of the war. Three years was a normal term of enlistment for the Union Navy early in the war. Prohibitions were in place against enlisting foreigners and the incompetent and "idiots," but as is true throughout history, recruiters often looked the other way. Although some Confederate enlisted personnel came into the navy through the traditional rendezvous method, most appear to have been drawn from the army.[27]

Both navies suffered from desertions, although no figures are available on the number. The number of deserters was sufficiently large in the U.S. Navy, however, to warrant for the department to hire detectives to try to chase down the culprits. Among the latter were "bounty jumpers," individuals who signed on, received a significant bounty payment, and then deserted at the first opportunity in order to repeat the process in another location and under a different name.

In the U.S. Navy a recruit was considered officially enlisted after he had signed a contract, commonly referred to as a "shipping article," in the presence of a commissioned officer. This included the recruit's date of enlistment; pay, with any advances and possible bounties; and rating.

Following his enlistment, the recruit reported to one of a number of receiving ships. These were obsolete vessels, several of them former ships of the line with space sufficient to accommodate up to one thousand men. They included the *Ohio* and *North Carolina*. The Confederates utilized for this purpose the old frigate *United States*.

During his short stay on a receiving ship, the recruit received a cursory physical exam and was issued his uniforms and eating utensils. In the U.S. Navy, the uniform issue might consist of a duffle bag in which to keep the clothes on board ship, a dark blue wool frock, a pair of white duck pants, a white shirt with blue collar, a pair of blue pants, a blue shirt with wide collar and white star worked into each corner, two pairs of wool stockings, undershirts and drawers, a black silk handkerchief to use as a rag, a pair of leather shoes, a canvas hammock with hair mattress, and a single or double blanket. The sailor's collar, or "jumper flap," originated as a means to prevent the uniform from being soiled, especially as sailors used tar to shape their hair into a pony tail, invariably soiling the uniform (and giving rise to the term of "tars" for sailors in general). By the time of the Civil War this flap had been permanently sewed into the uniform. A typical mess kit consisted of a metal cup, quart bucket, knife, spoon, and fork.

Sixteen-year-old U.S. Navy recruit Alvan Hunter described his three weeks on board the receiving ship *Ohio* as "boring," with little to do save clean his gear and perform routine ship maintenance. Other recruits, however, reported constant activity, including rudimentary training in military courtesy, knot tying, the parts of the ship and functions of ropes and rigging, and even some weapons work. Men had to be on guard regarding their possessions, as apparently there was a good deal of thievery, including of uniforms. The men had to purchase their uniforms with up to three months' pay, so clothing items were a favorite target for the unscrupulous.[28]

After an indeterminate stay on the receiving ship, the recruit received his permanent billet on a newly commissioned ship, one that had undergone refit, or a ship that had sustained personnel losses. Once the recruit arrived on his assigned ship, he learned about it and how it operated, his duties, and how to function as a member of the crew. On-the-job training included learning the names, maintenance, and working of the various rigging and sails, as well as regular gunnery drill.

Warships were divided into specific divisions and tasks for battle. The master's division was responsible for keeping the ship under way and for its maneuvering and rigging. The engineer's division operated the engines and repaired damage as required. The surgeon's division set up below deck, usually in the wardroom, and prepared to receive and treat any wounded. Gun divisions varied in number, depending on the ship, as did the number of men in a particular gun crew, depending on the size of the gun. The powder division was stationed in the magazine and was responsible for its security and safety. Headed by the ship's gunner, it supplied bags of cannon powder or cartridges to the ship's boys, one of whom was assigned to each gun.[29]

Warships had to be ready for action at all times and were thus manned twenty-four hours a day. Although most of the crew members were awakened at 4 AM, according to the ship's log, days officially began at noon and ended at that point the next day. Watches and activities varied somewhat from ship to ship, but generally the "morning watch" was from 4 AM to 8 AM; the "forenoon watch" from 8 AM to noon, when most of the crew had dinner; the "afternoon watch" from noon until 4 PM; and then two short watches, known as the first and second "dog watches," from 4 PM to 6 PM and from 6 PM to 8 PM, intended to allow time for each half of the ship's crew to have supper. "Evening watch" was from 8 PM to midnight, and "midwatch" from midnight to 4 AM.

Once he was assigned to a watch, a deck division sailor stood a four-hour watch, followed by four hours off and then four hours on watch again (two on the dog watches). Because of the extreme conditions of heat in which they worked, engineering division sailors stood four-hour watches, followed by eight hours off. A two-watch system kept half of the sailors immediately ready at any time, day or night. Each watch was further divided into divisions, each of which covered a major part of the ship, so that all areas of a ship were manned twenty-four hours a day.

Seamen fell into different categories. The youngest, aged fourteen (later thirteen) to seventeen, were known as "boys." They performed odd tasks aboard ship and often acted as servants to the officers. In combat, the boys, also known as "powder monkeys," delivered powder cartridge cases from the magazine to the gun crews.

"Landsmen" formed the largest number of enlisted men aboard ship. These unskilled recruits comprised perhaps half the crew of any given ship. Landsmen performed the bulk of the labor-intensive tasks, such as scrubbing and holystoning (a term said to be derived from English seamen who took bits of sandstone monuments from St. Nicholas Church, in Great

Yarmouth, England, to use to scrub the decks), cleaning the bright work aboard ship, and working the rigging. Landsmen were expected to learn on the job under the supervision of more skilled seamen.

"Ordinary seaman" were the next highest rating. They possessed nautical skills and achieved this rating by having served at sea for at least two years. "Seamen" would have served four years and had to pass an examination. They often assisted the petty officers and officers in training the landsmen.

"Petty officers" were the highest-ranking seamen aboard ship. All had major leadership responsibilities, supervising the seamen under the direction of the officers and providing a communications link between the officers and the enlisted men. Petty officers also played a key role in training the landsmen. The highest-ranking petty officer on board ship was the boatswain's mate (Bo'sun). Boatswain's mates signaled by pipe to the crew the commands given to them by the officers. Gunner's mates were second only to the boatswain's mates. They had charge of the ship's guns, ordnance stores, and magazines. Other petty officers included quartermasters, carpenters, coxswains, quarter gunners, and captains of various masts. The chief-appointed petty officer was the master-at-arms. Very much like a chief of police, he was charged with enforcing regulations on board ship, assisted by the marine guard and ship's corporals.[30]

In addition to the deck sailors associated with the age of sail, there was the new breed of men aboard ship identified with the age of steam. Ironclads in particular required significant numbers of engineering personnel, officers as well as enlisted men. Engineers made up 11 to 20 percent of the total on the steamers that had both sail and steam, but they formed about 40 percent of the crewmen of the new monitors. They were a larger percentage on these ships because of their absence of traditional sail rigs and the small number of guns to work. Engineering division enlisted personnel included firemen first-class, fireman second-class, and coal heavers. Firemen first-class supervised the operation of the boilers, steam engines, and associated equipment aboard a ship and made up about 20 to 25 percent of the engineering personnel. Firemen second-class had similar duties and made up perhaps 25 percent of the engineering personnel. The coal heavers were at the bottom of the engineering division and constituted the remainder of its personnel.

The fire room on a typical large steam warship had four vertical boilers, each of which held four furnaces. To achieve a speed of five knots without sails, the four boilers would consume thirty-four hundred pounds of anthracite coal per hour! To sustain a speed of six knots, a *Cairo*-class river ironclad consumed two thousand pounds of coal per hour. The physical work of sustaining such operations was thus very demanding.[31]

The Confederate Navy had much the same enlisted ranks. These were, in ascending order, boy, landsman, coal heaver, fireman second-class, ordinary seaman (at least one year of service at sea), and seaman (at least two years of sea service). As with the Union Navy, petty officer was the highest seaman rating.[32]

The new warfare waged under steam power brought new hazards. Regardless of training, there was no way to prepare for a boiler explosion or ruptured steam tubes. During the Battle of Plum Point Bend on the Mississippi River on 10 May 1862, Union rifled shells smashed into the boilers of the Confederate steamers *General Sumter, Colonel Lovell,* and *General Earl Van Dorn,* disabling them and releasing clouds of steam that killed more than one hundred Confederate crewmen. Another constant threat was injury or death from asphyxiation on board the monitors if the ventilation system failed, as happened on the *Monitor,* with near disastrous result, during its passage from New York to Hampton Roads in March 1862.

Although this varied from ship to ship depending in large part on the captain's whim, most warships had regular daily and weekly routines. The typical day began at 4 AM with reveille sounded by the ship's bugler. The men rolled and lashed their hammocks with rope, then carried them to the spar deck and placed them in the hammock rails atop the main bulwarks. Netting covered the hammocks, which were to provide modest additional protection against wood splinters and small arms fire in time of battle. The men then washed down and holystoned the decks. Other activities included washing clothes, polishing brass fixtures, and checking the ship's rigging. The first of many inspections throughout the day followed. Perhaps two-and-a-half hours into the day, the men had breakfast, after which they spent much of the day in training, practicing going to quarters and drilling in order to prepare for any eventuality, including fire on the ship. The men also trained with muskets, pistols, axes, pikes, and cutlasses both for boarding a hostile vessel or for repelling boarders.

One of the most important shipboard activities was certainly regular practice with the big guns, including running out and training them, as well as loading procedures. Occasionally the ship held live-fire practice, shooting at barrels dropped overboard, with competitions among the gun crews. The survival of the ship might well depend on the ability of the crew to deliver rapid and accurate cannon fire, and each man had an assigned place and specific duty to perform. Drills had to be sufficiently frequent to ensure close teamwork among the crew and optimum performance in the heat of battle.

Other activities might include painting (something was always in need of paint on the ship), coaling (a dirty and physically demanding task that required the participation of most of the crew), and routine maintenance and repairs. On Sundays there was church service, usually conducted by the chaplain or ship's commanding officer. Although attendance was not mandatory, it was encouraged.

Such routine activities were usually not hazardous. Far more dangerous was working aloft in the rigging and on the masts and spars, when sailors might be seventy-five to one hundred feet above the sea or the ship's deck. It was not an uncommon occurrence for men aloft to lose their footing and fall to the deck or into the sea, often with fatal result.

Following dinner, the afternoon saw additional work details, inspections, drills, a light supper, and another inspection. The normal day on board ship ended at 8 PM with the playing of tattoo. Nighttime was not a period to relax vigilance, particularly for Union ships on blockade duty, as blockade runners inevitably tried to use darkness to slip past the Union ships.

This routine might be broken by short periods of intense activity, such as the onslaught of bad weather or, if the ship was on blockade duty, the chasing of a blockade runner. Only infrequently did crews experience the extreme hazards of fighting to save their ship in a storm or actual combat with an enemy ship or shore battery. In fact, many sailors never experienced combat during the war.

The men spent such free time as was available to them washing, mending their clothing (regulations called for clothing to be inspected once a week), trying to sleep, writing letters home (or for a few, keeping diaries), reading (newspapers were especially sought after), or playing cards or other games. Occasional variety shows provided a welcome diversion. U.S. Navy Acting Ens. John W. Grattan on the *Minnesota* noted that in evenings there was often "singing or music fore and aft."[33]

Although living accommodations and conditions were much better for officers, all those aboard ship had to put up with a near total lack of privacy, as well as extremes of heat and cold, rain, and dampness within the ship. Dampness was especially a problem aboard the monitors, which had their crew accommodations below the waterline where the iron sides of the ship constantly sweated. A sickness rate of some 25 percent on board the monitors in 1863 prompted an investigation by a committee of the U.S. Sanitary Commission. Ventilation improvements helped, and reportedly the sickness rate dropped to just 5 percent by 1865. If anything, conditions on Confederate ironclads were worse, but their crews at least had the advantage of usually remaining in port with berthing ashore.[34]

Despite efforts to keep the ships clean, they were invariably infested with vermin of all sorts, including rats, lice, fleas, and roaches. Coastal blockaders also had to contend with omnipresent flies and mosquitoes. One sailor on a ship off New Orleans described an "abominable climate and atmosphere. . . . We are scorched through the day by the sun and at night we are oppressed by a sullen atmosphere and annoyed almost to distraction by bugs of all descriptions, including mosquitoes."[35]

The quality and quantity of food varied aboard ships, but in both the Union and Confederate navies it appears to have been quite plentiful and wholesome by the standards of the day. In July 1861, the U.S. Congress approved the following daily food ration for the navy:

> One pound of salt pork, with half a pint of beans or peas; one pound salt beef, with half a pound of flour, and two ounces of dried apples or other fruit; or three quarters of preserved [canned] meat, with half a pound of rice, two ounces of butter, and one ounce of desicated [dehydrated] mixed vegetables; or three quarters pound preserved meat, two ounces of butter, and two ounces of desicated potato; together with fourteen ounces of biscuits [hardtack], one quarter of an ounce of tea, or one ounce of coffee or cocoa, two ounces of sugar, and a gill [four ounces] of spirits [grog]; and a weekly allowance of a half a pound of pickles, half a pint of molasses, and half a pint of vinegar.[36]

Breakfast might consist of coffee and hard bread. Dinner was the main meal, the menu varying according to season and proximity to port. It

might be a combination of salt beef or pork, dried apples, dehydrated pota-
toes, rice, beans, vegetables, molasses, cheese, and butter. Supper was a light
meal. Although generally well-balanced and wholesome by the standards
of the day, shipboard fare sometimes spoiled from long storage and was
often accompanied by unwelcome worms, weevils, or cockroaches. One
welcome innovation that found its way to the fleet during the war was
canned meat. Hard, dry, baked "hardtack" crackers of flour, three inches
square and an inch thick, were the main source of carbohydrates.

This diet might be supplemented by packages from home, especially on
birthdays and Christmas, and the efforts of landing parties on an enemy
shore. Seamen on the western rivers had more opportunity to forage. A sailor
on the sternwheeler *Forest Rose* reported, "We left Natchez yesterday ... stopping at several plantations on our way up to procure forage. We succeeded
admirably, obtaining a good supply of vegetables and some poultry."[37]

The prescribed Union Navy diet was somewhat more ample than that
allocated for soldiers in the Union Army. Although sailors often did not
benefit from the proximity of fresh produce on land, in many respects
they enjoyed the benefits of a superior logistical system. Secretary Welles
made it a priority that the men receive "frequent supplies of fresh provisions and other necessities conducive to health," and a large number of
supply ships delivered every two or three weeks fresh meat, vegetables, and
ice, as well as mail, newspapers, spare parts, and replacement seamen to
the Union blockading vessels.[38]

Alcohol on board ship often posed problems. Seamen received a grog
ration at meal times, sometimes even at breakfast. Grog (half rum and half
water) was traditional in the naval service and grew out of the Royal Navy
practice of serving a mixture of half rum, half water twice a day, even to
ships' boys and midshipmen. In the U.S. Navy this usually meant rye
whiskey, which was cheaper than rum.

At the time liquor was both cheap and plentiful, and often water fit to
drink was hard to come by. Many Americans also believed that alcohol
had a positive health benefit in helping to prevent disease, but its only real
advantage was in helping to mask real feelings. As historian Christopher
McKee wrote about grog in the early sailing navy, "More often than not, it
was the best part of the meal and made the rest bearable."[39]

For many sailors, the grog ration was the most anticipated part of the day,
as life on board ship tended to be monotonous and dreary. In consequence,

there were more problems with alcoholism on board ship than among soldiers on land. Many did not exercise moderation. Union seaman Harry Browne expressed an opinion felt by many when he wrote of his shipmates, "All are great smokers and drinkers."[40]

For a number of seamen, drinking was already an important element of their lives. As one officer put it, the Union Navy was a "drunkards' asylum." Often in boarding another vessel, seamen sought out alcohol above all else. During the boarding of one seized blockade runner, sailors from the sloop *Brooklyn* became so drunk and difficult to control that an officer restored order only by slashing one man's throat with a sword.[41]

Flag Officer Andrew Foote led the crusade in the U.S. Navy for temperance. Beginning in 1831, seamen had been allowed to refuse their grog ration and receive a pay supplement in its stead. In July 1862, aided by the absence of Southern opposition and with the strong support of Secretary Welles, Congress passed and President Lincoln signed legislation abolishing grog aboard Union ships and mandating a five cents per day payment in its stead. The regulation went into effect on 1 September 1862.[42]

A number of sailors were quite displeased with the new regulation. One recalled the reaction of his shipmates:

> I well remember the day we received the news that grog was abolished. . . . Curses not so loud, but deep, were indulged in by old tars, some of whom, had seen years of service, and who, by custom, had become habituated to their allowance of grog, that the very expectation of it was accompanied by a feeling of pleasure. It was a long time before the men forgot the actions of congress, and in fact, they never ceased to talk about it.[43]

Fighting and gambling also caused problems on board ship. Thievery was rampant, and to help prevent it, the navy required the seamen to stencil their names into clothing. Nonetheless, Union Seaman Tim Finn noted, "you had to be on the lookout all the time or they would steal the Shirt off your Back." Union Seaman Chester B. DeWitt complained, "One cannot lay any thing down for a few minutes, but it is gone in the twinkling of an eye."[44]

Nonetheless, sailors could be extraordinarily generous on occasion, as in supporting a shipmate fallen on hard times. Union Lt. Francis Roe observed, "I never knew of an instance of a sailor hesitating to put his name on a charity subscription, or to share his purse even with a vicious comrade." White refugees as well as escaped slaves often were the beneficiaries of sailor kindnesses. Some sailors saw this as a form of atonement, one remarking, "Charity covers a multitude of sins."[45]

Major infractions on board ship were dealt with by summary court-martial proceedings. Convictions brought a wide variety of punishments. By congressional order, and much to the chagrin of many officers, the navy had abolished flogging in 1850. Afterward, the chief means of discipline on board ship were confiscation of pay and privileges, confinement in or without irons, solitary confinement on only bread and water, loss of liberty ashore, additional duties, and dismissal from the service with a bad conduct discharge.

Desertion remained a problem, even on board a successful ship at sea, such as the Confederate commerce raider *Alabama*. At almost every port it touched, seamen deserted that ship. Much to his surprise, Capt. Raphael Semmes of the *Alabama* discovered on board one of his captures George Forrest, a seaman from the first Confederate raider *Sumter*, who had deserted at Cádiz. He was promptly court-martialed and sentenced to serve on the *Alabama* for the duration of its cruise without pay or prize money, after which he was to receive a dishonorable discharge. Proving incorrigible, Forrest was again court-martialed, this time for drunkenness, and abandoned on Blanquilla Island off Venezuela.[46]

Pay was low for seamen, but there was always the hope of extra income from the capture of an enemy prize. Many sailors, in fact, enlisted in the false expectation of making their fortune in prize money, no doubt encouraged in this by recruiters. In fact, large sums were awarded only rarely. Once a prize vessel was condemned, all court costs were deducted from the sum as well as half the value of the prize and its contents, which went to the naval pension fund. Nonetheless, a rich prize taken by a small crew could produce remarkable results. In 1864 the Union tug *Eolus* captured the blockade runner *Hope*. Following distribution of the money, the cabin boy on the tug netted $432, a sum amounting to more than four years' pay.[47]

Although combat was infrequent for the sailors of the Civil War, when it did occur it could be both intense and traumatic. Later in the war, for Union ships close to Confederate-controlled territory there was also the constant threat of torpedo attack. Although casualties in a sea fight never approached those for land battles, such contests could be extraordinarily bloody in the close confines of the ship with a shell explosion or a ruptured boiler. Such engagements would smash the illusion held by many that by joining the navy they would escape the war without personal cost. Combat scarred a number for life and disillusioned others, who had already found much to complain about in conditions on board ship and the lack of prize money. It is safe to conclude that the happiest sailors during the war, be they Union or Confederate, were those on board ships that were returning home.

CHAPTER TWO

Resources, Facilities, Warships, and Naval Ordnance

⸺〰⸺

RESOURCES

The Civil War was the world's first industrial war. The North, superior to the South by virtually any economic measure, enjoyed tremendous advantages. At the time of American independence, North and South had been relatively equal in population, but slavery in the South, with which free men could not compete economically, led the large influx of immigrants to settle in the North. In 1861, the twenty-three Northern states had 22.3 million people, whereas the eleven seceded states of the South contained only 9.1 million (nearly 4 million of them slaves). In white males age fifteen to forty, the Union advantage was perhaps 4 million to 1.5 million. The North also had a much higher number of educated people, an important factor in waging modern war.

The North had some 85 percent of the prewar industrial capacity of the United States but produced 92 percent of its industrial goods and had a like percentage of the industrial workers. The entire South had less manufacturing capacity than New York City! The South also had no facilities for forging steel and was unable to construct machine tools, major liabilities in the age of machine war. In 1860, Northern states produced 93 percent of the nation's pig iron and manufactured 97 percent of its firearms. In 1860, very little of the North's industrial might was devoted to arms and related manufacturing. Although it would take time to mobilize its great industrial assets for military production, at least the resources were there.

The South possessed abundant natural resources, including substantial iron and coal deposits and vast amounts of timber, but facilities to transport the raw materials to manufacturing sites were inadequate. In 1861 the North had 21,827 miles of railroad; the South only 8,947 miles of track; and, with the South unable to manufacture or secure rails or steam locomotives in any number, its railroads continued to deteriorate throughout the conflict.

The North also had 82 percent of the prewar U.S. banking capital. Overall, the Northern economy was self-sufficient, whereas that of the South was export driven. The South exported agricultural goods, chiefly cotton but also rice and tobacco, in return for industrial goods, mostly from Great Britain.[1]

All these factors played out in the naval sphere. The North could build large numbers of technologically advanced ships, whereas Southern facilities to construct and repair ironclad vessels were lacking, and skilled labor was in short supply. Although the South accomplished much in many areas, it simply was not enough. Manufacturing limitations severely limited Southern naval construction and thus had a direct impact on strategy. Given these disparities, it is hardly surprising that the war turned out as it did.

FACILITIES

At the beginning of the war, the U.S. government operated eight navy yards. The original six were Washington, DC; Philadelphia; New York; Boston; Portsmouth, New Hampshire; and Norfolk (Gosport), Virginia. By the Civil War, two more had been added at Pensacola, Florida, and Mare Island, California. The Navy Department and Congress debated the merits of either New London, Connecticut, or League Island near Philadelphia for a new yard devoted exclusively to serve iron steam vessels, but sharp division over the exact location prevented action.

In the spring of 1862, Flag Officer Andrew H. Foote established a naval depot at Cairo, Illinois. Later, Mound City, Illinois, on the Ohio River became the most important naval station for Union ships on the western waters. Although Foote recommended a permanent yard in the West and the project was much discussed, Congress took no action before the end of the war.

To compensate for the loss of the Norfolk yard, seized by the Confederates in April 1861, the navy established a repair and supply station at Baltimore, Maryland. Nonetheless, the considerable distances from a naval station for the ships of the South Atlantic Blockading Squadron prompted one of the earliest U.S. Navy operations of the war, against Port Royal, South Carolina. Port Royal became the chief station of the South Atlantic Blockading Squadron. After the Union secured New Orleans, the navy also organized a station there.[2]

At the beginning of the conflict, all prewar yards save Pensacola were in Union hands, and the Confederacy acquired the Norfolk yard on the secession of Virginia. Pensacola and Norfolk were not long in Southern hands, however; Federal troops took back both in May 1862.[3]

The Union yards were soon working to capacity. They readied ships then in ordinary for active service, repaired and refitted ships, and built new ships. With only limited capacity for shipbuilding, their chief role was operational support. The New York yard was by far the most important. Located in a key manufacturing center with abundant skilled labor, in a one-year span it repaired some 150 ships. All the yards underwent moderate expansion during the war, but the vast majority of new Union warships were constructed in civilian facilities.

The seceded Southern states had only limited construction and repair facilities, and the yards they did briefly control were never utilized to full capacity. On secession, Southern state militias seized the Federal arsenals on their territory as well as many of the key coastal forts, including Moultrie in Charleston Harbor, Fort Pulaski off Georgia, Forts Gaines and Morgan in Mobile Bay, Caswell near Wilmington, North Carolina, and St. Philip and Jackson below New Orleans. Of the Federal naval yards, the Confederacy initially secured only Pensacola. Of only modest size and little more than a coaling and repair station, it was in any case effectively neutralized by the Federal occupation and reinforcement of Fort Pickens on Santa Rosa Island and by a Union blockading squadron that closed off Pensacola Bay. With the significant Union threat to the western Confederacy that followed the capture of Forts Henry and Donelson, officials in Florida decided to give up part of the west Gulf Coast, and in May 1862 the Confederates evacuated and burned the Pensacola facility, whereupon Federal troops from Santa Rosa occupied it.

The Norfolk Navy Yard was a different story. The largest of the prewar yards, it boasted a dry dock and extensive stores, shops, and a number of ships were there undergoing repair or in ordinary. Union forces did, however, retain Fortress Monroe at the entrance of Hampton Roads and held it throughout the war. It proved a useful enclave and staging area.

UNION SHIPS

In March 1861, the U.S. Navy numbered only ninety ships. Most were in ordinary or serving as receiving ships; only forty-two ships were actually in commission. Twenty-three of these were steamers; the other nineteen relied entirely on the wind for their propulsion. Thirty of the forty-two ships in commission were scattered across the globe, in Asia, South America, and Africa. Four ships were at Pensacola, and, apart from the paddle steamer *Michigan*, which remained on the Great Lakes during the war, only four were in Northern waters: three at New York and one at Washington. Although the U.S. Navy did possess some fine steam screw propeller-driven warships in the *Merrimack*-class frigates and *Hartford*-class sloops, the number of ships available was totally inadequate for the task at hand. The North would require many more ships if it was to fulfill its naval goals.

Most U.S. Navy ships were deep-draft and unsuited to coastal operations. The Lincoln administration soon ordered construction on what would ultimately be more than 200 new warships. It also purchased 418 civilian ships for conversion into warships. By the end of the war the U.S. Navy numbered 671 ships of all types, totaling 510,396 tons and armed with 4,610 guns. By 1865 it was the world's second largest navy, behind only that of Great Britain. It counted 113 screw steamers and 52 paddle-wheeler steamers especially constructed for naval purposes; 71 ironclads; 323 steamers, either purchased or captured, fitted for naval purposes; and 112 sailing ships of all kinds. The vast majority of the Union fleet, 559 ships, were steam-powered. All this constitutes a remarkable accomplishment.[4]

During the war the Federal Navy built or converted ships for four primary purposes. First, the navy required a large number of steamships to maintain the blockade of the Confederate coasts. Second, it required fast, powerful cruisers to chase down and destroy the Confederate commerce raiders on the high seas. Third, shallow-draft ships were required for joint riverine operations with the Union Army in the Western Theater. Finally, ironclad ships were necessary to counter Confederate ironclad construction; later they would be sent to attack Southern coastal forts, such as those at Charleston and Mobile.

Secretary Welles's most pressing task was to secure ships for the Union blockade to prevent the South from exporting its agricultural products and importing military and industrial finished products. Even assuming all ninety U.S. Navy warships could be brought into service and pressed into blockade duties, this would mean only one ship for nearly forty miles of Confederate coastline. Welles immediately initiated a large naval construction program. In this he relied heavily on Chief of the Bureau of Construction, Equipment, and Repairs John Lenthall and Chief Engineer Isherwood.

Bringing new ships on line would take considerable time, and, to meet the needs of immediate service, government purchasing agents scoured the Northern ports to purchase ships that could be modified for naval use.

In 1861 the United States had the world's second largest merchant marine, behind only Great Britain. Cotton was the largest single prewar commodity carried in American ships, and now with the blockade and uncertainty of war, a great many of these ships were lying idle and available, including large numbers of steamers. Naval agents were soon purchasing these ships.

Quickly concluding that ship owners were taking advantage of the naval officers he had entrusted with buying ships for conversion, Welles appointed two purchasing agents: his brother-in-law George D. Morgan at New York and John M. Forbes at Boston. Morgan in particular had great success, securing eighty-nine ships at a cost of $3.5 million and saving the navy an estimated $900,000.[5]

Purchased ships soon went to the yards to undergo quick conversions and then were assigned to blockade duty. Few changes were necessary, as the blockaders were generally lightly armed ships. Modifications consisted mainly in reinforcing their decks to bear the ordnance and the construction of magazines. Steamships were the priority; they were essential if the blockade was to be effective. Although the steamer conversions were weak as warships, they were nonetheless generally faster than sailing ships and could thus eventually overtake them. Their lighter armament would also be sufficient to deal with the blockade runners, many of which were sailing ships relying primarily on speed and stealth. The blockade did cement the U.S. Navy's commitment to steam warships. As Welles put it,

"No sailing vessels have been ordered to be built, for steam, as well as heavy ordnance, has become an indispensable element of the most efficient naval power."[6]

The growth in numbers of navy ships was both rapid and dramatic. By December 1861, the navy had purchased 136 ships, including 26 side-wheeler steamers and 43 screw steamers. It also had under construction 49 warships: 14 screw sloops, 23 gunboats, and 12 side-wheeler steamers.[7]

The navy's steamers at the start of the war included six powerful warships: the five first-class screw frigates of the Lenthall-designed *Merrimack*-class (the *Merrimack, Wabash, Minnesota, Colorado,* and *Roanoke*) and the screw sloop *Niagara*. Authorized in 1854, the ships had been commissioned during 1856–58. At 4,536 tons, the *Merrimack*-class ships were typically armed in 1861 with two 10-inch shell guns, twenty-nine IX-inch Dahlgrens, and fourteen 8-inch guns.[8]

Guns intended to fire shell were lighter than those designed to fire shot. After the appearance of Dahlgren guns in the 1850s, U.S. Navy shell guns were often designated by Roman numerals to distinguish them from shot guns. From that time on most writers referred to shell guns, regardless of their type, by Roman numerals. In this book Roman numerals are used to designate Dahlgren guns only.

An interesting design by George Steers, the large sloop *Niagara* boasted a clipper-type hull and carried its guns all on one deck. Commissioned in 1857 and displacing 5,546 tons, it was the largest ship in the United States at the time. Following a rebuild in 1862, the *Niagara* mounted one 6.4-inch Parrott rifle and eleven XI-inch Dahlgrens.

Size was sometimes a disadvantage in blockade duties, where light-draft ships were required for operation in coastal shoals. The *Merrimack*-class, *Niagara,* and the large paddle-wheeler sloops *Susquehanna* and *Powhatan* drew too much water to be of great use in such duty along the Southern coasts. More important during the war were the twelve large sloops of war authorized by Congress in 1857 and 1858. Entering service beginning in 1859, these included the five-ship *Hartford*-class (the *Brooklyn, Hartford, Lancaster, Pensacola,* and *Richmond*). Probably the best Union warships at the start of the war, these 2,900-ton ships carried in 1862 an armament of two 3.67-inch Parrott rifles and twenty IX-inch Dahlgrens. During the war the *Lancaster* served on Pacific station, but its four sister ships rendered important war service. The *Hartford* was the

U.S. Navy screw frigate Merrimack, *engraving by L. H. Bradford after a drawing by*
G. B. Pook. NAVAL HISTORICAL CENTER (NH 46248)

U.S. Navy screw sloop Hartford. *Note sails and laundry drying.*
NAVAL HISTORICAL CENTER (NH 90535)

most famous of them and the one with the longest service life. With their relatively shallow draft and large batteries, these sloops proved invaluable in coastal and riverine operations.

Other highly effective screw sloops utilized both in coastal operations and for hunting down Confederate cruisers on the high seas were the two-ship *Mohican*-class (the *Mohican* and *Kearsarge*). One of the best-known ships to come out of the war, the *Kearsarge* displaced 1,550 tons and was armed in 1864 with one 4.2-inch Parrott rifle, two XI-inch Dahlgrens, and four 32-pounders. It engaged and sank the Confederate raider *Alabama* off Cherbourg, France. The *Kearsarge* enjoyed a long service life but succumbed to a shipwreck off Central America in 1894.

Other screw sloops included the three-ship *Iroquois*-class (1,488 tons, two XI-inch Dahlgrens, and four 32-pounders), two-ship screw-sloop *Wyoming*-class (1,457 tons, two XI-inch Dahlgrens, six 32-pounders, and one 4.2-inch Parrott rifle), the *Dacotah*, the two-ship *Narragansett*-class, and the *Pawnee* (1,553 tons and four XI-inch Dahlgrens). After the start of the war, many additional screw sloops joined the fleet, including the four-ship *Ossipee*-class authorized in February 1861. Among these was the ill-fated *Housatonic* of 1,533 tons, mounting in 1863 one 6.4-inch and three 4.2-inch Parrott rifles, one XI-inch Dahlgren, and four 32-pounders. There were also the six-ship *Sacramento*-, ten-ship *Contookcook*-, eleven-ship *Algoma*-, and six-ship *Swatara*-classes.

After the Confederates had initiated commerce raiding, Welles convened a board of officers to recommend a class of warships to hunt down these Southern ships. This resulted in the powerful screw sloop *Sacramento* of 1863 (2,100 tons armed with one 8-inch and one 4.2-inch Parrott rifle and two XI-inch Dahlgrens).

In addition to chasing Confederate commerce raiders, screw sloops were useful in blockade duties, and they participated in the bombardment of Charleston and Fort Fisher. They also fought in the Battle of Mobile Bay. Under sail and with its funnel lowered, only the greater length of the ship betrayed the fact that the screw steamer was not a traditional sailing warship. Unlike the paddle-wheelers, which carried a reduced armament of a few heavier guns on the upper deck and relied on long range fire, screw steamers could, and did, mount the traditional broadsides armament; most, however, retained the paddler arrangement of fewer but heavy guns on the upper deck.

The most pressing need in the blockade was for fast, smaller gunboats capable of operating effectively in coastal shoal waters and along rivers. In 1861 the navy had just one such ship available, the *Princeton*. Commissioned in 1852, it was a receiving ship at Philadelphia and continued in that capacity during the war. Isherwood suggested the design utilized in the construction of two small (691-ton) shallow-draft gunboats built for the Russian Navy to operate on the Amur River.

In July 1861 the Navy Department contracted for twenty-three of these ships. The first of the class and its namesake, the *Unadilla*, was completed in only ninety-three days, leading to the appellation of "ninety-day gunboats" for the entire class. All ships of the class were commissioned by March 1862. Displacing 691 tons and sporting a two-mast schooner rig, they were armed with one XI-inch Dahlgren, two 24-pounders, and one 3.67-inch Parrott rifle. The *Unadillas* proved their worth in operations throughout the war. Four were completed in time to take part in the expedition against Port Royal in November 1861, and ten took part in Flag Officer David G. Farragut's forcing of the lower Mississippi River in April 1862 that led to the capture of New Orleans. The *Unadillas* made 146 captures during the blockade. Although effective as steamers, they did have problems; machinery frequently broke down, steering was sluggish, the ships rolled heavily, and their maximum eight- to nine-knot speed was slow for blockade responsibilities.

In August 1862 the Navy Department authorized a second class of eight shallow-draft gunboats. These *Nipsic*-class (also known as *Kansas*-class) ships entered service beginning December 1863, with the last commissioned in November 1864. Displacing 836 tons, they had an armament of one 8-inch smoothbore and two IX-inch Dahlgrens, and one 4.2-inch and two 3.67-inch Parrott rifled guns. The *Nispics* performed well during the war, although they did not see extensive service because of their relatively late commissioning date.

One interesting innovation occurred in twelve "double-ender" side-wheeler gunboats laid down in 1861, the first of which was the 730-ton *Miami*. Entering service beginning in early 1862, these ships were built specifically to operate in shallow coastal waters and rivers, and, with rudders at each end, they could operate in either direction, a great advantage in shallow rivers where it might be difficult to turn a ship around. Lenthall designed their hulls and Isherwood the engines. The best known "double-enders," however, were the *Sassacus*-class ships, displacing 1,173 tons. Twenty-eight were laid down but only twenty-seven of them were commissioned, some after the war. Joining the fleet beginning in October 1863, the typical armament for these ships was two 6.4-inch rifled guns, four IX-inch Dahlgren smoothbores, and six Dahlgren boat howitzers.

Wooden ships were essential in the vast Union effort at sea, but the warships that excited the most interest at the time and thereafter were the ironclads, and specifically the monitors. It was an open secret that the Confederates had raised the *Merrimack* at Norfolk and were refitting it as an ironclad. In response, Welles urged the creation of a board to study ironclad designs, and in August 1861 Congress approved both it and an appropriation of $1.5 million for ironclad construction. Welles appointed three senior officers to the Ironclad Board. Chaired by Commo. Joseph Smith, the head of the Bureau of Yards and Docks, it included Commo. Hiram Paulding and Cdr. Charles H. Davis.

The board decided on light-draft ironclad ships capable of operating off the Southern coasts. Although it received proposals for ironclads from some British yards, the board chose to rely on U.S. firms alone, and the department placed advertisements in a number of Northern newspapers inviting proposals for the construction of "Iron-Clad Steam Vessels . . . for sea or river service." Interested parties were instructed to provide both plans and a construction timetable, as well as a guarantee for "proper execution of the contract."[9]

The board received sixteen proposals, with the cost of the individual ships ranging from $32,000 to $1.5 million. In September the board recommended the awarding of three contracts: the first to C. S. Bushnell and Co. of New Haven, Connecticut, the second to Merrick & Sons of Philadelphia, and the third to John Ericsson of New York. Their completed ships were, respectively, the *Galena*, *New Ironsides*, and *Monitor*.

The *Galena* was designed by Naval Constructor Samuel Pook. Displacing 950 tons, it was 210 feet in length. Commissioned in April 1862, the ironclad mounted two 6.4-inch Parrott rifles and four IX-inch Dahlgrens. Equipped with a two mast schooner rig to supplement its single-screw propeller, the *Galena* had tumblehome sides protected by 3.25-inch armor formed of interlocking iron bars. The *Galena* disappointed as a ship type from its very first combat action, when it was severely damaged during a duel with Confederate shore batteries at Drewry's Bluff on the James River in May 1862. Its armor proved susceptible to plunging fire that struck at almost straight angles. The armor was removed in 1863, and the *Galena* was converted to an unarmored screw sloop with a three-mast sail rig.

The second experimental ironclad, the *New Ironsides*, was the least revolutionary of the three in design and yet, in almost every respect, by far the most successful. Strangely, the *New Ironsides* has always been over-shadowed by the *Monitor*. Despite the fact that this type of ship offered a considerable tactical advantage in offensive firepower, the *New Ironsides* was the only broadsides ironclad in the Union Navy during the war. It proved its great worth in sixteen months of service with the South Atlantic Blockade Squadron off Charleston.

Launched in May 1862 and commissioned that August, the *New Ironsides* was designed by Barnabas Bartol for Merrick & Sons of Philadelphia. It was much more conventional in appearance with an extreme length-to-beam ratio (a 230-foot length between perpendiculars and a 56-foot beam) to ensure a shallow draft of 15 feet, 8 inches for coastal operations. To a considerable extent patterned after the French *Gloire*, the *New Ironsides* displaced 3,500 tons, and 170 feet of its length was protected by a 4.5-inch iron belt. The *New Ironsides* boasted an iron ram on its prow and mounted a formidable battery of two 8-inch Parrott rifles and fourteen XI-inch Dahlgren smoothbores.

The *New Ironsides* was the most powerful warship of the U.S. Navy in the Civil War. It was slow—only seven knots instead of the design-specified ten knots—but this was in consequence of its bulky hull. In combat, the ship proved virtually indestructible to enemy fire. It was far superior to the *Monitor* and its successors in seaworthiness, armament, rate of fire, and even in armor. The *Monitor* had laminated armor, which Ericsson chose because of the need for speedy construction, but the *New Ironsides* utilized superior solid plate. The only advantages of the monitors over this type were their shallower draft and small target area.

Off Charleston, the "guardian of the blockade," as the *New Ironsides* came to be known, proved an effective deterrent to Confederate ironclad attacks against the wooden Union blockading fleet. Clearly its service at Charleston was unmatched by any other Union warship. Always the primary target for return fire during Union bombardments of Confederate shore positions, the *New Ironsides* came off with only minor damage, whereas the monitors often suffered severely and even, in some cases, fatally.

The *New Ironsides* could place at least ten times the firepower on target per hour as the *Monitor* and five times as much as the later *Passaic*-class monitors, and this fire could also be concentrated on a particular point. While the XV-inch guns of the *Passaic*-class monitors were much more powerful individually than the XI-inchers on the *New Ironsides*, the monitors were at a severe disadvantage in fighting at sea. The earliest monitors had only 1–2 feet of freeboard, and even the "seagoing" monitors had only 2 feet, 7 inches. The *New Ironsides* had a full 13 feet of freeboard, putting the bores of her guns 9–10 feet above water, where there was no fear of interference by the sea. Its higher free-board also enabled the *New Ironsides* to keep its speed in a seaway, which the *Monitor* could not. The *New Ironsides* also enjoyed the advantage of there being no possibility of a jammed turret. Its most serious weakness was that its armor did not extend to the ends of the vessel.

Although smaller than the French *La Gloire* or the British *Warrior*, the *New Ironsides* was their equal in armor protection and was superior to them in armament. The European ships had the advantage only in speed. The *New Ironsides* also had significant advantages when compared to the Confederate *Virginia*. These pluses would have been critical had the Confederacy been able to acquire the "Laird Rams" building in Britain.[10]

The *Monitor*, which is discussed in detail later in connection with its engagement with the *Virginia*, was a low-freeboard, single-turret ironclad with many technological innovations. In service for only a relatively short period, it nonetheless had wide influence. In February 1862, before the *Monitor-Virginia* clash, Congress appropriated $10 million to build twenty additional ironclads, and advertisements for proposals went out the same month. These ships were intended both to enhance the nation's defense posture against Great Britain (relations between Washington and London were near the breaking point over the *Trent* Affair) but also to enable the U.S. Navy to take the offensive against Southern ports. Several weeks later, the clash between the *Monitor* and the *Virginia* occurred. Among those witnessing the battle from shore was Assistant Secretary Fox, who became an enthusiastic *Monitor* advocate. Welles also embraced the design. Indeed, virtually the entire North succumbed to so-called "monitor mania." Of fifty-six ironclads laid down by the North during the war, fifty-two were of the *Monitor* or turreted type.[11]

Three weeks after the clash between the *Monitor* and the *Virginia*, the navy contracted for ten improved Ericsson monitors. Both the

Passaic- and *Canonicus-*class ships were essentially modified monitors. The *Passaic* and its nine sister ships were 200 feet between perpendiculars and 46 feet in beam, and at 2,335 tons, they were nearly twice the displacement of the *Monitor*. Drawing only 11 feet, 6 inches, they were designed to mount two XV-inch Dahlgrens, but several carried one XI-inch or one 8-inch Parrott rifled gun instead of the second XV-incher. The *Passaic-*class ships joined the fleet in November 1862 and saw more service than any other Civil War monitors. They participated in operations against Charleston and Savannah and in the Battle of Mobile Bay.

The nine ship *Canonicus-*class monitors, only seven of which were commissioned, each displaced 2,100 tons. Most were 235 feet in length and mounted two XV-inch Dahlgrens. Ericsson also designed the large single-turreted *Dictator* and *Puritan*. Commissioned in November 1864, the *Dictator* displaced 4,438 tons, was 312 feet in length, and was armed with two XV-inch Dahlgrens. It had a formidable 15-inch armor protection on the turret, 12 inches on the pilothouse, 6 inches on the sides, and 1.5 inches on the deck. Largest of the Ericsson monitors, the *Puritan* was a longer *Dictator*. Displacing 4,912 tons, it was a whopping 340 feet long and was designed to carry two XX-inch Dahlgren smoothbores, which, however, did not see service in the Civil War. Launched in July 1864, the *Puritan* was never commissioned and was officially rebuilt as a new ship in 1874.

The twenty *Casco-*class monitors were the major Union ship design blunder of the war. Identified by a turtleback deck and with their construction supervised by Chief Engineer Alban C. Stimers, they displaced 1,175 tons and were 225 feet in length. The *Casco* was launched in May 1864 and commissioned that December, but most ships of the class were not delivered until after the war, the last in May 1866. Poor planning and faulty calculations meant that they had only 3 inches of freeboard before they were fitted for turrets. This, of course, necessitated raising their decks. Some *Cascos* served without turrets and were armed with spar torpedoes. All were scrapped in the mid-1870s.

The *Keokuk* and *Dunderberg* were among later Union ironclads. Ericsson partner Charles W. Whitney designed the *Keokuk*. Of 677 tons burden, it had a turtleback hull that mounted a single XI-inch Dahlgren in each of two cylindrical fixed armored gunhouses pierced for three gunports. The *Keokuk's* weakness lay in its armor protection of horizontal iron bars alternating with wood, the whole covered with iron plate. The *Keokuk* proved so vulnerable to heavy close-range fire that it sank after its first day of battle off Charleston in 1863.

The ironclad ram *Dunderberg* displaced 7,060 tons. Designed by Lenthall and built by Webb of New York, it was 159 feet, 6 inches in overall length and had a casemate along the lines of the CSS *Virginia*. Intended as a seagoing ironclad frigate ram and brigantine rigged, it was designed for broadside fire. The *Dunderberg* had a double bottom, a collision bulkhead, and a massive solid oak ram. Although laid down late in 1862, construction was so delayed that the navy refused to accept it in 1866. France bought the ship to prevent its sale to Prussia. Renamed the *Rochambeau*, it took part in the naval blockade of Prussia in 1870.

Perhaps the most unusual turreted design of the war was the 6,300-ton *Roanoke*. Cut down from the wooden screw frigate of the same name and 178 feet in overall length, it was rebuilt and recommissioned in June 1863 with three centerline turrets, the only such ship of the war. It also had high freeboard and thus was not a monitor-type vessel. The *Roanoke* mounted one 8-inch Parrott rifle and one XV-inch Dahlgren in the forward turret, one XV-inch and one XI-inch Dahlgren in the middle turret, and one 8-inch Parrott rifle and one XI-inch Dahlgren in the aft turret. Unstable and of deep draft, the *Roanoke* was retained at New York City to defend that harbor against possible Confederate attack.

The Union also converted and built from scratch a number of ships for the Western Theater. The army contracted for the initial ships, although Cdr. John Rodgers and Naval Constructor Samuel Pook oversaw their conversion and naval officers commanded them. The first of the Union western gunboats were the side-wheeler river steamers *Conestoga*, *Lexington*, and *Tyler*, purchased in June 1861. Rapidly converted to military use, they entered service two months later. Known as "timberclads," they were protected only by the addition of five-inch-thick oak planks. Displacement was 572 tons for the *Conestoga*, 362 tons for the *Lexington*, and 420 tons for the *Tyler*. Initial armament was as follows: the *Conestoga*, four 32-pounders; the *Lexington*, two 32-pounders and four 8-inch shell guns; and the *Tyler*, one 32-pounder and six 8-inch smoothbores. All of the timberclads provided highly effective service. The *Conestoga* was lost in a ship collision in the Mississippi River in March 1864 but the other two survived the war. Other converted river ships received iron protection.

These included the 633-ton *Benton*, a former catamaran snagboat (designed to pull debris from the river) and the most powerful of the early river ironclads. Commissioned in February 1862, it mounted sixteen guns: two IX-inch Dahlgrens, seven 42-pounder (7-inch bore) coast defense rifles, and seven 32-pounders. The *Essex*, a converted merchant river ferry of 355 tons, was at first a timberclad, but in early 1862 it received a 3-inch ironclad casemate protection. It mounted five IX-inch Dahlgrens.

The army also ordered the construction of purpose-built ironclad warships for western river service. The first of these were the highly effective *Cairo*- or city-class ships, named for towns on the western waters. The name ship of the class, the *Cairo*, was sunk by a mine in the Yazoo River in December 1862. The other ships were the *Carondelet, Cincinnati, Louisville, Mound City, Pittsburg*, and *St. Louis*. Built by James Eads, they were designed by Lenthall but modified by Eads and Pook. The *Cairo*-class vessels were often referred to as "Pook Turtles" for their rectangular casemates and sloped sides, which gave them a turtlelike appearance. Although underpowered, these river ironclads were heavily armed, although less than the twenty guns each originally planned (probably the consequence of the weight of their iron plating). In January 1862 each mounted thirteen guns: three 8-inch smoothbores, four 42-pounder coast defense rifled guns (7-inch bore), and six 32-pounder rifled guns. Three of the guns fired forward. Each gunboat was protected with 2.5 inches of armor on the casemate and 1.25 inches on the conical pilothouse forward.

James Eads also designed highly effective monitors for western service. In early 1862 he secured a government contract to design and build three single-turreted monitors. The first two to enter service were the 523-ton burden *Neosho*-class (the *Neosho* in May and *Osage* in July 1863). They were unique in being propelled by stern wheels, which, however, would not allow full 360-degree fire for their two turret-mounted XI-inch Dahlgren guns. The 578-ton *Ozark* was commissioned in February 1864. It combined a single turret mounting two XI-inch Dahlgrens and a casemate with one X-inch and three IX-inch Dahlgrens.

Eads then secured a contract to build four double-turreted river monitors, known as the *Milwaukee*-class of *Chickasaw, Kickapoo, Milwaukee*, and *Winnebago*. They had one turret designed by Eads and the other by Ericsson. The forward-mounted Eads turret was a sophisticated design that turned on a ball-bearing race. It employed steam power for moving and elevating the guns and operating the gunport shutters and an elevator that moved the guns down to a lower deck for reloading. Laid down in 1862, the four monitors were commissioned in the spring and summer of 1864. They had an 8-inch turret and 1.5-inch deck armor, and were each armed with four XI-inch Dahlgrens.

The U.S. Navy would retain its coastal monitors into the twentieth century. Unfortunately, the Civil War monitor craze inhibited the construction of true seagoing ironclads. Until the 1880s the U.S. Navy had no seagoing armored ships that could fight other ironclads.

Other specialized ships, such as the Mississippi rams, are discussed later, but among innovative ships of the war were the navy's first hospital ships. In March 1862 the navy converted the *Ben Morgan* from a hulk into a hospital ship with the North Atlantic Squadron. In December 1862 the navy also placed in commission in the Mississippi Squadron the former Confederate steamer *Red Rover*. Featuring two operating rooms and a special space for amputations, it also had an elevator to shift patients between decks as well as several flush toilets. The *Red Rover* achieved another first for a U.S. Navy ship by taking aboard female nurses from the Order of the Holy Cross.

CONFEDERATE SHIPS

The Confederate States Navy hardly enjoyed an auspicious beginning. Although counts of the number of ships vary, there is agreement that Secretary Mallory had to create a navy almost from scratch. He inherited five ships from the seceded states and secured through seizure or purchase four revenue cutters, three slavers, two privately owned coastal steamers, and the side-wheeler *Fulton*, laid up at the Pensacola Navy Yard. None of these had been purpose-built as warships, with the exception of the old *Fulton*. As with the U.S. Navy, the Confederates also purchased merchant steamers for conversion into warships, but, unlike the Union, it faced a paucity of resources both in ships to purchase and in facilities for their conversion, let alone for new construction. Only Richmond, New Orleans, and Memphis (which had boasted a navy yard during 1844–53, but for the making of rope from hemp) had properly equipped civilian facilities at the start of the war that could, given the opportunity, construct and repair ironclad ships. Compounding Mallory's problems, the shipbuilding facilities of New Orleans, Norfolk, and Memphis were all taken by the Union early in the conflict.

The South also faced a major problem in building the steam engines required for the new ironclad ships. Skilled artisans were in short supply, compounded by the need of manpower for the army. Only Tredegar Iron Works (J. R. Anderson & Co.) of Richmond could manufacture entire propulsion systems. Most of the steam engines that powered Confederate naval ships were requisitioned from civilian ships. As a result, throughout the war the vast majority of the Southern steam warships were inadequately powered. The ironclad ram *Virginia* is but one example.

Although the Confederacy never built any cruisers in its ports during the war (the *Sumter* was a conversion), it did construct a great many wooden gunboats. These fell into three major categories: one class of at least four large side-wheeler steamers; three classes of screw steamers designed by Confederate Chief Naval Constructor John L. Porter; and a variety of small ships conceived by oceanographer and former U.S. Navy officer Matthew Fontaine Maury and intended for coast defense.

The first category of ships included the two *Carondelet*-class (*Carondelet* and *Bienville*) and two *Gaines*-class (*Gaines* and *Morgan*) ships. The first two, tonnage unknown but 196 feet in length and commissioned in March and April 1862, were constructed at Bayou St. John, Louisiana, and built to help protect New Orleans against Federal attack. Each mounted five 42-pounder smoothbores and one 32-pounder rifled gun. The two fell prey to Flag Officer David G. Farragut's West Gulf Coast Squadron: the *Bienville* was destroyed in Lake Pontchartrain on 21 April 1862, prior to completion in order to prevent capture. The *Carondelet* fought in the Battle of Pass Christian on 4 April 1862 and was also destroyed on 21 April 1862 to prevent capture.

The 863-ton two *Gaines*-class side-wheeler steamers were constructed at Mobile in 1862 as part of the Confederate squadron protecting access to Mobile Bay. Each was armed with six guns: one 7-inch, one 6-inch, and two 32-pounder rifles and two 32-pounder smoothbores. Both fought in the Battle of Mobile Bay on 5 August 1864. The *Gaines* was run aground to prevent capture, whereas the *Morgan* escaped upriver and was not taken until the surrender of Mobile on 4 May 1865.

Porter designed a number of gunboats. Of two of the *Chattahoochee*-class, only the *Chattahoochee* was completed. Seven *Macon*-class gunboats were completed but only two, the *Macon* and *Peedee*, were commissioned. Two *Hampton*-class gunboats (*Hampton* and the *Nansemond*) reached commissioning. These eleven gunboats were 116 to 170 feet in length and mounted three to six guns. As with all Confederate warships, steam power plants varied widely, even within classes, and many, if not most, of the gunboats were underpowered. The *Macon*, one of the largest of the Porter designs, was 150 feet in overall length. Armed with one IX-inch Dahlgren, four 32-pounder smoothbores, and one 32-pounder rifled gun, it participated in the defense of Savannah and was surrendered at Augusta, Georgia, in May 1865. The Porter-designed gunboats, although small, rendered effective service but were employed mostly as auxiliaries.

Maury's gunboats were by far the most extensive Confederate ship-building program of the war. Despite Mallory's well-publicized interest in ironclads and his opposition to the small wooden gunboats, he could not overcome Maury's great political influence, and in December 1861 Maury secured Confederate Congress approval for the construction of one hundred of them. The program was reminiscent of Thomas Jefferson's gunboat program at the beginning of the nineteenth century, which was based on the notion that swarms of small gunboats could protect coasts and harbors against attack. Maury noted the inability of the South to build larger ships and assumed that numbers of his small, easily built, relatively inexpensive shallow-draft steam gunboats, armed with two to four guns each, would be a match for the larger Union warships—precisely the same argument used to justify the Jeffersonian program earlier.

The Maury gunboats, which were 106 to 116 feet in length, were not to have cabins or accommodations. Fifteen of them were laid down in various Virginia yards, including five at the Norfolk Navy Yard during 1861–62. Others were laid down at Pensacola, Florida, and Edwards Ferry and Elizabeth City, North Carolina; however, all were destroyed before their completion. Armament was projected as two guns: one rifled 32-pounder forward and a IX-inch Dahlgren smoothbore aft. The *Torch*, the *Isondiga*, and perhaps the *Yadkin* may have been of this class. As their critics had feared, the gunboats were too small to combat the larger Union warships, and those that may have been completed of this class ended up as auxiliaries or spar torpedo boats.

It was natural for the Confederates, who lacked both warships in being and the potential to build any significant numbers of them, would seek to offset the Union numerical advantage through technologically advanced ships in the form of ironclads. Mallory understood their importance much more clearly and earlier than did Welles. On 10 May 1861, Mallory wrote Chairman of the Committee on Naval Affairs of the Confederate Congress C. M. Conrad a long letter in which he pointed out the ironclad revolution then under way in Europe and the need for a Confederate offensive strategy based on these ships:

> I regard the possession of an iron-armored ship as a matter of the first necessity. Such a vessel at this time could transverse the entire coast of the United States, prevent all blockades, and encounter, with a fair prospect of success, their entire Navy.
>
> If to cope with them upon the sea we follow their example and build wooden ships, we shall have to construct several at one time; for one or two ships would fall an easy prey to her comparatively numerous steam frigates. But inequality of numbers may be compensated by invulnerability; and thus not only does economy but naval success dictate the wisdom and expediency of fighting with iron against wood, without regard to first cost.
>
> Should the committee deem it expedient to begin at once with the construction of such a ship, not a moment is to be lost.[12]

The Confederate Congress agreed, and on 10 May 1861 it appropriated $2 million to purchase or construct one or two ironclads in European yards. A week later Mallory sent Confederate Navy officer Lt. James H. North to Europe in an effort to secure one or two ironclads there, preferably the French ironclad frigate *La Gloire* or a similar ship. If he was unsuccessful, North was to arrange for the construction of two similar ironclads that would mount six to eight guns. Soon after North's departure, however, Mallory attempted to have some of the new ironclads constructed in the South. On 10 June he directed Lt. John M. Brooke to design an ironclad, and within two weeks, Brooke had come up with a plan for a casemated ship with inclined sides. On 23 June, Brooke, Mallory, Naval Constructor Porter, and Chief Engineer William P. Williamson from the Norfolk Navy Yard met and approved the concept. With no engines of the size required available in the Confederacy, Williamson suggested they use the hull, engines, and boilers on the former U.S. steam frigate *Merrimack*. Brooke and Porter agreed, and on 11 July Mallory ordered that work proceed to rebuild the *Merrimack* as an ironclad, the outcome of which is discussed in Chapter 6.

The South experienced serious problems with ironclad construction throughout the war. Iron production capacity was so limited that the navy was forced to rely on iron from militarily nonessential railroad lines, including the Richmond streetcar tracks. The navy was also forced to compete with the army for the limited supply of railroad iron available. In January 1863, Flag Officer William F. Lynch, the naval officer charged with construction of the ironclad *Albemarle* at Edwards Ferry in North Carolina, reported to Mallory:

> I think it is impossible to obtain any iron unless it is seized. The Petersburg Railroad agent says that he must have the old iron on the Petersburg road to replace the worn out rails on that road. The Kinston and Raleigh road requires the iron taken below Kinston to replace the iron on the Charlotte and N.C. road, and these roads are considered a military necessity[.]
>
> The whole subject of R.R. iron was laid before the North Carolina legislature and I am unable to obtain any iron.[13]

Although iron was eventually secured for the *Albemarle*, in late 1864 Chief Naval Constructor Porter reported that a dozen vessels were on the stocks awaiting their armor, "but the material is not on hand." At least ten ironclads had to be broken up for lack of iron plate.[14]

The Tredegar could roll iron plate and cast heavy guns, but in 1861 it was the only such facility in the South. In 1863 the navy bought and staffed the Selma Foundry Works in Alabama to produce guns and to roll iron plate. It is rather surprising, given the myriad problems in lack of manufacturing resources and construction facilities, that the Confederacy was able to experience such success in the construction of ironclads. By May 1863, Mallory had under construction twenty-three warships, and all but three were ironclads.

While conversion of the *Merrimack* into the *Virginia* was still in progress, Mallory let contracts for five ironclads to be built from scratch. These were the *Arkansas, Tennessee, Mississippi, Louisiana*, and *Georgia*. With the exception of the *Georgia*, a steam-powered, floating battery to help protect Savannah, these were projected as the major instruments of Mallory's offensive policy of building large, powerful seagoing ships to engage and defeat Union blockaders. All were laid down in October 1861.

For the most part, the Confederates opted for casemated ironclads along the lines of the *Virginia*. Two of the new ironclads were built at Memphis, the *Arkansas*-class of the *Arkansas* and *Tennessee*. These casemated ironclads had a ram bow and sloping sides. Hastily built with poor engines, they were smaller, at 165 feet between perpendiculars, and were protected by 18 inches of iron and wood. They were armed with two IX-inch Dahlgrens, two 8-inch shell guns, two 6-inch rifles, and two 32-pounders. The *Arkansas* was commissioned in May 1862 but taken to Yazoo City, Mississippi, to prevent capture at Memphis. It was destroyed that August. Never commissioned, the *Tennessee* was burned on the stocks at Memphis in June 1862 to prevent its capture.

The *Mississippi* and *Louisiana* were larger, at 1,400 tons and with lengths of 260 feet and 264 feet, respectively. Both were constructed at Jefferson City, Louisiana. The *Mississippi* was launched in April 1862. Powered by three steam engines for triple screws, it was designed to carry eighteen guns but had not yet received its armament when it was burned following the Union capture of New Orleans the same month.

The *Louisiana*, launched in February 1862, had four steam engines and six boilers to power two paddle wheels mounted in tandem in a central well. Two steering propellers were situated at the stern. Designed to mount twenty-two guns, the *Louisiana*'s power proved insufficient to move it against the Mississippi River current, and it was towed to Fort St. Philip below New Orleans while still incomplete. There it became a floating battery. The *Louisiana* was burned to prevent capture following the passage of the Union fleet upriver to New Orleans.

Some 250 to 260 feet in length with a 12-foot-high casemate, the *Georgia* was launched in October 1862. Its battery is variously reported at five to ten guns ranging from 6-inch rifles and 32-pounders to IX-inch Dahlgrens. The *Georgia*'s engines were so inefficient that it could hardly get about, and in consequence, it became simply a floating battery. Anchored off Fort Jackson near the big bend in the Savannah River northeast of the city, it became the principal barrier to a Union approach to Savannah. It was scuttled in the river at the end of the war.[15]

By any measure, Mallory's strategy of offensive operations by heavy ironclads was a failure. Excluding the *Georgia*, only three of the five above vessels designed for offensive operations saw combat, and of these only the *Virginia* and *Arkansas* were operational under their own power.

Successful Union operations against a number of leading Confederate coastal ports in late 1861 and early 1862 led Mallory to abandon an
offensive naval strategy centered on large seagoing ironclads to break the
blockade in favor of one centered on smaller, shallow-draft ironclads to
defend Confederate harbors and rivers. This found expression in the six-
ship *Richmond*-class of ironclad rams: the *Chicora*, *North Carolina*,
Palmetto State, *Raleigh*, *Richmond*, and *Savannah*. Designed by Porter and
laid down in early 1862, they resembled the *Virginia* in that they had a conventional hull and casemate of similar inclination and thickness but with
an intended armament of only four guns. Their completion was delayed
for a variety of reasons, and commissioning dates ranged from July 1862
(the *Richmond*) to April 1864 (the *Raleigh*). These ships were 172 feet, 6
inches in overall length. Propelled by a single screw, they were also underpowered. Armor consisted of 4 inches of iron backed by 22 inches of wood.
Actual armament varied from four to ten guns. Most of the *Richmond*-class
ships were burned or sunk to prevent capture.

Ironclads following the *Richmond*-class ships were for the most part
stretched versions that could carry more guns. These included the two-
ship *Charleston*-class (the *Charleston* and *Virginia II*). Intended for the
defense of Charleston and designed by Naval Constructor William Graves,
the *Charleston* was commissioned in September 1863 and was 1,050 tons
and 189 feet in overall length. It mounted two IX-inch Dahlgrens and four
rifles. The *Charleston* was burned to prevent capture in February 1865.
The *Virginia II* was similar. Completed in June 1864 and mounting one
XI-inch Dahlgren, two 6.4-inch rifles, and one 8-inch rifle, it participated
in the defense of Richmond on the James River and was blown up on
3 April 1865 following the fall of the Confederate capital.

Porter designed the two-ship *Columbia*-class of the *Columbia* and
Texas. They were 1,520 tons displacement and mounted six guns. The
Columbia was 213 feet overall and commissioned in 1864. It was lost in
January 1865 when it ran into a sunken wreck near Fort Moultrie.
Occupying Union forces salvaged it four months later. The *Texas*, which
was 217 feet overall, had a shorter casemate, never saw active service, and
was seized by Union forces at Richmond in April 1865.

The *Tennessee* was a modified *Columbia*. Commissioned in February
1864, it was 1,273 tons and 209 feet overall. It had two screws and side-wheels.
The *Tennessee* was one of the most celebrated ironclads of the war. As the

Confederate flagship in the Battle of Mobile Bay in August 1864, it was disabled and captured. It had a 5-inch casemate, 6-inch forward, and 2-inch deck armor and mounted six guns: two 7-inch and four 6.4-inch rifles.

Other later Confederate ironclads included the Porter-designed *Nashville*, a side-wheeler to take advantage of available riverboat machinery. Never commissioned, it was surrendered in May 1865. Porter also designed twin-screw, shallow-draft ironclads with intended drafts of only 9 feet. Patterned after the *Richmond*-class, these included the *Milledgeville*-class of four ships and the *Wilmington*. Only the *Milledgeville* was ever launched, and none of the ships were ever commissioned.

Mallory also ordered a simplified standardized design for ironclads that could be built inland. Designed to have only eight-foot drafts, all save one paddler were to be propelled by twin screws. Several were laid down in Tidewater Virginia but were not completed by the time of the Confederate evacuation of that area in spring of 1862. The two-ship *Huntsville*-class of the *Huntsville* and *Tuscaloosa* were shallow-draft ironclads. They had an overall length of 152 feet and 4 inches of armor, and each mounted one 6.4-inch rifle and three 32-pounders. Commissioned in 1863, their inadequate power plants forced their employment as floating batteries. Both were sunk as blockships in the Mobile River in April 1865.

Finally, of shallow-draft Confederate ironclads there was the Porter-designed *Albemarle*-class of the *Albemarle*, *Neuse*, and another unnamed ship never commissioned. Both the *Albemarle* and the *Neuse* entered service in April 1864. Of some 376 tons, they were 152-feet-long twin-screw vessels that mounted two 6.4-inch rifles. The *Albemarle* was one of the most famous Confederate ironclads. It attacked and routed Union blockaders below Plymouth, North Carolina, in May 1864 before being sunk by a Union spar torpedo boat that October. The *Neuse* was run aground off Kinston, North Carolina, in May 1864, where it remained until sunk to prevent capture in March 1865.

Porter also designed a lengthened four-gun version of the *Albemarle*-class, the *Fredericksburg*, which was commissioned in March 1864 as part of the James River flotilla. Some 700 tons and 188 feet in overall length, it was armed with one XI-inch Dahlgren, one 8-inch rifle, and two 6.4-inch rifles. The *Fredericksburg* was blown up on 4 April 1865 following the loss of Richmond.

Only one ship, the *Missouri*, was completed of a Porter-designed center-wheel class of ironclads. Built at Shreveport, Louisiana, and completed in

September 1863, it was 183 feet in overall length with 4.5 inches of rail armor protection and armed with one XI-inch Dahlgren, one IX-inch Dahlgren, and two 32-pounders. It served in the Red River, but low water prevented it from leaving Shreveport, where it was surrendered in June 1865.

In 1865 the Confederacy began construction of its one-turreted, monitor-type ironclad. Under construction at Columbus, Georgia, to mount two XI-inch Brooke smoothbores in a single 23-foot diameter turret, it did not see service. Construction was halted by the end of the war.

Mallory had much less success in his efforts to purchase ironclads overseas. Confederate Lt. James H. North was unsuccessful in efforts to purchase *La Gloire* or other ironclads in France, and it was the spring of 1862 before North contracted with J & G Thomson of Glasgow, Scotland, for the construction of a large, seagoing ironclad ram. Identified in the yard by its hull number of *No. 61*, it was 270 feet in length and was designed for 4.5-inch armor supported by 18 inches of teak and to mount a standard broadsides battery of twenty guns. With its 20-foot draft, however, *No. 61*, also known as the "Scottish Sea Monster," would have been unable to operate effectively off the Southern coasts. It also required a sizeable 530-man crew. The obvious clash of this warship with British neutrality laws led to the cancellation of the contract in December 1863. On completion, the ship was sold to the Danish government as the *Danmark*.

James D. Bulloch, Mallory's second agent, had more success. By August 1861 the former U.S. Navy lieutenant, who had resigned from the service in 1853, was charged with securing cruisers to act against Union commerce. By August 1861 he had placed contracts with British yards for the ships that would become the Confederate cruisers *Alabama* and *Florida*. Then in June 1862 Bulloch arranged with the firm of John Laird and Sons to build two smaller armored ships. More suited to Confederate requirements, the two ships, known thereafter as the "Laird Rams," were 224 feet, 6 inches in length and drew only fifteen feet of water. They were to mount four 9-inch rifled guns in two rotating iron turrets. Each also sported a 7-foot iron ram at the bow. The ships were protected by the midships hull armor of 4.5 inches supported by 12 inches of teak, with an inner .625-inch iron belt. The turrets had 5.5 inches of iron protection, supported by 12 inches of teak. Screw propulsion and auxiliary sail were to provide ten-knot speed. Bullock did all he could to conceal the true destination for the ships, putting out the cover story that they had been ordered by the

Egyptian government as the *El Toussan* and *El Monassir*. U.S. agents were not fooled, and heavy pressure by Washington on London, assisted by changing Southern military fortunes in the summer of 1863, led the British government to seize both ships that October. The next year the government purchased them for the Royal Navy as the *Scorpion* and *Wivern*.

Bulloch was also active in France, where he contracted with Bordeaux shipbuilder Lucien Arman for two small steam rams. Tentatively named the *Cheops* and *Sphinx*, they were 171 feet, 10 inches in length with a 14-foot, 4-inch draft. Armament was to be a 9-inch rifle in pivot mount forward and two 6.4-inch pivot-mounted rifles in a stationary turret-shaped casemate aft. Each ship mounted a large submerged ram at the bow. The armor belt was 3.5 to 4.75 inches backed with 16 inches of wood, while the forecastle and casemate had 4.5-inch plate armor.

As with the British government in the case of the Laird Rams, and despite pledges to the contrary, the French government interfered. The *Cheops* was sold to Prussia as the *Prinz Albert*, and the *Sphinx* went to the Danes as the *Staerkodder*. With the Danes defeated by the Prussians in war in 1864, the *Staerkodder* went back to Arman, and Bulloch was then able to purchase it. Commissioned as the CSS *Stonewall* in January 1865 and the only foreign-built ironclad in Confederate service, by the time the *Stonewall* had reached Havana in May 1865, the war was over. Transferred to the United States by Spain, the *Stonewall* was sold to Japan as the *Kotetsu*. Later renamed the *Azuma*, it was Japan's first armored warship and took part in the Meiji Restoration War of the late 1860s.[16]

As noted earlier, Bullock contracted abroad for construction of commerce raiders. The *Alabama* and its consorts are dealt with later. The Confederate government also owned a number of blockade runners, although most of these ships remained privately held. These ships are also discussed later.

UNION NAVAL ORDNANCE

U.S. naval ordnance in 1861 was as advanced as any in the world, and, as in shipbuilding, the North held the advantages. Four of the five large prewar foundries capable of casting the heaviest iron guns were located north of the Mason-Dixon Line, and the single such facility in the South, the Tredegar in Richmond, did not employ the Rodman Process, acclaimed as the most advanced technique for producing the strongest guns. Despite shortcomings in manufacturing, the South's navy was so small that it did not suffer materially from ordnance shortages.

One man, John Dahlgren, dominated American naval ordnance of the era. Dahlgren joined the navy at age sixteen, and in 1847, as a lieutenant, he was assigned to direct ordnance activities at the Washington Navy Yard. He soon had developed new sights and firing mechanisms for heavy guns, and in 1848 he conducted experiments with the various classes of the navy's standard 32-pounder broadside guns and 8-inch pivot guns and produced the first ranging data for them.[17]

U.S. Navy sailors exercising with a 12-pounder Dahlgren smoothbore boat howitzer on board the monitor Lehigh. U.S. NAVAL INSTITUTE PHOTO ARCHIVE

In 1849 Dahlgren designed and produced a new boat howitzer. Cast of bronze, it appeared in a variety of types, chiefly 12-pounders (light, 660 lb, and heavy, 750 lb) and 24-pounder smoothbores (1,300 lb), but also 3.4-inch (12-pounder, 870 lb) and 4-inch (20-pounder, 1,350 lb) rifles. These were undoubtedly the finest boat guns of their day in the world. Capable of being mounted both in boats and on field carriages, as many as four of them were included in the armament of Union warships, and they formed the sole armament on some ships. They played an important role in the Civil War, especially in riverine warfare in the West, but also in amphibious operations along the coasts. Dahlgren boat howitzers continued in service with the U.S. Navy until the 1880s and were copied by other navies, most notably that of Japan. Boat howitzers were not included in the rating or official armament of warships, however.[18]

Dahlgren also designed shoulder arms, but he is chiefly known for his system of heavy smoothbore, muzzle-loading ordnance employed by both sides in the Civil War. The first prototype IX-inch gun was cast in May 1850. Dahlgren was familiar with the latest scientific knowledge relating the endurance of the gun to its exterior shape, and his guns had a smooth exterior, curved lines, and preponderance of metal at the breech, the point of greatest strain. Dahlgren guns resembled soda water bottles in appearance and were often referred to as such.

Dahlgren's IX-inch was the most common broadside, carriage-mounted gun in the U.S. Navy in the Civil War; his XI-inch, the prototype of which was cast in 1851, was the navy's most widely used pivot gun. Shell from an XI-inch gun could penetrate four-and-a-half inches of plate iron backed by twenty inches of solid oak.

Dahlgren guns appeared in a variety of sizes: 32-pounder (3,300 and 4,500 lb), VIII-inch (6,500 lb), IX-inch (12,280 lb), X-inch (12,500 lb for shell and 16,500 lb for shot), XI-inch (16,000 lb), XIII-inch (34,000 lb), and XV-inch (42,000 lb). There was even a gun of XX-inch bore (97,300 lb), although it came too late to see service afloat during the war. The XV-inch guns were the largest at sea during the war and were employed aboard the heaviest Union monitors. The basic philosophy behind such heavy guns was that their armor protection would allow the new monitors carrying a few of the heaviest weapons to close to short range where the massive projectiles would simply batter the target to pieces.

Both sides also employed rifled guns at sea. Rifles had the advantage of greater accuracy and higher velocity, but their very close tolerances combined with the state of metallurgy at the time made such guns problematic. And a gun bursting at sea could have far more disastrous consequences in the close confines of a ship than on land.

The first of the naval rifled guns were smoothbores converted into rifles. The most common rifled gun early in the war was the old army

42-pounder. To reinforce the area of greatest strain, some cast-iron rifled guns received a wrought-iron band on their breech ends. It was applied when hot and contracted as it cooled, gripping the breech tightly (the French knew this finishing touch as the pièce de résistance).

Dahlgren was among those who experimented with rifled guns. His rifles were somewhat similar in shape to his smoothbores, but many of them had separate bronze trunnion and breech straps. Dahlgren rifles appeared as 4.4-inch/30-pounder (3,200 lb), 5.1-inch/50-pounder (5,100 lb), 6-inch/80-pounder (8,000 lb), 7.5-inch/150-pounder (16,700 lb), and 12-inch (45,520 lb, only three of which were cast). The rifled guns were Dahlgren's singular ordnance failure. A number of them burst, and in February 1862 most were withdrawn from service.

The most well-known and widely used rifles at sea were the banded guns designed by Robert P. Parrott of the West Point Foundry. Parrott guns, some of which also burst, were nonetheless more reliable than those designed by Dahlgren, and by 1864 Parrott was the only founder producing rifled guns for the U.S. Navy. Although Parrott produced a large number of 2.9-inch (10-pounders) for the U.S. Army, as far as is known the navy never took delivery of any of these. The smallest U.S. Navy Parrott was the 3.67-inch (20-pounder). Parrott also made his rifled guns for the navy in the sizes of 4.2-inch (30-pounder), 5.3-inch (60-pounder), 6.4-inch (100-pounder, also known in the navy for its short shell as an 80-pounder), 8-inch (150-pounder, 200-pounder Army), and 10-inch (250-pounder, 300-pounder Army). Through February 1864, the navy had taken delivery of 790 Parrott guns. Still, rifled guns were in the minority in Union ship batteries during the war, and, where they did appear, it was in tandem with shot guns. By the end of the war, about one-fifth of the U.S. Navy ordnance inventory consisted of rifled guns.[19]

CONFEDERATE NAVAL ORDNANCE

As noted, the sole prewar source for the manufacture of heavy guns in the South was the Tredegar at Richmond, and during the conflict it produced the bulk of ordnance for the Confederacy. Not until February 1863 did the Confederate government purchase a new facility, which became the Selma, Alabama, Naval Works. It cast guns chiefly for use against Union ironclads, but it never turned out more than one gun a week.

Production of heavy guns at Selma was limited by the shortages of skilled labor and of proper gun iron.[20]

A principal difference between Union and Confederate naval guns is that Confederate pieces were not turned smooth. All U.S. Navy guns were so finished. Because this contributed nothing to the functioning of the gun and was a costly operation, the exteriors of Confederate guns were often the same as when they left the molds.

Despite myriad problems, Confederate ordnance production was sufficient to meet its more modest requirements, although the lack of manufacturing facilities and skilled labor led to difficulties in mounting guns, as well as shortages in shells and wrought-iron bolts.

The Confederates favored rifled guns. They converted a number of smoothbores to rifles, cast their own, and purchased some abroad. The Southerners also copied the Union Parrott design. The Tredegar produced some 2.9-inch (6-pounder) Parrott rifles for the Confederate Navy, one of which may be the weapon captured aboard the tug *Teaser*.[21] They also banded other cast-iron guns. Among favorites early in the war was the U.S. Navy heavy 32-pounder of 57 or 63 cwt, rifled and banded with wrought iron.

Dahlgren's counterpart in the Confederate Navy was Lt. John Mercer Brooke. Known for his work on the CSS *Virginia*, Brooke's ordnance accomplishments are particularly remarkable, given his lack of experience in that area. Brooke was responsible for the *Virginia*'s slanted armor casemate that was subsequently copied in other Confederate ironclads, as well as the idea of bow and stern extensions under water. Friction between Brooke and Naval Constructor Porter, who claimed full credit for the *Virginia*'s design, contributed to Brooke's subsequent lack of interest in the ironclad program. Promoted to commander in September 1862, Brooke in March 1863 was named chief of the Confederate Bureau of Ordnance and Hydrography, where he remained until the end of the war.

Brooke designed a variety of heavy guns for the Confederacy, including 8- and 9-inch smoothbores, 10- and 11-inch double-banded smoothbores, and the 11-inch triple-banded smoothbore. He is, however, best known for his double- and triple-banded rifled guns, which were produced in 6.4-inch, 7-inch, and 8-inch bore sizes. Brooke rifled guns were probably the finest such heavy guns at sea on either side in the war. As with Dahlgren, Brooke understood that a hemisphere offered the strongest cap for a cylindrical pressure vessel. He also understood the increase in strength gained from a wrought-iron band around the breech of a cast-iron gun.

Brooke-designed guns are identified, with few exceptions, by a fully hemispheric breech contour; layers of welded-on reinforcing bands; a plain tapered chase extending from the reinforcing bands to the muzzle; the general Confederate practice of not turning and merely leaving the exterior of the guns rough; and, save in the smoothbore guns, seven-groove rifling of right-hand twist.[22]

Union and Confederate Navy ordnance practices were the same, and, contrary to what some Union naval officers thought at the start of the conflict, Southern naval ordnance arrangements during the war were on a par with their own. The chief difference, and it was a significant one, lay in the amount of resources that each side could bring to bear.

There was a direct correlation between the size of a gun crew and rate of fire. Fourteen men was the suggested number for a heavy 32-pounder long gun on a truck carriage, whereas the 1864 U.S. Navy *Ordnance Instructions* specified sixteen men for the IX-inch Dahlgren on a Marsilly carriage and twenty-four men for the XI-inch pivot-mounted Dahlgren. The general rule of thumb was one man per 500 pounds of metal in the gun if it was on a truck carriage, or one man per 450 pounds of gun metal if on a pivot mount. In case both sides of the ship had to be fought at once, the size of each gun crew was halved.

Each gun crew member had a precise assignment. The fourteen-man crew for a heavy 32-pounder included the first gun captain, who had actual charge of the gun, the second gun captain, sponger and assistant sponger, loader and assistant loader, and tacklemen, handspikemen, and auxiliaries. Not counted a formal part of the gun crew, but essential to its operation, the boy or "powder monkey" assigned to each gun retrieved individual cartridges from the magazine and carried them to the gun.

The preliminary to battle was the command calling the crew to quarters, generally effected by a drum roll. The men placed their hammocks in the hammock rails along the sides of the ship, if not already there, to provide some additional protection against small arms fire. Among other preparations, the crew stowed furniture and other articles not necessary to battle, distributed small arms, made ready the rigging axes and boarding axes, filled fire buckets and water tubs from which the men might drink, and dropped the ship's boats astern.

Ordnance instructions during the Civil War provided for ten-step commands for both broadside and pivot guns. For broadside guns, the first command was "Silence! Man the starboard (or port) guns!" Generally the guns were kept loaded in a hostile environment, but they could be made ready for action in as little as three minutes of the first beat of the drum. Assuming that the guns were not loaded, the following was the general sequence of commands, all of which were given by the gun captain.

When the order was given to clear for action ("Cast loose and provide!"), the gun crew cast loose the portsill lanyard and cleared the gun and made it ready for action. On "Run in!" the crew worked the train tackle and handspikes to run the gun in, and then placed quoins (wedges) in front of the trucks (wheels) to prevent the gun from moving with the roll of the ship. "Serve the vent and sponge" was the command to ram a dampened wool sponge with a worm down the muzzle to the end of the bore both to extinguish any sparks and remove any debris. At the same time, the gun captain cleared the vent with a priming wire and sealed it with thumbstall.

On the command of "Load!" the charge in the form of a powder bag was placed in the muzzle end of the bore and rammed home. (Pass boxes were colored with the type of charge: red for short, white for medium, and blue for long range.) Marks on the rammer shaft indicated that the cartridge, and later the shot or fused shell, were properly seated against the cartridge. The shot or shell then followed.

On the next command, "Run out!," the crew removed the truck quoins, opened the port shutters, and used the tackles and handspikes to return the gun to its proper position for firing. On "Prime!" the gun captain again made certain the vent was clear and, by running the priming wire down the vent, punched a hole in the cartridge bag. He then inserted a primer and turned the hammer down on it.

The next command was "Aim!" Under the direction of the gun captain the crew used the handspikes and elevating screw (or a wooden quoin in the case of older guns) to train and elevate/depress the gun on its target. The men then assumed their stations well to the sides of the gun so as not to be caught when it recoiled against its breaching.

The last command for firing was the two-part "Ready—fire!" The gun captain held the lock lanyard taut until, according to the rise and fall of the vessel, the gun was properly aligned on the waterline of the enemy vessel, and on "fire" he sharply pulled the lanyard, which fired the gun and caused the gun and its carriage to recoil sharply back on its rope breeching. The firing sequence would be repeated as many times as necessary until the command of "Secure!" when the crew either secured or housed (in the case of the lower deck) the gun.[23]

Naval battles were usually not of long duration, but they could be bloody. Wooden and metal splinters caused by the explosion of a shell or hit of a shot were the chief causes of personnel casualties. Only on rare occasions during the Civil War would a crew be called upon to board an enemy ship. The men had no assigned weapons but would be issued a variety of small arms, including carbines, muskets, rifles, revolvers, boarding pikes and axes, cutlasses, and bayonets.

Both sides in the war followed these standard procedures. Given two ships of equal size, success in battle depended on thorough training, with the side that could fire its guns the faster and with the most accuracy the more likely to triumph. As with warfare generally, however, luck always played a role.

CHAPTER THREE

Union and Confederate Naval Strategies and the Start of the War

—~~~—

S ecession was already in the air when Republican Party candidate Abraham Lincoln won the U.S. presidential election of 6 November 1860. Although Lincoln captured only a plurality of the popular vote, he won an overwhelming majority in the Electoral College. Six weeks later, on 20 December, believing that Lincoln's election portended a move against the institution of slavery, the South Carolina legislature voted to secede. Other states soon followed: in order, Mississippi, Florida, Alabama, Georgia, and Louisiana, all in January 1861. Texas seceded on 1 February. Waverers on the issue of slavery were told that the South could negotiate its way back into the Union on more favorable terms. Southerners also assumed that Northerners would not fight to preserve the Union, whereas Northerners believed that most Southerners were loyal to the Union. Both were mistaken.

On 8 February, delegates from the seceded states met at Montgomery, Alabama, and formed the Confederate States of America. The next day the Confederate Congress elected Jefferson Davis as president. Meanwhile, the seceded states seized Federal property within their borders.

U.S. President James Buchanan took no action, nor did his successor, Lincoln, for three weeks. Buchanan opposed secession, but he believed he did not have the constitutional power to suppress it, and he was also reluctant to antagonize Virginia and other border states that he rightly feared might then join the Confederacy. Legal concerns notwithstanding, several of Buchanan's cabinet members resigned in protest over his failure to act.

The governments in the seceded states abruptly took control of all Federal forts and naval facilities within their territory. Alabama militiamen took Fort Morgan at Mobile on 5 January; Louisiana troops seized possession of Forts Jackson and St. Philip on the lower Mississippi River on 10 January; and Alabama and Florida units took over Fort Barrancas and the Pensacola Navy Yard on 12 January. By the time of Lincoln's inauguration in Washington on 4 March 1861, of national forts in the seceded states only Fort Pickens on Santa Rosa Island off Pensacola in Florida and Fort Sumter at Charleston, South Carolina, remained under Federal control. Sumter's situation was the most precarious. Located on an island in Charleston harbor, the fort was vulnerable to land artillery fire. Major Robert Anderson and his 127 officers and men at Sumter were also almost out of provisions. Sumter had neither been reinforced nor supplied since the troops had rowed out there from Fort Moultrie on the night of 26 December 1860.

On 2 January President Buchanan authorized reinforcements for Sumter, but, in order not to provoke the South, the two hundred men were to be sent out on an unarmed merchant vessel, the *Star of the West*. Word of the operation leaked out, and when the ship arrived off Charleston flying a large American flag and began moving past Morris Island, newly erected Confederate batteries there opened fire. Although the *Star of the West* made it past Morris Island, it then came under fire from Fort Moultrie and was obliged to turn back. With Sumter now masked by Confederate artillery, on 11 January 1861 authorities at Charleston demanded that Major Anderson surrender, but he refused.

Although there were those in the navy who believed they could reinforce Sumter without the introduction of ground troops, the army demurred. Major Anderson estimated that it would require up to twenty thousand troops in order to reduce the Charleston shore batteries before ships would be able to reach Sumter. U.S. Army general-in-chief, Brevet Lt. Gen. Winfield Scott, concurred with Anderson, but he placed the estimate at twenty-five thousand men: five thousand regulars and twenty thousand volunteers. Putting this in perspective, the entire U.S. Army numbered about sixteen thousand men, many of whom were scattered in outposts across the western frontier.

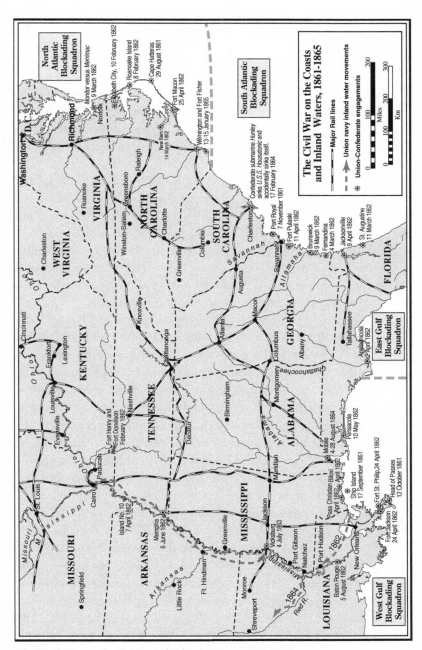

The following labels appear on the map:

North Atlantic Blockading Squadron

Monitor versus Merrimac, 9 March 1862
Elizabeth City, 10 February 1862
Roanoke Island, 8 February 1862
Cape Hatteras, 29 August 1861
Fort Macon, 25 April 1862

Norfolk
Richmond
Washington, D.C.

South Atlantic Blockading Squadron

Wilmington and Fort Fisher, 13-15 January 1865
New Bern, 14 March 1862
Raleigh
Greensboro
Winston-Salem
Roanoke
VIRGINIA
WEST VIRGINIA
Charleston
NORTH CAROLINA
Charlotte
Greenville
Columbia
SOUTH CAROLINA
Charleston
Augusta
Savannah

Confederate submarine Hunley sinks U.S.S. Housatonic and accidentally sinks itself, 17 February 1864

Port Royal, 7 November 1861
Fort Pulaski, 11 April 1862
Brunswick, 9 March 1862
Fernandina, 4 March 1862
Jacksonville, 11 March 1862
St. Augustine, 9 April 1862

FLORIDA

East Gulf Blockading Squadron

Apalachicola, 3 April 1862
Tallahassee

The Civil War on the Coasts and Inland Waters, 1861-1865

Major Rail lines
Union navy inland water movements
Union-Confederate engagements

0   100   200
Miles
0   100   200   300
Km

Cincinnati
Frankfort
Lexington
Louisville
Evansville
KENTUCKY
Knoxville
Chattanooga
TENNESSEE
Nashville
Decatur
Birmingham
ALABAMA
GEORGIA
Atlanta
Macon
Columbus
Montgomery
Albany
Chattahoochee
Alabama
Altamaha
Savannah

Fort Henry and Fort Donelson, February 1862
Paducah
Cairo
St. Louis
MISSOURI
Springfield
Ohio
Missouri
Mississippi

Island No. 10, 7 April 1862
Memphis, 6 June 1862
ARKANSAS
Little Rock
Ft. Hindman
Arkansas
Greenville
Natchez
Monroe
Shreveport
Vicksburg, 4 July 1863
Port Gibson
Port Hudson
MISSISSIPPI
Jackson
Meridian
Mobile, 4-28 August 1864
Pensacola, 10 May 1862
Ship Island, 17 September 1861
Cass Christian Biloxi, April 1862
Baton Rouge, 5 August 1862
Fort St. Philip, 24 April 1862
Head of Passes, 12 October 1861
Fort Jackson, 24 April 1862
New Orleans
LOUISIANA
Red R.
1864
1862

West Gulf Blockading Squadron

The Civil War on the Coasts and Inland Waters, 1861–1865

Reluctantly, Secretary of the Navy Welles and Secretary of War Simon Cameron concurred with Scott's gloomy assessment. Secretary of State William Seward also pointed out that a relief expedition to Sumter would probably lead to war and bring the secession of Virginia. Seward favored evacuating Sumter and holding Pickens. Scott concurred with Seward's view but favored evacuating both forts. When Lincoln polled his cabinet in mid-March, only Postmaster General Montgomery Blair and Interior Secretary Caleb B. Smith favored an expedition to Sumter. The other five members were opposed.[1]

Lincoln was torn, but he believed he had to take some action. Northern opinion was hardening against the South, and the press was demanding that something be done to reinforce Sumter. Gustavus Vasa Fox, introduced by his brother-in-law Blair to Lincoln, assured the president that the navy could run boats filled with supplies and men to Sumter under the cover of darkness and protected by that fort's guns and those of nearby ships. The persuasive Fox seems to have reinforced Lincoln's own view that both Anderson and Scott were unduly pessimistic.

On the evening of 28 March, following a dinner at the White House, Lincoln met with his chief advisors. Scott had left early and was thus not present when Lincoln read Scott's letter urging evacuation of both forts and claiming that this might "instantly soothe and give confidence to the eight remaining slave-holding States, and render their cordial adherence to the Union perpetual." Some professed to see Virginia native Scott as tainted in his views, and it became clear as the discussion wore on that Lincoln wanted something done to reinforce both forts. The next morning in a cabinet meeting, Seward concluded that Lincoln was determined on action and that a majority of the cabinet were now prepared to support this position, but he did not inform Scott.[2]

Ignoring the simpler course of evacuating Sumter and holding on to Pickens, on 30 March Lincoln ordered Secretary of the Navy Welles to prepare a relief expedition for Sumter based on the plan drawn up by Fox. The expedition was to be ready to sail by 6 April, with Lincoln to make the final decision at that point. The key warship in the planned relief of Sumter was the side-wheeler steam frigate *Powhatan*, with one pivot-mounted XI-inch Dahlgren and ten broadside IX-inch Dahlgrens. Located at the Brooklyn Navy Yard, the ship had only recently returned from a lengthy cruise in poor repair and had been ordered to be decommissioned and its engines disassembled. Welles revoked these orders and instructed that the ship be readied for the Sumter expedition.

Lincoln was still vacillating on a decision regarding the relief of Forts Pickens and Sumter when on 1 April Seward, accompanied by Army Capt. Montgomery Meigs and Navy Lt. David Dixon Porter, presented the president with his own plan to reinforce Fort Pickens. In company of the *Powhatan*, the large steam transport *Atlantic* would ferry six hundred men, artillery, and supplies to Fort Pickens. Porter assured Lincoln that if he were given command of the frigate, he could guarantee success. Following discussion, Lincoln agreed with Seward's proposals and personally signed the orders. Seward and Porter convinced Lincoln to bypass Welles, claiming that if the Navy Department was involved, disloyal clerks there would immediately inform Confederate authorities and that any chance to save Fort Pickens would thus be lost. Nonetheless, Lincoln's decision to bypass Welles and appoint a lieutenant to command a frigate were major breaches of established naval procedure.[3]

On the morning of 2 April, Porter presented himself to Capt. Andrew H. Foote at the Brooklyn Navy Yard. Foote was immediately suspicious of Porter, concerned that this might be a ploy to turn the *Powhatan* over

U.S. Navy side-wheeler frigate Powhatan. NAVAL HISTORICAL CENTER (NH 48103)

to the South. Porter eventually convinced Foote to proceed and not to inform Welles. Working around the clock, men at the yard managed to have the frigate ready for sea in only four days.[4]

Welles, unaware of Seward's machinations, was himself meanwhile assembling the squadron for Fort Sumter. Several telegrams from the secretary, however, convinced Foote that Welles did not know what was planned for the *Powhatan*, and Foote hinted at the true situation in a telegram that immediately aroused Welles's suspicions. Matters came to a head late on the night of 5 April when Welles confronted Seward. The two men then met with Lincoln at the White House, and, over Seward's protests, the president ordered the *Powhatan* restored to the Sumter expedition.

Seward continued his duplicitous ways. Instructed by Lincoln to notify the Brooklyn Navy Yard immediately, he delayed sending the telegram until 2:30 PM on 6 April. He also did not note that this decision was by Lincoln's order. Thus Foote did not receive the telegram until 3 PM, a half hour after the *Powhatan* had sailed. Foote immediately sent a tug with an aide to overhaul the frigate, but Porter refused to obey the telegram, stating that his orders came directly from the president and that it was too late for him to change his plans. The *Powhatan* continued out into the Atlantic.

The Sumter expedition with Fox in charge that sailed from New York and Hampton Roads during 8–10 April thus consisted of two warships only: the screw sloop *Pawnee* (eight IX-inch Dahlgrens) and the side-wheeler *Harriet Lane*, the only steamer in the Revenue Service (three IX-inch Dahlgrens and a 4.2-inch Parrott rifle). These escorted the *Baltic*, an unarmed troop and supply ship with two hundred men and supplies. Although the absence of the *Powhatan* probably did not change the outcome at Sumter, the chain of events involving the frigate says much about the Lincoln administration decision making at the beginning of the war.[5]

On 6 April Lincoln had dispatched State Department clerk Robert L. Chew to Charleston to inform South Carolina Governor Francis Pickens that a Federal supply expedition was being sent to Fort Sumter, in effect leaving it up to Confederate authorities whether there would be war. Chew arrived in Charleston on the night of 8 April and immediately met with Pickens. At the same time Anderson at Sumter received word via letter from U.S. Secretary of War Cameron of the relief expedition. Meanwhile, Confederate Brig. Gen. Pierre G. T. Beauregard had established new shore batteries facing Sumter and had trained guns on Sumter from Forts Moultrie and Johnson.

Pickens immediately informed Jefferson Davis of Lincoln's message, and, following a meeting and concurrence of the Confederate cabinet, on Davis's order, Confederate Secretary of War Leroy Pope Walker instructed Beauregard to demand Sumter's surrender and, if this was refused, to reduce the fort. Confident of the arrival of the relief expedition, Anderson rejected the demand, whereupon Beauregard ordered his shore batteries to open fire before the Union ships could arrive. At 4:30 AM on 12 April the first shot of the Civil War boomed out across Charleston harbor, opening a lopsided thirty-four-hour artillery duel. In order to conserve ammunition, Anderson restricted Sumter's return fire to only six guns.

Although Fox's ships arrived off Charleston harbor, rough weather precluded any attempt to launch boats to resupply Sumter. Lacking the most powerful ship assigned to his squadron, Fox was also reluctant to expose his ships to enemy fire. With the Confederate batteries holding the Federal ships at bay, and with Sumter nearly out of food and fires having broken out in the fort, Anderson surrendered the next day.

On 14 April, having received Beauregard's permission, Sumter's garrison began a last act of firing a hundred-gun salute to the U.S. flag. On the fiftieth shot, however, one of its guns exploded, killing a Union soldier and wounding several others, the only casualties in the battle that began the bloodiest war in U.S. history.

The shelling of Fort Sumter galvanized opinion on both sides. As Confederate Secretary of State Robert Toombs had warned Davis, it ended any sympathy in the North for the Confederate cause. With the South having fired on the U.S. flag, a patriotic fervor swept the North. On 15 April, citing existence of an "insurrection," Lincoln issued a call for seventy-five thousand volunteers to serve for three months. What had long been dreaded was now reality; America was at war with itself.

Meanwhile, Federal troops and supplies arrived in Pensacola Bay in the *Brooklyn*. The men went ashore at Fort Pickens on 13 April. Five days later, the steam ferry *Atlantic* came in, followed a few hours later by the *Powhatan*, which had been plagued by defective boilers. Fort Pickens, at least, was secure for the Union.

As Scott and others had feared, Lincoln's decision to reinforce the two forts brought the defection of much of the Upper South. Virginia, North

Carolina, Tennessee, and Arkansas joined their Southern sisters in secession. The losses of Virginia, with its important manufacturing center of
Richmond and the Norfolk Navy Yard, and Tennessee, with its considerable natural resources, were particularly grievous to the Union side.

Union material losses at Norfolk were needlessly heavy. In April 1861
the yard held eleven ships in various states of repair and construction,
ranging from the *Pennsylvania*—in its heyday the largest sailing ship in
the U.S. Navy but now stripped of its armament and serving as a receiving ship—to the dispatch brig *Dolphin.* Undoubtedly the most important
was the modern, powerful 3,200-ton steam frigate *Merrimack.* It had been
sent to the yard to have its weak, unreliable engines rebuilt.

Uneasy about the future of both the yard and this prize ship, Secretary
Welles on 11 April ordered commandant of the Norfolk Navy Yard
Commo. Charles F. McCauley to prepare the *Merrimack* "in as short a time
as possible for temporary service." That same day Welles ordered two hun-
dred seamen, including twenty firemen and coal heavers, there from New
York, and he sent Cdr. James Alden to Norfolk to take command of the
steam frigate and bring it to Philadelphia. The next day he ordered Chief
Engineer Benjamin F. Isherwood to Norfolk to reassemble its engines.[6]

These efforts were largely negated by McCauley's bumbling. A
veteran of the War of 1812 who should have long before been retired,
McCauley was easily influenced by junior officers sympathetic to the
South. They took advantage of Welles's earlier admonition to McCauley
not to do anything that might alarm Virginia authorities and bring that
state into the war. The Southern sympathizers informed McCauley that
sending the *Merrimack* to sea would do just that, even bring an attack by
Virginia militia on the yard. As a result, although Isherwood managed to
reassemble the ship's engines in working order, McCauley resolutely
refused to allow the *Merrimack* to depart.

Furious at the inaction, Welles ordered Capt. Hiram Paulding to
replace McCauley, but Paulding arrived back at Norfolk at 8 PM on 20 April
from a quick trip to Washington only to find that McCauley, believing the
yard was about to be attacked, had ordered the scuttling of all its ships.

Paulding had no choice but to continue the work begun by McCauley
and was able to get away only two ships. Early on the morning of 21 April
the screw sloop *Pawnee* towed off the sailing sloop *Cumberland.* Once they
were safe, Paulding gave the signal to torch the yard.[7]

The work of destruction was only haphazard. Barrels of powder at the dry dock failed to go off. The occupying Confederates discovered intact valuable machinery and castings, ammunition, and stores. The next day Confederate Navy Lt. G. T. Sinclair telegraphed Secretary Mallory:

The *Pennsylvania, Merrimack, Germantown, Raritan, Columbia,* and *Dolphin* are burned to the water's edge and sunk. The *Delaware, Columbus,* and *Plymouth* are sunk. All can be raised; the *Plymouth* easily; not much injured. The *Germantown* crushed and sunk by the falling of shears. Her battery, new and complete, uninjured by fire; can be recovered. The most abominable vandalism at the yard. Destruction less than might be expected. . . . About 4,000 shells thrown overboard; can be recovered. The *Germantown's* battery will be up and ready for service to-morrow. In ordnance building all small arms broken and thrown overboard will be fished up. The brass howitzers thrown overboard are up. The *Merrimack* has 2,200 10-pound cartridges in her magazine in water-tight tanks. . . . Only eight guns, 32-pounders, destroyed. About 1,000 or more from 11-inch to 32-pounders taken, and ready for our cause. . . . Many thousands of shells and shot, from 11-inch to 32-pounders, safe. All the machinery uninjured. Magazine captured, with 2,000 barrels of powder and vast numbers of shells and quantities of fixed ammunition.[8]

In all, the South secured 1,195 heavy guns, including 52 IX-inch Dahlgrens. A number were soon on their way to coastal defenses throughout the Confederacy. The Confederates also raised the *Merrimack,* took apart and reassembled its machinery, and rebuilt it as the ironclad *Virginia.*[9]

Rear Adm. David Dixon Porter wrote scathingly of the fiasco:

The department did not seem to reflect that a few armed tow-boats with marines on board, could have been sent from New York to tow all the vessels under the guns of Fortress Monroe. One tug with a twenty-four pounder howitzer on board, properly handled, would have been master of the situation. . . . The broadside of the *Germantown,* which was all ready for sea and only waiting a crew, or the *Portsmouth,* in the same condition, would, with a few men on board, have saved the Navy Yard against attack, overawed Norfolk and Portsmouth, and prevented the channel from being obstructed by the Confederates.[10]

Despite the serious losses sustained at Norfolk, the North still enjoyed overwhelming material advantages, and these resources helped determine strategy. Although its own resources were far inferior to those of the North, the South did not have to defeat the North militarily in order to achieve its aims. Its leaders hoped that they could remain on the defensive, wearing down their opponent to the point that the Northern population tired of the war and prevailed on Washington to recognize Southern independence. In order for it to triumph, however, the North would have to invade and physically conquer the South. The South was a vast territory, and how and where to attack it were major issues that Northern leaders would have to resolve.

Seventy-five-year-old Union General-in-Chief Scott was one of the few who understood the enormity of the task facing the North. He warned Lincoln that the war would be both difficult and protracted. Scott estimated it would take an army of three hundred thousand men three years just to subdue only the Deep South. While this great army was being trained, Scott wanted a naval blockade of the Confederacy's Atlantic and Gulf coasts to strangle the South economically and prevent it from importing military supplies from Europe. Once the Northern armies were trained, Scott wanted to send them along the principal Southern rivers with flotillas of steam gunboats. These would bisect the South, cutting it in two along the eleven-hundred-mile-long Mississippi River. Although Scott soon retired from the military, his strategy lived on. Known as the "Anaconda Plan," for the giant snake that strangles its victims to death, its broad outlines formed the basis of the Northern victory. Thus Secretary of the Navy Welles did not have grand strategic dilemmas to resolve but generally fitted navy operations into the overall national plan.[11]

Although the Civil War witnessed no great fleet battles, such as during the Napoleonic Wars or World Wars I and II, there were some spectacular small engagements. The struggle that now unfolded on the high seas and along the South Atlantic and Gulf Coasts and great interior rivers was immensely important to the war's outcome and a prime example of the advantage of command of the sea in war. Throughout, the North dominated on the water, its advantage growing steadily during the course of the conflict.

In his annual report at the end of 1861, Welles spelled out the Union naval goals as the "closing of all the insurgent ports," combined naval and military expeditions against the Confederate coasts, and hunting down on the high seas of the "piratical" Confederate cruisers. Certainly, by far the major effort was the blockade of the Confederate coasts. Numbers of ships involved alone confirm this. The North employed its crushing naval superiority to ruin the South's commodities export trade, denying the Confederacy the means to pay for manufactured goods that would enhance its war effort. The Union also used its naval strength to mount amphibious operations along the Confederate coasts and on the interior rivers of the West with its few and inadequate roads. Finally, Welles was forced to send out increasing numbers of fast, powerful cruisers to hunt down and destroy the few Southern state-sponsored commerce raiders attacking Union merchant shipping on the high seas.[12]

Confederate naval strategy centered on efforts to break the Union blockade. At the same time, however, Mallory hoped to carry the war to the North by attacking its shipping and even its ports. Mallory's initial strategy was aggressive and offensive. Largely ignoring coastal defense, which he left to the army and land fortifications, he made breaking the Union blockade his top priority. As he could never hope to match the North in numbers of ships, Mallory hoped to achieve this end with a few powerful, technologically advanced ironclad vessels, armed with large, powerful rifled guns. Secondarily, Mallory sought to send out commerce raiders to cause financial hardship in the North by destroying its shipping on the high seas. Mallory had no confidence in privateers, and the raiders he envisioned were regular commissioned naval vessels that would operate in conformity with established international law. As the war progressed, Mallory shifted to a more defensively oriented approach and increasingly experimented with new methods of warfare, including mines and the submarine.

At the very beginning of the war, President Davis committed a major strategic blunder. The South exported the bulk of its cotton crop to Britain, and Davis embraced a plan—although it was never officially announced Confederate policy—to suspend cotton exports in the mistaken belief that "Cotton Diplomacy" would bring British intervention. The assumption here was that withholding the cotton would be such economic pressure as to force the British government to dispatch warships to assist in breaking the Union blockade. Neither occurred. Not only were cotton markets accessible to Britain in Egypt and India, but Northern "corn" (grain) was also immensely important to Britain.

As a result of this mistaken decision, the Confederacy lost a splendid opportunity to secure the sinews of war. Before the Union blockade could become effective, the South should have rushed every available bale of cotton to European markets in order to purchase as many arms and manufactured goods as possible. Much of the embargoed cotton later rotted on Southern wharfs. Its gold reserves soon exhausted, the Confederacy then reversed its policy, attempting to ship cotton to pay for the goods received. By then it was too late, for the Union blockade had become much more effective.

THE ATTITUDE OF BRITAIN AND FRANCE

The leaders of the Confederacy placed great stock in securing diplomatic recognition from Britain and France. There was indeed considerable initial support for the Confederacy in both countries, especially among the upper classes, although many working people tended to regard African-Americans as inferior in general and saw white Southerners as struggling to break free of Northern oppression. Such attitudes changed during the war, particularly with Lincoln's Emancipation Proclamation.

Both the French and British governments feared the loss of the chief source of their nations' raw cotton and the cutting off of a lucrative market for manufactured goods. Paris had initially opposed the division of the United States as it sought a strong and united America to help counter British naval power. French leaders also feared that France and Britain might be drawn into the war on opposite sides. To avoid the latter, Paris was willing to coordinate with London its policies toward the Civil War.[13]

On 14 May 1861, Queen Victoria issued a proclamation through the Palmerston ministry that recognized the Confederate States as a belligerent power. This rejected the Lincoln Administration's contention that Confederate privateers were pirates. At the same time, however, on 1 June the Queen forbade armed ships of either the United States or the Confederacy from bringing their prizes into British home or colonial ports. France and the other major maritime powers promptly followed suit. Not really appreciated in the North at the time, this policy of neutrality was a serious blow to the Confederacy. For prizes to be legal, captured vessels had to be taken into port and there adjudicated by a prize court as a legal capture. Privateering involved the capture of civilian property by private individuals and thus could not mean simple destruction of enemy vessels. On the other hand, international law held that state warships could legally destroy captured vessels. Thus without access to prize courts, privateers would be little more than pirates. Not only did a declaration of neutrality prohibit the entry of prize vessels to ports but it prohibited that nation's citizens from fitting out privateers under the flag of either belligerent. One factor at work behind the British government's refusal to try to break the Northern naval blockade was that London had always insisted that other powers respect British blockades, even when these existed largely on paper.

At the same time that it proclaimed British neutrality, London invoked the Foreign Enlistment Act of 1819. This legislation prohibited its citizens from taking part in the wars of other nations. This decision produced anger in the North, particularly in some western states, over the insistence of some British citizens applying for U.S. citizenship that they could not be made to serve in the army. Lincoln defused the situation by ordering all foreigners who had expressed the intention to seek U.S. citizenship but had refused to serve in the army to leave the country in sixty-five days or face the possibility of military service. To Lincoln's relief, the Palmerston ministry recognized this action as entirely correct.

Of course, relations were sometimes rocky between Washington and London and Washington and Paris. British citizens were very much involved in financing and manning the blockade runners to the South, and such individuals routinely fell into Union hands. To prevent their imprisonment from becoming a diplomatic crisis, Secretary Seward adopted a lenient policy. Generally speaking, British citizens who were apprehended in blockade-running activities were imprisoned only a few days or months and then handed over to British authorities on the pledge that they would in the future refrain from assisting the Confederacy. This did not mean that there were not major crises that threatened war between Britain and the United States. The first such test occurred in the *Trent* Affair of November 1861.

THE *TRENT* AFFAIR

In order to try to intercept the Confederate commerce raider *Sumter*, Secretary Welles detached a half dozen U.S. warships from the blockade, among them the screw frigate *San Jacinto*, commanded by Capt. Charles

Wilkes. On 8 November 1861, Wilkes put into Havana to coal and there learned that the two newly appointed Confederate commissioners to Britain, James M. Mason and John Slidell, had recently sailed for England on board the British mail packet *Trent*. The overzealous Wilkes pursued the *Trent*, caught up with it east of Cuba, and forcibly removed Mason and Slidell, placing the two men in irons.

As Wilkes no doubt had hoped, much of the North lionized him for this action, but the British government saw it as a clear violation of international law and demanded the immediate release of the Confederate commissioners. Prime Minister Lord Palmerston threatened war if the incident was not resolved to London's satisfaction, and to make the point he ordered eight thousand British troops to Canada and instructed the Admiralty to prepare for war against the United States.

Cooler heads prevailed. In Britain Benjamin Disraeli urged a "generous interpretation" of Wilkes's action, and Prince Albert helped draft the note to Washington so as to allow the U.S. government a graceful escape. Lincoln was indeed furious at Wilkes's action and stressed the need to fight only "one war at a time." He agreed that both Mason and Slidell would be released, and in January 1862 the two Confederate commissioners were quietly transferred to a British warship off the New England coast, although Northern leaders could not resist pointing out to London the parallels between the event and Royal Navy impressment practices earlier in the century. Resolution of the crisis again revealed the commonsense approach of Lincoln, who had gone against Northern public opinion in order to maintain the diplomatic isolation of the Confederacy. Other difficult tests between London and Washington came later in the building of Confederate commerce raiders in British yards and the Laird Rams controversy.[14]

SOUTHERN PRIVATEERS

Since the Confederacy had so few ships available to it at the beginning of the war, President Davis turned to private vessels. On 17 April, two days after Lincoln called for seventy-five thousand volunteers, Davis and Secretary of State Robert Toombs issued a statement that proclaimed Lincoln's "intention of invading this Confederacy with an armed force for the purpose of capturing its fortresses, and thereby subverting its independence and subjecting the free people thereof to the domination of foreign power." Davis thus invited "all those who may desire, by service in private-armed vessels on the high seas, to aid this Government in resisting so wanton and wicked an aggression, to make application for commissions or letters of marque and reprisal to be issued under the seal of these Confederate States." The Confederate Congress passed, and Davis signed into law on 6 May, a bill recognizing a state of war with the United States and establishing regulations for "letters of marque, prizes, and prize goods" similar to those employed by the United States in the War of 1812.[15]

Davis and other Southern leaders believed that privateering was legally justified because, alone among major powers, the United States and Spain had failed to ratify the 1856 Declaration of Paris, the signatories of which foreswore the employment of privateers. In 1861 privateering seemed a natural recourse for a nation without a navy and thus dependent upon private assistance.

In retaliation for the Southern action, on 19 April Lincoln proclaimed a blockade of the Confederate coasts and warned that anyone who "shall molest a vessel of the United States, or the persons or cargo on board of her, such person will be held amenable to the laws of the United States for the prevention and punishment of piracy."[16] Lincoln also offered to bind the United States to adhere unconditionally to the 1856 Declaration of Paris, an idea rejected by British Secretary of State for Foreign Affairs Lord John Russell, who pointed out that any European power signing such a convention with the United States would be bound to treat all Confederate privateers as pirates.[17]

Mallory had little confidence in privateers, but even modest success in this quarter would force up insurance rates in the North and adversely affect the business sector there. Also even a few privateers would oblige the U.S. Navy to shift warships from the blockade to hunt for them. Mallory was strongly in favor of commerce raiding per se, but he favored national cruisers, which, however, were not available at the start of the conflict.

Lincoln's threat did not deter applications for letters of marque in the Confederacy, with the first coming in the day after Davis's invitation. On 10 May, the same day the regulations were published, the government granted the first commission, to the 30-ton schooner *Triton* of Brunswick, Georgia. One of the smallest privateers, it was armed with a single 6-pounder and had a crew of twenty men. The largest of the Confederate privateers, the 1,644-ton steamer *Phenix*, was fitted out in Wilmington, North Carolina, at the end of May. It mounted seven guns and had a crew of 243. Although by mid-summer letters of marque and reprisal had been issued to ships in most of the major Confederate ports, the chief venues remained Charleston and New Orleans. In all, the Confederacy issued letters of marque for fifty-two privateers.[18]

The few Confederate privateers that got to sea in May found easy hunting. The first success came on 16 May, when the *Calhoun* of New Orleans, of 509 tons and five guns (one 18-pounder, two 12-pounders, and two 6-pounders), captured the 290-ton Union merchant bark *Ocean Eagle* of Rockland, Maine, off the Mississippi River mouth. The Union ship carried 3,144 barrels of lime consigned to a New Orleans firm. Over the next two weeks, the *Calhoun* took five other Union ships, three of them whalers. Two other New Orleans privateers, the steamers *Music* and *V. H. Ivy*, captured four Union ships.

The heady atmosphere of these early days, along with a premonition that this period would be brief, may be seen in a letter written by a crewman of the *V. H. Ivy* on 21 May:

> Last Friday I left New Orleans for this place and boat for a little privateering—to assist in annoying the enemy's commerce. . . . On board the *Ivy* are guns and men enough to accomplish great destruction, were we called on to open with our cannon . . .
>
> We lie in or near the river every night, but start out soon after midnight, and keep a sharp lookout for any speck on the horizon, and when the cry of "sail-ho!" is heard the *Ivy*'s "tendrils" don revolvers, swords, knives and rifles with great excitement and good nature. We have exceedingly good times . . . but I fear all will be closed with the appearance of the blockading force.[19]

Indeed, the arrival at the end of May off the mouth of the Missisippi of the screw sloop *Brooklyn*, with its IX-inch Dahlgrens, soon put an end to privateering from the Crescent City. Although such activity at New Orleans was brief-lived, it was just reaching its heyday along the Atlantic coast.

Typical of the Atlantic coast privateers was the fast 53-ton schooner *Savannah*, with a crew of twenty men and armed with a single short 18-pounder of War of 1812 vintage turned into a rifled gun, as well as an array of muskets, pistols, and cutlasses. Commissioned on 18 May, it was ready for sea two weeks later. No Union blockaders were in evidence when the *Savannah* departed Charleston on 2 June. Commanded by Harrison Baker, the *Savannah* soon captured and sent into port the merchant brig *Joseph* of Philadelphia, the first prize taken by a Charleston privateer.

At dusk that same day, the *Savannah* spotted a sail and ran toward it. The ship in question turned out to be the U.S. Navy brig *Perry*, with six 32-pounders. The *Savannah* had lost part of her top rigging in a storm the night before and could thus not hope to outrun the Union ship. Baker ordered the *Savannah*'s remaining sails lowered to try to avoid detection in the approaching darkness, but lookouts on the *Perry* spotted the privateer nonetheless. The *Perry* quickly closed on the *Savannah*, and both ships ran up their respective colors. It was 7:50 PM and almost dark when the *Perry* opened fire. Gun flashes from both ships illuminated the scene in the gathering darkness, but the shots went wild. Most of the privateer's crew took cover during the fight, with only four men manning its single gun. His ship hopelessly outclassed and fearing its imminent destruction, Baker surrendered after twenty minutes.

Sailed to New York, the *Savannah* was there condemned and sold. Its crew became something of a *cause célèbre*. Branded as "pirates" by the Northern press and Federal government, the men were brought to trial, and, under public pressure, were threatened with the death penalty. President Davis promptly issued a statement to the effect that if they were executed, he would hang Union officers on a one-for-one basis. For whatever reason, the Federal government soon backed down. In February 1862 it decided that privateersmen would be treated as prisoners of war and moved from jails to military prisons. As for the crew of the *Savannah*, two died in captivity, and the remainder were exchanged.[20]

Union warships soon ran down the remaining Confederate privateers. Some of the privateers were taken at sea, whereas others succumbed to cutting-out operations in which Union forces went into a harbor and seized the ship by storm. Still others, such as the brig *Jefferson Davis*, fell prey to natural causes. One of the more successful Confederate privateers, the *Jefferson Davis* received its commission on 18 June 1861. Privateers more often than not found armament hard to come by, and the *Jefferson Davis* was no exception; it mounted five old cannons manufactured in England in 1801: two 32-pounders and two 24-pounders in broadside and one long 18-pounder on a pivot mount amidships. It sailed from Charleston on 28 June and took nine prizes (one of which was recaptured).

The lure of privateering sometimes led captured crew members to enlist, and this occurred when two seamen from one of its prizes joined the crew of the *Jefferson Davis*. Nonetheless Louis Coxtetter, the privateer's captain, found himself desperately short of crewmen from the need to man his prizes; he was also running out of provisions. Coxtetter tried to put in to St. Augustine, but his ship grounded and was wrecked on 10 August while trying to enter that harbor.[21]

Privateers were in fact not much used in the war. The British government decision, copied by the other maritime powers, to ban privateer prizes from British ports dealt a death blow to Confederate privateering. As the Union blockade improved in effectiveness, it became more difficult to send prizes to the South, and increasing numbers of them were recaptured. Subsequently many privateer vessels were simply converted into blockade runners. Privateering out of Pamlico Sound ended when Flag Officer Silas H. Stringham led his squadron there in August, and most Confederate privateers were gone within a year. Two of the most unusual Confederate privateers were at New Orleans: the ironclad ram *Manassas* and the submarine *Pioneer*. The Confederate war against Union commerce was nonetheless carried on with considerable effectiveness by Mallory's regularly commissioned naval warships.

Despite the early threat, Secretary Welles resisted strong political pressure in the North that ships be detached from blockade duties to defend the Federal coastline. For the most part, Welles insisted that, as they came available, new warships be employed in blockading the Confederacy or in securing the great rivers of the West.

EARLY FIGHTING

As the Union blockade went forward, albeit it slowly and with scant effectiveness at first, numerous small engagements took place between Union ships and shore batteries. The first of these occurred on 7 May when the Union armed tug *Yankee* came under fire from a Confederate battery at Gloucester Point at the mouth of the York River. Along the Potomac, the Confederates set up shore batteries to disrupt Union river traffic. Indeed, officials in Washington were greatly concerned about a possible Confederate coup de main against the Federal capital.

On 22 April 1861, Cdr. James H. Ward proposed to Welles the creation of a "flying flotilla" for duty in Chesapeake Bay and its tributaries. Welles approved the request five days later. Soon the Potomac Flotilla, Ward's scratch force of small, lightly armed steamers, was patrolling the river to secure the movement of Union transports and supply ships to the capital.[22]

In this activity, the Washington Navy Yard played an important role. Located on the Eastern branch of the Potomac, it was the chief defense of the capital. On or about 22 April, most naval officers at the yard, including its commandant, Capt. Franklin Buchanan from Maryland, resigned their commissions. Cdr. John Dahlgren then took over for Buchanan. With the Washington Navy Yard an important element in the capital's defense, Lincoln became a frequent visitor there and often conferred with Dahlgren. The two men soon became fast friends.[23]

Centered on the Potomac and Rappahannock Rivers and Chesapeake Bay, the Potomac Flotilla was specifically charged with the defense of Washington. Increasing numbers of Confederate shore batteries, especially at Alexandria, rendered flotilla activity hazardous. Army troops were then assigned to operate with the flotilla and carry out limited land assaults. During 29 May–1 June the steamers *Thomas Freeborn*, *Anacostia*, and *Resolute* (joined by the *Pawnee* on 31 May) engaged and silenced Confederate shore batteries at Aquia Creek, Virginia. Then on 27 June, Ward's flagship, the three-gun *Thomas Freeborn*, supported a Union landing at Mathias Point. The landing party encountered a sizable Confederate force, which forced the attackers back to their ships. In the ensuing exchange of fire, Commander Ward was struck and mortally wounded by a Confederate musket ball as he sighted one of his ship's 32-pounders, becoming the first Union naval officer killed in the war.[24]

Both sides mounted raids. Meanwhile, the Potomac Flotilla steadily increased in size and firepower, and by March 1862 the Confederates, who needed the guns elsewhere, had withdrawn their shore batteries from the Potomac. More serious fighting was occurring on land between the two sides to the interior.

At the beginning of the war, Union forces secured western Virginia, control of which was vital for Federal westward communications. But expectations in the North of a quick victory over the South were dashed in the first important battle of the war, in which Union forces sought to secure Manassas Junction, a key Confederate rail junction west of

Washington, as a necessary preparatory step to an overland drive on Richmond. The (First) Battle of Manassas (Bull Run) on 21 July 1861 involved significant numbers of inexperienced troops and great confusion on both sides but ended in a clear Confederate victory and Union troops streaming back to the defenses of Washington. The battle served to confirm Scott's gloomy predictions, and both sides now settled in for a long war.

CHAPTER FOUR

The Blockade and Early Atlantic Coastal Operations

—◦∿∿◦—

O n 19 April 1861, President Lincoln announced a naval blockade of Southern ports from South Carolina to Texas. On 27 April a second proclamation extended the blockade to Virginia and North Carolina. To help man the vessels required, on 3 May the president called for the enlistment of an additional eighteen thousand seamen.

Lincoln saw the blockade as fulfilling two important functions. First, reducing the Confederacy's access to foreign markets would make it more difficult for the South to wage war. Second, the blockade would demonstrate to foreign governments the president's resolve to crush the rebellion. The downside was that the declaration could be construed as a de facto recognition of the Confederacy's independent existence; indeed, European states responded by recognizing the South's belligerent status.

According to the 1856 Declaration of Paris, foreign powers were not obligated to respect a blockade unless it was effective—that is, maintained by force sufficient to prevent access to an enemy coast. Neutrals would not be bound by a "paper blockade"—a blockade by proclamation alone or with an inadequate number of ships to enforce it. Nonetheless, the North was aided by the fact that Britain, the world's leading naval power, had for its own purposes interpreted the notion of blockade very loosely. The blockading force had only to be "adequate," and this could be as little as one ship in constant attendance off a Confederate port sufficient to prevent ready communication. Once the blockade had begun, however, at least one vessel had to be on station off

the port at all times. Failing this, the blockade would have to be rein-
stated. In November 1861 London formally agreed with Washington's
position that the blockade was effective.

Following Lincoln's initial proclamation, Home Squadron commander Flag Officer Garrett J. Pendergast immediately attempted to
implement it. On 30 April he reported to Welles that he had notified the
Norfolk and Baltimore newspapers of his intention to begin the blockade
and that his ships had halted passenger and mail service between Norfolk
and Baltimore.[1]

Few vessels were available at first. Ships returning from foreign stations
required repairs before they could join the effort, and it was many months
before the navy legally was able to blockade many Southern ports. On 1 May
Flag Officer Silas H. Stringham took command of what was known as the
Coast Blockading Squadron, charged with blockading the Southern coast to
Key West. Three weeks later it became the Atlantic Blockading Squadron.
It consisted of fourteen gunboats and the Potomac Flotilla. At first,
single warships took up station off key Confederate ports. On 10 May the
screw sloop *Niagara*, just returned from Japan, initiated the blockade of
Charleston, while on 26 May the *Brooklyn* arrived off the Mississippi River,
and on 8 June the *Mississippi* set the blockade of Key West.

At first the blockaders were in two commands: Stringham's Atlantic
Blockading Squadron and Flag Officer William Mervine's Gulf Coast
Blockading Squadron. Stringham arrived off Charleston on 28 May, and
Mervine took up station in the Gulf on 8 June. By 4 July, Stringham had
at his disposal twenty-two vessels mounting 296 guns, and Mervine had
twenty-one ships with 282 guns.[2]

The distances involved were vast. From Alexandria, Virginia, to the Rio
Grande in Texas, the Southern coastline stretched more than 3,500 miles.
And for much of this distance, the outer banks presented a double
coastline. There were 189 harbors, river mouths, and indentations to be
guarded. The Mississippi and its tributary rivers counted 3,615 miles, and
sounds, bayous, rivers, and inlets along the Atlantic and Gulf coasts constituted another 2,000 miles. The Union blockaders were also handicapped
by the fact that the largest Southern ports boasted substantial defensive
works of stone or brick, the so-called Third System fortifications.[3]

Only one day off Charleston led Stringham to conclude that the means
available to him were totally inadequate. On 29 May a steamer exited

Charleston. Stringham closed on it in his flagship, the screw frigate *Minnesota*, but the steamer easily returned to port, making twice the speed of the big Union warship. Above all, Stringham needed fast steamers able to carry a good quantity of coal.[4]

Union naval strategy was set by the Commission of Conference, organized on 27 June 1861 and most often referred to as the Blockade Board. Welles created it in response to a suggestion by Superintendent of the U.S. Coastal Survey Alexander Dallas Bache for such a body to advise the secretary. Capt. Samuel Du Pont chaired the Commission on Conference. Its other members were Bache, Chief Engineer of the Army Department of Washington John G. Barnard, and Capt. Charles H. Davis. The board worked tirelessly. Its members studied charts and maps, then produced six major and four supplementary reports that set priorities for Union naval operations. The board recommended that in order to render the blockade effective, the U.S. Navy undertake a number of amphibious operations along the Confederate Atlantic and Gulf coasts.[5]

The extensive Confederate coastline that posed such a problem for Union naval forces to blockade also presented an opportunity for the U.S. Navy. The coastline was far too long for Confederate forces to be able to defend everywhere at once, especially as Southern land units were already stretched thin to meet an anticipated invasion from northward. Indeed, the South had been forced to confine its defensive efforts along the coast to a half dozen key points. It would thus be relatively easy for Union forces to attack from the sea at selected locations. Indeed, the problem for the Union would come only later, when it sought to expand these enclaves and to attack the principal, well-defended Confederate ports.

Securing the coastal enclaves would bring a number of advantages for the North. Not only would these provide bases and coaling stations at shorter ranges for the blockading warships, but the enclaves could be jumping-off points for future advances inland. It must be pointed out, however, that the initial Union coastal objectives were selected *not* for access inland but rather for their ability to defend against attack from inland.

Taking into account the major Confederate Atlantic seaboard ports of Wilmington, Charleston, and Savannah, the Blockade Board's initial recommendations for bases were Bull's Bay, north of Charleston, and Fernandina, north of Jacksonville, Florida. These were subsequently dropped in favor of Hatteras Inlet (one of several gaps in two hundred miles of North Carolina barrier islands) and Port Royal, South Carolina (approximately midway between Charleston and Savannah). The principal Confederate Gulf Coast ports were Mobile and New Orleans, and the board recommended that bases be secured in the Gulf at Ship Island, near Biloxi, Mississippi, and Head of the Passes, Louisiana.[6]

THE UNION ASSAULT ON HATTERAS INLET

Just as he urged offensive action on his generals, President Lincoln wanted the earliest possible action by his naval commanders against the Confederate coasts, but it was four months after the start of hostilities before the navy was able to mount a significant offensive operation. This was the attack at Hatteras Inlet, one of several access points to Pamlico Sound, a major staging area for blockade runners and Confederate privateers.

In Union hands, Hatteras might become a staging area for operations against the North Carolina coast. Two weakly manned log and earthen forts on Hatteras Island controlled the inlet: Fort Clark, a small earthen works on the ocean side mounted five guns; the more powerful Fort Hatteras a half mile away on the other side had twenty-five guns. Maj. W. S. G. Andrews commanded the forts. Unfortunately for the Confederates, the two forts were separated from the land by the very sounds they were supposed to protect.

On 26 August 1861, Flag Officer Silas H. Stringham departed Hampton Roads with six warships: the screw frigates *Minnesota* (flag) and *Wabash*, the paddle frigate *Susquehanna*, the screw sloop *Pawnee*, the converted merchant steamer *Monticello*, and the ex-revenue cutter *Harriet Lane*. The squadron also included the tug *Fanny* and two chartered steamer transports, the *Adelaide* and *George Peabody*, lifting some nine hundred army troops under Maj. Gen. Benjamin F. Butler from Fortress Monroe. The two transports towed schooners carrying surfboats, whereas the *Monticello* and *Pawnee* towed surfboats only.

The Union plan was straightforward. Stringham's ships would bombard the forts from their water face, while Butler's troops assaulted them from the rear on the land face. The operation was conceived as a raid.

The squadron anchored off Hatteras Inlet on the afternoon of 27 August. At 6:45 AM the next day, Stringham ordered that marines and troops be put ashore by the surfboats at a point about two miles east of

Fort Clark and beyond the range of its guns. The squadron provided launches mounting Dahlgren boat howitzers for covering fire should it be required by the troops during their landing. In addition, the smaller ships—the *Pawnee, Monticello,* and *Harriet Lane*—hovered offshore at the landing site to provide heavier cannon fire if needed.

At 8:45 AM the larger Union ships began the bombardment of Fort Clark. The *Wabash* led, towing the recently arrived razee (cutdown) sloop *Cumberland,* and the *Minnesota* following. Stringham ordered the bombardment ships to steam in a large oval, an innovative approach. Fort Clark returned fire for a time. Heavy surf, meanwhile, meant that by 11:30 AM Butler managed to put only 320 men ashore. Despite this, under pressure of the naval bombardment, about noon the Confederates abandoned Fort Clark. The Union land force then worked their way overland to it, and by 2 PM the American flag was flying over Clark.

At 4 PM, mistakenly believing both Confederate forts had surrendered, Stringham ordered the *Monticello* into Hatteras Inlet, but it had advanced only a short distance up the channel when it came under fire from Fort Hatteras. Seamen on the *Monticello* also observed a steam tug approaching the fort from the south, towing a schooner filled with Confederate reinforcements. Stringham then ordered the remainder of the Union squadron in to shell Fort Hatteras. The *Monticello* was in an exposed position, separated from the remainder of the squadron, and was struck five times by shot from the shore, although without major damage, before it was able to withdraw.

Meanwhile, the weather had turned bad, preventing the landing of additional Union troops. The Union squadron then anchored for the night. The Confederate defenders on the island were bolstered by the arrival of 230 officers and men under Flag Officer Samuel Barron, commander of the naval defenses of Virginia and North Carolina. This brought Confederate strength at Fort Hatteras up to some 650 men. On Anderson's invitation, Barron assumed command. Barron wanted to attack and retake Fort Clark, but when additional men did not arrive, he dropped that plan in favor of simply strengthening Fort Hatteras.

At 5:30 AM the next day, 29 August, Stringham ordered the big Union ships to get under way and recommence shelling Fort Hatteras. The action began at 8 AM, the *Susquehanna* leading, followed by the *Wabash* and *Minnesota*. All three ships anchored and then opened fire. At about 9 AM the

Cumberland came in under sail, anchored, and joined the fight. Because the Union ships were firing at long range, many of their shells were falling short, and Stringham ordered a temporary halt in the firing and crews to switch to fifteen-second fuses and fire only from the largest guns. This change had the desired effect. The *Harriet Lane* also joined the action with its longer-range rifled guns. Although the Confederates replied, their shot fell short.

Barron then met with his officers to consider the situation. The Southerners' shorter-range guns could not reach the Union ships, ammunition was in short supply, and the fort would not be reinforced. A Union shell that penetrated the fort's ventilator shaft next to the magazine while Barron was meeting with his officers may have hastened the decision, for not long afterward, at 11 AM, a white flag appeared over the fort. Union troops then marched to it and took possession. Some Union ships also entered the inlet. Although the *Harriet Lane* grounded, it was able to get free.

At 2:30 PM Barron and several Confederate Army officers came aboard the *Minnesota* to make formal surrender. In the battle, the Union side secured between six hundred and seven hundred Confederate prisoners. There were no Union casualties. Too late, Commandant of the Norfolk Navy Yard Flag Officer French Forrest ordered Cdr. Thomas T. Hunter to prepare an expedition to Hatteras "to defend the inlets of North Carolina" and cooperate with Barron.[7]

The Hatteras Inlet victory was the first real Union naval triumph of the war, indeed the first noteworthy Union victory—land or sea—and it did much to restore morale in the North, shaken by the earlier Union defeat on land at Manassas (Bull Run). It also proved the great value of steamships in engaging land forts. Securing the inlet allowed the Union to seal off Pamlico Sound to Confederate privateers and blockade running. Stringham urged, and Washington concurred, that Hatteras be kept. In Union hands, it became a base for the blockaders and a depot for coal and supplies.[8]

THE UNION DESCENT ON PORT ROYAL

Apart from Charleston, the best natural harbor on the South Atlantic coast was Port Royal, South Carolina, approximately halfway between Savannah and Charleston. The Confederates well understood Port Royal's importance and made it one of the first coastal areas to be fortified. Following the success at Hatteras Inlet, the Blockade Board recommended that Port Royal be the next objective, and Lincoln urged that the operation go forward as soon as possible. All agreed that Port Royal's deep harbor would be ideal for a major Union naval base.

Meanwhile, Stringham came under criticism, both from within the Navy Department and in the Northern press, for the inadequacies of the blockade effort and for failing to follow up his Hatteras victory by venturing into the North Carolina sounds. Stung by these unwarranted attacks, Stringham submitted his resignation on 16 September. This came at an ideal time because the Blockade Board had concluded that the Confederate Atlantic seaboard was too long for one man to supervise. Welles agreed, and the result was that the Atlantic Blockading Squadron was split into two commands. On 18 September 1861 Welles named sixty-year-old Capt. Louis M. Goldsborough, a veteran of forty-nine years of navy service, to head the northern division (the North Atlantic Blockading Squadron); Capt. Samuel F. Du Pont took command of the southern division (the South Atlantic Blockading Squadron). Du Pont thus had charge of preparations for the Port Royal operation.

Reflecting the strength of the Confederate defenses, the force assembled for the attack on Port Royal was considerably larger than that employed against Hatteras. On 29 October, flying his flag in the screw frigate *Wabash*, Du Pont departed Hampton Roads with fifty ships, the largest task force under single command to that point in U.S. Navy history. The day before, he had sent on ahead to Tybee Bar off Savannah twenty-five sloops converted into coal ships for the squadron, escorted by the *Vandalia*. Du Pont's fleet lifted a sizable invasion force of sixteen thousand army troops commanded by Brig. Gen. Thomas W. Sherman. The Northern press had reported the assembly of the expeditionary force, and Southern authorities had a good idea of its intended target.

On 1 November, as the Union expeditionary force approached Port Royal, it was struck by a severe storm out of the southeast. Winds approaching hurricane force scattered the ships, and by the next morning only one other Union ship was visible from the *Wabash*. The mission appeared in jeopardy, but the wind soon died down and gradually the ships rendezvoused off Port Royal, acting according to Du Pont's prior sealed emergency instructions.

The storm had, however, forced the captain of the *Isaac Smith*, a converted warship, to order the ship's entire battery overboard. Thus lightened,

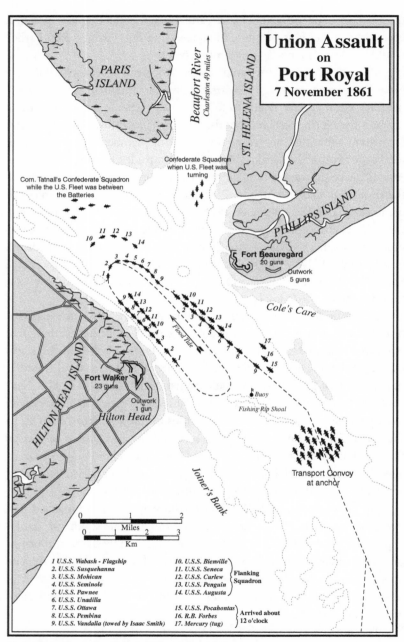

Union Assault on Port Royal, 7 November 1861

the *Isaac Smith* had been able to go to the rescue of the chartered steamer *Governor* with an entire battalion of marines. All save seven marines were rescued before the *Governor* sank. Another transport, the *Peerless*, also went down, but all aboard were gotten off safely.

In the early morning of 4 November, the flagship *Wabash* arrived off the bar, ten miles east of Port Royal with twenty-five ships in company and others coming up. There Du Pont concluded that the losses in the storm were insufficient to prevent the operation from proceeding, and he immediately ordered a reconnaissance, necessary as the Confederates had removed all the navigation buoys.

Two Confederate earthworks, Fort Beauregard on the southern tip of Phillips Island at Bay Point and Fort Walker on the northern end of Hilton Head Island, guarded the harbor entrance. Together the well-sited forts mounted forty-three guns. Unfortunately for the Confederates, the wide distance of the entrance of the inlet—2.2 miles—precluded effective artillery coverage.

The Union ships quickly located the channel and took soundings, while a survey ship that Du Pont had insisted be included in the fleet marked it with buoys. Du Pont then ordered in his lighter gunboats and transports. The Union gunboats drove off three small Confederate gunboats under Flag Officer Josiah Tattnall and escorted the transports into the roadstead beyond range of the Confederate forts, where they anchored for the night.

The next morning, under the supervision of Cdr. John Rodgers, four of the Union gunboats—the *Ottawa*, *Seneca*, *Curlew*, and *Pembina*—made a reconnaissance in force, drawing sufficient fire from the forts to learn their strength.

Pilots having determined that there was sufficient water for the *Wabash* to cross the bar, Du Pont ordered in the flagship, followed by the frigate *Susquehanna*, the *Atlantic*, the *Vanderbilt*, and other deep-draft transports. The original plan had been for a joint army–navy attack, but much of the army's equipment had been lost in the storm, and, after conferring with his subordinates, Du Pont decided on a naval effort alone. Because of this and the estimate of at least several days to reduce the forts from long range, all agreed that, despite the risk of grounding, the ships, and especially the powerful forty-four-gun *Wabash* (two X-inch, twenty-eight IX-inch, and fourteen VIII-inch guns), should engage the forts at close range.

Since the distance between Forts Beauregard and Walker precluded engaging both simultaneously save by the largest rifled guns, Du Pont decided to attack one at a time. Fort Walker, regarded as the most powerful, was the first. It mounted twenty-three guns, but only thirteen of these were on the sea face, the remainder being for land defense. Fort Beauregard contained twenty guns; thirteen of them commanded the water approaches, but only seven faced the channel. This, the tide, and the presence of the Confederate flotilla all determined the timing and mode of the Union attack.[9]

At about 9 AM Tattnall steamed out with his small flotilla to exchange long-range fire with the Union ships. He then retired, followed by some Union ships, which also dueled with the Confederate shore batteries for about forty-five minutes, although with little effect on either side. Then at 3:30 PM Du Pont ordered a signal hoisted for the ships to get under way for the attack. But as the ships stood in, both the *Wabash* and the *Susquehanna* grounded on Fishing Rip Shoals. It took two hours to get the big ships free, forcing Du Pont to cancel the attack for that day. The following day was too windy, leading to another postponement.

At 8:30 AM on 7 November the Union ships again got under way, and an hour later Du Pont in the *Wabash* led nine warships into Port Royal Sound. Following the flagship were the frigate *Susquehanna*; the sloops *Mohican, Seminole,* and *Pawnee*; the gunboats *Unadilla, Ottawa,* and *Pembina*; and the *Issac Smith* towing the sailing sloop *Vandalia*. Steaming northwest, the ships kept in mid-channel and exchanged long-range fire with both forts until they were well past them. The ships then turned south and reversed course, heading southeast close by Fort Walker on its northern face. This circular plan of attack, similar to that employed by Stringham at Hatteras, had been suggested by Du Pont's flag captain, Charles H. Davis, while the ships were under way. Meanwhile, a flanking squadron of the gunboats *Bienville, Seneca, Curlew, Penguin,* and *Augusta* interposed itself to the northwest of the circling Union ships so as to be between the latter and Tattnall's flotilla of seven small Confederate gunboats in the upper harbor. These Union gunboats had the task of preventing the Confederate vessels from firing on Du Pont's bombardment ships as they turned and to keep the Confederates from cutting out any disabled Union ship.

The action began at 9:26 AM when a IX-inch Dalhgren at Fort Walker fired on the *Wabash* and a gun at Fort Beauregard immediately followed suit. The *Wabash* returned fire, followed by the *Susquehanna*, and the fighting then became general. After passing through the channel, the ships turned in succession according to plan, passing eight hundred yards from Fort Walker. They then circled and turned to mid-channel, again following it in while engaging both forts at long range before turning south. The second Union pass was at only six hundred yards from Fort Walker. While the Union ships poured shells into the fort, the inexperienced Confederate gunners found it difficult to hit the moving Union ships. Fire from the fort steadily diminished in intensity, and by the time the *Wabash* was in position to commence fire for a third time with its starboard guns against Walker, Confederate fire had entirely ceased and the engagement was over.

At 11:15 AM the *Ottawa* signaled that the Confederates had abandoned the works, and seamen in the tops of the Union ships confirmed the flight of the defenders from the fort. Du Pont then sent Cdr. John Rodgers ashore under a flag of truce, and at 2:20 PM Rodgers raised a Union flag over the deserted Confederate works. Du Pont then ordered signals hoisted to bring up the transports and sent Cdr. C. R. P. Rodgers ashore with a party of marines and seamen "to take possession and prevent, if necessary, the destruction of public property."[10] A brigade was ashore by nightfall, with Fort Walker firmly in Union hands.

During the engagement, all but three of Fort Walker's guns on the water side had been dismounted or otherwise put out of action. Du Pont had proven that the best defense against an enemy battery was an accurate and high volume of fire; during the engagement, the *Wabash* alone had fired 880 shells, including grape shot with excellent effect near the end of the action. Although the Union ships had been hit in the exchange, the Confederates tended to fire high, and most of the damage was thus aloft and of little consequence. Aboard the fleet, eight men had been killed. Another twenty-three were wounded, six of these seriously. Confederate casualties totaled eleven killed and forty-eight wounded.

Two late-arriving Union ships, the *Pocahontas* and the *R. B. Forbes*, also participated in the action, as did the tug *Mercury*, which employed to good effect its lone Parrott gun. Tattnall's gunboats had been utterly unable to intervene in the battle, although they did rescue some of the fleeing defenders from Hilton Head and ferry them to the mainland.

Immediately after the situation at Fort Walker had been decided, Du Pont ordered some of his ships to reconnoiter Fort Beauregard and to prevent the Confederates from ferrying men and equipment from that place. Near sunset, lookouts reported that Beauregard was deserted and that the Confederate flag had been hauled down. Early the next morning a Union landing party hoisted the U.S. flag over that fort as well. Du Pont then turned over both forts to Sherman. Fort Walker was renamed Fort Welles, and Fort Beauregard became Fort Seward. [11]

The triumph at Port Royal was an important event, preceding as yet any major battlefield victory for the Union Army and coming immediately on the heels of another Union land defeat, at Ball's Bluff on 21 October. On learning of the capture of Port Royal, Welles wrote to Du Pont: "The success is all that was expected, and more than we ought to have asked."[12]

Port Royal's deep harbor provided an ideal base for extended South Atlantic Blockading Squadron operations and was soon a major naval station and supply depot. There was a negative for the Union in this victory, however. Many in the North, including Welles and Fox, now came to believe that steam warships could defeat all forts. This mistaken belief became an important element of future Union naval strategy.

The Union victory had widespread strategic ramifications. In early November President Davis gave Gen. Robert E. Lee charge of reorganizing the Confederacy's South Atlantic defenses. Noting growing Union naval strength and the North's ability to project power at almost any point along the coast, Lee within weeks ordered abandonment of a number of scattered Confederate coastal positions and the withdrawal of their defenders beyond the range of Union naval guns, save in the case of Charleston and Savannah, which were to be strengthened. The Confederates thus shifted from a perimeter to a mobile defense based on interior lines, relying on the railroads to concentrate against any major Union amphibious operation. As Lee explained:

> Wherever his [Union] fleet can be brought to bear no opposition to his landing can be made except within range of our fixed batteries. We have nothing to oppose to its heavy guns, which sweep over the low banks of this country with irresistible force. The farther he can be withdrawn from his floating batteries the weaker he will become, and lines of defense, covering objects of attack, have been selected with this in view.[13]

Upon securing Port Royal, Du Pont concentrated on strengthening the blockade. Off South Carolina, Union ships closed North Edisto, Stono, and Bull's Bay. At the same time, blockaders watched Georgetown, and Du Pont was able, thanks to newly arrived ships, to double the number of blockaders off Charleston. His ships also secured Tybee Island near the estuary of the Savannah River. This action provided a coaling base, and heavy guns placed here closed the Savannah River to blockade runners. At the same time, the *St. Lawrence, Mohican,* and *Seminole* carried out blockade duties along the Georgia coast. There were problems, nonetheless. Du Pont reported that, with skilled pilots, blockade runners were often able to utilize night and fog to run by the Union ships.[14]

By the end of 1861, Union naval strength had increased dramatically. In his annual report, Secretary Welles noted the capture of 153 ships, most of them blockade runners. He also reported that the Union Navy now numbered some twenty-two thousand seamen, and that, when ships then under construction joined the fleet, the navy would number 264 ships with 2,557 guns.[15]

In October and November 1861 the Navy Department purchased a number of hulks, many of them former whaling ships, with the intention of loading them with stone and sinking them as block ships in the channels off Charleston and Savannah. The plan called for twenty-five to be placed off Savannah and twenty off Charleston. Welles also promised Du Pont any additional hulks required for similar operations elsewhere.[16]

The assembly of the large number of ships constituting this "stone fleet" off Savannah may have led Confederate leaders to assume that a major Union amphibious operation was imminent. In any case, it helped bring the Confederate decision to abandon their fort on Wassaw Island, which dominated one means of access (the other being Tybee Roads) to the Savannah River. Early on the morning of 5 December, Cdr. C. R. P. Rodgers led the gunboats *Ottawa, Seneca,* and *Pembina* across the bar of Wassaw Sound to the island and there discovered an enclosed fort with platforms for eight guns. The guns themselves had been recently removed, the platforms cut, and the fort's magazines blown.[17]

The "stone fleet" was not a success, however. Seventeen of the hulks ultimately made it to Savannah on 4 December, although a number were in sinking state and four of these went down before they could be properly placed. Others were indeed scuttled off Tybee Island. Then, on 20 December

Capt. Charles H. Davis supervised the placement of sixteen "stone fleet" ships in the main ship channel on the bar at Charleston. Although this action did block that channel for a time, blockade runners could still access the port through North and Maffitts Channels, and the operation had little long-range advantage. Indeed, it was something that Welles preferred to forget. Gen. Robert E. Lee, then commanding the Southern Military Department of South Carolina, Georgia, and Florida, called it an "abortive expression of the malice and revenge of a people," but he also correctly concluded that the "stone fleet" revealed the North was not then considering an attack on Charleston and that the Confederates should therefore prepare for attacks elsewhere along the coast.[18]

The capture of Tybee Island enabled Union forces to assault Fort Pulaski at the mouth of the Savannah River. Pulaski was situated on mile-long Cockspur Island, about seventeen hundred yards from Tybee. Its island location precluded a boat attack. Built of brick with seven-and-a-half-foot-thick walls and completed by the Corps of Engineers in 1847 after eighteen years of work and a cost of $1 million, Fort Pulaski mounted forty-eight heavy guns and was probably the most impressive of the Totten coast defense system fortifications erected before the Civil War. Many observers, including General Lee, believed the fort would be impervious to Union attack. This view, however, did not take into account the range and penetrating power of new heavy rifled guns.

In February 1862 U.S. Army troops came ashore on Tybee Island a few miles from Fort Pulaski. Over the next several months Union Brig. Gen. Quincy A. Gilmore directed the siting of heavy smoothbore Colombiads and Parrott rifles to fire on Pulaski. When Fort Pulaski's commander, Col. Charles H. Olmstead, refused a surrender demand, Gilmore opened fire on the morning of 10 April 1862. Federal fire concentrated on the southeast face of the fort, with the Parrott rifled guns doing the damage. By nightfall their rounds had opened a breach in the walls, and the next morning the Union gunners began to exploit it. With shells flying into the fort and striking the magazine, Pulaski was in danger of being blown up by its own powder. Olmstead surrendered on the afternoon of 11 April after thirty hours of bombardment. The reduction of Fort Pulaski revealed the vulnerability of the old masonry forts to new rifled guns. The estuary of the Savannah River was now closed to blockade runners, although access to Savannah was still possible by means of Wassaw Sound and the Ogeechee River.

Union forces also carried out other small joint operations to harass the Confederates and to occupy islands and some ports along the 150-mile coastal strip from Savannah to Cape Canaveral, Florida. This part of the coast was particularly important because of its proximity to Bermuda and Nassau, the principal ports from which the blockade runners operated.

Typical of such operations was that led by Cdr. C. R. P. Rodgers during 31 December 1861–2 January 1862 against Confederate positions at Port Royal Ferry and the Coosawhatchie River. Rodgers commanded the gunboats *Ottawa*, *Pembina*, and *Seneca* and four boats armed with 12-pounder boat howitzers operating in conjunction with an army brigade under Brig. Gen. Isaac Stevens. The gunboats covered the landing of the troops in order to disrupt Confederate plans to construct batteries to close the river and isolate Federal forces on Port Royal Sound. Although individual Union operations such as this invariably met success, the Confederate coastline was too long and the Union assets committed were too few to seal the coast entirely.[19]

In the Gulf, Union forces took Ship Island and Head of Passes, south of New Orleans. But the Union blockade was not limited to the immediate coastal waters. Union ships plied the high seas, especially off Bermuda as well as Nassau, principal entrepot for the blockade trade. On 27 April 1862, the converted merchant steamer *Mercedita* stopped the merchant steamer *Bermuda* off the Bahamas and seized it as a prize. Although the *Bermuda* was registered as a British vessel, its papers included Confederate signals for Charleston, indicating that it was intending to run the blockade there. A prize court subsequently upheld the seizure.

This ruling was an important one because it meant that neutral ships no longer meant neutral goods and that the British flag would not offer protection. A ship might be stopped anywhere on the high seas and seized if its papers indicated it was bound for the Confederacy. Although the ruling did cause some shippers to stop carrying cargoes bound for the South, the majority simply repacked the goods and changed the ship manifests to indicate Nassau as their final destination.

The loss of the *Bermuda* was a heavy one for the Confederacy because the cargo taken aboard it included thousands of small arms and eight heavy rifled guns ranging from a 5.5-inch Whitworth to a large 8.5-inch Blakley. The big guns were all intended for the defense of Confederate harbor.[20]

Blockade runners continued to get through, however. One prominent example was the new fast steamer *Memphis*. Owned by an English firm, it sailed from Liverpool in May 1862. On its approach to Nassau, the *Memphis* was stopped by the Union gunboat *Quaker City*, but the owners were well aware of the fate of the *Bermuda* so its papers were in good order, and the ship was allowed to proceed. A month later the *Memphis* departed Nassau, arriving off Charleston on the night of 22 June 1862. Approaching Forts Moultrie and Sumter, the blockader showed a red light, undoubtedly on instructions received at Nassau. The forts returned the signal and the blockader slipped into the channel past the Union blockaders. While entering the harbor, however, the *Memphis* grounded, and in the darkness gunners at Fort Sumter opened fire on the ship until it again showed a red light.

At dawn the Union blockaders discovered the stranded *Memphis* and opened long-range fire on it. Loaded with 112,000 pounds of gunpowder, the ship was virtually a bomb. During all of 23 June, Confederate soldiers from Sullivan's Island worked to remove the gunpowder before it could be set off by an exploding Union shell. Miraculously, not one Union shell hit the ship, and late that afternoon the *Memphis* had been sufficiently lightened that two Confederate steam tugs were able to pull it free and take it to safety in the harbor. Over the next days the remainder of the ship's cargo was offloaded. It included 11,000 small arms, a million percussion caps, twenty-five tons of lead, and medicine and other goods. The ship then immediately took on a cargo of 1,446 bales of cotton and departed Charleston on the night of 29 June. Before the *Memphis* could gain Nassau, however, it was stopped and seized by the Union gunboat *Magnolia*.[21]

THE UNION SEIZURE OF ROANOKE ISLAND, NORTH CAROLINA

The year 1862 opened with a series of major Union joint navy–army operations. In February in the Western Theater, gunboats under Flag Officer Andrew H. Foote operated in conjunction with Brig. Gen. Ulysses S. Grant's troops to capture Forts Henry and Donelson; that same month in the Eastern Theater there was a comparable Union victory at Roanoke Island.

Union possession of the Hatteras Island forts offered a base for further amphibious operations against eastern North Carolina. West of the Outer Banks were six sounds, the two largest being Pamlico and Albemarle.

The Confederacy had no effective means of preventing Union ships from operating on these sounds against a number of major cities that lay directly on them or were accessible to them by means of navigable rivers.

Roanoke Island lay at the northern end of Pamlico Sound. The island controlled passage between Pamlico Sound to the south and Albemarle Sound to the north and west. It also dominated access to the southern termini of the Dismal Swamp Canal and the Albemarle and Chesapeake Canal, both of which reached to Norfolk, Virginia. Federal forces already controlled Pamlico Sound. Securing Roanoke Island would give them access to Albemarle Sound, with its rivers leading into interior North Carolina and over which railroads ran north on bridges to Norfolk. In Union hands, troops might strike from Roanoke Island against Norfolk, and shallow-draft Union warships could use the sound as an anchorage.

Flag Officer Goldsborough and Army Brig. Gen. Ambrose Burnside commanded the Roanoke Island operation. Sometimes known as the Burnside Expedition, it departed Hampton Roads in mid-January. Because of the shallow water in which they would have to operate, Goldsborough's twenty vessels were all converted tugs, river steamers, and ferry boats. Most were lightly armed. Goldsborough's flagship, the *Philadelphia*, was hardly impressive. The 504-ton iron-hulled side-wheeler steamer had before the war plied the Norfolk to Baltimore route. Employed by the U.S. Navy as a transport, its armament consisted of two 12-pounder Dahlgren rifled boat howitzers.[22]

Goldsborough gave the captain of the *Delaware*, Cdr. Stephen C. Rowan, charge of the fighting ships, but command problems were compounded by the fact that Burnside had actual charge of the army's warships, including some gunboats. Goldsborough was unhappy with the arrangement and wrote Fox that "in case of another joint expedition, everything concerning all the vessels should be arranged exclusively by the Navy, & kept under Naval command. Duality, I assure you, will not answer."[23]

Goldsborough's ships were to provide protection for some seventy Union transports, lifting twelve thousand troops and supplies. Once all the ships were in position, the navy was to shell Confederate shore installations and engage any hostile warships as well as provide fire support once the troops were ashore.

Goldsborough had to overcome major and unanticipated problems in assembling the task force. Once at Hatteras Inlet a number of the deeper-draft army ships had to be substantially lightened and then reloaded. Troops were also taken off and then reembarked. Other ships were kedged over the bar.

A severe storm then scattered many of the ships. The army lost three ships: the *City of New York* with ordnance and supplies, the *Pocahontas* with one hundred horses, and the army gunboat *Zouave* (ex-*Marshall Nye*). As a result, the warships and transports were not all in place until 5 February. Early that morning, Goldsborough ordered the *Philadelphia* to signal for the ships to get under way, and that night all anchored at Stumpy Point.[24]

On the morning of 6 February Goldsborough transferred his flag to the *Southfield* and ordered the flotilla to proceed. Goldsborough sent ahead two light-draft steamers, the *Ceres* and *Putnam*, to report on Confederate activity and possible obstructions. In late morning the weather turned foggy and rainy, forcing the squadron again to anchor.

The morning of 7 February was clear, and that morning the ships were again under way, the *Underwriter* joining the other two light-draft steamers in advance. The Union ships carefully threaded their way through the narrow channel west of the southern tip of Roanoke Island and entered Croatan Sound, which in the best of conditions was only seven and a half feet deep. The ships were in two divisions, the warships leading and the transports behind. Once in Croatan Sound and "being anxious to make a decided impression upon the enemy early in the contest," Goldsborough ordered all ships with IX-inch Dahlgren guns to concentrate around the flagship.[25]

Although they were well aware of the Union preparations, Confederate authorities had few troops available. Heavy guns were also in short supply, as were ammunition and warships. Former Virginia governor now Confederate Brig. Gen. Henry A. Wise commanded Roanoke Island with two North Carolina regiments of 1,435 men in all. Another 800 Confederates were in reserve at Nags Head.

Roanoke Island contained five forts with a total of thirty guns. The largest, Fort Huger on Weir's Point, mounted twelve guns but was at the narrowest northern part of Croatan Sound between the island and the mainland and thus beyond the range of the proposed Federal landing site. The chief concern to the Federals was Fort Bartow, with nine guns located at Pork Point. Another fort, Fort Forrest, with eight guns, lay directly across the sound from Pork Point. Spanning the two miles of water between these two forts, Wise had ordered placed a double line of piles about ten feet apart. On the Federal approach, the Confederates also sank a number of small vessels to strengthen this barrier. Behind it, Flag Officer William D. Lynch commanded seven small steamers mounting a total of only eight guns.[26]

At 10:30 AM on 7 February as the Union ships moved slowly up Croatan Sound, lookouts spotted Lynch's ships hovering behind the obstructions. The *Underwriter* signaled that there was no Confederate defenses at Sand Point on Roanoke Island, and this news allowed the transports to move in and prepare to disembark their troops at nearby Ashby's Harbor south of Sand Point, several miles south of the main Confederate defenses.

At the same time, Goldsborough ordered his nineteen gunboats forward to shell the Confederate forts and ships. By noon the firing became general. Because of their distance from the battle scene, the Confederate forts north of the obstructions could not participate, and only four of Bartow's guns could engage the Union gunboats. At 1:30 PM Union shells set on fire the barracks behind Fort Bartow, which soon was burning out of control.[27]

The Union gunboats mounted a total of fifty-seven guns; many of these were larger and of greater range than the eight Confederate guns. Lynch reported that whenever his ships approached the barrier, the Union ships concentrated their fire on them:

> As his force was overwhelming, we commenced the action at long range, but as our shells fell short, whilst his burst over and around us, we were eventually compelled to lessen the distance. . . .
>
> Repeatedly in the course of the day I feared that our little squadron of seven vessels would be utterly demolished, but a merciful Providence preserved us.[28]

There were few personnel casualties in the exchange. Only six Confederates were wounded, three seriously. Damage to the Southern ships was extensive. The largest warship, the side-wheeler steamer *Curlew*, mounting a single rifled 32-pounder, took a shell that passed through its magazine without exploding but then drove out one of the iron plates forming the ship's bottom. Its crew promptly ran the steamer ashore, where it sank. The screw steamer *Forrest*, also armed with a single 32-pounder, was disabled by a displaced propeller. The Union warships escaped serious injury, thanks to the accuracy of their own fire and their continued maneuvering.

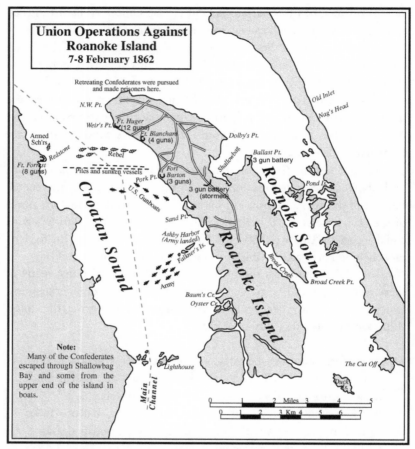

Union Operations against Roanoke Island, 7–8 February 1862

The Confederate ships kept up an intermittent fire but were soon short of ammunition. As Lynch could secure only a few rounds from the upper land battery, in late afternoon he ordered his remaining ships to take the *Forrest* in tow and proceed to Elizabeth City, thirty-five miles up Albemarle Sound, for resupply. With little ammunition there as well, Lynch sent an officer to Norfolk to obtain it. Securing fuel and ammunition sufficient for only two of his warships, Lynch was en route back to Roanoke Island when he learned of the surrender of Confederate forces there.[29]

During the Union bombardment on 7 February, the earthen works of Fort Bartow on Pork Point had been hard hit. At times the fort was almost hidden by smoke, sand, and debris thrown up by Union shot and shell. Lynch reported afterward, "The soldiers in the battery sustained their position under a terrific fire. . . . At times the entire battery would be enveloped in the sand and dust thrown up by shot and shell. . . . The earthwork . . . was very much cut up, but doubtless repaired during the night."[30]

The ex-ferryboat and side-wheeler *Commodore Perry* steamed in to within eight hundred yards of Bartow and was hit seven times by Confederate fire. Its crew was fortunate. One shot passed through the ship's magazine and an empty powder tank; another passed between the engine and boiler, but there was no major damage. In all, the *Commodore Perry* fired from its two IX-inch Dahlgrens a total of 172 shells and twenty rounds of shrapnel. At about 5 PM, with darkness coming on, Goldsborough ordered his ships to cease fire.

Meanwhile, beginning at 3 PM on 7 February, Union troops began going ashore on Roanoke Island. They soon came under fire from a Confederate field gun, and the *Delaware* moved in to clear their way, firing shrapnel from its IX-inch Dahlgren. At the same time, Midshipman Benjamin H. Porter brought ashore in launches six Dahlgren howitzers on field mounts. Once they were ashore, Porter positioned the howitzers to provide security for the landing area. Other troops continued to land, and by midnight some ten thousand were on the island.

The next day, 8 February, the Union soldiers got under way at first light, and by 9 AM the fighting was general. The Union ships moved in to support the land advance by again taking the forts under fire. The Union soldiers had little difficulty with the outnumbered Confederates. Aided by army personnel, the sailors moved the guns by drag ropes about two miles to fire on a Confederate battery guarding a road that allowed access to the rear of the Confederate forts. Employing shell, grape, canister, and shrapnel, the howitzers greatly assisted the Union advance, and at about 4 PM the troops raised the American flag over Pork Point, while the Confederates set fire to the *Curlew* and blew it up.

Meanwhile, Union gunboat crews cleared a path through the obstructions across the sound, and by 4 PM the ships were through these and into Albemarle Sound. Unable to do more than offer token, long-range resistance, Lynch withdrew with his gunboats up the Pasquotank River.[31]

The battle of Roanoke Island ended in a major Union victory, won at surprisingly little cost. Although the ships had been hit numerous times in the exchange of fire, Union Navy losses were only 6 men killed, 17 wounded, and 2 missing. These figures also include 3 killed and 5 wounded in Porter's boat howitzer battery. The U.S. Army sustained just over 250 casualties, with 47 of them killed. In turn the Union soldiers captured nearly 2,000 Confederates, 500 reinforcements arriving just in time to surrender. [32]

Early on the morning of 10 February, Cdr. Rowan led thirteen Union gunboats with marines up the Pasquotank River to pursue Lynch's remaining gunboats. This move caught Lynch and the Confederates by surprise. The *Forrest* was on the ways at Elizabeth City undergoing repairs and Lynch had sent the *Raleigh* up the Dismal Swamp Canal toward Norfolk to expedite the delivery of ammunition. Learning that Federal marines were going ashore near Cobb's Point, and with its battery the only means of preventing the Union ships from reaching his gunboats, Lynch went there to organize the defense. Finding only a half dozen militiamen present, he ordered most of the crew of the *Beaufort* ashore to assist. The militia soon ran away, and the remaining Confederates could only man two of the fort's 32-pounders.

After a spirited hour-long engagement, Rowan's ships passed the shore battery and closed in on the gunboats, sinking the *Sea Bird* and making its crew prisoners and also boarding and capturing the *Ellis*. The crew of the steamer *Fanny* ran their vessel ashore and set it on fire, and the crew of the schooner *Black Warrior*, with two 32-pounders, also fired it. Although Union seamen sought to extinguish the flames, neither gunboat could be saved.

The Union gunboats now outflanked the fort, the guns of which could not be brought to bear. Seeing this, Lynch ordered the guns spiked and his men to withdraw. He also ordered the *Forrest* at Elizabeth City fired to prevent its capture. The *Beaufort, Raleigh,* and *Appomattox* escaped. The battle cost Lynch four men killed and six wounded.

Driven up the Dismal Swamp Canal, the *Beaufort* and *Raleigh* joined the ironclad *Virginia* at Norfolk. The *Appomattox* proved too wide for the canal lock above Elizabeth City, however, and Lynch decided to destroy both it and the lock with explosives for fear that the Union forces would mount a pursuit.

In the battle, the men of the Union screw steamer gunboat *Valley City* experienced a close call. A Confederate shell struck the ship and passed through its magazine, exploding in a locker containing pyrotechnics. The *Valley City*'s captain, Lt. Cdr. James C. Chaplain, went to the magazine to help fight the fire and there discovered Quarter Gunner John Davis seated on an open barrel of powder as the only means of keeping the fire from reaching it. At the same time Davis was passing powder to other seamen so that the upper deck gun division could return fire. For this brave action that likely saved his ship, Davis received the Medal of Honor in April 1863. Rowan sent marines ashore to occupy both Elizabeth City and Edenton and to obstruct the Albemarle and Chesapeake Canal. Others of his men destroyed Confederate property and brought off ammunition, ordnance, and other useful stores.

In early March Goldsborough was recalled to Hampton Roads during the threat from the Confederate ironclad *Virginia*, and Rowan took charge of the naval portion of the Union expedition against New Berne on the Neuse River at the south end of Pamlico Sound. On 13 March Rowan's gunboats and Burnside's transports anchored at the mouth of the Neuse, sixteen miles below New Berne. The next day the Union ships overcame Confederate obstacles in the river, working their way upstream in conjunction with Burnside's eleven thousand troops and eight artillery pieces ashore. Confederate Brig. Gen. Lawrence O. Branch's defenders put up a stiff fight for several hours, but superior Union numbers told. When the Confederate center gave way, it precipitated a general retreat. A number of Confederates escaped across the Trent River under shelling from the gunboats, and then set the bridge on fire behind them.

New Berne fell that same day, Branch moving what remained of his command to Kinston by rail. At New Bern, Union forces took several hundred small arms, military supplies, and a three-masted schooner. Union losses in the operation totaled some 520 men, 50 of them naval personnel; the Confederates suffered nearly 600 casualties.[33]

Shortly thereafter Union land and naval forces moved against Fort Macon on Bogue Island at the southernmost point of Pamlico Sound forty miles from Beaufort, South Carolina. Col. Moses L. White commanded the fort of sixty-seven guns and a garrison of some five hundred men. The federals first took Carolina City and Morehead City, followed by Beaufort on 25 March. Although heavily outnumbered, White refused demands to surrender, and Burnside was obliged to conduct a siege beginning on 23 March. Finally, heavy Union artillery pieces, including siege mortars, were landed and sited, and on 25 April they and three Union steamers, the *Chippewa*, *Daylight*, and *State of Georgia*, opened fire on the fort. Subjected to ten hours of furious fire, White surrendered that same day, giving the

Union control of perhaps the most strategic stretch of the North Carolina coast and complete control of the North Carolina sounds.[34]

These victories, coupled with those in the West in which the navy also took a leading role, helped restore Northern morale. The capture of Roanoke Island and its attendant operations also cut Norfolk off from its main supply lines and helped bring about its capture three months later, an event that had far-ranging repercussions for the war. At the same time, the Port Royal operation reduced the amount of Atlantic coastal area under Confederate control to a short stretch from Wilmington to Charleston, together with the isolated port of Savannah, Georgia.

The blockade continued, but after January 1862 the Union Navy had four blockading squadrons: the Atlantic Blockading Squadron was divided into two: the North Atlantic Blockading Squadron, with responsibility for the Chesapeake Bay, its tributaries, and the coast south to the South Carolina boundary near Wilmington; and the South Atlantic Blockading Squadron, operating principally from Port Royal, South Carolina, that continued the blockade southward from near Wilmington to Cape Canavarel, Florida. The original Gulf Coast Blockading Squadron was similarly divided: the East Gulf Coast Blockading Squadron had responsibility for the coastline from Cape Canavarel to St. Andrew's Bay, whereas the West Gulf Coast Blockading Squadron operated from St. Andrew's Bay to the Rio Grande boundary with Mexico.

The blockade steadily strengthened as new ships, especially steamers, entered service. The Confederates also relied on steamers: small, fast, shallow draft ships that could run back and forth between Southern ports and the West Indies. To thwart Union warships on the high seas checking ships bound for the South, large ships carried cargoes with their manifests declaring them for the British West Indies (Nassau was the favorite destination, but goods also went to Bermuda and Havana) or even Halifax. At these locations, cargoes were offloaded and transferred to the small, swift steamers for the run to Wilmington, Charleston, and Mobile. These ports were from the West Indies only one-seventh to one-ninth the distances from the same ports to England.

The Northern public and press never understood the difficulties of the blockade or what went into it. Union success in this effort was attributable to being able to keep ships in constant operation. This supply and repair effort, largely overlooked in histories of the Civil War at sea, was vital to the success of Union Atlantic and Gulf coastal operations.

Resupply problems were greatly eased by the capture of Port Royal. The chief base for the South Atlantic Blockading Squadron, it was equidistant from the squadron's operational limits. The seizure of Ship Island by Union forces was similarly vital for Flag Officer David Farragut's move up the Mississippi to New Orleans. From these bases, navy colliers and supply steamers regularly visited the blockaders on station, bringing food, including fresh vegetables in season, and mail.

Indecisive leaders in Washington made no effort to capitalize on the capture of Port Royal, Fernandina, Beaufort, and other points along the coast. The capture of Fort Pulaski and James Island in 1862 and Morris Island in 1863 should have led to Union land campaigns from the coast. Although problems in carrying out such operations would have been considerable, the War Department remained uninterested in projecting military power in this fashion.

Following the failure of its initial embargo on cotton shipments in order to bring about European recognition, the South did all it could to get its goods to European markets, running a fair amount of cotton out through the blockade between 1862 and 1865. This was nonetheless only a small fraction of its prewar exports, and increasingly production of cotton was shifted over to food, although not nearly as much as was needed. Probably the cotton carried out by blockade runners amounted to no more than three hundred fifty thousand bales, most of it from the southeastern Atlantic coast. Another fifty thousand or so bales went overland through Texas to Mexico, where it was then shipped out through Tampico and Matamoras.[35]

The inability of the South to ship out large amounts of its chief product severely affected Confederate government finances. Taxes could not be paid, and paper money steadily declined in value. Depreciation and shortages in essential goods also pushed prices to astronomical levels. From 1861 to 1865, flour shot up from $7.90 to $412.50 a barrel, sugar from $.10 to $7.20 a pound, and bacon from $.13 to $6.87 per pound. Such prices also meant that it was difficult to induce blockade runners to bring in essential raw materials or sinews of war. Much more money was to be made in items for the consumer economy.[36]

President Davis's mistaken belief in the power of cotton also caused the South to go slow with its own construction of ships to run the blockade. Yet the potential worth of blockade running was amply demonstrated in September 1861, when the first steamer to challenge the blockade, the privately owned British iron hulled screw steamer *Bermuda*, arrived from England with at least eighteen rifled field pieces, four heavy smoothbore guns, sixty-five hundred Enfield rifles, and twenty thousand cartridges that the owners planned to sell to the Confederate government. The *Bermuda* also carried an unreported quantity of arms and ammunition destined for private individuals, either to resell to the highest bidder or to be used to equip their own units. Col. Wade Hampton of South Carolina secured for his command two hundred Enfield rifles, twenty thousand Enfield cartridges, and two 6-pounder field guns. The civilian side of the *Bermuda*'s cargo included shoes, blankets, dry goods, and drugs.[37]

With fortunes to be made on one successful voyage, too often patriotism took second place to the quest for profit. In any case, much of the blockade running was in the hands of foreign shippers. English citizens organized private firms for blockade-running operations, and speedy low-silhouette ships were built specifically for such operations. Small, fast, shallow-draft coastal packets capable of working their way in shallow channels and eluding the larger and almost always slower Union warships came to be the preferred ships for blockade running. Such ships lacked the carrying capacity of the large seagoing ships and were unsuited for transatlantic voyages.

The earliest steamer blockade runners were modified British coastal and cross-Channel ships used to transport mail, passengers, and freight. Many of them were built in the Clyde district of Scotland, and the term "Clyde-built steamer" became synonymous with blockade runner. Modifications included removal of the passenger cabins to provide additional space for coal and cargo. Attracted by the potential for high profits, British entrepreneurs operated some eighty of these ships.

As the war went on, purpose-built iron-hulled blockade runners appeared. Such ships were noted for their rakish swept-back appearance and were most often side-wheelers with two or more smokestacks. Longer ships with narrower beams and lighter thin-skinned iron or steel hulls produced greater speed. Shallow draft and easy maneuverability were other prerequisites. Streamlined "turtleback" forward decks enabled such ships to knife through the waves, but this required raised bridges and enclosed helms, the forerunner of today's bridge structures. Twin screws increased both speed and maneuverability, but side-wheeler steamers had a slight advantage in speed, in consequence of the shallow draft size required that severely limited propeller size.

Side-wheeler steamer and blockade runner Advance, *sepia wash drawing by*
R. G. Skerrett. NAVAL HISTORICAL CENTER (NH 61882)

Their low freeboard and minimal deckhouses, coupled with telescoping funnels, produced slight silhouettes and made the blockade runners difficult to spot. To reduce visibility further, blockade runners were painted a slate gray to render them almost invisible. Builders also worked to render the ships as quiet as possible during operation.[38]

One of the reasons that the Confederates continued to enjoy success in passing blockade runners in and out of Charleston was the construction of "trifling draft" ships. Designed specifically for operations in the Gulf of Mexico, such ships had drafts of only seven feet or less. They proved especially effective at Charleston, where they were able to operate anywhere off that port without fear of running aground.[39]

Blockade runner captains bragged about the speed of their ships, but sometimes speed was not sufficient to save the ships from capture. Perhaps the fastest of the blockade runners was the side-wheeler *Margaret and Jessie*. Originally the *Douglas* and reputedly the fastest ship in the world when built in 1855, it was purchased in November 1862 and converted into a blockade runner. It had made five trips in and out of Charleston and Wilmington, when in late May, bound for Nassau from Wilmington with fouled boilers, it was overtaken by the Union warship *Rhode Island*, which opened fire when the *Margaret and Jessie* refused to come to. When a Union shell crashed through one of its boilers, the blockade runner's captain beached his ship on

Eleuthera Island. The ship was later salvaged and placed back into service, making another half dozen round trips to the Confederacy. But on 4 November 1863, commanded by Capt. Robert Lockwood, the *Margaret and Jessie* was approaching Wilmington when the Union gunboats *Niphon* and *Howquah* moved to intercept it. Lockwood turned his ship back to sea and that night outran his pursuers. The next morning, however, the gunboats *Keystone State* and *Nansemond* and the army transport *Fulton* all spotted it and joined the chase. Too late the blockade runner began jettisoning its cargo. The *Nansemond* closed within range to open fire, but rough seas soon forced it to reduce its speed; however, the large *Fulton* cut through the waves and, firing a shot with its bow gun, forced Lockwood to surrender his ship.

The *Margaret and Jessie* was taken into the Federal Navy as the blockader *Gettysburg*. Armed with a single 4.2-inch Parrott rifle and six boat howitzers, it subsequently took three prizes of its own. The *Gettysburg*'s captain, Roswell Lamson, claimed the ship once made sixteen knots. Even this speed was not sufficient to catch some of the blockade runners. On 26 July 1864, the *Gettysburg* chased a blockade runner all day but was unable to overtake it.[40]

Blockade runners were not armed. This was because under international law if the crew of a nonbelligerent ship were to use arms in its defense, the men might be tried as pirates. Crew members were usually foreigners, which created a problem for Federal authorities, who were bound to release all foreign nationals captured.[41]

The Confederate government left most of the blockade running effort in the private sector, with private ships transporting the bulk of its cargoes. This decision was attributable to concerns about states' rights. But with profit in luxury goods considerably greater than in war supplies, much of the trade was in consumer goods rather than more important military supplies, and the government needed to get cotton to market to be able to import necessary war supplies.

In February 1864 the Confederate Congress passed a bill that went into effect on 1 March authorizing President Davis to regulate foreign commerce. The bill gave Davis full control over the exportation of cotton, rice, tobacco, sugar, molasses, and other goods. It also prohibited importation of a number of goods that were taking valuable space on the blockade runners, including such diverse items as brandy and spirits, carpets and rugs, carriages, furniture, marble, bricks, coconuts, gems, antiques, and coin collections. A second bill, passed on 5 March 1864, required shippers to make full disclosure regarding their ships and cargo before departing any Southern port. All ships were liable to have one-half of their outward and inward cargo space taken by the Confederate government at specified rates. British owners in particular bitterly protested the new regulations, and a number swore they would remove their ships from service. Few if any did so, and before long they had accepted the regulations and were working with Confederate authorities to deliver the supplies.[42]

Blockade duties were tedious, routine-centered, and sometimes difficult. Blockaders had to keep on station in all kinds of weather: tropical summer heat or the gales and cold of winter. Close to shore, insects were a major problem in summer, and the crews had to be on constant guard against a sudden attack by a Confederate ironclad ram or a spar-torpedo boat.

Sailors on blockade duty found it often frustrating. It could also be hazardous, especially as the blockade runners attempted to pass in or out of port at night and in difficult weather conditions. The blockaders also had to contend with operations in generally unfamiliar coastal shoal waters.

Captains of blockade runners routinely sought a dark, moonless night, often under the cover of foul weather, to run the blockade. Speed was essential, and a typical blockade-running steamer might burn sixty tons of coal a day, but two hundred tons of coal, sufficient for the trip from Wilmington to Bermuda, weighed as much as seven hundred bales of cotton. The best coal was Pennsylvania anthracite; it burned without the telltale black soot of North Carolina soft bituminous coal, which also did not burn as hot. To secure even higher heat in the boilers and a few extra knots of speed, captains might burn cotton soaked in turpentine.

Union blockaders kept as close to shore as their captains dared, occasionally cruising for short distances along the coast. Captains kept their ships with banked fires so that they could get under way on a moment's notice. Runners and blockaders also worked to develop techniques to outwit the other. For example, signal rockets on the Union side used to alert consorts to the presence of a runner might be countered by false Confederate signals to lure off the blockaders in another direction so that the runner might then dash for shore. Blockade runners sought the protection of shore guns as quickly as possible. As a last resort, a ship could be run aground on the shore, with its cargo to be salvaged later at some convenient time. When this occurred, Union ships would try to send shore parties to burn the ship; if this were not possible, they would endeavor to set the ship afire with hot shot.[43]

Wilmington and Charleston were the chief ports for blockade running, although Charleston became more difficult for the blockaders to use with the seizure of Morris Island at the end of 1863, and the fact that Union warships could then watch the narrow harbor entrance from inside the bar. Access to Wilmington on the Cape Fear River was fairly easy because of its separate entrances—that is until after Union forces took Fort Fisher in January 1865. Savannah, another principal blockade running port, was rendered virtually inaccessible with the Union capture of Fort Pulaski at the harbor entrance by joint military-naval assault in the summer of 1862.

Texas, with its 325 miles of Gulf Coast shoreline, was especially difficult to blockade. Incoming ships would arrive at the mouth of the Rio Grande that formed the boundary between Texas and Mexico, and then discharge their cargoes at Matamoras, Mexico. It would then be transferred by barge to the Texas side. This could be done without interference by Union seagoing ships because the river was too shallow for them to enter. The goods might then be transhipped from central Texas by rail to any point in the Confederacy—that is until Union forces secured control of the Mississippi in 1863.

Despite Union efforts, most blockade runners made it through. Runs out were safer than runs in, simply because captains would have the benefit of knowing the location of the Union blockaders and could plan their attempt accordingly. During all of 1863, in nearly 170 attempts, only eleven ships were taken trying to clear Wilmington and Charleston; thirty-six were lost in more than 200 tries to enter those ports. The most dangerous time to attempt to pass in was in daylight. If a blockade runner arrived off the coast in daytime and was sighted by Union warships, it became largely a matter of speed as to whether the blockade runner would escape.[44]

Although few blockade runners returned substantial profits, the financial rewards could be considerable, even if a ship were ultimately lost. The *Ella and Annie*, capable of carrying up to 1,300 bales of cotton, made eight trips through the blockade. Combined with profit on inbound cargo, it returned a profit of about $200,000 per round trip. The *Alice and Fannie*, averaging 925 bales of cotton per trip, returned more than $100,000 per circuit. Financial reward was the chief motivation for blockade running, and such returns explain why so many people participated in the activity.[45]

Sailors on blockade duty could hope for prize money from any captures, but the sums realized were far less than supposed. Unless the ship was more powerful than its captor—a rare occurrence—half of the money realized went to the navy's pension fund. The remainder was heavily weighted in favor of the more senior officers, with all the sailors and marines sharing only 35 percent. Commanders of squadrons made out the best; they received one-twentieth of any prize money awarded to ships in their squadrons. Thus Samuel Lee received $110,000 for his time in command of the North Atlantic Blockading Squadron, and David Farragut realized $56,000.

If other ships happened to be in the vicinity, their crews could claim a share of the prize money. Thus, on 31 July 1862 the blockader *Magnolia* (itself an ex-blockade runner) captured the runner *Memphis*. No other Union ships were present, and the prize was judged worth more than half a million dollars. At the other extreme was the sloop *Secesh*, taken off Charleston in 1863. It brought $17,685.69, but this sum was shared among the men of twelve ships.[46]

Slowly but surely, the Union tightened its blockade of the South. By January 1865 the Union Navy had 471 ships with 2,245 guns in blockade service. During the course of the war these took a total of about 1,500 vessels of all classes:[47]

	Captured	Destroyed
Steamers	210	85
Schooners	569	114
Sloops	139	32
Ships	13	2
Brigs	29	2
Barks	25	4
Yachts	2	—
Small Boats	139	96
Rams	6	5
Gunboats	10	11
Others	7	—
Totals	1,149	351

These totals may be compared with the steadily decreasing number of successful runs through the blockade, with a growing proportion of the runs by steamers:[48]

	Atlantic Ports		Gulf Ports		
Year	Steam	Sail	Steam	Sail	Total
1861	1,036	763	371	1,293	3,465
1862	79	184	45	229	537
1863	347	66	78	193	684
1864	414	30	84	91	619
1865*	22	2	50	11	85
Total	1,898	1,047	628	1,817	5,390

* to end of war only

With Confederate domestic production never reaching 50 percent of military needs, goods brought in by blockade runners were essential to the Southern war effort. Historian Stephen Wise has estimated that the South brought in through blockade running at least 400,000 rifles (more than 60 percent of the Confederacy's modern arms), 2.25 million pounds of saltpeter (two-thirds of that needed), and 3 million pounds of lead (one-third of army requirements). He concludes, "Without blockade running, the nation's military would have been without proper supplies of arms, bullets, and powder." The blockade runners also brought clothing, chemicals, and medicine. Without these supplies, the Confederacy could not have survived as long as it did.[49]

Despite the undoubted success of the blockade in taking many ships and restricting supplies, it nonetheless remains a hot topic of debate among historians.[50] Its critics note that the majority, even the vast majority, of blockade runners were successful, even to the end of the war. They charge that the economic collapse of the Confederacy was due not to the blockade but to the deterioration of the Southern railroad system. Others point out this vast, costly Union effort was ineffective—that the blockade was easily penetrated and the vast majority of blockade runners got through. Runners were still passing through the blockade at the end of the war. Critics argue that because the Confederacy showed a great ability to improvise and was largely independent of imports to continue the war, even a more effective blockade would not have prevented the South from continuing the war. In point of fact, the Confederacy never lost a major battle for want of arms or ammunition. Critics of the blockading effort admit that the blockade disrupted traditional trading patterns and cost the South heavily in financial terms, but they do not see it as in any way war-winning. Confederate defeat did not result from lack of materials; rather, the South simply ran out of manpower.

Defenders of the blockade acknowledge its shortcomings. Although they admit to its incomplete nature and the fact that the South never lacked the essential weapons with which to fight and win battles, they note that the Confederacy was hard pressed in such essential items as artillery, clothing, shoes, harnesses, medicines, and even blankets. The blockade also affected the entire Southern economy. The loss of rolled iron rail was particularly harmful, as it led directly to the collapse of the Confederate transportation system. With this came serious distribution problems, even of food, affecting soldiers and civilians alike.

It is hard to disagree with the conclusion that the blockade was the chief cause, directly or indirectly, of Southern economic distress. The figures given above of successful passages through the blockade are also misleading. For one thing, this includes ships exiting as well as entering Southern ports. Thus each successful stop by an individual coastal packet making stops at many different ports is counted as a "successful attempt." Two coastal steamers making up to ten stops per trip made almost eight hundred of the runs in 1861. The total also includes small river vessels. The number of successful runs must also be compared to the number of ships entering Southern ports in normal circumstances. Thus in a typical peacetime year, New Orleans alone had nineteen hundred ships entering the Gulf.

Historian David G. Surdam notes the role played by cotton, by far the most important prewar Southern export, in the blockade equation. He believes that the effectiveness of the blockade should be measured not in goods smuggled through it or the success rate of the ships. Rather, the points to remember are that the total volume of trade was sharply reduced and the cost of shipment dramatically increased. This was especially true regarding cotton. As U.S. Secretary of State William Seward put it, "the true test of the efficiency of the blockade will be found in the results. Cotton commands a price in Manchester, and Rouen, and Lowell, four times greater than at New Orleans. . . . Judged by this test of results, I am satisfied that there was never a more effective blockade." Economic historian Stanley

Lebergott noted an even greater price differential in 1864, when cotton sold for six cents a pound in Houston and fifty-six cents in New York.[51]

Although a majority of blockade runners got to sea during the war, the trade was increasingly in steamers and in specially designed, hence more expensive, ships. Also the statistics of successful runs do not include ships forced to turn back when sighted by Union ships, or the ships that did not even attempt the effort.

The Federal government spent $567 million on the navy during the war (1879 calculation). This was roughly one-twelfth of the expenses of the entire war ($6.8 billion). Yet the entire cost of the navy was equal to or exceeded by the loss in revenue to the South from the export of raw cotton. As Surdam makes clear, the underindustrialized Confederacy had to import manufactured goods to win the war, yet the higher shipping costs consumed much of the South's purchasing power and sharply eroded its ability to make purchases overseas. The increased cost in transporting cotton to Europe accounted for almost all the war's increase in its price in Europe and the North. The sharp rise in transportation costs precluded the South from importing the heavy items it so desperately needed for the war effort, such as machinery, steam engines, and iron rails. Although European goods could always reach the South, this increasingly occurred through less convenient ports, such as via the Mexican port of Matamoros to Brownsville, Texas. Increased shortages of consumer goods sharply affected civilian morale.

The blockade also disrupted patterns of intraregional trade by water, sharply increasing the burden on an already inadequate Southern railroad net that progressively deteriorated during the war. Thus in early 1865, millions of rations were at Augusta and Columbus, Georgia, awaiting shipment. The bottleneck resulted from the inability of the Southern railroads to haul them. Such logistical breakdowns may be directly attributed to the blockade. Given the fact that the North was far richer than the South, it was far easier for it to bear the expense of the blockade than it was for the South to sustain the loss in export revenue.

For all of the reasons stated, the Union blockade of the South appears to have been an effective use of resources. Had there been a concurrent commitment of major Union ground forces, the blockading warships would have made an even more substantial contribution to the ultimate Confederate defeat.[52]

CHAPTER FIVE

Early Union Riverine Warfare in the West

—⁓—

A lthough the Union naval preoccupation was always with the blockade and related operations along the eastern seaboard, the navy nonetheless provided important assistance to army operations in the West. The Western Theater was every bit as important as the East. A vast area, it was bounded by the Appalachian Mountains on the east and the Mississippi River on the west. Its battlegrounds were Kentucky, Georgia, and Tennessee, with the latter its key. Roads in the West were poor and railroads insufficient. If the Union could control the region's major rivers, it would possess avenues along which it might invade the lower South.

On 16 May 1861, Welles ordered Cdr. John Rodgers to Cincinnati to report to Maj. Gen. George B. McClellan, commander of the Department of the Ohio. Rodgers was to establish "a naval armament on the Mississippi and Ohio rivers, or either of them, with a view of blockading or interdicting communication and interchanges with the States that are in insurrection." Because "interior intercourse" was under its control, the army was to provide whatever Rodgers needed, save for guns and men. Although operating under the army, Rodgers would nonetheless report to the Navy Department.[1]

The great western rivers were for the most part shallow and winding, precluding employment of sailing warships mounting traditional broadside batteries. River gunboats were required: broad-beamed, shallow-draft warships mounting as many as four guns forward and two aft, with others in broadsides. In the race to build gunboats, the North had the advantage in manufacturing facilities, skilled workers, adequate marine engines, and the production of iron-plate protection. The navy began the western naval struggle with three converted Ohio River steamers; it ended the conflict with more than one hundred warships on the Mississippi and its tributaries.[2]

In early May 1861, McClellan had recommended to Union General in Chief Scott the construction of three gunboats to support Federal troops at Cairo, Illinois. Strategically located at the junction of the Ohio and Mississippi rivers, Cairo offered direct access to the river traffic of Illinois, Kentucky, and Missouri. From Cairo, gunboats might control both the Ohio and the upper Mississippi.

Scott supported the idea as part of his Anaconda Plan. Also lending support was attorney general Edward Bates from Missouri. In mid-April, Bates wrote to his friend James B. Eads, suggesting the civil engineer come to Washington. Eads was involved in a salvage business in St. Louis that employed powerful twin-hulled, steam-driven vessels to pull snags from the rivers.

In Washington, Eads met with Welles and proposed that Cairo become the principal base for Union operations on the Mississippi and the Ohio, and that a number of the "snag boats" be converted into gunboats. Welles, preoccupied with the blockade, rather surprisingly referred Eads to the War Department, "to which the subject more properly belongs." Later Welles said that the army had insisted on jurisdiction over the western naval forces.[3]

Meanwhile, Rodgers had taken up his assignment. An experienced officer familiar with steam propulsion, Rodgers came from a distinguished naval family (his father was Commo. John Rodgers of War of 1812 fame) and enjoyed important political connections. His brother-in-law was Brig. Gen. Montgomery Meigs, the army quartermaster general. With the army paying for the western ships, no doubt Wells thought this connection would prove valuable. The only negative was that Rodgers knew virtually nothing of riverine warfare. This was true of most navy officers, however; they would have to learn on the job.[4]

McClellan gave Rodgers a free hand, and over the next few months Rodgers made great strides in creating an inland navy. On his own initiative, he purchased three side-wheeler steamboats and converted them into the gunboats *Conestoga, Lexington,* and *Tyler.* The three became known as

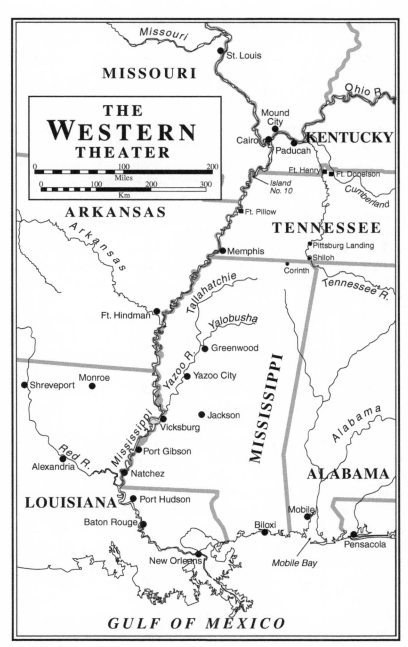

Western Theater of Operations

"timberclads" for their 5-inch-thick oak plank installed as protection against small-arms fire. After securing both cannon and crews, on 15 August Rodgers sent Lt. Seth L. Phelps and two of the timberclads down the Mississippi to above New Madrid, Missouri. There they chased two Confederate gunboats back to New Madrid, but Phelps did not proceed farther, afraid to risk his lightly protected gunboats to the Confederate shore batteries.[5]

In late July, meanwhile, McClellan was called east to assume command of the Union Army. His replacement was Maj. Gen. John C. Frémont, who took command of the newly created Department of the West. Known as "the Pathfinder" for his western explorations, Frémont had parlayed important political connections into a major generalcy of volunteers. He proved hopelessly inadequate in higher command and was soon at loggerheads with Rodgers, demanding his removal. Bowing to the inevitable and hoping that a more senior naval officer would have greater success, in late August Welles selected the commandant of the Brooklyn Navy Yard, Capt. Andrew H. Foote, to replace Rodgers.[6]

Foote proved an excellent choice. A veteran of thirty-nine years of naval service, he was popular with his subordinates and had a reputation as an aggressive, capable commander. Most important for this assignment, he was a proven administrator and diplomat. His experience commanding amphibious operations against the barrier forts near Canton, China, was another plus. Of strong moral principles, Foote had led the campaign for temperance in the navy. Later he became one of the first U.S. Navy admirals.[7]

Foote arrived at St. Louis on 6 September to take up his position as commander of Union naval forces on the upper Mississippi. Work was then proceeding around the clock, seven days a week, on nine ironclad gunboats and thirty-eight mortar boats. In addition to seven ironclads contracted for with Eads, Frémont had authorized the purchase and conversion into ironclads of two snagboats. The first was the 633-ton *Submarine No. 7*. Renamed the *Benton* by Frémont, in honor of his father-in-law, Thomas Hart Benton, it mounted sixteen guns and became Foote's flagship. The second was the 355-ton *New Era*. It mounted five guns and was renamed the *Essex* by its captain, Cdr. William D. Porter, brother of David D. Porter, in honor of their father's ship in the War of 1812.

With most design work already completed, Foote concentrated on bringing the flotilla into being and securing the resources for its operation.

U.S. Navy Rear Adm. Andrew Hull Foote. NAVAL HISTORICAL CENTER (NH 46248)

Later Foote said that he regarded the creation of the flotilla as the greatest achievement of his life and the fighting of it as secondary. Certainly, problems were immense. Foote wrote his friend Fox, "I only wish that you could have spent one day here for the last six weeks, as no imagination can fancy what it is to collect materials and fit out western gunboats with western men without a navy yard, in the west, where no stores are to be had."[8]

Foote established a naval depot at Cairo for repair and replenishment of his ships. Initially this was afloat, but later he ordered construction of a ten-acre navy yard at Mound City, just above Cairo, although the machine shops and carpenter shops remained afloat in steamers. Foote's most difficult procurement task was finding trained crewmen. The navy sent some men and the army released others, but in large part the crews learned on the job.[9]

On 12 October 1861, the ironclad *St. Louis* slid down the ways. The first of Eads's *City*-class gunboats (named for river cities), it was also the first U.S. ironclad. In September 1862, it was renamed the *Baron de Kalb*. During the next three weeks, its five sisters were launched, with the *Benton* added in November. The ironclads were all underpowered and had an unfortunate design flaw: the vulnerable steam drums had been crowded into the holds, with the result that water as well as steam went into the engines, forcing relocation of the drums on top of the boilers. (Alone among these ironclads, the *Benton* had both its steam drums and its boilers fully protected in its hold.) Their exposed machinery would later lead to disaster for two of the *City*-class ships and some two hundred crewmen.[10]

While the ironclads were being readied, Foote kept his timberclads busy conducting intelligence and raids, sometimes in conjunction with the army. An example of these operations came in the Battle of Lucas Bend on 10 September 1861, when Union land forces skirmished with the Confederates near Norfolk, Missouri, about eight miles below Cairo. The *Conestoga* and *Lexington* provided covering fire and damaged and drove off the Confederate steamer *Yankee*.

On 6 November the *Lexington* and *Tyler* also escorted six transports lifting 3,110 troops under Brig. Gen. Ulysses S. Grant, commander of the Cairo Military District, in a demonstration down the Mississippi against Columbus, Kentucky. Frémont ordered this operation in an attempt to mask a Union effort in southeastern Missouri and to prevent Confederate Maj. Gen. Leonidas Polk from dispatching reinforcements thence from Columbus. Grant had no precise plans when he set out, although he intended to fight rather than merely stage a demonstration.[11]

With Columbus far too powerful for his force, early on 7 November Grant landed twenty-five hundred men across the Mississippi to attack twenty-seven hundred Confederates at Belmont, Missouri. The Union troops went ashore three miles above Belmont, then marched to attack it. Meanwhile, the Union gunboats circled and exchanged fire with the heavy Confederate guns in the upper batteries across the river. Grant's force defeated the Confederates ashore, but the Union troops stopped to loot the Confederate camp, allowing their adversary an opportunity to regroup. Protected by the lower batteries at Columbus, Polk also dispatched reinforcements across the river in an effort to cut off the Union soldiers from their transports. The timberclads returned to the landing as Grant's now-outnumbered force managed to cut its way through the Rebels. As the last Federals hurriedly reembarked, the Confederates struck in strength, only to be met, and stopped, by grape and canister fire from the timberclads.

The Battle of Belmont claimed 610 Union and 642 Confederate casualties. It was not a battle that Grant could point to with great pride, but Lincoln was pleased to have a general willing to fight. The battle also spread concern in the South over possible future Union amphibious operations. Although Polk trumpeted a great victory, he also demanded additional men and artillery and was thereafter reluctant to heed Johnston's calls for manpower. In this sense, Belmont played a key role in the subsequent Union operations against Forts Henry and Donelson.[12]

In early November 1861, Lincoln reorganized the Western Department. Brig. Gen. Don Carlos Buell replaced Brig. Gen. William T. Sherman at Louisville as commander of the Department of the Ohio, including Ohio, Michigan, and Indiana; Maj. Gen. Henry Halleck took command of the newly designated Department of the Missouri, embracing Missouri, Iowa, Minnesota, Illinois, Arkansas, and Kentucky west of the Cumberland River. The ambitious Halleck proved a capable administrator but a poor field general. Certainly, Foote did not think highly of him. It did help Foote in his dealings with his army counterparts that he received promotion to the new rank of flag officer, equivalent to army major general, the same month.[13]

Union western land operations now centered on Tennessee. The state was a major food-producing area and its capital of Nashville was a key rail center and arms-manufacturing depot. Along the Cumberland River northwest of Nashville lay the South's largest gunpowder mills, and Tennessee held two-thirds of the South's mineral wealth, including its largest iron-producing regions and 90 percent of its copper. Tennessee also supplied more soldiers to the Confederacy than any other state save Virginia.[14]

With Union forces in the West outnumbering the Confederates two to one, Lincoln pressed his commanders to take the offensive, but both Buell and Halleck held back, citing logistical problems and insufficient resources. Each wanted to make a major attack, but only if supported by the other, and the result was inaction. Dividing the Union command in the Western Theater proved to be a major mistake.[15]

In Gen. Albert Sidney Johnston, the Confederates did have unity of command in their Western Military Department, but Johnston also had a vast area to defend. Hopes of a Confederate frontier on the Ohio had been dashed by Kentucky's proclamation of neutrality, but that state at least provided a shield for Tennessee. On 4 September, before Johnston arrived to take command, however, Polk committed a major blunder in ordering Brig. Gen. Gideon J. Pillow to fortify Columbus, twenty miles below Cairo.

This violation of Kentucky's neutrality gave the Union an excuse to intervene. On 6 September, believing that the Confederates would next move on Paducah at the confluence of the Tennessee and Ohio rivers, Grant dispatched a force there in transports escorted by the *Tyler* and *Conestoga*. Seizing Paducah, Grant then sent troops to occupy Smithfield, at the mouth of the Cumberland. These moves gave Union forces access to the Ohio, Tennessee, and Cumberland rivers.

The Confederate defense of Tennessee extended in a great arc centered on the Tennessee and Cumberland rivers, with the two flanks in advance. Johnston regarded the western terminus of Columbus as the key to the Western Theater and had vowed to turn it into a "Gibraltar of the West." Polk soon had ten thousand men and a large number of heavy guns at Columbus. Although Halleck could not take Columbus without a siege, he knew that it could be flanked and forced into surrender.[16]

Columbus lies close to where the Ohio is joined by its two main tributaries, the Cumberland and the Tennessee. The 650-mile-long Tennessee rises in eastern Tennessee above Knoxville, flows through northern Alabama and a corner of Mississippi, returns to Tennessee, and then moves north into Kentucky west of Bowling Green to join the Ohio at Paducah. The circuitous 700-mile-long Cumberland rises in eastern Kentucky and joins the Ohio at Smithland, a few miles above Paducah.

In January 1862 McClellan ordered Grant to mount a demonstration against Nashville. With Buell supposedly about to begin his long-delayed offensive on that city, McClellan hoped that Grant, accompanied by appropriate publicity, would fix Confederate forces at Columbus and prevent men at Forts Henry and Donelson from reinforcing Brig. Gen. Simon Bolivar Buckner at Bowling Green. Grant sent Brig. Gen. Charles F. Smith from Paducah up the western bank of the Tennessee to threaten Fort Henry, while he accompanied Brig. Gen. John McClernand's division into western Kentucky to threaten Columbus. The *Conestoga* and *Lexington* supported Smith from the Tennessee, while the *Essex* and *St. Louis* performed the same function for Grant and McClernand on the Mississippi. On 11 January the latter two gunboats fought an hour-long battle with three Confederate gunboats from Columbus, in which the Union gunboats drove off their opponents.[17]

Buell was slow to move, however. Under pressure from both McClellan and Lincoln, he finally sent Brig. Gen. George H. Thomas and four thousand men toward Knoxville, leading to the Union victory of Mill Springs, Kentucky (or Logan's Crossroads). This battle on 19 January 1862 shattered Johnston's right flank and led to his decision to abandon eastern Kentucky. But Buell, claiming poor roads and supply difficulties, failed to follow up the victory. Thomas then moved his army to Burkesville, Kentucky, about seventy-five miles northeast of Nashville on the Cumberland. He and Buell wanted Foote's gunboats to push up the Cumberland past Fort Donelson and join them in a Union attack on Nashville, but Halleck favored a concentration in middle Tennessee, with both armies within supporting distance. He wanted to attack Fort Henry while Buell moved against Fort Donelson. Such a move would flank the powerful western Confederate fortress of Columbus and the Confederates to the east at Bowling Green.

Grant and Foote repeatedly urged Halleck to authorize a move against Forts Henry and Donelson, but Halleck consistently refused. Halleck wanted to counter Buell's Kentucky success, and Lincoln was also applying pressure, but he was not prompted to act until he received an erroneous report that the Confederates were sending reinforcements west. On 30 January, Halleck finally ordered Grant to take Fort Henry.[18]

Confederate Brig. Gen. Lloyd Tilghman commanded Forts Henry and Donelson. Westernmost Fort Henry was located on the east bank of the Tennessee River. It occupied three acres of ground in a solidly built five-sided earthwork parapet. Rifle pits extended to the river and two miles east toward Fort Donelson. Although Henry lay in a bend of the river commanding a straight stretch of water some three miles long, it was also on low ground. In early February 1862 the Tennessee was in flood, and some of the land within Henry's perimeter was two feet under water.

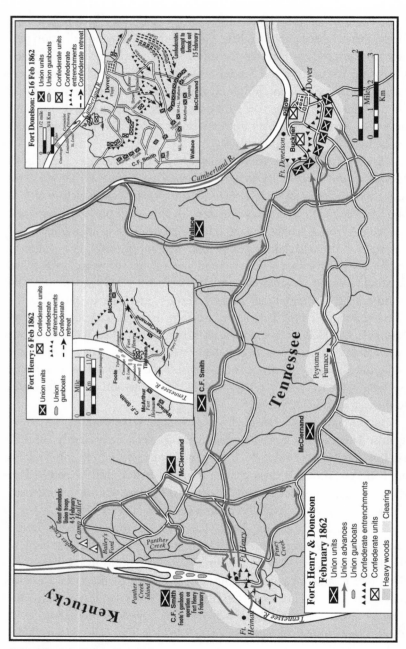

Forts Henry and Donelson, February 1862

Work to fortify the heights on the west bank, known as Fort Heiman, was incomplete at the time of the Federal attack.

Fort Henry mounted seventeen heavy guns. Twelve faced the river and five guarded the land approaches, but the Confederates also had no ammunition for their 42-pounders, leaving only nine guns able to contest a water approach. Fort Henry's garrison was only 2,610 men, many of them raw recruits armed with shotguns and hunting rifles; some had only flintlocks.[19]

On 2 February, the Union flotilla departed Cairo, led by the ironclads *Cincinnati* (the flagship), *Carondelet*, *Essex*, and *St. Louis*. The transports were next, followed by the timberclads *Conestoga*, *Lexington*, and *Tyler*. Two lifts were necessary to transport all of Grant's seventeen thousand men. Early on 4 February, the Confederates learned of the Union advance. Tilghman immediately telegraphed Polk at Columbus for reinforcements, but none were sent.

The Confederates had placed some torpedoes (mines) in the river, but the strong current swept away a number of them. The wife of a Confederate officer inadvertently revealed their presence to Union scouts, and Foote set crews on the timberclads to work dragging for the torpedoes. They recovered six, soaked and harmless.

Union gunboats advancing up the Tennessee River toward Fort Henry, 6 February 1862; engraving copied from Harper's Weekly. NAVAL HISTORICAL CENTER (NH 59016)

Grant debarked his troops some three miles from Fort Henry, just beyond the range of its guns. He then returned to Paducah with the transports to hurry the second lift of Smith's division. Late on the 5 February, meanwhile, three of Foote's gunboats approached Fort Henry and opened fire, killing one defender and wounding three others. The Confederates replied with six shots, and the gunboats withdrew.

All Union troops were not ashore until the night of 5 February, when it rained heavily. Although he did not yet have all his men in place, Grant believed that prompt action was imperative to forestall Confederate reinforcement. Hopeful that all his men would have arrived in time, he ordered the advance to begin at 11 AM on 6 February.

Grant planned a simultaneous land and water attack. During the night of 5 February he sent Smith and two brigades along the west bank of the river to prevent reinforcement from that direction, to cut off a Confederate escape, and to seize Fort Heiman as a possible artillery emplacement, but Smith's men discovered Heiman deserted. General McClernand's division along one of Smith's brigades made the main Union land effort on the east bank.

Estimating Grant's strength at twenty-five thousand men and knowing he could not withstand such an attack, at 10 AM on 6 February Tilghman ordered all the fort's defenders, save the artillerymen manning the batteries, to withdraw by foot to Fort Donelson. Only about a hundred men remained, including those too sick to move. Tilghman's goal was simply to delay the attackers long enough for the rest of his command to escape.

At 10:50 AM Foote ordered the flotilla to get under way. The ironclads formed in line abreast: the *Essex* on the right, then the *Cincinnati*, *Carondelet*, and *St. Louis*. A half mile behind them came Lieutenant Phelps's division of timberclads. As the flotilla approached Fort Henry, there was no sign of the Union troops, and Foote decided to begin the battle alone. At 11:45 AM, from about seventeen hundred yards' range, the *Cincinnati* fired a shot, signaling the other gunboats to open fire. At about a mile's range, Taylor ordered the water battery to respond. The firing then became general. During the engagement, the vulnerable timberclads remained at long range, lobbing shells into the fort.

Confederate fire was both lively and accurate. Although Fort Henry had only nine guns that could respond, their shells struck all the gunboats many times. Most of the damage from their fifty-nine hits was slight, save to the *Essex*, when a Confederate shell tore into its middle boiler, killing or wounding thirty-two men, including Commander Porter. The gunboat then drifted out of control downriver, where it was towed to safety by a tug. A seaman was also killed and nine others wounded on board the *Cincinnati*, and another man was killed aboard the *Essex* by a musket ball.

Union gunboats attacking Confederate Fort Henry, 6 February 1862; engraving after sketch by Thomas Nast. NAVAL HISTORICAL CENTER (NH 60823)

From the beginning of the engagement, Union fire was quite accurate. The crews could see shell explosions throwing up earth around the Confederate guns. Disaster struck on shore when the 6-inch rifled gun blew up, killing or wounding its crew. A priming wire stuck in the vent of the 10-inch Columbiad, spiking it, and two 32-pounders were struck at almost the same time.

With only four of his guns able to return fire and Union fire sweeping the fort, Tilghman surrendered at 2 PM. He had, however, saved the bulk of the garrison. Only ninety-four men, including sixteen aboard a Confederate hospital boat, were taken prisoners. Confederate personnel losses were five dead, eleven wounded, and five missing. The victors also captured the fort's guns as well as supplies and equipment. With the roads mired in mud, Union land forces did not arrive at the fort until an hour after its surrender.[20]

In his after-action report, Foote wrote that his gunboats "after a severe and rapid fire of one hour and a quarter, have captured Fort Henry and have taken Gen. Lloyd Tilghman and his staff, with 60 men, as prisoners.

The surrender to the gunboats was unconditional, as we kept an open fire upon them until their flag was struck." [21]

Foote's characterization of the battle to his wife was quite different, however. "I never again will go out and fight half prepared," he wrote. "Men were not exercised & perfectly green. The rifle shots hissed like snakes. Tilghman, well he would have cut us all to pieces had his best rifle not burst & his 128-pounder been stopped in the vent."[22]

Upon securing Fort Henry, Foote immediately sent Phelps and his timberclads up the Tennessee to raid as far as depth of water would allow. In a daring foray, the Union ships reached Mussel Shoals, Alabama, before returning to Fort Henry on 10 February. The five-day raid captured three Confederate steamers and brought the destruction of six others. The large *Eastport* was a particularly valuable capture. It had been undergoing conversion into an ironclad at Cerro Gordo and was about half complete when it was taken on 7 February, along with the materials sufficient to complete the work. The *Eastport* became a Union ironclad of the same name, mounting eight large guns. The expedition also secured a considerable quantity of small arms, as well as lumber, iron plate, and other stores. News of the raid soon spread across the South and also had some psychological impact.[23]

Following the capture of Fort Henry, Grant announced his intention to move against Fort Donelson as soon as possible. On the west bank of the Cumberland River two miles north of Dover, Tennessee, Fort Donelson was situated on a steep bluff that overlooked a straight stretch of several miles of river. The fort was only about fifteen acres in size, but its outer works extended over one hundred acres. Donelson had two river batteries cut into the slope of the ridge facing downriver. The lower battery contained ten guns, whereas the upper battery mounted three. The fort itself contained eight additional guns. On 7 February, the day after the fall of Fort Henry, Fort Donelson had a garrison of about six thousand men, including those from Henry.

Johnston now decided to abandon Kentucky for the time being, extracting the garrisons at Bowling Green and Columbus. Johnston could have concentrated some thirty thousand men at Donelson or he could have evacuated it altogether. Instead, he blundered. Johnston assumed, based on what had happened at Fort Henry, that Donelson was lost, and so he sent only twelve thousand men there, merely to hold Grant long enough until he could withdraw most of his eastern forces to Nashville.[24]

Johnston appointed Brig. Gen. John B. Floyd to command Fort Donelson. Floyd was at best incompetent; his second in command, General Pillow, was both ambitious and incompetent. The third-ranking Confederate, Brig. Gen. Simon Bolivar Buckner, was the one capable senior commander present.

Bad weather imposed a delay on movement by land, but on 12 February Grant proceeded from Fort Henry to Fort Donelson. At the same time, Foote retraced his steps with his gunboats and the Union troop transports. He expressed serious reservations about what lay ahead:

> I go reluctantly, as we are very short of men. . . . I shall do all in my power to render the gunboats effective in the fight, although they are not properly manned. . . . If we could wait ten days, and I had men, I would go with eight mortar boats and six armored boats and conquer.[25]

Necessary repairs to the *Essex* and *Cincinnati* meant that they could not participate. Foote departed with the *St. Louis* (the flagship), *Louisville*, and *Pittsburg*. On 12 February they encountered the *Conestoga* and *Lexington*. The *Conestoga* joined the flotilla, but the *Lexington*, damaged in an accident, continued on to Cairo for repairs. At Paducah the flotilla joined twelve loaded troop-transport steamers. The flotilla did not arrive in the vicinity of Fort Donelson until the night of 13 February, there to discover that Grant had already invested it from the land.[26]

The *Carondelet* had preceded the remainder of the flotilla. Near Fort Donelson on the morning of 13 February, Cdr. Henry Walke received a message from Grant asking him to occupy the Confederates while the Union troops improved their lines. Masked by a heavily wooded point on the riverbank, the *Carondelet* fired 139 shells at the Confederate positions from long range. The Confederates returned fire and, although most of their shot passed high, two hit home. One of them, a 128-pound solid shot from the rifled gun in the upper battery, burst through the ironclad's front casemate, wounding a half dozen men and slightly damaging the ship's machinery. The *Carondelet* halted fire briefly to transfer the wounded, then lobbed another forty-five shells into the fort. One of the shots struck a Confederate gun, disabling it and killing two and wounding five men. According to the Confederates, the *Carondelet*'s shelling that day had more effect than that of 14 February from the entire Union flotilla.[27]

The situation on land initially favored the Confederates, with fifteen thousand unentrenched Union troops confronting twenty-one thousand entrenched Southerners. Fortunately for Grant, Floyd made no effort to attack. In fact, Union troops initiated what little fighting occurred. Although Grant was displeased with this, the Union initiative served to mask his inferior numbers.

The afternoon of 13 February the weather changed dramatically from near summer to winter conditions; driving wind brought sleet and snow and freezing temperatures, with much suffering to both sides. By 14 February the Confederates were completely invested, save along the Cumberland above Dover where the river had flooded the land. As Grant continued to strengthen his lines, the Confederate commanders decided to break out, but Floyd countermanded an attempt on the afternoon of 14 February on the insistence of Pillow, who thought it too late that day.

Grant now called on Foote to mount a naval attack. Grant's plan was to hold the Confederates within the fort from the land while Foote reduced the water batteries. If possible, some of the gunboats would then run past Fort Donelson to south of Dover, cutting off Confederate river resupply.

Although Foote preferred a delay until he could make a personal reconnaissance, he complied with Grant's request. On the morning of 14 February the Union crews placed chains, lumber, and bags of coal on the upper decks of the gunboats and around their boilers to protect them from plunging shot. Preparations were completed by the afternoon, and the assault began shortly before 3 PM. Foote employed the same formation as at Fort Henry. The *St. Louis*, *Carondelet*, *Louisville*, and *Pittsburg* were in front, while the timberclads *Tyler* and *Conestoga* formed a second division about a thousand yards astern, beyond the range of Donelson's guns.

Surprise was impossible and the Confederates had an excellent field of fire up the long, straight stretch of the river, while at the same time their earthen works were difficult to locate from the water side. At about 3:30 PM and at fifteen hundred yards' range, the Confederates fired two shots from a 10-inch Columbiad against the advancing Union ships. Both fell short. When the Union ships were about a mile from the fort, the *St. Louis* opened fire, the other gunboats following suit. Foote attempted to reduce the accuracy of the Confederate fire by varying his speed from time to

Union gunboats engaging Confederate batteries at Fort Donelson, 14 February 1862; engraving published in Harper's Weekly. NAVAL HISTORICAL CENTER (NH 58898)

time. The Union ships fired rapidly until they were within two hundred to four hundred yards of the shore positions.[28]

The battle extended over an hour and a half. The height of the water battery and guns on the bluff permitted plunging fire that nullified the sloping Union armor by hitting it at right angles. This soon began to tell. Commander Walke reported that shot "knocked the plating to pieces, and sent fragments of iron and splinters into the pilots, one of whom fell mortally wounded, and was taken below . . . and still they came, harder and faster, taking flag-staffs and smoke-stacks, and tearing off their side armor as lightning tears the bark from a tree."[29]

The nearness of the Union ships also aided the inexperienced Confederate gunners by allowing them to bring more of their guns into action and to fire more accurately. The gunboats, meanwhile, could use only their three bow guns, and the gunners found it difficult to locate the Confederate positions and to elevate the guns sufficiently to bring the Confederate positions under fire.

Confederate shot soon took away the steering mechanisms of two of the Union warships and badly damaged pilothouses of two others. On board the flagship *St. Louis*, splinters from a shell explosion wounded Foote in the left foot; the same shell killed the pilot standing next to him and took away the ship's wheel. Because the ironclad could no longer be controlled, Foote ordered it left to drift downriver. Another shell then struck the *St. Louis*, knocking down five of six men manning a gun and wounding Foote a second time, in the left arm. The *Louisville*, disabled by a shot that carried away its rudder chains, also drifted out of action. On board the *Carondelet*, a rifled gun blew up on firing, wounding more than a dozen men, and two Confederate shell hits killed four others. There would have been many more Union casualties had not lookouts shouted warnings of the incoming Confederate shot to allow crewmen time to duck. Still, Walke reported that there was so much blood on the decks "that our men could not work the guns without slipping."[30]

The *Carondelet* sustained the most damage. The *Pittsburg*, also in difficulty, crashed into the other Union ship, breaking its rudder. The *Tyler* then disabled the *St. Louis*, smashing into its steering gear. Three of the four ironclads were now hors de combat. The Confederate soldiers broke into cheers as the Union ships withdrew. In the engagement as a whole, eleven men in the flotilla were killed and forty-three were wounded, half of these on the *Carondelet*.

In his subsequent report to Welles, Foote said he had taken his ships in against Fort Donelson at the "urgent request of General Halleck and General Grant, who regarded the movement as a military necessity, although, not in my opinion properly prepared." He claimed that the assault, if continued for fifteen additional minutes, would have resulted in the capture of the two forts: "The enemy's fire had materially slackened and he was running from his batteries" when the St. Louis and Louisville were forced to retire.[31]

Both sides suffered from misconceptions. Damage to the gunboats was not as severe as it first seemed. The *St. Louis* was hit fifty-nine times, the *Louisville* thirty-six, the *Carondelet* thirty-five, and the *Pittsburg* thirty, but none of these hits proved fatal. On the other hand, Foote's assertion to Welles that Donelson was close to surrendering was simply not true. In truth, much of the Union fire had gone high, and there were no casualties among the defenders. The batteries themselves were but little damaged. As Confederate Army Capt. B. G. Bidwell observed, "their fire was more destructive to our works at 2 miles than at two hundred yards. They over fired us from that distance."[32]

Foote had already departed for Cairo with the disabled gunboats on 15 February, leaving behind the *St. Louis* and *Carondelet* to protect the transports, when a dispatch arrived from Grant asking that the gunboats continue to harass the fort. Cdr. Benjamin Dove of the *Louisville*, the senior naval officer present, ordered his own ship and the *St. Louis* upstream. The *St. Louis* lobbed a few shells into Fort Donelson, and toward dusk both ships returned to the anchorage. The next morning Dove again cleared for action and got under way for Fort Donelson, although events made this unnecessary. Certainly, the navy had little impact on the battle. David Porter later wrote, "we feel obliged to say that all the credit for the capture of Fort Donelson belongs to the Army. . . . This victory belonged exclusively to General Grant."[33]

Despite the failure of the naval attack, Union troop reinforcements continued to arrive by water. At 6 AM on 15 February the Confederates had begun their belated attempt to break out to the south. The attack caught the Union troops by surprise and drove them back. Having opened up the road to Charlotte, Pillow then threw away the chance to escape. Imagining that he was in position to defeat Grant, he continued the attack. Arriving on the scene from a meeting with Foote, Grant ordered that the lost ground be retaken.

Correctly assuming that the Confederates must have weakened their lines elsewhere, Grant also ordered an immediate assault on the Confederate right. The Union troops soon breached the fort's breastworks, placing the entire Confederate position in jeopardy. At the same time, Grant's men recovered the ground lost earlier. That evening, additional Federal troops brought Union strength to twenty-seven thousand men. It was now no longer possible for the bulk of the Confederates to escape, and Generals Floyd and Pillow abandoned their command and escaped across the Cumberland. Col. Nathan Bedford Forrest also got away with some five hundred men on horseback, fording a swollen creek between the Union right flank and the river. In all, perhaps five thousand Confederates escaped.

Accepting the inevitable, early on 16 February Buckner asked for terms. Grant's reply of "No terms except unconditional and immediate surrender" became famous. The Union forces took some 15,000 Confederates prisoner. Grant also secured a considerable number of small arms, a number of guns, and substantial quantities of equipment and rations. Estimates of Confederate killed and wounded vary from 1,500 to 3,500. Union losses were 500 killed, 2,108 wounded, and 221 captured or missing.[34]

The twin victories at Forts Henry and Donelson gave the Union control of Kentucky and most of middle and western Tennessee, with devastating long-term economic consequences for the Confederacy. In the short run, they broke the backbone of the South's western defensive line and captured a third of Johnston's forces, with the remainder now divided between Nashville, Tennessee, and Columbus, two hundred miles apart. On 14 February Johnston evacuated Bowling Green, and on 17–18 February he moved the majority of his troops from Nashville to Murfreesboro. The Confederates evacuated Columbus on 2 March. The Mississippi was now clear down to Island No. 10.

Grant believed at the time that only a failure of Union leadership prevented a rapid conquest of the entire West. Halleck's refusal to act, the division of Union forces between himself and Buell, and logistical overreach all prevented a decisive drive in that theater. Grant and Foote urged Halleck to mount an immediate assault on the Cumberland to take Nashville by coup de main, but Halleck refused to allow Union forces beyond Clarksville. Although Nashville fell to Union forces on 25 February, the delay enabled the Confederates to remove from that place cannon, small arms, ammunition, food, uniforms, and vital foundry equipment. Johnston's troops then headed to Alabama and a stand south of the Tennessee River. Ultimately Johnston gathered some forty thousand men at the key rail hub of Corinth, Mississippi, twenty miles inland from the river.[35]

On 1 March the *Tyler* and *Lexington* attacked Confederate troops fortifying Pittsburg Landing on the Tennessee. There the gunboats neutralized half a dozen Confederate field pieces and landed troops. The Union side suffered two killed, six wounded, and three missing in the exchange. Confederate losses were estimated at twenty dead and one hundred wounded.[36]

Grant prepared to move against Corinth, but Halleck halted him at Savannah, Tennessee, ordering him to await Buell's arrival from Nashville. On 6–7 April, Johnston struck first in a surprise attack on Grant's bivouac at Pittsburg Landing. The resulting bloody contest came to be known as the Battle of Shiloh. Johnston was among the many dead, the highest ranking general, North or South, killed in the war. There is controversy as to how close the South came to victory at Shiloh, but one historian concluded that five thousand more men would have given the South a victory. This puts the fifteen thousand Confederates lost at Fort Donelson in proper perspective.[37]

Meanwhile, Grant kept his nerve as his troops were driven literally to the banks of the Tennessee, going personally among his men and urging them to hold. The *Tyler* and *Lexington* played an important role in the battle. As Lt. William Gwin, the commander of the gunboats, reported, the two Union ships "opened a heavy and well-directed fire" against the advancing right wing of the Confederate line and "in conjunction with our artillery on shore, succeeded in silencing their artillery, driving them back in confusion."[38]

Much of the fire from the gunboats went long, landing in the rear where General Beauregard, Johnston's replacement, had his headquarters, but this helped bring about his decision at dusk to call off the attack. The arrival of Buell's twenty-one thousand fresh Union troops that night allowed Grant to go on the offensive and win the battle the next day. That these troops could cross the river, bring in supplies, and evacuate wounded was owing to the U.S. Navy, an important fact often overlooked in accounts of the battle.

The cost of Shiloh was high, however; the 10,600 Confederate and 13,000 Union casualties made Shiloh the bloodiest day in the history of North American warfare to that point. Five days later, Halleck arrived to take personal command of the combined Union armies, but his subsequent advance on Corinth covered only about a mile a day. Not until 29 May were Union forces before Corinth, and that same day Beauregard abandoned the city for Tupelo.

Grant had been inhibited in moving more forcefully against Johnston earlier because of the division of Union resources and because Halleck had initiated another offensive, this one down the Mississippi against Columbus. Halleck's goal here was to secure both New Madrid, Missouri, and nearby Island No. 10. Both sides saw control of the Mississippi as vital. Union control of the river would cut off the Trans-Mississippi West from the remainder of the Confederacy and allow the transit of goods along it to the Gulf of Mexico, thus binding the northwest region to the Union. In the ensuing Mississippi campaign, Flag Officer David G. Farragut would take New Orleans and then move north, while Foote's flotilla worked its way south.

Island No. 10 no longer exists. Now a part of the Missouri shore, in 1862 it was about a mile long and a quarter-mile wide and lay at a long inverted S-bend in the river about forty miles below Columbus. Surrounded by cypress-entangled swamps, Reelfoot Lake, and the great river itself, Island No. 10 was not easily accessible to land forces. Its Confederate defenders there were, however, dependent for communications and resupply on the river and on a single road on the Tennessee side through Tiptonville. Were Union troops able to sever these, the garrison would be trapped.

Utilizing heavy guns from the 3 March evacuation of Columbus, the Confederates turned Island No. 10 into a formidable defensive position. Its outer works consisted of field batteries along the riverbanks commanding the channel for ten to twelve miles north. The island itself held nineteen guns and the land bluffs another forty-three, with the batteries arranged to deliver concentrated fire. Confederate Cdr. George N. Hollins had charge of Confederate naval forces on the upper Mississippi. A former U.S. Navy officer of great longevity who had fought in the War of 1812, he had positioned a floating battery, the *New Orleans*, in the river. This battery, which Union Commander Walke referred to as the Confederacy's "great war elephant," had been adapted from a floating dry dock and towed up the Mississippi all the way from the Crescent City. Some 60 feet wide by 180 feet long, it mounted nine guns—eight 8-inch Columbiads and a rifled 32-pounder—and was intended to be moved about as required.[39]

At Island No. 10 the Mississippi made a sharp bend and then ran to the northwest. The town of New Madrid, Missouri, six miles downriver, was thus actually farther north than Island No. 10. There the river resumed a southerly direction. In order to prevent the island from being attacked by land forces from the Missouri side, the Confederates fortified New Madrid with two earthen forts and twenty-one guns. They also fortified the Tennessee side of the river. Brig. Gen. John P. McCown commanded the Madrid Bend area with seventy-five hundred men.

In order to take Island No. 10, Union forces first had to capture New Madrid, cutting the island off from communication downriver. Halleck assigned this task to Brig. Gen. John Pope's new Army of the Mississippi. Pope marched his eighteen thousand men fifty miles overland and brought New Madrid under siege on 3 March. His attention centered to the north, McCown had failed to anticipate this Union move and appealed to Beauregard for reinforcements. Any possibility of Maj. Gen. Earl Van Dorn's sixteen-thousand-man army in Arkansas arriving was, however, shattered by its defeat at the hands of eleven thousand Union troops under Maj. Gen. Samuel R. Curtis in the 7–8 March Battle of Pea Ridge. When Van Dorn was ready to move, time had run out for New Madrid.

On 12 March, Union siege guns arrived at New Madrid, and the next day Union gunners opened a heavy bombardment. McCown precipitously abandoned New Madrid the same night, his move masked by a heavy thunderstorm. The fifteen-day-long land campaign had seen only about fifty killed and wounded on each side, but Island No. 10 was now cut off from most river communication and means of supply. Hoping the defenders of

Island No. 10 would at least buy time for the Confederates to strengthen Fort Pillow farther south and enable General Johnston to attack Grant's forces at Pittsburg Landing, Beauregard ordered the Madrid Bend Garrison to Fort Pillow and informed McCown that he would not be reinforced.[40]

Foote had resisted Halleck's calls to move to Island No. 10 following the capture of Fort Donelson. Bitter over what he perceived to be Halleck's lack of accolades for the navy's role, he nonetheless needed time to carry out repairs to his ironclads. Foote also ordered the addition of iron plating and chain to protect his ships' pilothouses. He was also apprehensive about fighting downstream, especially because the boats could not be held by a stern anchor in the Mississippi; unlike in the Cumberland and Tennessee rivers, ships disabled in the Mississippi would drift downriver under the Confederate guns and be lost.[41]

Not until 14 March did Foote, his flag in the *Benton*, set out from Cairo. His force numbered seven gunboats and ten mortar boats, accompanied by an assortment of steamers and tugs. At Columbus the flotilla joined Union transports carrying twelve hundred troops and convoyed them south. Just below Island No. 8, early on 15 March the Confederate steamer *Grampus* suddenly appeared out of the fog. It stopped engines and struck its colors, but its captain evidently had second thoughts for he quickly got his ship under way again, escaping downriver with blasts of its whistle under a hail of Union shells.

At about 9 AM the Confederate positions on Island No. 10 came into view, and the squadron hove to. The next morning, 16 March, Foote positioned his mortar boats along the shore, with the plan that their fire would reduce the Confederate positions, enabling his gunboats to run to New Madrid.

The 13-inch mortar was a formidable weapon. Weighing 17,250 pounds, it rested in a 4,500-pound bed. With a 20-pound charge of powder and an elevation of 41 degrees, the mortar could hurl a 204-pound shell loaded with 7 pounds of powder three miles. At this range the shell took thirty seconds in flight.

At 2:40 PM mortar boat *No. 12* fired the first shell against Island No. 10. Because the mortar boats were firing diagonally across Phillips Point, their crews could not see the target, and the only immediate effect was to drive some of the Confederate defenders from their positions. That day the mortars fired nearly three hundred shells, the *Benton* joining in with forty-five rounds from its own guns.[42]

The mortars seem to have been of little worth, although Foote would never be as critical of them as the commander of the South Atlantic Blockading Squadron, Flag Officer Samuel Du Pont, who wrote of them against Fort Pulaski, Georgia:

> One item has disappointed me—those great mortars are a dead failure; they did nothing at all, went wild, burst in the air, and caused no apprehension at all to the garrison. I am worried about this because this is the great dependence, those 13-inch mortars, that our friends in the Gulf are looking to, to reduce the forts in the Mississippi.[43]

On the morning of 17 March, Foote attempted a long-range attack on the Confederate positions with fire from his ironclads, but the net effect was one Confederate gun dismounted and one man killed and seven others wounded. The flotilla took some hits in return, but the most costly blow was self-inflicted; an old army rifled 42-pounder burst on one of the gunboats, killing and wounding fifteen officers and men. Foote now settled in for a long siege, shelling the defenses around the clock from long range. But the small, dispersed forts proved difficult targets.

Union night bombardment of Island No. 10 by 13-inch mortars, 18 March 1862.
NAVAL HISTORICAL CENTER (KN-969)

Aerial view of the Union gunboats and mortar boats shelling the Confederate batteries at Island No. 10, March 1862; engraving published in Harper's Weekly *in April 1862.*
NAVAL HISTORICAL CENTER (NH 58888)

Meanwhile, on the other side of Island No. 10, Union troops moved a 24-pounder upriver along the shore and, on the morning of 18 March, opened fire on steamers unloading supplies across the river at Tiptonville, damaging several of them. Commander Hollins commanded only five wooden gunboats. Unwilling to risk them to heavy Union guns, he soon withdrew below Tiptonville, taking with him much of the garrison's provisions.[44]

Although Pope now held New Madrid, swamps prevented his men from reaching the vicinity of Island No. 10 on the Missouri side. And with no transports, he had no means of crossing over to the Tennessee side to attack the Confederate rear. Foote rejected Pope's repeated requests that he send gunboats past Island No. 10. By 24 March a stalemate existed, with little action save daily shelling by the Union mortar boats of the Confederate positions, which, however, did little damage and inflicted few casualties. Occasionally the gunboats joined in. Halleck summed up, "Commodore Foote will not attempt to run past the batteries and he can not reduce them."[45]

On 23 March, meanwhile, work had begun on one of the more innovative engineering achievements of the war. During a three-week period, hundreds of Union soldiers and sailors, supported by four shallow-draft steamers and six coal barges, employed a variety of tools and two million feet of lumber to cut a canal fifty feet wide and twelve miles long from the bend of the Mississippi near Island No. 8 across the swampy peninsula to near New Madrid. Three-fourths of a mile of the canal cut through solid earth; another six miles ran through timber that had to be cut off and dragged out from under water.

Although not deep enough for Foote's gunboats, the canal could take light steamers, tugs, and transports. Confederate Commander McCown did nothing to try to interrupt the work, convinced that it would fail. Beauregard, meanwhile, replaced McCown with Brig. Gen. William W. Mackall, who took up command on 31 March.[46]

Bombardment of Island No. 10 by Union gunboats and mortar boats, March 1862; lithograph published by Currier & Ives. NAVAL HISTORICAL CENTER (NH 59201)

Pope was determined to get over the Mississippi. He had some steamers but he informed Foote that he would have to have at least one gunboat to control the opposite bank. On 30 March Foote finally authorized Commander Walke of the *Carondelet* to make an attempt on the next stormy night. As Walke prepared, on the night of 1 April sailors from the flotilla landed fifty soldiers from boats and took out one of the Confederate shore batteries without loss. Then on 4 April, Foote's ironclads and mortar boats shelled and disabled the Confederate floating battery, causing it to drift downriver.

The *Carondelet*'s crew piled planks from a wreck on its deck to provide additional protection against plunging shot, strung surplus chain around the more vulnerable parts of their ship, and wound a large 11-inch hawser around the pilothouse up to its windows. They stowed hammocks in the netting against small-arms fire and piled cordwood up against the boilers. Crewmen were issued small arms and hand grenades for repelling borders, should the gunboat become disabled, and the *Carondelet* took on board twenty-three army sharpshooters. Finally, the crew piled baled hay on a barge lashed to the side of the ship for additional protection from shore batteries on the Tennessee side of the river.

A bad storm on the night of 4 April provided cover. Slipping from her anchorage at 10 PM, the *Carondelet* got under way with lights extinguished and gunports closed. The Confederates soon detected the ship, however, most probably from flames from the stacks as soot inside took fire, for in order to muffle puffing sounds from the stacks Walke had run pipes aft from the boilers to exhaust excess steam into the paddle-wheel house, and this no longer dampened the stacks. Sheets of rain prevented accurate Confederate observation, and their shot went high as the "vivid lightning" allowed the Union gunboat to keep to the channel. Only two Confederate shot hit home, one lodging in the barge. There were no casualties. Three hours after beginning its run, at 1 AM on 5 April the *Carondelet* arrived at New Madrid.[47]

Early on 7 April another heavy thunderstorm provided cover for the *Pittsburg* to run the gauntlet unscathed. That same day the two Union ships shelled and neutralized Confederate batteries opposite Point Pleasant; they then covered Pope's steamers ferrying troops across the river. The Union soldiers moved inland and secured the Tiptonville Road, cutting off Island No. 10.

Caught in a trap with a Union Army–Navy assault imminent and large numbers of his men deserting, Mackall ordered a withdrawal. On the evening of 7 April, Capt. W. Y. C. Hume, commanding Island No. 10, sent officers to Foote asking for terms. Foote demanded unconditional surrender, which Hume accepted early on 8 April. Only about one thousand Confederates, principally from the upper batteries on the Tennessee side of the river, managed to escape, most of them through the swamps.[48]

The loss of Island No. 10 was more grievous for the South than the carnage of Shiloh. Union forces took forty-five hundred prisoners, five thousand small arms, and 109 cannon and mortars. They also secured four steamers and the floating battery, as well as quantities of ammunition, supplies, and provisions. It was also a cheap victory in terms of Union casualties: seven men killed, fourteen wounded, and four missing, more than half to accidental causes.[49]

The Union ironclad Carondelet *running the Confederate batteries at Island No. 10, 4 April 1862; engraving by Henry Fenn after a sketch by Henry Walke.*
NAVAL HISTORICAL CENTER (NH 42912)

Fort Pillow was the next Union objective. Located sixty miles south of Island No. 10 and just north of Fulton on the Tennessee shore, it guarded the northern approach to the vital Confederate railhead of Memphis forty miles downriver. The Confederates made the fort into a strong defensive position, locating batteries on the high, nearly vertical Chicakasaw Bluffs and in their face at the water's edge. The fort mounted some forty heavy guns, including 10-inch Columbiads. Manned by some six thousand men, it also boasted extensive earthworks.

On the evening of 11 April, Foote moved his five gunboats, along with mortar boats, tows, transports, supply ships, and tugs, south from Island No. 10 to New Madrid to join the *Carondelet* and *Pittsburg*. Foote then went ashore and conferred with Pope, where he learned of the presence of additional Confederate gunboats in the river.[50]

The Confederate gunboats introduced a new element in the fight for the Mississippi. The Confederate River Defense Fleet, as it was officially known, consisted of more than a dozen lightly armed and poorly armored gunboats. Constructed with double-pine bulkheads bolted together and stuffed with compressed cotton, these "cottonclads" mounted only one or two guns each but were somewhat faster and more agile than their Union counterparts. A number had reinforced bows of oak and iron, enabling them to act as rams. Former riverboat Capt. James E. Montgomery and Capt. J. H. Townsend commanded the River Defense Fleet. The crews came from civilian steamboats and fought on the condition that they would not be subject to the orders of naval officers.[51]

On 13 April the Union flotilla traversed some fifty miles of river to Hale's Point, just below the Arkansas state line. At daybreak on 14 April, the transports arrived there with General Pope and twenty thousand troops. Then at 8 AM that same day five Confederate gunboats steamed out to meet the Union ships. The Rebel ships were soon in retreat, the *Benton* leading the charge against them. Some twenty shot were exchanged before the Confederates gained the protection of Fort Pillow's batteries. The Union gunboats closed to a mile from the fort to undertake a reconnaissance, at which time the fort's guns opened fire, but their shot went high. At 11 AM Foote ordered a retirement. At 2 PM that same day the Union mortar boats opened fire on Fort Pillow. The bombardment continued for the next seven weeks.

The original plan of attack developed by Foote and Pope called for the mortar boats, protected by the gunboats, to bombard the land batteries while Pope's troops went ashore upriver and outflanked the fort from the rear and Foote's gunboats assaulted it from the front. But Pope quickly determined that he could not reach the rear of Fort Pillow from any point of the river above it, and he decided to repeat the plan of Island No. 10 by digging a six-mile-long canal on the Arkansas side of the river across Craigshead Point to allow Federal gunboats below the Confederate position.

Any possibility of a quick strike at Pillow was dashed, however, when Halleck withdrew Pope's troops for his own snail-like campaign against Corinth. Foote and Pope learned of this decision the evening of 16 April, and the bulk of the Union land force departed upriver in twenty transports the next day, taking with them tools for cutting through the swamps and leaving behind only twelve hundred infantry to garrison Fort Pillow should the Confederates decide to evacuate it.[52]

The Union naval bombardment of Fort Pillow continued, but it was chiefly harassing fire. One eyewitness, First Class Boy George R. Yost of the *Cairo*, described the Union shelling in his diary:

> I frequently saw as many as a dozen shells in the air at one time, crossing each other's fiery tracks; some of them burst in mid air, some landing in the water, others in the heavy woods of the Arkansas shore. One shell, a very large one passed directly over our upper deck, where I was sitting, missing our wheel house about twenty feet, and dropping into the water twenty yards way, where it burst, making a tremendous splashing of the water.[53]

The Confederates were not entirely quiescent. Deserters had for some time been warning that their gunboats would attempt an attack on the Union flotilla, and on 8 May Union lookouts sighted smoke downriver, a sure sign of approaching steamers. Three Southern rams—the *General Sumter*, *General Bragg*, and *General Earl Van Dorn*—soon rounded the point and made for the area where the Union mortar boats were usually positioned during firing. These, however, had been moved a short time before and were now protected by the *Cairo*, *Cincinnati*, and *Mound City*. Soon the Confederate gunboats were in precipitous retreat, pursued by the Union gunboats. The range was too great, however, and Foote soon ordered his ships to cease fire.

The very next day Foote bid an emotional farewell to the flotilla. Sick and largely immobile, the consequence of his leg wound from the battle at Fort Donelson having failed to heal, Foote had requested he be relieved.

Welles assigned Flag Officer Charles H. Davis to replace him. In July, Foote was one of four U.S. Navy officers raised to the rank of rear admiral.[54]

The Confederate sortie on 8 May should have been sufficient warning. The Union gunboats were in two divisions: three on the Tennessee bank and four on the Arkansas side of the river. Although Foote had ordered them headed downstream by securing their sterns to the bank, no lookouts had been posted downriver.

On the morning of 10 May Union mortar boat *No. 16*, with a crew of fourteen men, had just fired its fifth shell of the day, while crewmen of the covering gunboat *Cincinnati* nonchalantly went through their usual morning routine. Suddenly, eight Confederate gunboats hove into view around Craigshead Point. These were the *General Bragg, General Sterling Price, General Earl Van Dorn, General Sumter, General Thompson, General Beauregard, Colonel Lovell,* and the flagship *Little Rebel.* Captain Montgomery hoped to cut out or destroy the mortar boat and its covering gunboat. The two Union vessels were vulnerable because they were separated from the rest of the flotilla and unprepared for an attack.

The Confederate ships made straight for the *Cincinnati,* its crew desperately trying to get their ship under way. Although it took a broadside at only fifty yards from the *Cincinnati,* the *General Bragg* continued on, crashing into the Union gunboat. Capt. Stembel of the *Cincinnati* swung the bow so that the impact was at an angle, but it nonetheless tore a large hole in the Union ship's starboard quarter just abaft the armor plate and flooded its magazine. As the *General Bragg* wrenched free, another Union broadside tore into it, and it soon drifted downstream out of action. Both the *General Sterling Price* and *General Sumter* also rammed the *Cincinnati.* The *General Sterling Price* struck the Union ship on the port side near the stern, carrying away its rudder, sternpost, and part of the stern. This blow threw the *Cincinnati*'s stern around so that it now caught the entire force of the *General Sumter,* which had run in at full speed. The *Cincinnati* was now sinking rapidly, and Confederate sharpshooters began to pick off members of its crew, among them Commander Stembel, who had exposed himself on deck and fell badly wounded. Nonetheless, with the arrival of two Union tugs, the *Cincinnati* made it to shallow water along the shore, where it went down in twelve feet of water. The crew found their way to the upper deck with Commander Stembel and two other wounded men, where they watched the ensuing action.

When the fight began, the remainder of the Union gunboats were at anchor with hardly any steam up. Now they arrived. The *Mound City* and *Carondelet* led, followed by the slower *Benton* and then the *Pittsburg*. The other Union gunboats did not come up in time to participate.

As the *General Earl Van Dorn* passed by to engage the *Mound City*, it sent two 32-pounder shots as well as several volleys of musket fire into *No. 16*. The shells went completely through the mortar boat, but miraculously no one was injured. Its crew had lowered the mortar's elevation and, firing with reduced charges and dangerously short fuses, the men managed to burst shells over the Confederate gunboats. Even after their own boat was hit, the men of *No. 16* continued to fire their mortar, expending fifty-two shells that day, including the five before the battle.

Meanwhile, the *General Earl Van Dorn* rammed the *Mound City*. The Union gunboat received a glancing blow, which tore away part of its bow, causing it rapidly to ship water. Cdr. Alexander H. Kilty got off a punishing broadside before he grounded his ship to prevent it from sinking. The *Mound City* had one man wounded.

The arrival of the more powerful Union ships, however, caused Montgomery to signal a retirement. As the Confederate ships fled downriver, a shell from one of the *Carondelet*'s rifled guns smashed into the *General Sumter*'s boilers, releasing clouds of billowing steam, which its crew desperately attempted to escape. Rifled rounds from the *Benton* also shattered the boilers of the *Colonel Lovell* and then the *General Earl Van Dorn*, disabling both.

During the hour-long battle the Union side suffered only 4 wounded, 1 of whom later died; deserters later reported up to 108 Confederate dead. But apart from the heavy personnel losses, the Southerners had won a tactical victory, temporarily disabling two much more powerful Union gunboats. Refloated, the two were sent back to Mound City for repairs.[55]

Over the next three weeks, Davis continued a slow bombardment of Confederate positions. By 25 May all seven steamers of the War Department's new Mississippi Ram Fleet had joined the flotilla. Hastily purchased by the Army Quartermaster Department, these stern and side-wheeler Ohio River steamers were converted into rams under the supervision of engineer Charles Ellet Jr., who had early in the war suggested to Welles the construction of purpose-built steam rams. Welles had initially rejected the idea as impractical but changed his mind following the ramming of the *Cumberland* by the *Virginia* in Hampton Roads. Secretary of War Stanton, meanwhile, secured an army colonelcy of engineers for Ellet, who now took charge of the conversions.

Transforming the steamers into rams included reinforcing their hulls with additional timbers and filling their bows with timber, all to enable them to withstand the shock of ramming. The rams ranged between 98 and 406 tons. Initially they carried no ordnance, although a good number of sharpshooters were assigned to each ram. The new ships were simply a counter to the Confederate river rams. They were under army command but for the most part operated under navy orders, an arrangement that pleased neither party.

The Switzerland *of the U.S. Army Mississippi Ram Fleet.* U.S. NAVAL INSTITUTE PHOTO ARCHIVE

Ellet wanted an immediate blow against Fort Pillow, which Davis resisted, but the Confederates took the decision out of Union hands. On 29–30 May, General Beauregard, deciding to save his fifty thousand men, abandoned Corinth to General Halleck's one-hundred-twenty-thousand-man army and retired to a new line along the Tuscumbia River in Alabama with his headquarters at Tupelo, Mississippi. This left Fort Pillow outflanked and untenable, and on 4 June the Confederates evacuated it as well.[56]

On 5 June Davis's flotilla, reinforced by Ellet's rams, moved south past Fort Pillow to attack the Confederates at Memphis, arriving just above the city that evening. The battle for Memphis began early on 6 June. At 4:20 AM with the Union ships about two miles above Memphis and the eight Confederate warships in view with steam up, Davis signaled the flotilla to raise anchor. Slowly the Union ironclads dropped downriver. Davis proceeded stern first, well aware of the problems of trying to maneuver in the fast river current. Should it be required, the ships would thus be in an easier position to proceed back upriver. At 4:50 AM the Confederate ships weighed in turn and steamed upriver. The battle thus began with the Confederate ships firing from their bow guns and the Union ships from astern. Thousands of Memphis citizens lined the shores to watch the contest to decide their city's fate. Heavy smoke from the discharge of the guns and the coal of the steamers soon obscured their vision and that of the participants.

Montgomery organized his gunboats into a double defensive line. He hoped to duplicate the Battle of Plum Point Bend by ramming and sinking the Union ironclads. After about fifteen to twenty minutes of an exchange of fire, Davis ordered the *Benton* to turn about and head downriver bow first, signaling to the other ships to duplicate his maneuver. As the bigger Union ships lumbered downriver against the Confederate ships, two of the Union rams, acting under Ellet's order, charged past them.

Ellet had arranged four of his rams in line, above the ironclads. When the Confederates first opened fire, he signaled the others to follow his lead in the *Queen of the West*. Only the *Monarch*, under his brother, Lt. Col. Alfred Ellet, responded. These two rams, the one following the other, now made for the advancing Confederate gunboats.

The *Colonel Lovell*, the leading Confederate ram, seemed headed for a bows-on collision with the *Queen of the West* when one of the Confederate ship's engines suddenly stopped, and it veered. Moments later the *Queen of the West* smashed into the side of the *Colonel Lovell*, inflicting a mortal wound. The Confederate ram *General Sumter* then struck the *Queen of the West* at its port wheelhouse. Ellet ran out on deck, where he was wounded in the leg by a Confederate pistol shot. Charles

The Naval Battle of Memphis, 6 June 1862; engraving from The Illustrated London News, *19 July 1862.* NAVAL HISTORICAL CENTER (NH 89626)

Ellet's brother, Lt. Col. Alfred Ellet, then smashed his ram, the *Monarch*, into the *Colonel Lovell*, which promptly sank with all but five of its crew. The *Queen of the West* was able to ground on the Arkansas shore. The remaining Confederate rams then concentrated on the *Monarch*, the *General Sterling Price* getting in a glancing blow while the *General Beauregard* came up from the other side. At the last possible moment, however, Alfred Ellet was able to slip his ship between the two Confederate ships, which then collided with one another. The *Monarch* then rammed the *General Beauregard*. By this time accurate cannon fire from the Federal ironclads was exacting a toll. One shell burst the *General Beauregard*'s boilers, and it went down. The disabled *General Sterling Price* also sank in shallow water.

The remaining five Confederate ships attempted to escape. With Union ships pursuing, the ongoing battle disappeared downriver. During the ensuing ten-mile-long fight, the *Little Rebel* was hit below the water-line. As the Confederate ship made for shoal water, the *Monarch* rammed it, pushing the Confederate ship up on the shore and enabling Montgomery and his crew to escape. Union cannon fire disabled both the *General Bragg* and *General Sumter*. The commander of the *General*

Thompson grounded his ship on the Arkansas shore. Set on fire by its crew, it soon blew up. Of the eight Confederate ships, only the *General Earl Van Dorn* managed to escape to Vicksburg. Meanwhile, Lieutenant Phelps took the surrender of Memphis.[57]

The naval Battle of Memphis was perhaps the most lopsided Union victory of the war. The Union side suffered only four casualties and one badly damaged ram. Charles Ellet, however, died two weeks later, his superficial wound complicated by dysentery and measles.

At slight cost, the Union had ended Confederate naval power on the Mississippi and added additional ships to its flotilla. The battle gave the Union the fifth largest city in the Confederacy, along with control of four key rail lines and important manufacturing resources, including a naval yard that soon became a principal Union base. Most important, the river was now open all the way south to Vicksburg.

At Memphis on 5 June the Confederates burned on the stocks the casemated ironclad *Tennessee* that they had been building. Well before the battle they did manage to move downriver a second uncompleted ironclad, the *Arkansas*. Completed at Yazoo City, Mississippi, and commissioned on 26 May 1862, it operated on the Yazoo River and became one of the best known Confederate ironclads of the war.[58]

On 13 June, a week after Memphis had been secured, Davis sent Cdr. A. H. Kilty and the *Mound City*, *St. Louis*, and *Lexington* up the White River, a tributary of the Mississippi where Confederate ships were thought to be active. Two days later he dispatched after them one transport with supplies and another carrying Col. G. N. Fitch's 46th Indiana Regiment. The *Conestoga* provided convoy. On 14 June the *Mound City* captured the *Clara Dolsen*, one of the largest and finest steamers on the river, soon incorporated into the Union Navy.

On the morning of 16 June, the *Conestoga* and transports having joined the other Union ships, the detachment proceeded to a point upriver about five miles from St. Charles, Arkansas, where it anchored for the night. Early on the morning of 17 June they again got under way, the *Mound City* leading and the transports bringing up the rear. Just north of St. Charles about eighty miles from the river mouth, the Confederates had positioned the gunboats *Maurepas* and *Pontchartrain* and two transports. There they sank in the river the *Maurepas* and both transports. Ordnance from the *Maurepas* and guns already ashore gave the defenders two 42-pounder rifled seacoast howitzers, two 12-pounder bronze pieces, and two small Parrott rifles. These were then concealed in the woods and on a bluff ashore.

As the Union ships approached, they came under fire from Confederate pickets ashore. The ships returned fire, landed Colonel Fitch's regiment, and continued on. Rounding a bend, the Union sailors could see the sunken Confederate ships about a mile upriver. Continuing upstream, the *Mound City* soon came under fire from the shore battery. At about six hundred yards from the obstacles, a well-aimed Confederate shot penetrated on the port side of the casemate, killing three men outright and bursting the *Mound City*'s steam drum. All Union boats immediately were sent in to rescue the crew, while the *Mound City* drifted across the river until it was brought under tow by the *Conestoga*. The *St. Louis* and *Lexington* moved forward and, silencing the lower battery, concentrated on the Confederate guns on the bluff. Meanwhile, several dozen Confederate soldiers opened fire on the Union sailors in the water. Ten minutes after the *Mound City* had been hit, Colonel Fitch signaled from shore for the Union ships to cease fire, and the Union infantry then charged the remaining Confederate battery, killing 7 or 8 of the defenders and suffering no losses of their own. They also took 29 prisoners including Confederate Navy Capt. Joseph Fry, who had commanded the position.

The *Mound City* was completely hors de combat, and personnel losses on it were devastating. Lt. Wilson McGunnegle reported: "To endeavor to describe the howling of the wounded and the moaning of the dying is far beyond the power of my feeble pen." Of its 175-man crew, 82 had died by 19 June in the bursting of the steam drum, another 43 had been shot and killed in the water or drowned, and 25 others were scalded and burned, including Commander Kilty. Only 3 officers and 22 men escaped unscathed.[59]

Towed to St. Charles, the *Mound City* was there repaired. The remainder of the Union ships proceeded up the White River for another sixty miles but, finding no sign of Confederate military activity and in dangerously shallow water, the ships returned to Memphis.

With the exception of a subsequent action involving the Confederate ironclad *Arkansas*, Union naval action north of Vicksburg now sharply diminished. With the Confederate forts and naval vessels on the upper Mississippi both gone, much of the Union naval effort was devoted to protecting slow moving noncombatant vessels on the river and its tributaries and engaging occasional small pockets of Confederates ashore, including small arms fire and occasional field artillery pieces.

On 15 October, the same month that Congress belatedly gave the Navy Department control over the river operations in the West, Acting Rear Adm. David D. Porter took command from Davis of the Mississippi Flotilla, now designated the Mississippi Squadron. Naval activity then sharply increased with the initiation of joint operations against Vicksburg.

CHAPTER SIX

The First Clash
of Ironclads

—⁓—

T he most important single-ship engagement of the Civil War and the first clash between ironclad warships in naval history occurred in Hampton Roads, Virginia, on 9 March 1862. The Peninsula Campaign provided its backdrop. During the Civil War the East was the principal theater of war and Virginia its chief battleground, with the Union military objective the capture of Richmond.

If the North could take the Confederate capital, it would mean the loss to the South of important war industries, most notably the Tredegar Iron Works, the only Southern facility in 1861 capable of casting the largest guns. Union strategists also hoped that the loss of Richmond would shatter both the South's morale and its hopes for European diplomatic recognition.

President Lincoln favored a direct overland advance in which the chief field army, the Army of the Potomac, drove south from the vicinity of Washington, encircled Richmond, cut it off from outside aid, and then forced its surrender. This approach would also have the advantage of covering the Federal capital, always a concern for Lincoln, who admonished commanders of the Army of the Potomac to keep their force between the city and the Confederate Army of Northern Virginia.

General McClellan, commander of the Union Army since November 1861, had his own plan, however. Modeled on Scott's campaign against Mexico City in 1847, McClellan sought to take advantage of Union command of the sea to outflank developed Confederate defenses north of

Richmond by moving his army by water down the Chesapeake Bay, and then up the Rappahannock River to Urbanna, a scant forty-five miles east of Richmond, Virginia, striking overland from that point. This approach offered the shortest possible land route to Richmond and, if executed quickly, would force the Confederates to quit their positions west of Washington at Manassas, Virginia, as well as isolate Confederate defenders in the eastern peninsulas formed by the Rappahannock, York, and James rivers.[1]

Lincoln opposed the plan but his only real option at this point was to replace McClellan. With no prospective commander in the wings, Lincoln yielded. McClellan then modified the plan, making the Union land base not Urbanna on the Rappahannock, but the more distant (seventy-five miles from Richmond) Fort Monroe on the Chesapeake. Fort Monroe had the advantage of already being in Union hands. Operating from that point, where it would be supplied by water, McClellan's army would supposedly move by detachments up the York and James, outflanking the Confederates, who would have no recourse but to withdraw west on the capital. As McClellan closed on Richmond, a Union corps under Maj. Gen. Irvin McDowell, left behind to guard Washington, would push south and link up with McClellan to take Richmond and end the war.

Lincoln acquiesced, and in late February 1862 the War Department began purchasing steamers and sailing ships to move the Army of the Potomac to Fort Monroe and Hampton for what became known as the Peninsula Campaign, the largest land campaign of the entire war.

Unfortunately for the Union side, McClellan's plan was deeply flawed in planning and execution. For one thing, it suffered from faulty intelligence. McClellan concluded, incorrectly, that the peninsula boasted "good natural roads," sandy and well drained. Speed was never a factor in McClellan's planning, and lengthy delays, in part because of poor planning, finally led an exasperated Lincoln to remove McClellan from his post as Union Army general-in-chief, supposedly so he could concentrate on command of the Army of the Potomac.[2]

Confederate authorities in Richmond were well aware that a major Union drive against the capital was imminent. To protect the river approaches, they ordered significant defenses constructed at Yorktown at the mouth of the York. To defend the James, they counted on the new ironclad ram *Virginia*.

The *Virginia* was the reincarnation of the U.S. Navy screw frigate *Merrimack*. As noted, in April 1861 it had fallen into Confederate hands with the loss of the Norfolk Navy Yard. Set on fire by the withdrawing Union forces, the ship sank in shallow water. Although its spar and gun decks were destroyed by the fire and its berth deck was damaged, its machinery and hull could be salvaged. The Confederates raised what remained, moved it to the yard's large dry dock, and began its conversion into an ironclad.

Lt. John M. Brooke drew up the basic plans and had charge of the ordnance and armor, Naval Constructor Porter oversaw the reconstruction, and Chief Engineer Williamson dealt with the overhaul of the engines. The *Merrimack's* two engines had on commissioning provided 869 horsepower and a top speed in ideal conditions of nearly nine knots, but they had been intended only as auxiliary power and were inadequate in the best of circumstances. Although Williamson took apart the engines and reassembled them, this did not solve the problem of inadequate power, now more pronounced than ever with the far heavier ironclad.[3]

Friction developed between Brooke and Porter (who later claimed sole credit for the ship's design), but by mid-July work was well under way, ultimately involving some fifteen hundred men. The yard workers first cut out the burnt portion of the ship to about three feet above the waterline. The berth deck remained, but the carpenters shortened the ship from 279 feet to 262 feet, 9 inches. They then built onto the cut-down hull a main deck two feet above the waterline. On top of this they built the ship's most distinctive feature: a central casemate sloping upward and inward 36 degrees on each side so as to deflect shot.

The casemate extended over the hull and into the water. It began 29 feet from the bow and ran aft for 170 feet. It was formed of 4 inches of oak laid horizontally, 8 inches of yellow pine laid vertically, and 12 inches of white pine laid horizontally, the whole caulked and bolted together. This was then sheathed in iron plate. Unique in Confederate ironclads, both ends of the casemate were rounded. The casemate itself was pierced by fourteen elliptical gunports, four unevenly spaced on port and starboard (so as to provide greater room for the gun crews to work inside the sloping casemate) and three each at bow and stern. The flat top of the casemate, also known as the shield or spar deck, was pierced by the funnel and three gratings that provided ventilation to the gun deck below. The gratings were formed of 2-inch-thick iron bars.

The *Virginia* was the first modern warship to completely do away with rigging. Unique to Confederate ironclads was its submerged bow and stern. A 1500-pound iron ram or beak about 3 feet long was placed at the bow underwater; it was, however, poorly secured to the rest of the ship.

The ram seems a strange throwback, as it formed the principal ship armament of antiquity, but it was nonetheless in the forefront of contemporary naval thinking. Noting that Russian shore fire had not been able to damage the French floating batteries in the Crimean War but that ships often sank after collisions with other vessels, a number of naval theorists opined that the ram might now replace the gun as the most effective weapon at sea. Mallory hoped that Buchanan would make use of it, in part to conserve scarce ammunition.

Plans called for the *Virginia* to be ready in November. Had the work proceeded on schedule, the technologically backward Confederacy would have had stolen an important march on the Union. Armoring the ship brought delays, however. Originally the *Virginia* was to have 1-inch plate, but in early October Brooke conducted firing tests against a target resembling the proposed wooden shield of the *Virginia* covered with three layers of 1-inch plate. The shield failed, but two thicknesses of 2-inch plate were found to be successful. Brooke reported to Mallory that the *Virginia* would have to have 4 inches of armor protection, preferably two layers of 2-inch plate, and Mallory concurred.

The Tredegar Works in Richmond was able to produce the plate from rolled railroad iron, but the 723 tons of plate required took nearly the entire activity of its rolling mills for five months. Transporting the plate to the yard also proved difficult because of a shortage of freight cars on the inadequate Confederate rail system. As the plate was delivered, workers applied it in two layers, the inner layer running horizontally and the outer layer running vertically.

In November, Mallory ordered Lieutenant Catesby ap Roger Jones to the navy yard as the new ship's executive officer. Jones was in charge of expediting construction, securing and mounting the ordnance, assembling a crew, and preparing the ship for sea. Despite Jones's best efforts, delays continued. By January, shipyard workers were laboring seven days a week until eight at night to complete the work, and there were concerns that the ship might not be completed before Union troops and ironclads descended on Norfolk. The last iron plating did not arrive at the yard until 12 February, and the *Virginia* was launched five days later, a full week after the launching of the Northern ironclad, the *Monitor*.

Problems were immediately apparent. The *Virginia*'s steering was so sluggish that it took thirty to forty minutes and four miles to bring the ship about 180 degrees. Its engines were unreliable and inadequate, and the top speed was only about five knots. Most serious, Constructor Porter had miscalculated the ship's displacement, with the result being that the *Virginia* rode too high in the water. The armor-plated casemate was to have extended two feet under water to protect the hull, but in places it was submerged only an inch or so. This would be the ship's greatest vulnerability and remained the chief concern. Adding one hundred fifty tons of coal, additional ballast, shot, and supplies lowered the *Virginia* in the water somewhat, but this problem was never completely resolved.[4]

Lieutenant Jones summed up the danger on 5 March, three days before the *Virginia* steamed out into Hampton Roads to engage the Union ships there:

> The ship will be too light, or should I say, she is not sufficiently protected below the water. Our draft will be a foot less than was first intended, yet I was this morning ordered not to put any more ballast for fear of the bottom. The eaves of the roof will not be more than six inches immersed, which in smooth water would not be enough; a slight ripple would leave it bare except the one-inch iron that extends some feet below. We are least protected where we most need it. The constructor should have put on six inches where we now have one.[5]

The *Virginia* was well armed. On its completion, it mounted ten guns: six IX-inch Dahlgrens and two 6.4-inch single-banded Brooke rifles in broadsides, and two 7-inch single-banded Brooke rifles in pivot at bow and stern. When it went into battle, the *Virginia* had shell for all its guns, but, owing to the delays in manufacture and transportation, possessed shot only for its smoothbores.[6]

On 24 February Mallory detailed Confederate Flag Officer Franklin Buchanan to command Confederate naval defenses in the James. A Marylander by birth, Buchanan had joined the navy as a midshipman in 1815. Ambitious and known as a consummate professional but also as an authoritarian, Buchanan had married into a powerful slave-holding Eastern Shore family and soon adopted its proslavery views. A prominent figure in the navy, Buchanan was the first superintendent of the U.S. Naval Academy and he played important roles in both the Mexican War and Commo. Matthew C. Perry's two expeditions to Japan. A captain when the Civil War began, Buchanan resigned his commission in the belief that Maryland would secede. When his home state did not leave the Union, he tried without success to retract the resignation. When Secretary Welles refused to have him back, Buchanan then made his way to Richmond and joined the Confederate cause, heading the important Bureau of Orders and Detail. In August 1862, Buchanan would become the first Confederate admiral.[7]

Originally Mallory had thought in terms of a joint army–navy attack on Newport News. Maj. Gen. John B. Magruder, commander of Confederate forces on the peninsula between the James and York rivers, initially agreed but then changed his mind, citing the poor condition of the roads. On 2 March Mallory advised Buchanan that he would have to proceed alone.[8]

Buchanan was determined to drive the Union ships from Fort Monroe. Although Lt. Jones had hoped to command the ironclad, Buchanan took the *Virginia* as his flagship. Jones remained the executive officer, so technically there was no captain aboard the ship. Jones continued supervising the *Virginia*'s preparation for combat, as Buchanan did not take formal command until 25 February.

The *Virginia* had a crew of 320 men, including 55 marines. Although there was no shortage of recruits, only a minority of the men were trained artillerymen or seamen, and many of these had been released from the army. In contrast, virtually all its officers had served in the U.S. Navy.[9]

As the *Virginia* neared completion, there was wild and completely unfounded speculation in both the Confederacy and the Union as to its capabilities. Pessimists feared that the weight of its iron armor would prove too much for the ship. Naval Constructor Porter wrote later, "Hundreds— I must say thousands—asserted she would never float." The day before the ironclad's launch on 17 February, Porter went to Capt. Sidney Smith Lee, brother of Gen. Robert E. Lee and executive officer of the Norfolk Navy Yard, to inform him that water would be let into the dry dock the next day. Lee inquired, "Mr. Porter, do you really think she will float?"[10]

Confederate Rear Adm. Franklin Buchanan, shown here as a U.S. Navy captain, probably as commander of the Washington Navy Yard just before the Civil War.
NAVAL HISTORICAL CENTER (NH 61920-A)

Optimists such as Mallory veered too far in the opposite direction. The secretary wrote Buchanan that he hoped the ship would proceed up the Potomac to Washington or past Old Point Comfort to New York "and attack and burn the city," destroying shipping, the Brooklyn Navy Yard, and all of the lower part of the city. This, Mallory believed, would "strike a blow from which the enemy would never recover. Peace would inevitably follow." Others thought the *Virginia* might be employed to drive the Union blockaders from the South Atlantic seaboard. But such plans were beyond its capabilities. Its draft was too deep for the *Virginia* to get up the Potomac, and it is doubtful that, even with the best pilot, it could have crossed the bar to New York City. Buchanan dashed Mallory's hopes when he informed the secretary that the *Virginia* was not a good sea boat and might well founder in a storm or even a heavy swell. There was also the matter of the ship's engines and the possibility that they would break down under the strain of prolonged steaming in a seaway.[11]

In late February, meanwhile, the Confederate cabinet, worried that Union forces would soon begin their drive on Richmond, ordered Gen. Joseph E. Johnston, who had charge of the capital's defense, to evacuate Manassas and transfer its resources to Richmond. Johnston worried that the Federals would detect this movement and attack while it was in progress but, during a period of several weeks, the Confederates shipped south by rail considerable quantities of cannon, equipment, and supplies without the Federals suspecting what was in progress. Finally, on the weekend of 8–9 March, Johnston's remaining troops burned what was left at Manassas and withdrew south to Richmond.[12]

At 11 AM on 8 March, the same day that Johnston's forces started south, the *Virginia* sortied from Norfolk. Conditions were ideal. The day was clear and bright and the water calm. Most of the crew assumed they had embarked on a trial run, but Buchanan was not about to delay. The *Virginia* thus went into battle without either trials or underway training.

Buchanan intended nothing less than destroying much of the Union blockading fleet and driving the remainder from Hampton Roads, while at the same time freeing Confederate warships in the James. "Old Buck" was delayed by the inability to secure sufficient cannon powder. The last consignment came aboard only on 7 March.[13]

Had Buchanan been able to attack on 7 March, he would have had two days to complete destruction of the Union warships before the arrival of the *Monitor*. But as fate would have it, a severe storm blew in, also affecting the *Monitor* in its passage south. It forced Buchanan to put off his plans for twenty-four hours.

Hampton Roads was the scene of the coming battle. A key strategic location for the Union naval blockade and land operations, it is the large basin into which the James, Nansemond, and Elizabeth rivers empty before Chesapeake Bay. The Roads is seven miles across, but the *Virginia* required at least twenty-two-foot deep water to operate, and this effectively confined it to an area never more than two miles across. Union troops occupied the northern shore of the Roads: Newport News, Hampton, and Fort Monroe; Confederate forces held the southern shore, including Norfolk and Portsmouth on the Elizabeth River. For two days thousands of soldiers in both armies and many more civilians thronged the shores to observe the events.

In addition to his flagship, Buchanan had available two small steamer tenders: the *Beaufort* (85 tons and one 32-pounder) and *Raleigh* (65 tons and two 6-pounders), both based at Norfolk. He also had the three gunboats in Cdr. John Randolph Tucker's James River Squadron: the former passenger steamers *Patrick Henry* (later the school ship for the Confederate Naval Academy) and *Jamestown* (1,300 and 1,500 tons, respectively, and each armed with one X-inch, one 64-pounder, six VIII-inch, and two 32-pounder rifled guns); and the former tug *Teaser* (64 tons with one 32-pounder rifled gun). These six Confederate ships mounting a total of 35 guns faced a Union naval force that mounted an aggregate 204 heavy guns. The larger Union ships were the screw frigates *Minnesota* (40 guns) and *Roanoke* (40 guns), the sailing frigates *Congress* (50 guns) and *St. Lawrence* (50 guns), and the razee (cut-down) sailing sloop *Cumberland* (24 guns).

As the *Virginia* slipped its moorings and steamed the ten miles down the Elizabeth River, trailed by the *Beaufort* and *Raleigh*, word of its departure spread quickly on land. Private James Keenan of the 2nd Georgia Infantry recalled, "women, children, men on horseback and on foot were running down towards the river from every conceivable direction shouting 'the *Merrimac* is going down.'"[14]

With nothing of the *Virginia* visible on the horizon save its casemate, the ship resembled a barn roof on the water. As the ironclad passed Craney Island and made its way toward Hampton Roads, Buchanan ordered the crew to its noon meal of "cold tongue and biscuit." He then briefly addressed the men, telling them that they had the opportunity to show their devotion to the Confederacy and strike a blow for their country. He concluded with a Nelsonian touch: "The Confederacy expects every man to do his duty."[15]

At about 1:30 PM at high tide, the *Virginia* rounded Sewell's Point and entered Hampton Roads. Although Union spies had kept Washington well informed about the progress of the *Virginia* and the fact that the Confederate James River Squadron was in close proximity and visible from the *Cumberland*, the appearance of the *Virginia* came as a surprise to the men aboard the Union ships. The crews had been attending to normal shipboard routine. They nonetheless had ample time to prepare, as it took the *Virginia* more than an hour to steam across the Roads.

The two nearest ships, the *Cumberland* and *Congress*, were the first likely targets, and at 2:20 PM the little *Beaufort* fired the opening shot of the battle from its lone 32-pounder against the *Congress*. Rated a forty-four, this Union sailing frigate mounted ten VIII-inch and forty 32-pounder smoothbore guns. Buchanan, meanwhile, made first for the *Cumberland*, which, while rated a twenty-two gun sloop, actually mounted a heavier battery (one X-inch smoothbore, twenty-two IX-inch Dahlgrens, and one "70-pounder" rifle—probably a 5.3-inch, 60-pounder Parrott gun) than the *Congress*.

Unfortunately for the *Cumberland*, the tide had shifted the ship athwart the channel. Its stern faced the oncoming *Virginia*, its keel in line with its spring anchors. The *Cumberland* thus could not be turned to deliver a broadside, and few of its guns could be brought to bear.

Buchanan opened fire at about fifteen hundred yards. A shell from the *Virginia*'s bow 7-inch Brooke pivot gun immediately told, causing considerable damage and casualties on the *Cumberland*'s starboard quarter. As the *Virginia* lumbered on, it came abreast of the *Congress*, which loosed a broadside against it, but none of the shot entered open gunports, and the *Virginia*'s response of hot shot and shell from the four guns of its starboard broadside caused extensive damage on the *Congress*, dismounting a gun, killing or wounding the gun crew, and starting several fires. Buchanan did not stop to finish off the crippled Union ship and kept straight on course for the *Cumberland*.

The firing was now general, with such Union ships and shore batteries as were able joining in. Union shot from the *Cumberland* created a great din inside the casemate of the *Virginia* when they struck the iron

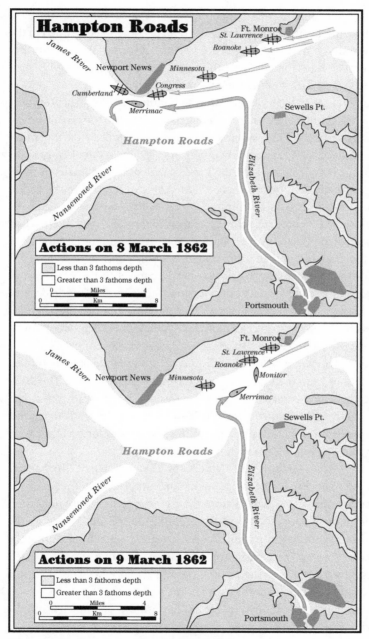

Hampton Roads

Actions on 8 March 1862

James River
Ft. Monroe
St. Lawrence
Roanoke
Newport News
Minnesota
Cumberland
Congress
Merrimac
Sewells Pt.
Hampton Roads
Nansemoned River
Elizabeth River

Less than 3 fathoms depth
Greater than 3 fathoms depth

Miles
0   4
0   8
Km

Portsmouth

Actions on 9 March 1862

James River
Ft. Monroe
St. Lawrence
Roanoke
Newport News
Minnesota
Monitor
Merrimac
Sewells Pt.
Hampton Roads
Nansemoned River
Elizabeth River

Less than 3 fathoms depth
Greater than 3 fathoms depth

Miles
0   4
0   8
Km

Portsmouth

Hampton Roads, Actions of 8 and 9 March 1862

plating, but they had no other apparent effect. Fearful that his ship, even at six knots, might strike so hard that it would become so embedded in the sloop's wooden hull that it would not be able to withdraw, at about fifty yards' distance Buchanan ordered the engines stopped. The *Virginia* simply glided forward on momentum alone.

The *Virginia* easily broke through the antitorpedo obstructions surrounding the *Cumberland*, its ram striking the Union ship forward at almost right angles on its starboard side and tearing a gaping hole below the waterline. The *Cumberland* immediately began to go down. As the Union sloop settled by the bow, it almost took the *Virginia* with it, but, when the pressure became too great, the poorly attached ram simply twisted off in the Union ship while the ironclad's seventeen-foot propeller managed to pull the *Virginia* away. Lt. Thomas O. Selfridge of the *Cumberland* later regretted that he had not attempted to drop his ship's starboard anchor on the *Virginia* in an effort to grapple it and take the Confederate ship down as well.

Once the *Virginia* was free, it was nearly parallel to the *Cumberland*, which got off three broadsides against the ironclad at about a hundred yards' range. Although the iron plate deflected the Union shot, two of the *Virginia*'s Dahlgren guns had their muzzles blown off. Although both guns continued to fire, one was so shortened that the muzzle blast set its gunport on fire.

Both ships were enveloped in clouds of dense white smoke, broken only by flashes from their guns, even as the Union sloop settled. The discipline of the *Cumberland*'s crew, which sustained 121 dead, prompted admiration from the Confederates. Buchanan reported of the *Cumberland*, "she commenced sinking, gallantly fighting her guns as long as they were above water. She went down with her colors flying."[16]

The *Virginia* then turned to attack the *Congress*, where Buchanan's brother, McKean Buchanan, was paymaster. Although the *Congress* was only several hundred yards away from the *Cumberland*, because of its deep draft and poor steering, the Confederate ironclad was forced to go up the James River to complete the turn. This took nearly half an hour, and in the process the *Virginia* twice passed by, and engaged, Union shore batteries, silencing several and blowing up one passenger schooner and sinking a schooner and capturing another, which was sent to Norfolk.

At about 4 PM the *Virginia* was at last in position. The *Raleigh* and the *Beaufort*, meanwhile, maintained a steady fire at the *Congress*, keeping the Union ship's gun crews occupied. At about this same time the three ships in the James River Squadron exited the river and began exchanging fire with Union shore batteries at Newport News.

While the *Virginia* was gaining position, Lt. Joseph B. Smith, captain of the *Congress*, ordered the armed tug *Zouave* to tow his ship under the Union batteries at Newport News. This proved a good idea for it prevented the *Virginia*, with its deep draft, from ramming. Unfortunately for Smith, the tide then swung the stern of his ship so that only two of its fifty guns could be brought to bear on the *Virginia*. Buchanan was thus able to position his ship about 150 yards off the stern of the *Congress* and open a deadly raking fire. In short order, one hundred men, a quarter of the Union ship's crew, were casualties. The *Zouave* also came under fire and its rudder became disabled, but another Union ship pulled it to safety.

The *Patrick Henry* now joined the *Virginia*, *Beaufort*, and *Raleigh* in shelling the *Congress*. The *Patrick Henry* took a disabling shot from a Union shore battery that struck its steam drum, but this was soon repaired. Meanwhile, both of the Union ship's stern guns were disabled, and Lieutenant Smith was killed, decapitated by a shell fragment. Still, the Union frigate took nearly an hour of punishment before it struck. Lt. John Taylor Wood of the *Virginia* concluded, "No ship was ever fought more gallantly." When Smith's father, Commo. Joseph Smith, learned in Washington that his son's ship had surrendered, he said simply, "Joe's dead."[17]

Buchanan then ordered the crews of the *Beaufort* and *Raleigh* to go alongside the *Congress*, take its officers and wounded men prisoner, permit the remainder of the crew to escape, and burn the ship. Lt. William H. Parker of the *Beaufort* secured the surrender, and the *Jamestown* then came up on the other side of the doomed Union ship. But as the prisoners were being transferred, Union troops on shore several hundred yards away opened up with small arms. Several Confederates were killed, and Parker was among others wounded. He soon ordered the *Beaufort* to cast off and move to safety. Thirty prisoners were on board, but the *Beaufort* had suffered some ten casualties from the Union fire, and the ship was peppered with holes. Parker did not first inform Buchanan, who looked in vain for the telltale smoke showing that the Union ship had been torched.

Soon it became clear what had transpired. Buchanan was furious at Parker's unauthorized withdrawal, characterizing the lieutenant as "unfit to command." But Buchanan was also incensed at what he considered a breach of the laws of the sea, although the Union troops ashore certainly had not surrendered.

Robert Minor, the *Virginia*'s flag lieutenant, volunteered to complete the task, setting out with eight men in one of the ironclad's boats. Despite a white flag, he too came under fire. When Minor and several others were wounded, he ordered the boat back to the ironclad. Buchanan believed that the fire was coming from the *Congress*, which was not true. Insisting that the Union frigate be destroyed, he ordered the *Virginia*'s gunners to set it alight with hot shot.

The excitable Buchanan also foolishly seized a musket, climbed to the top exposed deck of the *Virginia*, and began firing at the troops on shore, aiming particularly at the officers who he believed were responsible for this "breach" of the rules of war. The troops ashore opened up en masse on anyone exposed on the *Virginia*, so it is not surprising that Buchanan soon fell victim to a musket ball. Hit in the thigh, he slumped to the deck and was carried below. The wound turned out not to be life threatening, but Buchanan was forced to transfer command to Jones. In the charges and countercharges afterward, the Union side pointed out that the *Beaufort* was a legitimate target, and that the *Congress* was flying a white flag, actually two of them, when Buchanan ordered renewed shelling of the ship.

Jones carried out Buchanan's order to continue firing hot shot into the *Congress* until it was alight. Sometime after 5 PM, with the *Congress* engulfed in flames, the *Virginia* also lobbed a few long-range shells at the distant *Minnesota* and *St. Lawrence*, using ricochet firing to try to reach them.

The *Virginia*'s pilots now insisted that the ship return to its base before dark or risk running aground. Also, the tide had receded and the *Virginia* would have to remain in the channel. With the ironclad also leaking at the bow and the crew exhausted, Jones decided to retire, confident he could return and complete the work of destruction the next day.

The day had been a Confederate triumph. The *Virginia* had destroyed two major Union warships with a cost of two hundred fifty dead, seventy-five wounded, and twenty-six captured. Confederate losses were two men dead and eight wounded. Considering that it had been struck more than one hundred times, damage to the *Virginia* was minor. It had been swept clean of boats, davits, railings, and the like, the smokestack was punctured in many places, the ship was leaking, and two of its guns had been damaged. Some armor plates were also loosened, and the ram was gone.[18]

At about 8 PM the *Virginia* dropped anchor off Swell's Point. An hour later the crew took their evening meal. Jones surveyed the damage and easily effected repairs were carried out. That same evening, one of the pilots on the ironclad spied a strange craft putting into the Roads, made visible by the light from the burning *Congress*. It was the Union ironclad *Monitor*, designed by John Ericsson.

Officials in Washington were well aware that the Confederates had raised the *Merrimack* and were rebuilding it as an ironclad. In consequence, in August 1861 Congress appropriated $1.5 million for Union ironclad construction. Ericsson's design was one of three selected by the Ironclad Board of naval officers appointed by Secretary Welles, and the first to be completed. Born in Sweden and a highly respected leader in warship design and steam engineering, Ericsson had designed the power plant and propulsion system of the world's first screw-propelled steam warship, the U.S. Navy sloop *Princeton*, as well as the first of its two large 12-inch wrought-iron guns. Ericsson had been unfairly blamed for the explosion in February 1844 of the second 12-inch gun, the "Peacemaker," and he had not been paid for his work on the *Princeton*. Ericsson vowed that he would have nothing more to do with the government, or even set foot in Washington. In consequence, he had not initially entered the ironclad design competition.

Connecticut industrialist Cornelius Bushnell received one of the ironclad contracts, for the future *Galena*. Questioned about its buoyancy, Bushnell went to Ericsson, who concluded that the ship would indeed be stable. Ericsson then showed Bushnell his design for an ironclad warship of low freeboard and a revolving turret. Bushnell immediately recognized the superiority of Ericsson's work over his own and convinced him to change his mind and submit a proposal.

Securing the support of the Ironclad Board was not easy. One of the three board members, Capt. Charles Davis, opposed Ericsson's highly unorthodox design and changed his mind only after the engineer traveled to Washington in mid-September and made a personal presentation. Welles then concurred with the board's decision and gave Ericsson a verbal contract that same day. In truth, the department accepted the design only because of the perceived threat from the *Virginia* and because Ericsson promised to complete the work so quickly.

The contract was most unusual and reflected doubts about the ship's viability. Ericsson and his partners had to assume all the risk. If the ship failed

Engineer John Ericsson. U.S. NAVAL INSTITUTE PHOTO ARCHIVE

in any way—with the navy to determine what constituted failure—then all sums advanced for the construction were to be refunded to the government.

In contrast to the lengthy delays that marked construction of the *Virginia*, the *Monitor* was completed in record time; the contract, formally signed on 4 October 1861, required that what some called "Ericsson's Folly" be finished in only one hundred days, by 12 January 1862. The ship was laid down in Brooklyn, New York, on 25 October 1861, but not even Ericsson's tireless efforts and his simplification of the original design enabled him to meet the specified deadline. Nonetheless, the *Monitor* was ready for trials on 19 February 1862.

Commissioned six days later on 25 February, the *Monitor* revolution-ized naval warfare. Entirely of iron, it incorporated such innovations as forced draft ventilation. Of only 987 tons' displacement, the ship was 179 feet long by 41 feet, 6 inches abeam and had a draft of only 10 feet, 6 inches, half that of the *Virginia*. Its two engines delivered 320 horse-power to a single screw propeller. Design speed was nine knots, although actual speed was slightly less.

For all practical purposes, the *Monitor* had two hulls: an upper or armored raft supported by a lower iron hull. The raft portion had 2 inches of iron on the deck and 4.5 inches on the sides. To shield the hull, this armor extended 3 feet, 6 inches below the waterline. The *Monitor*'s most visible part was its 120-ton, 9-foot-tall spindle-mounted turret amidships. The tur-ret had two side-by-side gunports and mounted a pair of XI-inch Dahlgrens taken from the *Dacotah*. The rotating turret enabled the *Monitor*'s gunports to be protected from enemy fire while the Dahlgrens were being reloaded. The turret and a small pilothouse (the command center of the ship) locat-ed forward and extending only 3 feet, 10 inches above the deck were both heavily protected. The turret had eight layers and the pilothouse nine layers of 1-inch iron plating. The turret had an interior diameter of less than 20 feet and was quite cramped with the two guns and their crews. Most of the ship's machinery was below the waterline.

The turret was a great advantage in that it provided protection for the gun crews and could fire on an opponent with the ship in almost any position, but the heavy weight of early turrets prevented them from being located high in a ship, and for that reason Ericsson designed the *Monitor* and other monitors to follow with very low freeboard. With only 18 inches of freeboard and the turret as its principal visible part, the *Monitor* came to be called "a hat on the water" or "cheesebox on a raft." Because of the inefficiency of early steam propulsion, early ironclads had sail rigs and used the wind for most of their cruising. But a sail rig was largely impractical on the *Monitor*, and Ericsson simply ignored that contract requirement. The early monitors were moreover coastal vessels rather than seagoing ships. They were also unsuited for blockade duties, because in rough seas the crews had no alternative but to batten down the hatches and remain below.[19]

Ericsson had high hopes for what he styled the "impregnable and aggressive character" of his ironclad. His proposed name for the ship of the *Monitor* was designed to convey the strength of Northern industry and military might but also to serve as a warning to Britain and its Royal Navy.[20]

Lt. John L. Worden of New York took command of the *Monitor*. Worden had joined the navy as a midshipman in 1834 and was serving at the Naval Observatory on the outbreak of the war. His confessed hopes of becoming a hero appeared to have been dashed when he was taken prisoner in April 1861 while returning overland from Pensacola. He had then spent seven months in prison before being exchanged and had only recently recovered his health.

The crew was a small one—just ten officers and forty-eight seamen. All were volunteers, the navy being reluctant to assign anyone to such an untried ship. As with the crew of the *Virginia*, the men would have to learn on the job. Following final fitting out at the Brooklyn Navy Yard, on 27 February the *Monitor* embarked on a shakedown cruise in New York Harbor, which revealed some problems, chiefly in the ship's steering, which Ericsson then corrected.

On 4 March, Worden was ordered to take the *Monitor* to Hampton Roads. Welles hoped that the *Monitor* might steam up the Elizabeth River and engage and destroy the *Virginia* before it sortied, but a major storm delayed departure. Not until 6 March did Worden believe it safe to leave the Brooklyn Navy Yard.

The ironclad proceeded south under tow by the steam tug *Seth Low* but under its own engines and with the steam gunboats *Currituck* and *Sachem* in company. Never designed as an oceangoing ship and in any case suffering the usual problems associated with any brand-new weapons system, the *Monitor* nearly sank during the passage south.

The day of 6 March was uneventful, but after midnight a storm blew in and grew ever stronger, starting a number of leaks and revealing a serious error by workers at the Brooklyn yard. Ericsson had designed the turret to fit snugly, with its own great weight serving as a seal against admission of seawater. On their own, the workers had jacked up the turret and inserted a gasket of oakum—bits of old rope—around the entire base to act as a seal. The storm dislodged some of the oakum, eventually creating a sixty-three-foot circumferential opening through which the sea now poured. The pumps were quite unable to keep up with the influx of water, and the ship was soon in danger of foundering.

There were other problems, including water entering the ship through the observation slits in the pilothouse forward and air-intake vents on the deck. The water stretched the belts on the blower fans, which then stopped, in turn halting the engines. Carbon dioxide began to spread through the ship.

In desperation, Worden organized a bucket brigade. This demanding physical activity also helped calm the men. Finally, after some five hours, the *Seth Low* managed to tow the *Monitor* into calmer waters near shore, and the crew was able to repair the blower belts and clear out the carbon dioxide, restarting the boilers and engines. Slowly the pumps voided the remaining water.

The second evening passed quietly, but shortly after midnight the ship was again in peril when the sea again became rough. The same workers at the navy yard who had inserted the oakum had also ignored Ericsson's instructions to plug the hawser pipe through which the anchor chain passed. Water now poured through that opening in a great stream, and the blowers were again in danger of stopping. The pitching of the ship then caused the wheel ropes to jump off the steering wheel and become jammed. Once again the *Seth Low* was able to tow the *Monitor* to calmer waters, and the danger passed.

Finally, about 3 PM on 8 March, the crew sighted Cape Henry, the southern part of the entrance to Chesapeake Bay. They were some fifteen miles from their destination. As they approached, they could hear the boom of cannon and see the smoke of exploding shells. When a pilot came aboard, he confirmed that the *Virginia* had sortied and was in the process of destroying the Union fleet, ship by ship.

At about 9 PM the *Monitor* pulled alongside the frigate *Roanoke*, where Worden conferred with Capt. John Marston, senior Union officer in the Roads in Goldsborough's absence. Here Worden learned for the first time that on 6 March Welles had ordered Commo. Hiram Paulding, commandant of the Brooklyn Navy Yard, to order him to bring the *Monitor* up the Potomac to Alexandria for the defense of Washington. Marston countermanded the order, instructing Worden to defend the *Minnesota*. At 1 AM on 9 March the *Monitor* anchored alongside the grounded Union flagship.

Shortly thereafter, fires on the *Congress* finally reached that ship's magazine. In a letter to his wife, Paymaster William Keeler described what occurred: "A volcano seemed to open instantaneously. Pieces of burning timbers, exploding shells, huge fragments of the wreck, grenades & rockets filled the air & fell sparkling & hissing in all directions." [21]

At about 6 AM on 9 March, the *Virginia* weighed anchor and got under way. Lieutenant Jones could see what remained of the *Congress* still burning; beyond it lay the *Minnesota*, and, further on toward Fortress Monroe, the *St. Lawrence* and *Roanoke*. Both these latter ships had grounded while under the tow of tugs but had been pulled free and taken where they could be covered by the guns of Fortress Monroe. The *Minnesota*, still aground, appeared easy prey, however. The sea was calm and the day clear, and Jones ordered the ironclad to make for the Union flagship. Soldiers and civilians again lined the shore, and a number of civilian craft filled with spectators also appeared.

Earlier, at 4 AM, supposing the *Virginia* to be already under way, Worden had ordered the *Monitor* to weigh anchor and stand out in the channel. Discovering the report to be false, at 5:30 AM Worden again anchored. At 8 AM Worden and his officers were on top of the turret when they saw the *Virginia* and its consorts *Patrick Henry*, *Jamestown*, and *Teaser* steam out into the main channel for Fortress Monroe, before turning and heading for the *Minnesota*. Black smoke belched from the Confederate ironclad's damaged funnel.

Worden ordered his crew to prepare for battle. The men had only coffee and hard bread for breakfast. They were also exhausted. Few had rested that night and many had not slept for several days. Executive Officer Lt. Samuel D. Greene estimated that he had not slept for fifty-one hours, but he and the remainder of the crew forgot their fatigue and set to work.

As the *Virginia* approached the *Minnesota*, the crew of the Confederate ironclad at last saw the *Monitor*. It appeared both strange and insignificant. Midshipman Hardin Littlepage of the *Virginia* thought the *Monitor* might be a raft carrying one of the *Minnesota*'s boilers for repairs.

The *Monitor* was far more maneuverable than the *Virginia*, but it also was only a fraction of the Confederate ironclad's size and mounted but two guns to the ten on the *Virginia*. Despite Worden's defiant letter to his wife just before the battle stating that nothing could harm his ship, there must have been serious doubts on the *Monitor* as to whether it would prove a worthy opponent.

Jones knew what the *Monitor* was, but he intended to ignore the Union ironclad until he had finished off the *Minnesota*. He planned to position the *Virginia* about a half mile from the Union flagship and destroy it with hot shot. When he was about a mile from the grounded frigate, Jones ordered his gun crews to commence fire. Almost immediately a round from the forward 7-inch Brooke rifle struck the *Minnesota* and started a fire. A stern gun on the *Minnesota* replied, but the shot simply ricocheted off the *Virginia*'s armor.

Worden had his orders, and he set the *Monitor* straight for the *Virginia* but ordered the crew to hold fire. Worden took up position in the pilothouse, while Lt. Samuel Dana Greene had charge of the turret and the ship's guns. The speaking tube Ericsson had installed between the two positions had broken, so members of the crew carried communications back and forth between the two officers.

The *Minnesota* and *Virginia* continued to exchange fire until the *Monitor* had closed the range. The *Monitor*'s pilothouse prevented the Union ironclad's guns from firing directly forward (Ericsson later admitted that not placing the pilot house at the top of the turret was a mistake), so Worden conned the *Monitor* parallel to the *Virginia* and, when the range had sufficiently closed, ordered the engine stopped and then "Commence firing!" At 8:45 AM Greene fired the first shot of the battle between the two ironclads, but the ball simply bounced off the *Virginia*'s casemate.

The duel between the two ironclads lasted three and a half hours, until 12:15 PM. The *Virginia*'s consorts were only spectators, for the *Monitor*'s heavy guns would have made short work of them. The battle was fought at very close range, from a few yards to more than one hundred, and both ships were constantly in motion, circling. At one point the *Virginia* grounded, and it was some time before it was able to get free. With his ship still grounded, Jones came down from the spar deck to see a gun division standing at ease. Turning to the officer in charge, Lt. John R. Eggleston, Jones demanded to know why the guns were not firing. Eggleston reportedly replied: "Why our powder is very precious, and after two hours' incessant fire I find that I can do her about as much damage by snapping my thumb at her every two minutes and a half."[22]

The crew of the *Virginia* were surprised that the guns of the *Monitor* did not inflict greater damage. Most of the Union shot struck obliquely, and it also seems to have hit everywhere save at the most vulnerable spot. Not a single shot struck the *Virginia* at its waterline. A few well-placed shots struck there and the ironclad would have been doomed. The Confederates believed that the *Monitor's* crew had simply fired their guns as rapidly as possible (every five or six minutes) without aiming.

The *Virginia* was also extremely vulnerable when it ran hard aground. The *Monitor*, with half its draft, could then circle its antagonist and fire at will. With the *Virginia's* very survival now at stake, Chief Engineer H. Ashton Ramsay ordered the boiler safety valves tied shut to provide maximum steam, and the *Virginia* at length pulled free.

Following two hours of battle, Worden disengaged to resupply with ammunition, for the cannonballs had to be hoisted up from a storage bin below deck through a scuttle that required the ship to be stationary. Jones took advantage of the respite to try to sink the *Minnesota*, but shoal water halted the deep-draft *Virginia* almost a mile away from its target. Nonetheless, shot from the *Virginia's* guns did damage the Union flagship and disabled a tug trying to tow it to safety. At this point, the *Monitor* then returned, and the struggle between the two ironclads resumed.

With his fire having no apparent effect and unaware of the loss of his own ship's ram in the *Cumberland*, Jones decided to ram. He explained this to the officers as well as his intention to board the Union ship thereafter. Ramming would not be easy, however. As one of the *Virginia's* junior officers put it, "the ship was as unwieldy as Noah's ark."[23]

Seeing a chance, Jones ordered the *Virginia* ahead full steam. But Worden turned the more nimble *Monitor* aside, and it received only a glancing blow. The attempt actually hurt the *Virginia* more than the *Monitor*, as it opened up another leak in its hull. In any case, crew members of the *Monitor* had hand grenades ready to hurl out of the gunports in an effort to thwart any boarding attempt. Worden, meanwhile, attempted to concentrate the *Monitor's* fire on his antagonist's vulnerable propeller and rudder.

The *Monitor's* rotating turret meant that the guns were targets only when the heavy shutters were open and the guns about to fire, which no doubt explains the Union crew's haste and lack of aiming. The *Virginia*, however, sustained damage from the twenty hits that registered from forty-one 180-pound 11-inch shells fired by the *Monitor*. The wooden backing behind the armor plate on the Confederate ironclad was cracked and splintered in places. Although the more numerous Confederate guns fired many more shot and shells than did the *Monitor*, most went high, and those that did strike effected little damage. The *Monitor* was hit only twenty-four times and, although the concussion of a shell striking the turret knocked down men inside, the only results were dents in the armor.

A few minutes after noon, Worden's attempt to ram the stern of the *Virginia* ended in a near miss about two feet from the Confederate ship. Just as the Union ship passed the stern of the *Virginia*, a 7-inch shell exploded in a direct hit on the *Monitor*'s pilothouse, stunning and temporarily blinding Worden. He ordered the *Monitor* to sheer off in order to assess damage, and the ironclad drifted away toward Fort Monroe. Executive Officer Greene, just twenty-two years old and a lieutenant for only a year, took command.

Engagement in Hampton Roads, Virginia, on 9 March 1862 between the USS Monitor *and CSS* Virginia; *print after a painting by J. O. Davidson.* NAVAL HISTORICAL CENTER (NH 45973)

Jones, meanwhile, decided to return to Norfolk for repairs. Greene declined to pursue, in keeping with his orders to protect the *Minnesota*. This decision was controversial, although most of the ship's officers defended it. Each side claimed the actions of the other meant that the opponent was beaten.[24]

The battle was in fact a draw. The *Virginia* had suffered some damage, whereas the *Monitor* was virtually unscathed. Aboard the *Monitor*, Worden was the only serious casualty, whereas the *Virginia* sustained two dead and nineteen wounded. The battle might have turned out differently had the *Virginia* concentrated its fire on the *Monitor*'s pilothouse, a difficult target in the best of conditions, or if solid shot or special bolts had been available for the rifled guns. On the other hand, the *Monitor*'s fire should have been directed at its opponent's vulnerable waterline. Its guns also should have employed 30-pound powder charges instead of the 15 pounds decreed. Following the 1844 Peacemaker explosion, the Navy Department had decreed that no gun could be fired with a powder charge more than half that for which it had been designed. This mistaken order was revoked only after the *Monitor–Virginia* engagement. Ericsson was furious. He claimed with considerable justification that if the *Monitor* had simply taken up position at two hundred yards range with its guns exactly level and fired with the 30-pound charges he had sought, that the shot would have gone clear through the *Virginia*.

Worden did get his wish of becoming a hero, and President Lincoln visited him at his bedside. A joint resolution of Congress brought promotion

U.S. Navy officers shown on the deck of the ironclad Monitor *following its engagement with CSS* Virginia. *Note dents in the turret and the muzzle of one of the 11-inch Dahlgren guns.* NAVAL HISTORICAL CENTER (NH 2780)

to commander. Although Worden remained blind in one eye and experienced physical pain for the remainder of his life, he recovered sight in the other eye and returned to duty late in the year. Promoted to rear admiral in 1872, he retired from the navy in 1886.[25]

Tactically, the engagement between the two ironclads was a Northern victory. The *Monitor* had saved the flagship *Minnesota*. In merely surviving, the *Monitor* assured the safety of the Union transports and supply ships and hence the continuation of McClellan's Peninsula Campaign. But the South could claim a strategic victory, for as long as the *Virginia* remained in being, Norfolk and Richmond were safe from Union warships, and its presence acted as a brake on McClellan's drive toward Richmond.

The battle signaled a new era in naval warfare. The first time that ironclad ships had fought one another, it gave new impetus to the naval warfare revolution then in progress. As Capt. John Dahlgren put it, "Now comes the reign of iron—and cased sloops are to take the place of wooden ships." The London *Times* opined that the Royal Navy had suddenly gone from having 149 first-class warships to just 2—its own ironclads—and that apart from them there was not a single ship "that it would not be madness to trust to an engagement with that little *Monitor*."[26]

Each ship type proved the model for naval construction on its own side in the war. Of eighty-four ironclads laid down by the North, sixty-four were of the *Monitor* or turreted type. Unfortunately, the monitor craze inhibited the construction of seagoing ironclads. Until the 1880s the U.S. Navy had no true seagoing ironclad vessels that could fight similar ships. At the same time, the *Virginia* was the prototype for most of the fifty ironclads built or laid down by the South during the war.

Meanwhile, the Peninsula Campaign went forward. On 17 March, when the Navy Department had positive information that McClellan planned to begin the campaign, Welles rushed every possible ship to Hampton Roads, including some chartered ships that might be used to ram the *Virginia* should it prove necessary. The movement from Alexandria of one hundred thirty thousand Union troops, fifteen thousand horses, eleven hundred wagons, and forty-four artillery batteries was completed by 5 April. The troops then advanced against the now strengthened Confederate positions extending across the peninsula from Yorktown in the north to the James just west of Newport News in the south.

McClellan, who became known as the "Virginia Creeper" for his glacial speed, first moved against Yorktown. He urged Flag Officer Goldsborough to employ his warships in either attacking the Confederate works there or running past them, but with the *Virginia* in being, Goldsborough refused to weaken his force at Hampton Roads, apart from detaching several gunboats to shell Yorktown's defenses, which they did intermittently until the Confederate evacuation.[27]

The Confederates, meanwhile, effected repairs to the *Virginia*. These included a new funnel and steam pipes, replacement of damaged outer iron plates, two new guns, a new anchor and boats, and a 12-foot-long steel-tipped ram. The Brooke rifles also received new iron bolt ammunition, designed by Brooke specifically to engage the *Monitor*.

Goldsborough's caution seemed justified when Buchanan's successor, Flag Officer Josiah Tattnall, took the *Virginia* out on 11 April. Mallory had instructed him to attack the Union transports in Hampton Roads, and Tattnall also hoped to draw the *Monitor* into a renewal of their duel. At 6 AM the *Virginia* sallied from Norfolk along with five smaller ships and steamed into Hampton Roads. Although the *Monitor* got up steam, it remained under the guns of Fort Monroe, Goldsborough steadfastly refusing to be drawn into battle and wisely choosing to cover the army's base and its essential water lines of communication east and north. After remaining in the Roads until late afternoon without result, Tattnall directed the *Jamestown* to capture three Union transports off Hampton. The Confederate squadron then returned with its prizes to Norfolk.[28]

Goldsborough was confident he could rebuff any Confederate thrust. His chief defense was the *Monitor*, but he also had the steamer rams and many large guns ashore, and on the afternoon of 11 April the *Vanderbilt* arrived. This powerful former transatlantic side-wheeler passenger ship had been donated to the navy by Cornelius Vanderbilt. Still, the great value to the Confederacy of the *Virginia* in being was apparent in Goldsborough's reluctance to initiate offensive operations involving the *Monitor*. He believed that losing it might spell disaster for the rest of the Union squadron. Union fears concerning the *Virginia* were lessened on 24 April with the arrival at Hampton Roads of the *Galena*, second of the experimental Union ironclads.

Meanwhile, the Federal advance on land stalled before Yorktown. Gen. Johnston, charged with the defense of Richmond, had opposed a fight for the peninsula where the Union could effectively utilize its substantial naval resources, but Davis overruled him and insisted that the army be committed there. Thus Johnston assumed command at Yorktown in mid-April.

Meanwhile, Confederate Maj. Gen. John Magruder, with only fifteen thousand troops, bluffed McClellan, with seven times his number, into believing he had many more men than was the case. The Union siege of Yorktown went on for a month. Not until the Union lines were nearly complete did the Confederates evacuate, on 3 May. Union forces occupied Yorktown the next day.

McClellan boasted of his "capture" of Yorktown, but he also demanded more troops, claiming that Johnston commanded forces greater than his own. In fact, McClellan had one hundred five thousand men, some eighty-five thousand of whom were ready for battle, whereas Johnston had only sixty thousand men, of whom but forty-two thousand were available for combat.

The Confederates fell back on Williamsburg, and from there to the vicinity of Richmond. Johnston's plan was to draw the Union forces away from their river gunboats, and then counterattack. The success of McClellan's plan rested on his strategic skills and on speed. Unfortunately, speed was a quality utterly unknown to the Union commander.

During the campaign, the Union gunboats routinely conducted reconnaissance missions. When the Confederates evacuated Yorktown, Cdr. William Smith in the *Wachusett* reconnoitered the mouth of that river, raising the Union flag at Gloucester Point across the York. On 6–7 May, with the *Wachusett, Chocura,* and *Sebago,* Smith escorted transports up the York to West Point. The three gunboats covered a Union landing there and dueled with Confederate shore defenses. Smith also sent another of his gunboats, the *Currituck,* up the Pamunkey, a tributary of the York, where it captured two Confederate schooners and destroyed others.

On 8 May the Union Army advance renewed but almost immediately bogged down. That same day, the *Monitor,* supported by the *Dacotah, Naugatuck, Seminole,* and *Susquehanna,* shelled Confederate batteries at Sewell's Point, chiefly to explore the possibility of landing troops in the vicinity to move against Norfolk. Also on 8 May, some men deserted Norfolk in a tug and brought word that a Confederate evacuation was under way there and that the *Virginia* would soon steam up the James along with other ships of the squadron. Goldsborough hoped that he could draw the *Virginia* into deep water, allowing his high-speed steamers to ram. Lincoln, then acting as commander-in-chief of Union forces at Hampton Roads, sent a message to Goldsborough suggesting that if he had confidence that his other ships could contain the *Virginia*, he should send the *Galena* and two gunboats up the James to support McClellan. Goldsborough did so, and this action silenced two Confederate shore batteries and forced the gunboats *Jamestown* and *Patrick Henry* to withdraw farther up the James.[29]

On 10 May the Confederates evacuated the Norfolk Navy Yard, setting fire to the buildings and destroying the dry dock. Union troops crossed from Fort Monroe to land at Ocean View and occupied Norfolk just behind the departing Confederates. That same day the Confederates evacuated Pensacola, Florida.

The *Virginia* was moored off Sewell's Point when Tattnall learned of the loss of Norfolk. This came as a surprise, for he had expected it to hold out for another week. Nonetheless, Tattnall hoped to get the *Virginia* up the James and was assured by river pilots that it could travel to within forty miles of Richmond, providing its draft could be reduced to eighteen feet. This would have to be accomplished quickly, for the morning of 11 May would undoubtedly find the Federals in possession of the Confederate shore batteries.

The *Virginia*'s crew worked most of the night to lighten the ship, but the pilots then informed Tattnall that it would be impossible to get above Jamestown because of low water from a prevailing western wind. Tattnall was furious, for the *Virginia* had been lightened to the point where it could no longer be safely fought. When the ship was fully loaded, the armor barely protected the waterline, and now about two feet of wooden hull was completely exposed.

Tattnall believed he had no other choice but to scuttle his ship. The *Virginia* departed its anchorage at 2 AM on 11 May, and Tattnall deliberately grounded it off Craney Island. Over a three-hour span the 350-man crew was ferried by boats ashore. Ten men then placed combustibles throughout the ship and laid powder trains, which Jones lit. The *Virginia* blew up just before 5 AM, the crew proceeding by land up the James to Drewry's Bluff. Tattnall reported to Mallory, "The *Virginia* no longer exists, but 300 brave and skillful officers and seamen are saved for the Confederacy."[30]

Although there were still five Confederate gunboats in the James, destruction of the *Virginia* removed the only Confederate threat to

Fortress Monroe and gave Goldsborough's more powerful ships the run of the river as far as Drewry's Bluff, a fact that may have saved the Union land campaign from disaster. Lincoln now pressed Goldsborough to take immediate action. On 11 May the *Galena* was at Upper Brandon, but there was no sign of the Federal troops, who were only leisurely pursuing the retreating Confederates. On Lincoln's request, Goldsborough dispatched the *Monitor* and *Naugatuck*. The latter, designed and built by John Stevens as a demonstration for his proposed ironclad "Stevens Battery," had been launched in 1844. Loaned by Stevens to the government at the beginning of the war and taken into the navy from the Revenue Service, the *Naugatuck* was a twin-screw ironclad. Its innovations included a system for flooding the forward and aft compartments in order to partially submerge the ship during battle, making it less vulnerable to enemy fire.

Goldsborough ordered Rodgers to proceed to Richmond with his three ironclads and the wooden screw gunboat *Aroostook* and side-wheeler *Port Royal*, and shell the city into submission. At 6:30 AM on 15 May, Rodgers's squadron came within sight of the Confederate defenses at Drewry's Bluff, eight miles from the Confederate capital. Named for property owner Augustus H. Drewry and officially designated Fort Darling, it continued to be known simply as Drewry's Bluff. Initially the Confederates had given little thought to building defenses there because they assumed the *Virginia* would prevent any Union advance upriver. Work began only in March and intensified following the loss of Yorktown.

Drewry's Bluff was the best—even the last—place for the Confederates to halt a Union advance up the James to Richmond. There the river took a sharp bend and narrowed. High, sheer ninety-foot cliffs dominated the south bank, and at their top Brig. Gen. George Washington Custis Lee, Gen. Robert E. Lee's oldest son, supervised installation of a battery of three heavy guns. In order to inhibit the passage of Union ships farther upriver, the defenders also sank a number of hulks midstream and used pile drivers to position cribs of stone and other debris. Knowing the wooden ships of his squadron were no match for the Union ironclads, Commander Tucker of the James River Squadron sacrificed one of his two most powerful ships, sinking the *Jamestown* as an added obstruction.

Tucker's squadron added five guns to the defenses. These were placed outside the works, giving the defenders a total of eight guns, divided equally between rifles and smoothbores. These commanded a mile of the river downstream. Appropriately enough, Augustus Drewry commanded the battery as captain of the Southside Heavy Artillery. Lieutenant Jones of the *Virginia* had charge of a detachment of marines and seamen from the ironclad who were determined to have another go at the *Monitor*. Gen. Robert E. Lee, now serving as military advisor to President Davis, dispatched an infantry brigade to Drewry's Bluff, and these men were positioned in rifle pits along the riverbank. Finally, the gunboat *Patrick Henry* took up position behind the obstructions, adding its 8-inch smoothbore cannon to the defense.

The Confederate defensive positions had been well placed. The James was too narrow at this point for the Union ships to maneuver, and the obstructions in the middle of the stream easily blocked the deeper-draft ironclads. Before Union crews could hope to work at removing the obstructions, they would have to neutralize both the shore batteries and Confederate infantrymen.

At 7:45 AM on 15 May Rodgers boldly brought up the *Galena* to about six hundred yards from the bluff and anchored broadside to the channel so that its guns could be brought to bear. Even before the *Galena* was positioned, the Confederate defenders began what subsequently became known as the First Battle of Drewry's Bluff, sending two shot into the Union ironclad's port bow. At about 9 AM the *Monitor* passed the *Galena* and attempted to join the fight but its guns could not be elevated sufficiently to fire on the batteries along the bluff, and so it retired downriver with the *Aroostook* and *Port Royal*.

The three-and-a-half-hour-long battle, which ended at about 11 AM, saw the Confederates fire perhaps one hundred shots and the Union ships half that number. The *Naugatuck's* 6.4-inch (100-pounder) Parrott rifle burst halfway through the engagement, putting that ship out of action, and the *Port Royal* was kept busy firing into the woods on the riverbank against the Confederate infantry. Most of the Confederate fire was directed against the *Galena*, however; it took a terrible pounding, particularly on its port side.

The battle revealed the serious shortcomings in the *Galena's* armor. The ship was struck forty-three times, and thirteen shot penetrated, one embedding itself in the opposite side of the hull. The *Galena's* timbers and frames were much cut up, and it took on water. Thirteen crewmen were killed and eleven were wounded. Cited for bravery in the action, Cpl. John B. Mackie of the ironclad was subsequently awarded the Medal of Honor, the first to a member of the Marine Corps. Confederate losses in the battle were seven killed and eight wounded.

Despite the serious damage, Rodgers withdrew his ship only when it was nearly out of ammunition. In his official report, he noted with some irony of the *Galena*, "We have demonstrated that she is not shot proof." A number of the dead had in fact been killed by fragments of the ironclad's own plating. But Rodgers claimed that, had troops been available to be landed, Drewry's Bluff would have been taken and the campaign against Richmond might have worked out differently. As it transpired, the Confederate stand at Drewry's Bluff was decisive in saving the capital.[31]

Following the rebuff, Rodgers fell back downriver to City Point, where he could keep the James and Chickahominy rivers under observation. The next day, Paymaster Keeler of the *Monitor* went aboard the *Galena* off City Point. He described the ship's interior as

> a slaughter house . . . of human beings . . . the decks were covered with large pools of half coagulated blood & strewn with portions of skulls, fragments of shells, arms, legs, hands, pieces of flesh & iron, splinters of wood & broken weapons were mixed in one confused, horrible mass.[32]

The Confederates later improved their defenses on the upper James. They strengthened Drewry's Bluff and established their naval academy there. By 1864 they also had three ironclads in the upper James: the *Richmond, Fredericksburg,* and *Virginia II.* The Confederates also deployed in the river an elaborate system of electrically detonated mines developed by Matthew Maury.

Meanwhile, the struggle on the peninsula continued. On 14 May, the day before the battle at Drewry's Bluff, the Army of the Potomac reached the Pamunkey about twenty miles from Richmond and drove Johnston's men into the capital's suburbs. Despite his overwhelming strength, McClellan then halted to await McDowell's corps.

The main Union base was at White House on the Pamunkey, in close proximity to the York. On 17 May, at McClellan's request, the gunboats *Sebago* and *Currituck* raided up the Pamunkey, twenty-five miles beyond White House. Later the *Cuttick* and *Corwin* conducted a similar foray up the Mattapony, paralleling the Pamunkey.

McClellan passed the bulk of his men across the Chickahominy, his forces extending in a great V on its side, the upper arm of which stretched out to meet McDowell, the lower to within five miles of Richmond, just beyond Fair Oaks Station. At this point, nature intervened to provide an opportunity for Johnston. Heavy rains washed out bridges and isolated two Union corps on the south bank of the Chickahominy near the villages of Seven Pines and Fair Oaks Station, and on 31 May General Johnston ordered an attack there. Only the timely arrival of another Union corps that managed to cross the river prevented a Union disaster. In this Battle of Seven Pines, both sides sustained heavy losses. Among Confederate casualties was Johnston himself, severely wounded, and on 1 June Gen. Robert E. Lee assumed command of the Army of Northern Virginia.

A daring raid by Maj. Gen. J. E. B. Stuart's cavalry completely around McClellan's army confirmed that McClellan's right flank was unsecured. In what became known as the Seven Days' Battles (25 June–1 July), Lee sent forces under Maj. Gen. Thomas J. "Stonewall" Jackson to attack the vulnerable Union right, while he himself struck McClellan's center. Jackson was uncharacteristically late. Convinced that he was outnumbered, however, McClellan withdrew across the Chickahominy to the protection of the Union gunboats on the James. On 1 July he sent Goldsborough an urgent appeal: "I would most earnestly request that every gunboat or other armed vessel suitable for action in the James River be sent at once to this vicinity, and placed under the orders of Cdr. Rodgers, for the purpose of covering the camps and communications of this army."[33]

Goldsborough quickly responded, and Rodgers positioned his ships so as to provide maximum gunfire support ashore. The *Monitor* guarded City Point, and the *Delaware* and *Satellite* were in the Chickahominy. The *Galena*, *Aroostook*, and *Mahaska* remained near Turkey Creek to protect the Union flank.[34]

In the 1 July Battle of Malvern Hill, the withdrawing Army of the Potomac withstood Lee's determined attacks. The heavy guns of the gunboats, including the much-maligned *Galena*, perhaps staved off Union disaster. On 2 July Union forces established a new position at Harrison's Landing, across the river from City Point. McClellan came aboard the *Galena* to help pick out the position.

On 2 July the Confederates disengaged, and the Peninsula Campaign came to a close. Although Confederate losses were heavier than his own,

McClellan had fumbled away victory. A little more energy on his part and the war might have been ended in 1862 or been drastically shortened. The U.S. Navy could be proud of its role in the campaign. Not only had it safeguarded the Union supply line, but its gunboats had provided effective support to the troops ashore.

Welles was unhappy with Goldsborough, however, believing he was not sufficiently aggressive. On 6 July Welles created the James River Flotilla, an independent command under Commo. Charles Wilkes, who was tapped for the position by Lincoln and Seward. Welles also transferred a number of gunboats from Goldsborough's North Atlantic Blockading Squadron to Wilkes, with the James River Flotilla to provide protection to McClellan's troops on the peninsula until the last of the men were evacuated to northern Virginia in August. Welles and Rodgers, Wilkes's predecessor on the James, both had a poor opinion of Wilkes. Rodgers commented, "My own opinion is that he is but little removed from an absolute fool." Wilkes, who seems to have suffered from a persecution complex, managed to live down to this judgment of him. Within a few weeks, the James River Flotilla was disbanded, the result of its commander's demonstrated incompetence and the end of the land campaign.[35]

The appointment of Wilkes and the loss by transfer of many of his own ships to him were, however, the final straws for Goldsborough. On 15 July, stung by criticism from Welles and the press, he asked to be relieved of his command. Welles acceded to Goldsborough's request a week later. In gratitude for his services, Congress voted him promoted to permanent rear admiral.[36]

The *Monitor*, meanwhile, underwent a refit and was then ordered to Charleston. The ironclad was off Cape Hatteras, North Carolina, headed south and under tow by the side-wheeler *Rhode Island* when a violent storm broke the afternoon of 31 December. For three hours the crew struggled to save their ship, but the pumps were insufficient for the rush of water produced by thirty-foot waves, and the *Monitor* went down. Launches from the *Rhode Island* brought off most of the crew, but fourteen sailors were lost, including several who refused to leave the turret. Lying upside down, the wreck was first located in 1973 and is now a protected National Historic Site. Parts of the ship, including its revolutionary turret, propeller, and guns, have been recovered and are currently undergoing conservation at the Mariners' Museum in Newport News, Virginia.[37]

Following the failure of the Peninsula Campaign, Lincoln ordered McClellan to bring his forces back north in favor of a direct push south from Washington toward Richmond. Before the North could concentrate its forces, however, the Confederates attacked and defeated Union forces in the Second Battle of Manassas (Bull Run, 29–30 August). Lee invaded the North but was halted at Sharpsburg (Antietam Creek) on 17 September. The Army of the Potomac then again took the offensive but was rebuffed in Lee's most lopsided victory, the 13 December Battle of Fredericksburg. The next spring, Lee won his most brilliant victory in the 2–4 May 1863 Battle of Chancellorsville. Lee then invaded the North a second time, only to be stopped by Union forces under Maj. Gen. George Gordon Meade at Gettysburg (2–4 July), the high-water mark of the Confederacy. Meanwhile, the Union naval blockade continued and Union troops took the offensive in securing the lower Mississippi.

CHAPTER SEVEN

Union Operations on the Lower Mississippi

—~~~—

The Capture of New Orleans

UNION OPERATIONS IN THE GULF

While the *Monitor* and *Virginia* dueled in the east and great battles took place on land in the Eastern Theater, Union forces were steadily expanding their control over the great western rivers, most notably the Mississippi. By early June 1862, the northern Union flotilla had secured the upper Mississippi. With the defeat of the Confederate River Defense Fleet at Memphis, it had opened the great river all the way to Vicksburg. At the same time, Union forces were working their way north from the river's mouth.

The Union navy had first set the blockade of New Orleans and the Mississippi mouth on 26 May 1861, with arrival there of the steam sloop *Brooklyn.* The blockade was rendered more difficult because about one hundred miles south of New Orleans and fifteen miles from the gulf at the so-called Head of the Passes, the river split into three major branches (passes) for its final movement to the sea. The Mississippi delta itself extended over some thirty miles. Although the arrival of additional Union ships largely ended Confederate privateering, the blockade was by no means complete.

In June 1861, Union ships in the Gulf of Mexico were organized into the Gulf Coast Blockading Squadron under Flag Officer William Mervine, a veteran of fifty-two years' service who had joined the navy as a midshipman in

1809! With only fifteen ships to cover a vast area, Mervine's problems were compounded by the loss of the Pensacola Navy Yard at the beginning of the war, leaving Key West as the only base open to him on the Gulf.

Securing a facility farther west was essential, especially in any operation against New Orleans. The Blockade Board recommended Ship Island. Located some twelve miles south of Biloxi in Mississippi Sound and midway between Mobile Bay and New Orleans, it would be ideal for operations against the entire eastern Gulf coast.

Although Confederate forces initially occupied Ship Island and began to fortify it, Union naval superiority rendered that infeasible, and on 16 September the garrison set fire to its barracks, sabotaged the lighthouse, and abandoned the island. The next day, the U.S. Navy screw steamer *Massachusetts* arrived and offloaded troops who took possession. In early December some two thousand men under Brig. Gen. John W. Phelps reinforced the garrison already in place.[1]

Meanwhile, Mervine's perceived lack of action led Welles to relieve him from his command. On 6 September Welles named Capt. William McKean to command, but the next month the Gulf Squadron was split into an East Gulf Coast Blockading Squadron and a West Gulf Coast Blockading Squadron. McKean retained command of the eastern squadron with responsibility from Key West to Pensacola. Capt. David G. Farragut received command of the western squadron that covered the coast from Pensacola to the Rio Grande. Because it had responsibility for blockading New Orleans, Mobile, and Galveston, the western squadron was by far the more important of the two.

As Union forces strengthened the blockade, the Confederates were not quiescent. In June 1861 Capt. Raphael Semmes embarrassed the blockaders by escaping into the Gulf with the *Sumter*, the first Confederate commerce raider. Because it was impossible with the few ships they had available for the Union blockaders to secure all Mississippi exits, it made sense to try to control the Head of the Passes. If the Union ships could establish control here, they could intercept any ship going up or down the river, cutting off New Orleans from blockade runners.

In early October, a Union squadron of four ships took up position at the Head of the Passes. Capt. John Pope had the screw sloop *Richmond* (the flagship), the side-wheeler gunboat *Water Witch*, and the sailing sloops *Preble* and *Vincennes*. The coal and storeship *Nightingale* provided logistics support.

To oppose the Union ships, the commander of Confederate ships on the lower Mississippi Commo. George N. Hollins at New Orleans had available a rag-tag little force of the flagship *McRae* (a former Mexican steamer seized by the U.S. Navy in 1860 as a pirate ship and planned for conversion into a commerce raider, mounting eight guns) and five converted tugs, mounting in all seven additional guns. These were no match for the more than forty guns aboard the Union ships at the Head of the Passes, and Hollins adopted harassing tactics. On 9 October the Confederate side-wheeler *Ivy* (two guns) passed down the river and lobbed some shot and shell toward the Union ships before retiring. Although neither side sustained any damage, a worried Pope reported to McKean, "We are entirely at the mercy of the enemy. We are liable to be driven from here at any moment, and, situated as we are, our position is untenable."[2]

Three days later, Pope's fears were realized when the Confederates struck in force with the ironclad steam ram *Manassas*. Built in 1855 as the icebreaker *Enoch Train*, from 1859 it had been a tugboat at New Orleans. On the outbreak of the war, John A. Stevenson, secretary of the New Orleans Pilots Benevolent Association, raised $100,000 to convert it into a privateer ironclad ram. Stevenson had selected the ship because of its powerful bow.

Working in some secrecy, Stevenson removed the *Enoch Train*'s masts and superstructure and replaced the upper works with a convex deck of 12-inch-thick oak, covered by 1.5 inches of iron plate. The bow was filled in solid with timber, producing a 20-foot-long ram. Powered by two antiquated engines, the *Manassas* mounted only one gun, a 64-pounder smoothbore that fired forward through a small bow gunport. To train the gun, the entire ship had to be turned. This first-ever Confederate ironclad was only 387 tons and 134 feet long. In appearance, apart from a large central smokestack, the ram resembled a cigar floating on the water.[3]

Because the *Manassas* was the most powerful warship available, Hollins was loath to see it act as a privateer. On 11 October, acting on his orders, Lt. Alexander Warley took possession of the ram, sending Stevenson and his crew ashore and replacing them with men from the squadron. Two months later, the Confederate government officially purchased the *Manassas*, but Hollins had no intention of waiting for this action.

That very night of 11 October was ideal, the moon having set, and Hollins ordered Warley to take the *Manassas* down the river. Following it were two tugs pulling three fire rafts and the armed steamers *Ivy, McRae,*

Tuscarora, Calhoun, and *Jackson.* Hollins planned for the *Manassas* to ram the nearest Federal ship; with only one gun and but twelve shells for it, there was hardly any other option. After this, the fire rafts were to be lit and set adrift in the river, while the Confederate gunboats took advantage of the confusion to close with and shell the Federal ships.

Early on 12 October the Confederates sighted the Union ships in the Passes. The crew of the *Manassas* then charged the ram's furnaces with tar, tallow, and sulphur to build up maximum pressure as rapidly as possible. Leaving the remainder of the squadron behind, Warley headed for the *Richmond,* faintly visible because with dimmed lights it was taking on coal from the schooner *Joseph H. Toone* moored alongside. Despite the earlier Confederate attack and Pope's expressed concern about the vulnerability of his ships, he had not taken the precaution of posting a picket boat upstream that might have sounded the alarm. At 3:45 AM on 12 October, the deck watch on the *Richmond* discovered the *Manassas* bearing down on the ship. By the time the ship's crew was alerted, the ram had struck the *Richmond* hard on its port side. The blow stoved in three planks and opened a small hole below the waterline, although the ship's pumps were able to offset the resulting flow of water.

As the ram then passed abreast of the *Richmond,* the latter loosed its entire port battery, but the shot and shell bounced off the *Manassas's* iron plating. The collision, however, had accomplished what Union shot and shell could not, for the ironclad's iron prow had been wrenched off, its smokestack had collapsed over a ventilator, and one of its two engines was dislodged and not working. The *Manassas* drifted toward the shore. Later it was barely able to steam back upriver against the current. The *Manassas* was not repaired and ready to return to service until the end of January 1862.

During the attack, the *Richmond* had raised a red danger signal, and the ships of the squadron soon got under way toward the sea. At this point the Confederates loosed their fire rafts, but these soon grounded on a shoal. Although the Federal ships, along with a prize (the *Frolic* that had been taken earlier), were all able to escape, in the process of trying to gain the sea both the *Richmond* and the *Vincennes* grounded on the bar. Mistaking Pope's signal to "get under way" for "abandon ship," Cdr. Robert Handy of the *Vincennes* took off his crew and ordered a slow match lit to its magazine. Fortunately for the Union side the match failed, and, after an appropriate wait, a chastened Handy and his crew returned to their ship.

Although the Confederate gunboats shelled the grounded Union ships, they did not take advantage of the temporarily abandoned *Vincennes*, and the larger, longer-range guns of the Union squadron soon drove the gunboats back upriver. Finally, both Union ships were gotten free, although not before the crew of the *Richmond* had jettisoned fourteen of its eighteen guns and much shot. Meanwhile, the Confederates took the *Joseph H. Toone* with its fifteen tons of coal.[4]

The action, trumpeted throughout the South as "Pope's Run," was a considerable embarrassment to the Federal Navy, and Pope and Handy were both removed from their commands. Writing after the war, Admiral Porter called it "the most ridiculous affair that ever took place in the American Navy. There is no instance during the war like it."[5]

"Pope's Run" hardly represented a shift in the naval balance. Although the Federals did not return to the Head of the Passes for several months, they continued to control the river's mouth, and the effectiveness of the Union blockade steadily increased with the arrival of additional ships.

Operations in the eastern Gulf, meanwhile, were largely confined to Union efforts to prevent ship traffic between ports along the western Florida coast and Bermuda, Cuba, and Nassau. During 22–23 November, however, McKean utilized the screw frigate *Niagara* (flag) and screw sloop *Richmond*, supported by batteries at Fort Pickens, to bombard Confederate Fort McRae and the Pensacola Navy Yard. The Union shelling largely reduced McRae but accomplished little else. Union casualties came to one dead and seven wounded; the Confederates suffered twenty-one wounded, one mortally.[6]

The only other action of note in the eastern Gulf occurred in early May 1862. Prompted by their defeat in the western Confederacy at Forts Henry and Donelson in February, Southern authorities decided to give up western Florida and reinforce Tennessee. Beginning in early March, they removed heavy guns and equipment from the Pensacola area without managing to alert the Federals across the bay on Santa Rosa Island. Believing that Federal naval units were bound for Pensacola, on 9 May the Confederates torched Fort McRae and the Pensacola Navy Yard, as well as sawmills and planning mills, stocks of cotton, and a number of boats. The Confederates then withdrew. Union forces, finally aware of what was transpiring, occupied Pensacola the next day. Rebuilt, the yard there became a major depot for the West Gulf Coast Blockading Squadron.

On 4 November the able Capt. Theodorus Bailey replaced the ailing McKean in command of the East Gulf Coast Blockading Squadron. Under Bailey's leadership, the squadron aggressively patrolled the Florida coast. Over the next year, of fifty-two ships attempting to run the blockade, only seven made it. The blockaders captured nearly a hundred ships during a six-month span. Bailey's ships also attacked ships at dockside taking on or offloading cargo, and they raided up bays and rivers, destroying Confederate salt works. Necessary in the curing and preservation of meats, salt was a critical commodity for the Confederacy, and many of these works were situated in western Florida.[7]

THE CAPTURE OF NEW ORLEANS

The incident involving Pope's ships in the Mississippi heightened interest in Washington for an expedition against New Orleans, the capture of which was in any case a key element of the Anaconda Plan. New Orleans was the Confederacy's most important seaport and its largest and wealthiest city. Beyond denying to the South this outlet for the shipment of cotton, securing the entire Mississippi would open the river to oceanic shipping for goods from the northwest, as well as split off the trans-Mississippi West from the remainder of the Confederacy.

Union Assistant Secretary of the Navy Fox was the strongest proponent of an assault on the Crescent City. He believed that Union victories at Port Hudson and Hatteras Inlet had proved that steam warships could successfully engage and defeat shore forts, and that Union ships could defeat Confederate Forts Jackson and St. Philip guarding the southern approach to New Orleans. Cdr. David D. Porter, who had recently returned from duty near the mouth of the Mississippi in the steam frigate *Powhatan*, convinced Fox and Welles that bombardment of the forts by a flotilla of mortar boats would be essential to success of the plan. He pledged that both forts would be rendered ineffective, if not destroyed, by shelling from 13-inch mortars within forty-eight hours.

President Lincoln gave his endorsement, but McClellan was opposed—that is until he learned that it would be essentially a navy operation with only about ten thousand troops required to garrison the city and its forts once the navy had forced its surrender. In December Welles called Captain Farragut to Washington and offered him command of the expedition, which Farragut immediately accepted. Porter received command of the mortar flotilla. Farragut took as his flagship the steam sloop *Hartford* at Philadelphia and arrived at Ship Island on 20 February 1862. In a letter to Farragut, Welles called this "the most important operation of the war. . . . If successful, you open the way to the sea for the Great West, never to be closed. The rebellion will be riven in the center."[8]

An outstanding naval officer and staunch Unionist, David Farragut was a veteran of fifty-one years of naval service. Sponsored as a midshipman by his guardian, Commo. David Porter, Farragut was the stepbrother of Cdr. David D. Porter and Cdr. William D. Porter. Joining the navy at age nine in 1810, Farragut served with his guardian on the *Essex* during the War of 1812 and participated in its sanguinary 1814 action with the HMS *Phoebe* and *Cherub*. In the years that followed, Farragut compiled an exemplary record. A resident of Norfolk when Virginia seceded from the Union, Farragut denounced the secession and abandoned his home and possessions to move north. There were those in the navy who doubted his commitment to the Union cause, but Welles was not among them.[9]

An energetic, "hands-on" commander who liked to be seen with and personally instruct his men, Farragut was both a careful planner and a bold leader. He spent nearly a month preparing for the expedition. Farragut ultimately commanded seventeen ships mounting 192 guns. The most powerful of these were eight steam sloops and corvettes: the *Brooklyn* (26 guns), *Hartford* (28 guns), *Iroquois* (11 guns), *Mississippi* (22 guns), *Oneida* (10 guns), *Pensacola* (25 guns), *Richmond* (22 guns), and *Varuna* (11 guns). These mounted in all 154 guns. There were also nine gunboats: the *Cayuga* (4 guns), *Itasca* (4 guns), *Katahdin* (4 guns), *Kennebec* (4 guns), *Kineo* (4 guns), *Pinola* (5 guns), *Sciota* (5 guns), *Winona* (4 guns), and *Wissahickon* (4 guns). Farragut also had Porter's squadron of twenty mortar schooners. Maj. Gen. Benjamin F. Butler commanded the thirteen thousand soldiers who would accompany the expedition.

On 16 April, following careful planning and preparations, Farragut moved his ships from the Gulf into the Mississippi River estuary, just below and out of range of the river forts. Once the ships had passed the forts, Butler's troops were to join the squadron by means of a bayou about five miles upriver. Welles hoped that Foote and Union naval forces on the upper Mississippi would steam south and join Farragut at New Orleans. If that proved impossible, Farragut was to proceed north as far as possible.

Vice Adm. David G. Farragut. U.S. NAVAL INSTITUTE PHOTO ARCHIVE

Confederate leaders in Richmond, including those in both the navy and army departments, bore considerable responsibility for subsequent events. Richmond believed the chief threat was from the north and thus sent the scant resources available there. This same attitude contributed to the failure to complete the ironclads *Louisiana* and *Mississippi* that were under construction at Jefferson City, just north of New Orleans.

Maj. Gen. Mansfield Lovell had charge of the New Orleans defenses. Initially commanding six thousand men, he had expressed confidence that he could hold the city against any land attack. By early April, however, more than half of his men and much equipment had been siphoned off from New Orleans to Corinth, Mississippi, in order to challenge Grant's forces at Pittsburg Landing. Another major problem lay in a divided command structure that included multiple army and navy commanders. Thus, Brig. Gen. Johnson Kelly Duncan, not Lovell, commanded Forts St. Philip and Jackson. The naval command was even more fractious.[10]

Despite the paucity of Confederate manpower, it would not be easy for Union forces to ascend the Mississippi. The Union ships would first have to pass the two Confederate forts. Fort Jackson was a star-shaped works of stone and mortar mounting seventy-four guns and situated some hundred yards from the levee on the right or west bank of the river. Fort St. Philip, about a half mile upstream on the opposite bank, was of brick and stone covered with sod and mounted fifty-two guns. High water in the river had flooded portions of both works, but Confederate engineers worked around the clock to control the water and strengthen the forts against attack. Another liability was that the eleven hundred men in the forts were inexperienced and largely untrained. This played a role in the battle to come, especially in conditions of poor visibility.

On the river itself, the Confederates counted fourteen warships, most of which were small and mounted a total of only forty guns. There was no unity of command, and the ships were in three major divisions. Capt. John A. Stephenson commanded the Confederate River Defense Fleet of six small converted river tugs, mounting a total of seven guns and fitted with iron-reinforced prows for ramming. These were the *Defense, General Breckinridge, General Lovell, Resolute, Stonewall Jackson,* and *Warrior.* Stephenson was a Confederate Army officer who reputedly disliked naval officers and refused to obey orders of the senior Confederate naval officer in the lower Mississippi, Cdr. John K. Mitchell.

The Louisiana State Navy provided two side-wheeler gunboats, the *Governor Moore* and *General Quitman*, mounting two guns each, and the Confederate Navy contributed six warships under Mitchell: the gunboats *McRae* (eight guns) and *Jackson* (two guns) and the launches *No. 3* (one gun) and *No. 6* (one gun). The other two ships were the ironclads *Manassas* and *Louisiana*, but only the ram *Manassas*, with a single gun, was operational at the time of the Union assault.

The *Louisiana* posed the only real naval threat to the Union squadron, and many in the Crescent City regarded it as the strongest defense for the city, after the forts. The 1,400-ton *Louisiana* was an immense casemated warship, 264 feet by 62 feet in size. Builder C. C. Murray designed a unique propulsion system of both paddle wheels and propellers. In addition to two 4-foot propellers, the *Louisiana* had two paddle wheels in a well on the centerline, one behind the other, as well as twin rudders.

The *Louisiana* was to be powered by four large steam engines and protected by 4 inches of iron plate. Unfortunately for the South, the ironclad was not yet ready when Union forces began their attack. Nonetheless, Mitchell had it towed downriver, mechanics still working on it. The ship was then moored to the shore north of Fort St. Philip as a floating fort. Pierced for twenty-two guns, during the battle the *Louisiana* mounted sixteen: two 7-inch and seven 42-pounder rifles and three IX-inch and four 8-inch smoothbores. Soldiers drawn from the Crescent Artillery worked the guns.

Stephenson also had ordered fire rafts prepared so that they might be set loose in the current against any Union ships advancing upriver. Although the river was too swift and deep for obstructions, Lovell strongly advocated, and the Confederates built, a river barrier. It took the form of two long chains, formed of those from ships idled at New Orleans. Seven anchored hulks supported the chains, which passed across the river, over the forward part and amidships of the hulks, from abreast of Fort Jackson to the opposite shore.

Assembling off Pass a l'Outre, by mid-March all the heavier Union ships had been gotten over the bar with assistance from Porter's steamers. A month later all the other ships had assembled at Ship Island, along with Butler's troops. On 15 April Farragut gave the order for the operation to begin. On the evening of 18 April Porter's twenty mortar boats, towed into position by seven steamers and moored along the riverbank some three thousand yards from Fort Jackson where they were protected by a bend of the river and woods, opened a bombardment. Each boat mounted one 13-inch mortar. Although these powerful weapons had been employed against Island No. 10 and Fort Pillow without notable success, Porter was convinced they would be successful here.

The mortars fired at the rate of about 1 shell every ten minutes. At night, in order to provide some rest to the crews, they fired at a rate of 1 shell every half hour. For six days and nights the mortars fired 16,800 shells, almost all of them at the fort and without notable result. The problem seems to have been the fuzing, the shells either burst in air or buried themselves in the soft earth before exploding without major effect. The Confederates responded by sending fire rafts down the river at night, but Union boat crews grappled these and towed them off without damage. Although the Union shells did dismount some of the guns in Fort Jackson, most of the Confederate crews bravely kept to their positions and were able to remount the guns. Indeed, Confederate counterbattery fire on 19 April sank the mortar schooner *Maria J. Carlton*, killing and wounding some Union sailors. Nonetheless, Porter claimed that the first days' fire "was the most effective of any during the bombardment, and had the fleet been ready to move at once, the passage could have been effected without serious difficulty."[11]

Although the Union bombardment accomplished little physical damage, there can be no doubt that it did affect the Confederate gunners, exhausting them physically and emotionally. What role that may have had in ensuing events is hard to measure. The shelling and the delay that it brought in the movement upriver must also have been a source of anxiety and sleeplessness for the Union crews, especially those who had never before experienced combat.

Farragut's clerk, Bradley Osbon, who had at one point commanded a ship in the Argentine Navy, reported that Farragut ordered him to visit one ship where morale appeared to be low, saying: "I hear they are as blue as indigo in that wardroom over there. . . . Tell them some stories of the fights you've been in and come out of alive. It will stir their blood and do them good."[12]

Farragut knew, however, that too much delay would have a negative effect, and on the night of 20 April, while Porter's mortars kept up a steady fire so as to distract the gun crews in the Confederate forts, he sent the screw gunboats *Itasca* and *Pinola* against the river obstructions. Under heavy but inaccurate Confederate fire, the Union crews worked to open a gap through which the squadron might pass. Lt. Pierce Crosby of the *Pinola* attempted to blow up one of the hulks with an electronically detonated torpedo (mine), but the wire broke when the gunboat backed off. Lt. Charles Caldwell then brought the *Itasca* alongside another of the hulks, where some of the crewmen managed to break the chains with a chisel, opening a passage that Farragut thought would be sufficient for his ships to pass through. Also on 20 April, Farragut issued orders to his captains outlining the operation and specifying the order by which the ships would proceed upriver.[13]

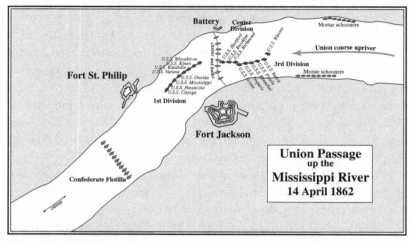

Union Passage Up the Mississippi River

While they waited for the mortars to do their work, the Union crews prepared their ships. The men landed anything that might be a potential fire hazard or inhibit smooth operations, including extra spars, rigging, boats, and all but a few sails. They also strung heavy iron cable chains on the outsides of the ships to provide additional protection to the most vulnerable areas housing the engines and steam boilers. These acted as a kind of chain-mail armor. The men also packed around the boilers bags of ashes, extra clothing, sand, and anything else readily available. Clearly, protecting the boilers was the major concern. As had been so terribly demonstrated in the case of the *Mound City*, clouds of steam from a punctured boiler could inflict heavy personnel casualties. Also, such an event could immobilize the ship, perhaps jeopardizing the entire operation.

The crews also worked to distribute weight so that their ships would draw more water forward than aft. This was so that if a ship grounded while heading upstream, the bow would strike bottom first and the ship would not be turned around by the swift current. The crews also whitewashed their ships' decks so that the gunners' tools would stand out more clearly at night; at the same time they gave the hulls a coating of oil and mud to render them more difficult to distinguish from the shore.[14]

On 22 April Farragut met aboard the *Hartford* with his subordinate commanders to discuss his plans in detail. The ships were to proceed one at a time through the obstructions. Porter's mortars would provide covering fire to occupy the Confederate gun crews and hopefully drive them from their guns. Once the ships had passed the forts, Butler's troops would be put ashore at Quarantine from the Gulf side through that bayou, allowing the Union land and naval forces to move in tandem to New Orleans. Farragut reserved the option of reducing the forts but instructed his captains that, unless otherwise ordered, they were to steam past the forts.

The prevailing view among the captains, freely stated during the meeting, was that the risk was such that any attempt should be delayed until the mortars had reduced the forts. Farragut answered that Porter himself favored an immediate attempt and thought that it would be successful. In any case, he said, Porter would soon run short of shells and his men were exhausted from the bombardment that had already extended over six days and seven nights. Farragut informed the captains that, because of these considerations, he had decided on an attempt that very night.

Gun deck of U.S. Navy screw sloop Hartford *showing IX-inch Dahlgrens in broadside mounts.* Naval Historical Center (HC 53678)

The attack was delayed for twenty-four hours, however, on pleas by two of the captains. On 23 April Farragut met with Porter aboard the *Harriet Lane* and expressed his displeasure with the delay when he had already fixed the time for the operation. Porter again expressed confidence that the attempt would meet success.

The attack was then fixed for early on 24 April. Osbon recalled the tension in the squadron the night before:

> At the usual hour the crews turned in, but I think there was little sleep. The men were cheerful and determined, but wakeful. Most of them had been green hands when we started, and scarcely one of them had been under fire. With a night attack just ahead it was natural that they should be anxious.[15]

Soon after midnight on 24 April, the crews were awakened; at 1:55 AM, Farragut ordered Osbon to hoist two red lanterns in the *Hartford* as the signal to get under way. The ships then moved upriver in two divisions to approach the opening in the obstructions made earlier. Capt. Theodorus Bailey commanded the first division of the *Cayuga, Pensacola, Mississippi, Oneida, Varuna, Katahdin, Kineo,* and *Wissahickon.* The center (second) division, under Farragut, consisted of the *Hartford, Brooklyn,* and *Richmond.* The third division, commanded by Capt. Henry H. Bell, included the *Sciota, Iroquois, Kennebec, Pinola, Itasca,* and *Winona.*

The *Cayuga* was the first ship through the water barrier, at about 3:30 AM. The Confederates did not discover the *Cayuga* until about ten minutes later, when it was well under the forts. Understandably, General Duncan at Fort Jackson subsequently complained that Mitchell had not sent any fire rafts to light the river at night, nor had he stationed any vessel below the forts to warn of the Union approach. The different naval commands and lack of cooperation between land and naval commanders indeed proved costly for the defenders.

As soon as they spotted the *Cayuga*, gunners at both Confederate forts opened up almost simultaneously, with the Union ships in position to do so immediately replying. Soon the river surface was filled with clouds of thick smoke from the black powder discharges of the guns. This smoke obscured vision from both the ships and the shore, but on balance this favored the ships. Porter, meanwhile, had brought forward the five steamers assigned to

Ships of the West Gulf Coast Blockading Squadron running the Confederate forts on the lower Mississippi, 24 April 1862. NAVAL HISTORICAL CENTER (76369 KN)

his mortar schooners, and these opened up an enfilading fire at some two hundred yards from Fort Jackson, pouring into it grape, canister, and shrapnel shell "while the mortars threw in their bombs with great fury." This fire did drive many of the Confederate gun crews from their guns and reduced the effectiveness of those who remained.[16]

The *Pensacola*, the second Union ship through the obstacles, was slow to get under way, and this meant that for some time the *Cayuga* faced the full fury of the Confederate fire alone. Lt. George H. Perkins, piloting the *Cayuga*, had the presence of mind to note that the Confederate guns had been laid so as to concentrate fire on the middle of the river and therefore took his ship closer to the walls of Fort St. Philip. Although the ship's masts and rigging were shot up, the hull largely escaped damage.

The *Pensacola*'s captain, Henry W. Morris, apparently interpreted Farragut's orders to mean that he was to engage the forts. Halting his ship in the middle of the obstructions, he let loose a broadside against Fort St. Philip, driving the gun crews on shore to safety. On clearing the obstructions, he ordered a second broadside against the fort. But stopping dead in the water made the *Pensacola* an ideal target. It took nine shot in the hull, and its rigging and masts were also much cut up. The *Pensacola* also suffered four killed and thirty-three wounded, more than on any other Union ship in the operation that day. Executive Officer Lt. Francis Asbury Roe wrote in his diary, "The guns' crews, right under me, were decimated. The groans, shrieks, and wails of the dying and wounded were so horrible that I shudder now at the recollection of it."[17]

The leading division continued upriver, engaging targets as they presented themselves. The remaining Union ships followed, firing grape and canister as well as round shot. The shore batteries had difficulty finding the range, and damage and casualties aboard these ships were slight.

About 4 AM the Confederate Navy warships above the forts joined the battle. The most powerful, the *McRae*, lay anchored along the shore three hundred yards above Fort St. Philip when its lookouts spotted the *Cayuga*. Lt. Thomas B. Huger, captain of the *McRae*, ordered the cables slipped and fire opened. The *McRae* mounted eight guns (one IX-inch Dahlgren on a pivot mount, six 32-pounders in broadsides, and a 6-pounder rifled gun) and opened up with its port battery and pivot gun, but the latter burst on its tenth round. The *Cayuga* continued upriver, passing the McRae. Two other Union ships, the *Varuna* and *Oneida*, then appeared out of the smoke and steamed past the *McRae* without firing on it, probably taking it for a Union gunboat. Huger ordered his ship sheered first to port and then to starboard, delivering two broadsides.

The *Varuna* and *Oneida* sheered to starboard and returned fire. Each of these ships mounted two XI-inch Dahlgrens in pivot, and these guns soon told. The explosion of one Union shell started a fire in the *McRae*'s sail room, and only desperate efforts by the crew kept the blaze from reaching the magazine.

Although most of the remaining lightly armed Confederate warships fled upriver on the approach of the Union ships, this was not the case with the *Manassas*. Its captain, Lt. Alexander Warley, was determined to attack the Union ships, even alone. Warley understood that the only Confederate chance for victory lay in an immediate combined assault by the gunboats and fire rafts to immobilize the Union ships long enough for the heavy guns in the forts to destroy them.

The *Manassas*, now armed with a single 32-pounder, lay moored to the left bank of the river above Fort St. Philip, when at about 3 AM gun flashes in the vicinity of the obstacles indicated action in progress. Warley immediately ordered his ship to get under way downriver. A first attempt to ram had to be aborted when the Confederate gunboat *Resolute* steamed into the *Manassas*'s path. Warley then made a second attempt, against the *Pensacola*. Skillful maneuvering by the Union pilot avoided a collision, and the *Pensacola* let loose with a broadside from its IX-inch Dahlgrens as the *Manassas* passed. Damaged in the exchange, the Confederate ram nonetheless continued on.

Warley then spotted the side-wheeler *Mississippi*. Lt. George Dewey turned that ship toward the onrushing *Manassas*. Dewey recalled that he was confident "that our superior tonnage must sink her if we struck her fairly."[18]

The ram was more agile than the Union paddle-wheeler, however. It avoided the Union parry while managing to strike the *Mississippi* a glancing blow on its port side. When the Union ship righted, Dewey could see a large hole in his ship. He immediately called out to the crew to man the pumps, but the ship was not leaking. Dewey recalled the incident:

> The impact of the ram, which would have sunk any other ship in the fleet, had taken out a section of solid timber seven feet long, four feet broad, and four inches deep. About fifty copper bolts had been cut as clean as if they were hair under a razor's edge. I remember seeing their bright, gleaming ends when I looked down from the hurricane deck in my first glimpse of that hole in our side.[19]

The Confederate forts and Union ships were trading heavy fire. As the ships cleared the forts they came under fire from the Confederate ironclad *Louisiana* along the riverbank. Its gunports were small and did not allow a wide arc of fire, so the gun crews scored few hits.

Proceeding north, the leading *Cayuga* overtook some of the fleeing Confederate warships and fired into them. Three of the Confederate gunboats struck their colors and ran ashore. The *Varuna* and *Oneida* soon came up, but in the confusion sailors in the *Varuna* mistook the *Cayuga* for an enemy ship and fired a broadside into it.

Impatient with the *Pensacola*'s slow progress, meanwhile, Farragut ordered the *Hartford* to pass it and then climbed into the mizzen rigging so as to secure a better view over the smoke. Osbon recalled the scene:

> Shot, shell, grape, and canister filled the air with deadly missiles. It was like the breaking up of the universe, with the moon and all the

stars bursting in our midst. As for seeing what the other vessels were doing, or what was going on about us, that was impossible. In that blinding smoke, and night, with everything flying in all directions, the only thing we could see was the flash of guns in our faces and the havoc on our own ship. Ropes were swinging, splinters were flying. . . . At first the enemy's aim had been high, but now they lowered it until their fire began to cut us through.[20]

As the *Hartford* proceeded upriver, Farragut saw a fire raft blazing off the port bow, pushed forward by the unarmed Confederate tug *Moser*. Farragut ordered his own ship to turn to starboard, but it was too close to the shore and its bow immediately grounded hard in a mud bank, allowing Capt. Horace Sherman of the *Moser* to position the raft against the *Hartford*'s port side. The blaze soon ignited the paint on the side of the Union ship, which then caught the rigging. With his ship on fire and immobilized, Farragut thought it was doomed. Fortunately, the gunners at Fort St. Philip were unable to fire into the now stationary target because the fleet's fire had dismounted one of the fort's largest guns and another could not be brought to bear.

Farragut came down out of the rigging to the deck where he exhorted the *Hartford*'s crew to fight the fire. Gunfire from the flagship, meanwhile, sent the *Moser* to the bottom. As Capt. Richard Wainwright directed the firefighting, Osbon brought up three shells, unscrewed their fuses, and dropped them over the gunwale of the *Hartford* into the fire raft. The resulting explosions tore holes in the raft and sank it, extinguishing the flames. With the raft gone, the *Hartford*'s crew was able to put out the fires. The men cheered wildly as their ship backed free of the mud bank and resumed course upriver.

In the confusion and smoke, accidents occurred. The gunboat *Kineo* collided with the sloop *Brooklyn*; despite sustaining serious damage, the *Kineo* was able to continue on past the forts. The *Brooklyn*, meanwhile, plowed into one of the Confederate hulks, and then suddenly ground to a halt just north of the obstructions, its anchor caught in the hulk and hawser taunt. The river current then turned the sloop broadside to Fort St. Philip. With the gunners ashore having found the range and the *Brooklyn* taking hits, a crewman managed to cut the cable and free the sloop.

Capt. Thomas T. Craven ordered the *Brooklyn* to pass close to Fort St. Philip, the sloop firing three broadsides into the Confederate works as it steamed past. The *Brooklyn* then passed the Louisiana at very close quarters. In the exchange of fire, a 9-inch Confederate shell struck the Union ship just above the waterline but failed to explode. Later the *Brooklyn*'s crew discovered that the Confederate gunners had failed to remove the lead patch from the fuse.

Smoke from the firing was now so thick that it was virtually impossible to see to take bearings. Craven merely conned his ship in the direction of the noise and flashes of light ahead. But the tide carried the sloop over on the lee shore, perfectly positioned for the guns of Fort Jackson. As the sloop touched bottom, Craven saw the *Manassas* emerge from the smoke.

Warley had previously tried to ram the *Hartford*, without success. The *Manassas* had taken a number of Union shell hits and its smokestack was riddled and speed sharply reduced. Warley decided to take the ironclad downriver to attack Porter's now unprotected mortar boats. But when the Confederate forts mistakenly opened up with their heavy guns on the ram, Warley thought better of the idea and resolved to return upriver. At that point he spotted the *Brooklyn* lying athwart the river and headed for Fort Jackson. Warley ordered resin thrown into the *Manassas*'s furnaces in order to produce maximum speed and maneuvered the ram so as to pin the *Brooklyn* against the riverbank.[21]

Seamen aboard the *Brooklyn* spotted the ram's approach and gave the alarm. Craven ordered the sloop's helm turned, but this could only lessen, not avoid, the impact. Only moments before the collision, a shot from the *Manassas* crashed into the *Brooklyn* but was stopped by sandbags piled around the steam drum.

The *Manassas* struck the *Brooklyn* at a slight angle, crushing three planks and driving in the chain that had been strung into the ship's side. Craven was certain his ship would go down, but the chain and a full coal bunker helped lessen the impact. Meanwhile, the *Manassas* disengaged and resumed its progress upriver.

The tail of Farragut's force, Porter's mortar flotilla, was also under way. This division included the sailing sloop *Portsmouth*, towed by tugs. When his vessels came under fire as they approached Fort Jackson, Porter ordered the mortar boats to stop and open fire. This was at about 4:20 AM. The mortars fired for about a half hour, sufficient time it was thought for the remainder of the Union squadron to have cleared the forts. When Porter signaled a halt in fire, some of the Union ships were still engaging the forts, however.

In the thick smoke the *Wissahickon*, the last ship in the first division, grounded. As the sun rose, Lt. Albert N. Smith, the *Wissahickon*'s captain, discovered he was near three third-division ships, the *Iroquois*, *Sciota*, and *Pinola*, but also in the vicinity of the Confederate gunboat *McRae*, soon hotly engaged with the much more heavily gunned *Iroquois*. In the exchange, the *McRae* was badly damaged and Lieutenant Huger was mortally wounded; three other men were killed outright and another seventeen wounded.

At this point the *Manassas* came on the scene. Warley tried to ram the *Iroquois*, but the Union ship easily avoided it. Warley then attempted to ram the other Union ships. The Union captains, realizing the danger if they were to be disabled close to the Confederate forts, broke off firing on the *McRae* and resumed their passage upriver.

Three of Farragut's ships failed to make it past the forts. The *Kennebec* and *Itasca* ran afoul of the river obstructions. In an effort to back clear, the *Itasca* collided with the *Winona*. The *Itasca* then took a 42-pounder shot through its boiler and had to abandon the effort. The *Winona* was able to retire before dawn. The *Kennebec*, caught between the two Confederate forts at daybreak, also withdrew. Fourteen of the seventeen ships in Farragut's squadron had made it past the forts, however.

Farragut now lost one other ship, the screw steamer *Varuna* in the first division. At about 4 AM, Lt. Beverly Kennon of the Louisiana state gunboat *Governor Moore* spotted the *Varuna*, which was faster than its sister ships and advancing alone. Kennon immediately ordered the *Governor Moore* to attack, but in order to reach the *Varuna*, it was obliged to run a hail of shot and shell from the other Union ships, which cut it up badly and killed and wounded a number of its crew. But the exchange of fire also produced so much smoke that the Confederate gunboat was able to escape and follow the *Varuna* upriver.

Some six hundred yards ahead of the trailing Union ships, the *Governor Moore* trailed the *Varuna* by one hundred yards. The Union warship engaged its adversary with its sternchaser gun and repeatedly tried to sheer, so as to get off a broadside, but Kennon carefully mirrored the motions of his adversary and was thus able to avoid this.

Nonetheless, the *Governor Moore* took considerable punishment. Shot from the *Varuna*'s sternchaser killed or wounded two-thirds of the men on the Confederate gunboat's forecastle. With his own ship then only forty yards from his adversary and his bow 32-pounder unable to bear because of the close range, Kennon ordered the gun's muzzle depressed to fire a shell at the Union warship through his own ship's deck. This round had a devastating effect, raking the *Varuna.*

Kennon ordered a second shell fired, with similar result. With the two ships only about ten feet apart and after firing a round from its after pivot gun, the *Varuna* sheered to starboard so as to loose a broadside, but Kennon could see the Union ship's mastheads above the smoke and knew what was intended. Swinging his own ship hard to port, he smashed it into the Union ship. Kennon recalled, "the crushing noise made by her break- ing ribs told how amply we were repaid for all we had lost and suffered."[22]

The *Governor Moore* than backed off and rammed the *Varuna* again, taking a full broadside from the Union ship in the process, which made casualties of most of the Confederates on the weather deck. Shortly there- after, however, another Confederate warship, the River Defense Fleet gun- boat *Stonewall Jackson*, appeared and rammed the *Varuna* on its opposite, port, side. This blow produced such damage that the *Varuna*'s pumps were unable to keep the ship afloat, and Cdr. Charles S. Boggs ran the *Varuna* ashore. Having absorbed two broadsides from the mortally wounded Union ship, the *Stonewall Jackson* was itself in a sinking state, and its captain ordered it also run ashore and the gunboat burnt to prevent capture.

As he watched the *Varuna* ground, Kennon was faced with a new problem in the remaining rapidly closing Union ships, which soon subjected the Confederate gunboat to a devastating fire. His own ship in danger of going down in the river, Kennon grounded it just above the stricken *Varuna* and ordered it burnt. The casualty toll on the *Governor Moore* was appalling. Fifty-seven men had been killed in action and seven more wounded out of a crew of ninety-three.

As dawn broke, between 5:30 and 6:00 AM, the Union ships assembled at Quarantine Station. At this point the *Manassas* suddenly appeared, heading for the squadron. Standing on the hurricane deck of the *Mississippi*, Lieutenant Dewey saw the *Hartford*, blackened from the recent fire, steaming by:

> Farragut was in her rigging, his face eager with victory in the morning light and his eyes snapping. "Run down the ram!" he called. I shall never forget that glimpse of him. He was a very

urbane man. But it was plain that if we did not run the *Manassas* down, and promptly, he would not think well of us.[23]

But when Warley saw the extent of his opposition, he knew the battle was over. The ironclad's speed was so much reduced and it had sustained such damage that an attack would have been suicidal. As Warley later put it,

> My people had stood gallantly by me, and I owed to them a duty as well as to the country. I cut the delivery pipes, and headed the vessel inshore. . . . I had the opportunity of throwing my men into the swamp and getting them under the cover of the rise in the bank before the enemy commenced to grape us, which they did for an hour and a half.[24]

The battle for the lower Mississippi was over. With the Union fleet past the forts and the Confederate gunboats destroyed, there was now no barrier between Farragut's squadron and New Orleans. Union casualties had been surprisingly light: the total from April 18 to 26 was just 39 killed and 171 wounded. Farragut reported to Porter on 24 April: "We had a rough time of it . . . but thank God the number of killed and wounded was very small considering."[25]

After burying his dead and carrying out minor repairs to his ships, at 11 AM Farragut sent word to Butler to land his troops, leaving behind the gunboats *Kineo* and *Wissahickon* at Quarantine Station for support. He then ordered the squadron to proceed to New Orleans. Following a brief engagement with that city's last line of defense, a forty-gun Confederate shore battery at Chalmatte some four miles below New Orleans, the ships arrived at the Crescent City just after noon on 25 April and anchored near the custom house.

With the river up and near the top of the levee, the ships' guns could easily be brought to bear on New Orleans. The city was in chaos, with taunting crowds lining the waterfront to protest events. Farragut dispatched Captain Bailey and an aide, Lt. George H. Perkins, to meet with city leaders and demand that they surrender New Orleans and that the U.S. flag be raised over the custom house, mint, and post office. The city fathers, with Gen. Lovell in attendance, refused. Lovell then announced that he and his remaining troops would evacuate the city. Evidently he and the city fathers hoped that this step would prevent Farragut from bombarding New Orleans. That same day, on the Union approach the Confederates burned their unfinished ironclad *Mississippi*. Launched only on 19 April and armored with 3.75 inches of iron plate, it had been intended to carry twenty guns but its ordnance was never mounted and the engines had yet to be assembled.

On the morning of 26 April, Bailey returned ashore to meet with the city leaders. Again they refused his demand for surrender; but with the city poorly provisioned and indefensible, they said they would not resist a Federal takeover. At noon on 29 April, two hundred U.S. marines and several naval officers went ashore and assumed official possession, raising the U.S. flag over the custom house. General Butler and his troops reached the city on 1 May. Butler's subsequent order to execute a man who had taken down a U.S. flag and his so-called Woman Order, by which he ordered that any woman who failed to show proper respect to U.S. soldiers would be treated as a common prostitute, led to his being known by the locals as "Beast Butler."

The stretch of river to the south had already fallen to the Union. With Fort Jackson now cut off, on 25 April Porter sent Lt. Cdr. John Guest under flag of truce to demand that General Duncan surrender both that fort and naval vessels in the vicinity, including the *Louisiana*. Duncan refused, whereupon Porter commenced a mortar bombardment. Although neither Confederate fort had been seriously damaged in the lengthy earlier bombardment, by now the defenders had enough, and early on 28 April many deserted. Accepting reality, later that same day Duncan came aboard the *Harriet Lane* to surrender both forts. As this was taking place, Mitchell set fire to the *Louisiana* and cut it free from its moorings to drift downriver, the ironclad blowing up before it reached the Union ships. Duncan assured Porter that the ironclad was not under his command and hence not bound by his surrender order.[26]

Careful planning, effective leadership, and bold execution had given Farragut a great victory. He became an immediate hero in the North. Certainly, the loss of its largest and most important seaport was a heavy blow to the Confederacy. Vicksburg and Port Hudson were now the only remaining Mississippi River Confederate strongholds. With the fall of New Orleans, their capture was only a matter of time. The timing of the Union attack was certainly propitious; it probably prevented the *Louisiana* and *Mississippi* from defeating the Union assault and dominating the mighty river for six months or more.

THE VICKSBURG CAMPAIGN

Farragut remained at New Orleans until Butler's troops arrived on 1 May. Welles wanted Farragut to push up the river in order to link up with the Union squadron descending the Mississippi. At the same time, however, the Union naval secretary wanted to secure Mobile Bay.

Farragut directed Porter to return to Ship Island with his mortar boat flotilla to prepare to move against Mobile Bay as soon as the big ships of the squadron could join him. Then, to fulfill the first part of his orders, Farragut ordered Capt. Thomas Craven to take the *Brooklyn* and several gunboats upriver. Craven was to steam to Vicksburg and there shell and destroy its large rail center. The *Brooklyn* passed Baton Rouge without incident but, short of the destination, the gunboats *Itasca* and *Sciota* both developed engine problems, and, his own ship having scraped the bottom of the river in several places, Craven turned back. Near Baton Rouge the *Brooklyn* encountered Cdr. S. Philip Lee with the *Oneida*, *Pinola*, and *Kennebec*. Lee had new orders from Farragut. Learning that the river level was dropping, he ordered Craven not to risk his ship and to go no further than Baton Rouge. Craven was, however, to send three or four gunboats to Vicksburg. On 11 May, however, Farragut ordered Craven to proceed with the *Brooklyn* and gunboats to Natchez.[27]

On 7 May Farragut had ordered Cdr. James S. Palmer of the *Iroquois* to secure both Baton Rouge, Louisiana, and Natchez, Mississippi. That same evening Palmer arrived off the Louisiana state capital. The next day he sent ashore a landing party to seize the arsenal and take possession of the city without a shot being fired. Farragut arrived on 10 May, landing fifteen hundred infantry to secure the city.[28]

The *Iroquois* departed Baton Rouge that same day and soon overtook the *Oneida* and the gunboats. On 13 May, Palmer secured the surrender of Natchez. Despite reservations about taking his big ships there because of the low water and lack of river pilots, Farragut ordered the squadron to continue on to Vicksburg. The *Hartford* ran aground but was gotten off two days later following the offloading of coal and some of its guns. The ships of the squadron then straggled in and finally collected near Vicksburg.

With their defenses strengthened by the arrival both of heavy guns and troops evacuated from New Orleans and other points in Mississippi, on 18 May Confederate authorities at Vicksburg confidently rejected a Union surrender demand delivered from the *Oneida*. Farragut correctly determined that his resources were totally inadequate to take that city. He wrote Butler on 22 May that not only were the heavy Confederate guns on the two-hundred-foot high bluffs "so elevated that our fire will not be felt by them," but several thousand soldiers defended Vicksburg, and the authorities had "the facility of bringing in 20,000 in an hour by railroad from Jackson." Even if the Union ships could have shelled Vicksburg into submission, Farragut had only about fourteen hundred to fifteen hundred men under Brig. Gen. Thomas Williams, an insufficient force to hold the city. On 30 May, Farragut returned to New Orleans with most of his ships, leaving behind only half a dozen gunboats.[29]

Under orders from Welles and Fox, and Lincoln's express demand that the river be cleared, Farragut made yet another attempt against Vicksburg in late June in conjunction with Flag Officer Davis's Mississippi River Flotilla to the north. This time Farragut brought along Porter's mortar boats, recalled from Ship Island. With about three thousand men, General Williams positioned an artillery battery on the riverbank opposite the main Confederate upper forts to distract them during Farragut's passage, but the Union guns accomplished little against the Confederate artillery on the high bluffs.

With mortar boats positioned on both sides of the river, the Union ships began their attack at 4 AM on 28 June. The *Richmond* led, followed by the *Hartford*, *Brooklyn*, and the gunboats in a three-mile-long exchange of fire between the ships and the Confederate guns on the bluffs. Two and a half hours later, Farragut's ships had all passed through the gauntlet of Confederate fire at minimal cost (seven killed and thirty wounded; Porter's mortar squadron sustained eight killed and ten to twelve wounded) but had failed to damage the forts.[30]

Although Farragut's dash past Vicksburg proved that the Union ships could pass back and forth at relatively little cost, the flag officer was now more convinced than ever that taking Vicksburg was a matter for ground troops. That same day he sent a message to General Halleck at Corinth via Colonel Ellet informing the Union theater commander that although he was now above Vicksburg with most of his ships, the Confederates had

some eight thousand to ten thousand ground troops in place, a force sufficient to prevent the relatively small number of Union troops from landing. Farragut concluded, "My orders, general, are to clear the river. This I
find impossible without your assistance. Can you aid me in this matter to
carry out the order of the President?" Farragut's request did not seem
unreasonable, given that Halleck commanded some one hundred twenty
thousand men, but Halleck replied: "The scattered and weakened condition of my troops renders it impossible for me at the present to detach any
troops to cooperate with you on Vicksburg."[31]

On 1 July Farragut linked up with Davis below the Yazoo River,
about a dozen miles above Vicksburg. Union troops then began digging
a canal across the mile-wide peninsula formed by the U-shaped bend in
the river on which Vicksburg was located. If completed, this canal from
Young's Point would cause the Mississippi to bypass Vicksburg beyond
range of many of its land batteries. But with half his crews sick and the
river falling, Farragut was fearful of being trapped there with his big
ships, and the partially completed project was abandoned. Before the
Union ships could depart, however, the Confederates sent out the powerful ironclad *Arkansas*.[32]

The preceding May, Confederate authorities at Memphis had sent the
uncompleted *Arkansas* to Yazoo City to prevent its capture by Union forces.
Hastily constructed with poor engines salvaged from the sunken river
steamer *Natchez*, the *Arkansas* was a casemated ironclad with a ram bow;
however, unlike other Confederate ironclads, the casemate was perpendicular rather than sloping. The *Arkansas* mounted eight guns: two IX-inch
Dahlgrens, two 8-inch/64-pounders, two 32-pounder smoothbores, and
two 6-inch rifles. It had one advantage in terms of maneuverability: its two
propellers acted directly on the engines; thus, reversing one screw enabled
the ram to turn in a very short length.

Union commanders were aware of the presence of the *Arkansas* in the
Yazoo; indeed Union forces in the river learned on the evening of 14 July
from two Confederate deserters that the ram, facing the same difficulty of
falling water levels, would soon sortie. Farragut, Davis, and Williams met
and agreed to send a reconnaissance force of three ships up the Yazoo: the
Ellet ram *Queen of the West*, only recently returned to active duty following repairs and strengthened by army sharpshooters; the timberclad *Tyler*;
and the ironclad *Carondelet*.

On 15 July, rounding a bend in the river, the Union ships discovered the more powerful Confederate ironclad, which immediately attacked. As the Union ships fled back downriver, the *Arkansas* fired on them with its bow guns, scoring thirteen hits on the unprotected stern of the *Carondelet* and forcing it into shallow water where it went aground. Confederate fire also damaged the *Tyler*.

At 8 AM and under full power the *Arkansas* exited the Yazoo into the Mississippi. Steaming south, it passed some twenty unprepared Union ships without steam up, trading broadsides with many of them. Perhaps to the surprise of its own crew, the *Arkansas* then docked at Vicksburg.[33]

An embarrassed and angry Farragut attempted to destroy the *Arkansas* as he ran his ships south past Vicksburg later that same day. It was dark when the Union ships reached the city, and the attempt failed. Commander Porter volunteered to try with the *Essex*. The plan agreed upon called for Davis and Farragut to get both their squadrons under way at 4 AM on 22 July, Davis to shell the northern Vicksburg batteries, while Farragut's ships occupied those batteries south of the city. Cdr. William Porter's *Essex* and Lt. Col. Alfred Ellet's *Queen of the West* would then converge on the ram and destroy it. As it turned out, the Union attacks were not simultaneous, and the attempt failed, although the *Arkansas* took considerable punishment in an exchange of fire with the *Essex* and from glancing blows by both the *Essex* and the *Queen of the West*. Porter had hoped to board the *Arkansas* and capture it, but Confederate field pieces and sharpshooters ashore prevented this. Both Union ships were also damaged in the exchange of fire. The *Essex* was hit forty-two times but only penetrated twice. It lost one man killed and three wounded.[34]

Two days after the abortive attack on the Confederate ironclad, the Union troops in the Vicksburg area were taken aboard transports to return with Farragut's squadron to New Orleans. Farragut left behind only a token force of four ships at Baton Rouge, centered on the *Essex* and *Sumter*, in case the *Arkansas* ventured south.

Although repairs from the 22 July Union attack were not yet complete and its engines were in terrible shape, the *Arkansas* was not long idle. On 3 August Executive Officer Lt. Henry K. Stevens got the ram under way for Baton Rouge, ordered to support a land attack there by three thousand Confederates under Maj. Gen. John C. Breckenridge. General Williams commanded about the same number of Union troops in entrenchments around Baton Rouge, while four Union warships, including the *Essex*, protected the city from the river side.

A day after the *Arkansas* sortied, its engines broke down. While the ironclad anchored upriver for repairs, Confederate soldiers at Baton Rouge breached the Union lines and drove the Federals back against the river. The *Arkansas* finally got under way again, only to suffer another engine breakdown a few miles above Baton Rouge. The starboard engine quit, and torque from the port engine drove the *Arkansas* ashore. As its crew desperately sought to effect repairs, the Union gunboats downriver kept up a steady stream of fire against the advancing Confederate troops and drove them back, although General Williams was among the Union dead. Had the *Arkansas* been on the scene and occupied the gunboats, the battle would probably have gone the other way.

During the night of 5 August, Commander Porter learned of the presence of the *Arkansas*, and at 8 AM the next day he led his small squadron upriver against it. The Confederates completed repairs to the *Arkansas* just as the *Essex* was getting up steam. But as the *Arkansas* moved to engage the *Essex*, its engines broke down yet again, and the ironclad drifted back to the shore. Stevens then ordered his men to abandon ship and fire it. The burning *Arkansas* then drifted back out into the river, and then downstream for more than an hour until it blew up. Learning of the ship's destruction, Breckenridge decided to withdraw his troops from Baton Rouge rather than renew the attack. In retrospect, the *Arkansas* should have been kept at Vicksburg. With its engines properly repaired, it could have disrupted the subsequent passage by Rear Admiral Porter's Mississippi Squadron that made possible General Grant's final operations against Vicksburg.[35]

The 1862 Union effort to take Vicksburg soon lost momentum. Porter and his mortar schooners were called east to Hampton Roads to reinforce there. In December General Butler was also ordered east, replaced at New Orleans by Maj. Gen. Nathaniel Banks. Flag Officer Davis also withdrew from the vicinity of Vicksburg north to Helena, Arkansas. Concerns were voiced in Washington about whether Davis was sufficiently aggressive. When Davis was recalled to Washington to head the Bureau of Navigation, in a surprise move Cdr. David D. Porter received promotion to rear admiral and replaced Davis in command of the now upgraded Mississippi Squadron. Another consequence of this command change was that the

Navy Department now controlled all Union ships on the Mississippi, save for the Ellet rams, which remained under the army.

Porter arrived at Cairo on 15 October and immediately demanded control of Ellet's rams as well. The cabinet in Washington agreed on 7 November. Porter now had what neither of his predecessors possessed: complete control of all Union warships in the upper Mississippi. His squadron included the three original timberclads; seven Eads ironclads; the ironclad *Benton* (the flagship); three river gunboats from the Confederate river defense fleet operating under their same names but flying Union colors, the *General Bragg, Little Rebel,* and *General Price;* and the nine Ellet rams.

Other ships augmented Porter's force. On 13 July 1863, the U.S. gunboats *Manitou* and *Rattler* captured in the Little Red River the Confederate Army side-wheeler cargo ship *Louisville*. Renamed the *Black Hawk* and converted into an armored "tinclad," it became Porter's Mississippi flagship for the remainder of the war. This 572-ton ship carried a heavy armament for support of shore operations: five 4.2-inch Parrott rifles, eighteen 24-pounders, and sixteen 12-pounder boat howitzers.

Porter ultimately received five additional ironclads, two of which—the *Lafayette* and *Choctaw*—were conversions from large side-wheeler steamers. Designed by William D. Porter, they were two of the most heavily armored ships on the river. Both utilized iron over India rubber, a technique developed by Porter. The *Lafayette* had a sloping casemate protected by an inch of iron over an inch of India rubber. It mounted two XI-inch and four IX-inch Dahlgrens and two 4.2-inch Parrott rifles. The *Choctaw* had a shorter casemate mounting four guns and was armored with 2.5 inches of iron over 2 inches of India rubber.

The three new-construction ironclads were side-wheelers, each also having two screws and two engines. The *Chillicothe* (2-inch side armor, armed with two XI-inch Dahlgrens) joined the fleet in September 1862. Both the *Indianola* and *Tuscumbia* were commissioned in March 1863. The former had 3-inch casemate armor and mounted two XI-inch and two IX-inch Dahlgrens; the latter had 6-inch casemate armor and mounted three XI-inch and two IX-inch Dahlgrens. All three ships were, however, poorly built and had a tendency to hogging (a distortion of the hull whereby the bow and stern were lower than the amidships section of the ship).

In addition to the ironclads, Admiral Porter secured many lighter tinclads. These warships were armored with metal plate less than an inch thick, capable of protecting against only small-arms fire. In addition to their names, they sported numbers painted on their pilothouses, the only ships of the war to be so identified. Sternwheelers and of very light draft (only two feet for many), they were specifically developed for service on the shallow rivers emptying into the Mississippi and proved highly effective in patrol and interdiction operations. Although the larger tinclads mounted a few heavier guns, their principal armament consisted of 12- and 24-pounder Dahlgren boat howitzers, sufficient for patrol work. Finally, and largely untold, there was a vast number of smaller auxiliary tenders, tugs, floating machine and carpenter shops, hospital ships, ordnance and supply vessels, and transports. In a very real sense these presaged the U.S. Navy's "fleet train" concept in the Pacific Theater during World War II.

Finally there was the Mississippi Marine Brigade, organized in October 1862 by Brig. Gen. Alfred Ellet with the strong support of Porter. Intended as an amphibious strike force, it numbered six companies of infantry and four of cavalry, and a battery of mobile artillery, all supported by ten armed steamboat transports and six auxiliary steamers. At full strength the Mississippi Marine Brigade included more than one thousand officers and men and five hundred civilians. As an army command within the Mississippi Squadron, the Mississippi Marine Brigade was one of the first experiments in joint operations by the U.S. military. Porter soon grew disillusioned with the brigade, however, complaining to Welles that Ellet "was adverse to harmonious action; that he was determined to assume authority and disregard my orders." Porter finally secured transfer of its vessels in August 1864. That November the Mississippi Marine Brigade itself was disbanded.[36]

Whereas Union naval strength in the Western Theater increased, that of the Confederates dwindled. The South could mount no serious challenge to Porter's squadron. Few Confederate warships remained on the Mississippi or its tributaries, and, with the South deficient in manufacturing resources, most of what remained consisted of poorly armed wooden ships.

CHAPTER EIGHT

Union Riverine Warfare Continued: Vicksburg

—⁓—

B y late summer there were only two major obstacles to Union control of the entire Mississippi River: Vicksburg and Port Hudson. Of
these two, Vicksburg was by far the most important and a special
interest of President Lincoln, who called it "the key" to western operations. Lincoln believed that the war could "never be brought to a close
until that key is in our pocket."[1] This enterprise involved most of Admiral
Porter's sizable squadron, whereas General Grant, commander of the
Department of the Tennessee since October 1862, eventually fielded
sixteen divisions against the city, with another six serving elsewhere.

Essential to Union success, Porter established an excellent relationship
with Grant. Nonetheless, the Union campaign against Vicksburg opened
badly. For one thing, the Confederates enjoyed significant geographical
advantages. The now heavily fortified city stood on bluffs some two hundred feet above the eastern bank of the river, where they had an excellent
field of fire, thanks to the meandering Mississippi itself. Full of twists and
turns, the river headed north for a stretch until just above Vicksburg, where
it turned back on itself to flow south again. Ships making this hairpin turn
in either direction would be obliged to slow, providing ample time for the
batteries to fire on them. To the west of the city, the DeSoto Peninsula
formed by the river was a lowland of marshes and swamps. Protecting the
northern approaches was a sixty-mile-wide quagmire of swamps, bayous,
and low-lying land known as the Yazoo Delta, and just north of the city lay
the natural defensive line of the eighty- to one-hundred-foot Chickasaw

Bluffs. Vicksburg was most vulnerable from the south and east, but these were far removed from Grant's supply base at Memphis.

Given the topography and hydrography, Grant attempted an overland campaign south from his advanced base at Holly Springs along the Mississippi Central Railroad. Grant hoped to draw out the bulk of Confederate Lt. Gen. John C. Pemberton's forty-thousand-man Army of Mississippi defending Vicksburg, while at the same time sending his trusted subordinate Sherman and thirty-two thousand men down the Mississippi River in transports covered by Porter's gunboats to stage a surprise attack on the few defenders remaining at Vicksburg.[2]

On 11 December, Porter at Cairo put into effect the naval aspects of the plan. Commander Walke led a Union flotilla up the Yazoo River, a tributary of the Mississippi that joins the mighty river from the east just above Vicksburg itself. Walke's flotilla consisted of the ironclads *Carondelet* (the flagship), *Cairo*, *Baron de Kalb*, and *Pittsburg*, and the tinclads *Marmora* and *Signal*, later joined by the ram *Lioness*. The tinclads and their boats were to drag the river for the large number of Confederate torpedoes secured just below the surface, while the more powerful Union warships provided protection against any attempt at intervention, including by infantry ashore. Walke gave explicit orders that the big ships not proceed ahead until the torpedoes had been swept.

At midday on 12 December about a dozen miles up the river, the smaller ships and their boats were busy sweeping the river. The *Cairo* was behind, with the leading *Marmora*'s bow out of sight thanks to a sharp bend in the river. Suddenly the men on the *Cairo* heard small-arms fire ahead, and Lt. Cdr. Thomas Selfridge, the *Cairo*'s captain, rashly ordered full-speed ahead. The *Cairo* came alongside the *Marmora*, only to learn that its crew had been firing at a torpedo in the water. Selfridge ordered a boat lowered to inspect the target, which turned out to be remains of a torpedo destroyed the day before. In the meanwhile, the bow of the *Cairo* had turned in toward the shore, and Selfridge ordered his ship backed out to straighten it upstream, ordering the *Marmora* to go ahead. The *Cairo* had gone perhaps only half a ship length forward when it struck two mines in quick succession on its port side. These ripped large holes in the ship's hull. The damage was at first thought not to be fatal, but in only a dozen minutes the ironclad went down in about twenty feet of water, a total loss. Only the tops of its pipes were visible, but the *Lioness* hauled

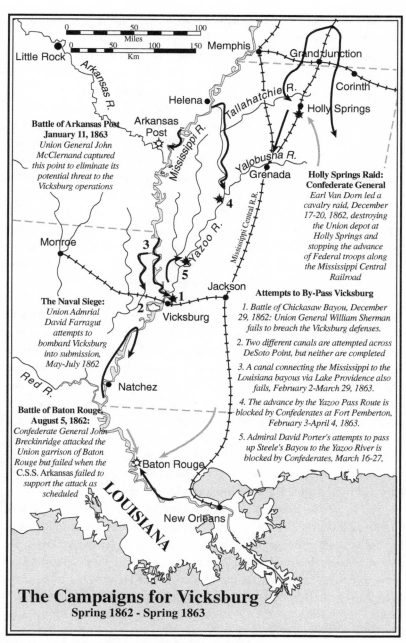

Little Rock

Memphis

Grand Junction

Arkansas R.

Helena

Corinth

Tallahatchie R.

Holly Springs

**Battle of Arkansas Post
January 11, 1863**
*Union General John
McClernand captured
this point to eliminate its
potential threat to the
Vicksburg operations*

**Arkansas
Post**

Mississippi R.

Yalobusha R.

Grenada

**Holly Springs Raid:
Confederate General**
*Earl Van Dorn led a
cavalry raid, December
17-20, 1862, destroying
the Union depot at
Holly Springs and
stopping the advance
of Federal troops along
the Mississippi Central
Railroad*

4

Mississippi Central R.R.

Monroe

3

Yazoo R.

5

Jackson

Attempts to By-Pass Vicksburg

1

2

The Naval Siege:
*Union Admiral
David Farragut
attempts to
bombard Vicksburg
into submission,
May-July 1862*

Vicksburg

*1. Battle of Chickasaw Bayou, December
29, 1862: Union General William Sherman
fails to breach the Vicksburg defenses.*

*2. Two different canals are attempted across
DeSoto Point, but neither are completed*

*3. A canal connecting the Mississippi to the
Louisiana bayous via Lake Providence also
fails, February 2-March 29, 1863.*

Red R.

Natchez

*4. The advance by the Yazoo Pass Route is
blocked by Confederates at Fort Pemberton,
February 3-April 4, 1863.*

**Battle of Baton Rouge
August 5, 1862:**
*Confederate General John
Breckinridge attacked the
Union garrison of Baton
Rouge but failed when the
C.S.S. Arkansas failed to
support the attack as
scheduled*

*5. Admiral David Porter's attempts to pass
up Steele's Bayou to the Yazoo River is
blocked by Confederates, March 16-27,*

Baton Rouge

LOUISIANA

New Orleans

The Campaigns for Vicksburg
Spring 1862 - Spring 1863

The Campaigns for Vicksburg, Spring 1862–Spring 1863

these out to prevent the Confederates from locating the spot and salvaging the ship and its contents.

Selfridge escaped reprimand for these events but nonetheless came in for much criticism. One fellow officer noted, "Selfridge of the *Cairo* found two torpedoes and removed them by placing his vessel over them." Selfridge himself wrote in later years, "As a young officer in command of a large ironclad . . . I had been so unfortunate, by pushing perhaps a little farther to the front than prudence dictated to lose my ship by the explosion of a torpedo in the Yazoo River." The Union side abandoned efforts to salvage the *Cairo* in 1863, and it remained hidden in the thick Yazoo mud for nearly one hundred years until it was located and raised in the 1960s.[3]

Meanwhile, the farther Grant moved south, the more vulnerable his supply/communication lines became. Brig. Gen. Nathan Bedford Forrest's cavalry soon threatened these communication lines all the way back to Columbus, Kentucky. Forrest's two thousand men tore up nearly fifty miles of railroad track, seized considerable quantities of military supplies, and inflicted some two thousand Union casualties. On 20 December, however, an even worse calamity befell Grant. As Porter prepared to depart Memphis with Sherman's troops down the Mississippi and with Grant having drawn off some twenty thousand Vicksburg defenders and engaging them outside the town of Granada, Confederate Maj. Gen. Earl Van Dorn led thirty-five hundred cavalry against Grant's supply base at Holly Springs, held by fifteen hundred Union troops. The raiders easily captured Holly Springs and there destroyed vast stocks of food and supplies bound for Grant's soldiers. Although Van Dorn soon departed ahead of reacting Union cavalry, Grant now had no choice but to call off his advance and retrace his steps to Grand Junction, Tennessee. He tried to get word to Sherman, but the telegraph lines had been disabled, and the message did not get through.[4]

Just before departure Sherman got word of Holly Springs, but not of Grant's withdrawal. Porter and Sherman, therefore, moved south from Memphis as scheduled on 20 December, stopping at Helena, Arkansas, the next day to gather additional forces that brought total Union troop strength up to about thirty thousand men. On 23 December, Porter in the *Black Hawk* and his flotilla of Union warships and transports entered the Yazoo. The Union ships then worked their way upriver, easily suppressing Confederate shore fire as they went. On 26 December, about ten miles from the river mouth, three of the four Union divisions disembarked.

Sherman's force was only about six miles north of Vicksburg itself, but before it could assault the Confederate positions on the Chickasaw Bluffs that formed the city's northern defenses, Union soldiers would first have to cross a morass of marshy low ground, bayous, swamps, thick forest, and felled trees. Only a few approach roads or causeways were available, and the defenders had these well covered by artillery. Heavy rain made an already difficult situation far worse.

During 27–28 December, as Sherman's men slowly worked their way toward the bluffs under covering fire from the Union ships in the river, the defenders doubled in number, from six thousand to twelve thousand men. Meanwhile, some of the Union gunboats continued upriver to feign an attack on Haynes's Bluff, which, however, failed in its design of drawing off some of the defenders.

The major fighting ashore occurred on 29 December, with Porter's gunboats again providing diversionary fire. Sherman struck the center of the Confederate line, advancing his men across open ground against the entrenchments. Union troops who managed to reach the Confederate rifle pits were driven back by heavy fire from the bluffs above.

Faced with deteriorating weather and resolute Confederate resistance, and learning at last of Grant's decision, Sherman ordered a withdrawal. By the morning of 2 January 1863, all his men were again on board ship and on their way to the Mississippi and a base at Milliken's Bend, Louisiana. Casualties in the Battle of the Chickasaw Bluffs testify to the superiority of the defense. Union losses, most of them on 29 December, came to 175 killed, 930 wounded, and 743 prisoners; Confederate casualties numbered only 63 killed, 134 wounded, and 10 prisoners.

Grant learned two important lessons from this campaign. The first was that his troops could to some extent live off the land. The second was that he would have to abandon the overland approach in favor of utilizing the Mississippi River as his main line of communications.[5]

Of major rivers flowing into the Mississippi, Union forces had yet to penetrate the Arkansas and Red, and the Union commanders now decided to send a sizable force up the Arkansas River, the largest river emptying into the Mississippi. The goal was to destroy Confederate Fort Hindman, also known as Arkansas Post, located some 50 miles from the river's mouth. Mounting fourteen guns, the largest of which were four IX-inch Dahlgrens, it guarded the river approach to Little Rock, 117 miles north. Arkansas Post was also an important staging area for Confederate raids that threatened Union control of the Mississippi. Here Brig. Gen. Thomas J. Churchill commanded some five thousand Confederate troops. A Union success at Fort Hindman would not only remove an important Confederate military threat but would also serve to restore lagging morale following the Chickasaw Bluffs reverse.

Maj. Gen. John McClernand had overall command of the expedition. A political appointee lacking a military background, he had arrived at the beginning of January 1863 and taken command from Sherman. The expedition set out on 4 January, Porter heading the naval contingent of the ironclads *Baron de Kalb, Louisville,* and *Cincinnati;* the ram *Monarch;* the gunboats *Black Hawk* and *Tyler;* and the tinclads *Rattler* and *Glide,* all escorting a large number of transports lifting some thirty-two thousand men. Following a feint against the White River, the flotilla headed up the Red, arriving several miles from Arkansas Post on the evening of 9 January. The troops then went ashore on both sides of the river in order to prevent the Confederates from either reinforcing or escaping.

In the afternoon of 10 January, the *Baron de Kalb, Louisville,* and *Cincinnati* opened fire on the Confederate breastworks, testing the range of the defending artillery. Porter then sent in the *Rattler* to fire on the rifle pits and breastworks, which were then silenced and occupied by Union troops.

At 5:30 PM, with the Union troops in position, Porter ordered in the three ironclads against the fort. Advancing to within four hundred yards, they opened up with three heavy guns, eight rifled guns, and musket fire. Directing operations from the steam tug *Thistle,* Porter next brought up the light-draft *Lexington* and *Black Hawk* to fire shrapnel and rifle shell. He ordered the *Rattler* to enfilade the fort. It provided effective fire from that position, although it also sustained extensive damage from shore fire. Although the fort was largely silenced by the naval gunfire, it was too late in the day for the Union troops to attack.

The next day, 11 January, McClernand sent word to Porter that his men were waiting for the navy to attack, when they too would assault the fort. The warships then resumed their shelling, this time from very close range and including shrapnel. At about 4 PM, with all of his guns save one Parrott rifle out of commission, Col. John W. Dunnington surrendered the fort to Porter. At the same time, Churchill surrendered the land forces to Sherman. Confederate losses in the battle numbered about 150 dead and 4,791 prisoners. Union casualties apart from prisoners were heavier because the troops had been forced to assault entrenchments. The Union tally ashore amounted to 79 killed and 440 wounded. The ships sustained about 30 casualties, the *Rattler* and *Baron de Kalb* being the hardest hit. The Union troops then destroyed what remained of the fort and its guns before rejoining the transports to return to Milliken's Bend, about seven miles above Vicksburg. The operation was, as Porter later put it, "one of the prettiest little affairs of the war."[6]

The pompous McClernand strutted and sought to take full credit for the victory, although both he and Grant had opposed the operation at the outset. Although fears that Grant would be made subordinate to him proved groundless, Grant, Sherman, and Porter all became concerned that McClernand might fatally handicap the entire Vicksburg operation. Sherman and Porter both wrote to Grant and urged him to come to Young's Point to minimize any potential damage by McClernand. Grant arrived on 29 January. Although he wanted Sherman to have charge of land operations, the latter was junior to McClernand, and Grant thus had no choice but to take the field command himself. He then divided his sixty thousand men into three corps commanded by Sherman, McClernand, and James B. McPherson.[7]

As Grant and Porter contemplated their next step, small engagements continued along the Mississippi and on other western rivers, most often between Confederates on land and Union ships. Occasionally the Southerners were able to ambush and capture or destroy a lightly armed Union vessel, as when they seized a tug at Memphis. But for the most part, the small Union warships used their boat howitzers to disrupt such attacks. Union naval patrols also interdicted Confederate trade, seizing cotton and other goods. Such actions, although for the most part small and receiving little public notice, were very important to the overall Union war effort.

Porter was anxious to renew offensive operations, and in the beginning of February he ordered Ellet to blockade the mouth of the Red River with the *Queen of the West*. Both Port Hudson and Vicksburg were receiving supplies from the western Confederacy via the Red. His ram somewhat protected by the addition of cotton bales, Ellet started down the Mississippi near midnight on 2 February. The need to shift the location of his ship's wheel en route, however, delayed his arrival of the first battery at Vicksburg by an hour until daylight, and Confederate pickets immediately fired a signal gun to alert the other batteries below.

Presuming that the *Queen of the West* would arrive at Vicksburg under cloak of darkness, Porter had ordered Ellet to ram the Confederate steamer *City of Vicksburg*, which had been brought down the Yazoo, as well as set it on fire with incendiary shells. Although such an attempt in daylight risked almost certain destruction, Ellet proceeded. Just as he was about to ram the *City of Vicksburg*, however, the powerful river current swung the *Queen of the West*, and its blow struck obliquely. Ellet had ordered one of his guns shotted with three incendiary shells, and at the moment of impact these were fired into the *City of Vicksburg*, setting it alight. The Confederates soon managed to put out the fires, and the *Queen of the West* was also ablaze from cotton bales set alight by the discharge of its own gun.

Ellet realized that if he pressed the attack, his own ship would be destroyed by fire. Reluctantly, he ordered the *Queen of the West* to withdraw and head downriver, the crew extinguishing the flames by tossing overboard the protecting cotton bales. Although exposed to Confederate fire for more than fifty minutes and hit twelve times, the *Queen of the West* somehow escaped the gauntlet of fire without serious damage.[8]

Arriving off Natchez on 3 February without the Confederates being aware of his presence, Ellet there captured and destroyed three Rebel steamer supply ships and their cargoes of food and provisions. Following the arrival of an unmanned coal barge sent down the river by Porter, Ellet left men on the 390-ton captured Rebel steamer *De Soto* to watch the mouth of the Red, while he took the *Queen of the West* up the smaller Atchafalaya River to destroy two Confederate wagon trains and burn several plantations.

Porter sent additional firepower to Ellet in the form of the powerfully armed *Indianola* under Lt. Cdr. George Brown. Towing two coal barges, it ran the Vicksburg batteries on 13 February and anchored off the Red River to await news of Ellet, the Union colonel having then gone up that river with the *Queen of the West* and *De Soto* in search of additional prizes.

On 14 February, Ellet captured the steamer *Era No. 5*, carrying Confederate soldiers and a cargo of corn. Taking on board the captured steamer's pilot, Ellet proceeded upstream. The *Queen of the West* was approaching a shore battery of four 32-pounders at Gordon's Landing when the Confederate pilot deliberately ran the ship aground. Shore fire soon inflicted heavy damage on the stationary *Queen of the West*. A smashed steam pipe and billowing clouds of steam forced the crew to abandon ship.

The Union sailors clung to bales of cotton in the water, hoping to reach the trailing *De Soto*, but an unshipped rudder caused that ship to run aground, destroying it. Ellet and his men finally found refuge on the *Era No. 5*, which then joined the *Indianola*. Meanwhile, the Confederates seized the *Queen of the West*, repaired it, and incorporated it into their own forces.

In order to put an end to Ellet's depredations, Confederate authorities in Jackson now ordered the 655-ton side-wheeler steamer transport *William H. Webb* converted into a ram at Alexandria, Louisiana. A privateer at New Orleans at the beginning of the war, it had escaped that city in advance of the Union arrival. As modified, the ram mounted one 8-inch rifled gun and two 12-pounder howitzers. Maj. Joseph L. Brent had command.

Learning of the presence of the *Indianaola* and determined to seek it out, on 24 February Confederate Army Lt. Col. Frederick B. Brand in the small steamer *Dr. Beatty* (one 6-pounder) joined the *William H. Webb* and repaired *Queen of the West*, both under Brent's command. With the *Grand Era* acting as a tender, the squadron steamed out of the Red River and headed up the Mississippi. The Confederates discovered the *Indianola* about thirty miles below Vicksburg, near Carthage, Mississippi, moored to the shore with two coal barges alongside. Knowing of the heavy guns on the Union ship, Brand hoped to mount a surprise night attack. But shortly before 10 PM, Union lookouts spotted the Confederates approaching.

The fight raged for about an hour, with the *Indianola* firing its four Dahlgrens a total of seventeen times. The *William H. Webb* and *Queen of the West* managed to ram and strip away the two barges protecting the *Indianola*, and on its third run the *William H. Webb* sliced into the Federal ship near its starboard wheelhouse, an action that also opened a large hole in the ram's own bow. The *Queen of the West*, meanwhile, braved the *Indianola*'s two stern IX-inch Dahlgrens to smash into the Union ship there, breaking the *Indianola*'s stern apart. On being informed that the Union ship was disabled, Brand positioned the *Dr. Beatty* alongside and grappled it with the intention of boarding, whereupon Brown surrendered. The *Indianola* had suffered one dead and another wounded from Confederate sharpshooters, as well as some ninety men taken prisoner. The attackers in turn had a number of guns disabled, with two men dead and three others wounded.

Brand took Brown's sword, then ordered the Union ship pushed to shore in order to prevent it from sinking in deep water. All damage to

Indianola had been inflicted by ramming. The Confederates placed it under tow with the hope of taking the ship up the Red River for repairs. But with the ironclad taking on a great deal of water, in part from Union efforts to sabotage the ship, the Confederates allowed it to settle in ten feet of water off Jefferson Davis's plantation as a water battery.

Meanwhile, the *Queen of the West* steamed up the Mississippi toward Vicksburg to secure a pump so that the captured Union ironclad might then be moved to safety. The Confederate ram soon aborted its mission and returned on 25 February with news that a large Union gunboat had cleared Vicksburg and was heading south. The ships of the small Confederate squadron immediately fled up the Red, even abandoning a Confederate salvage party and some boat howitzers on the *Indianola*. Although the Union ship did not approach closer than about two and a half miles, the salvage crew disabled the *Indianola*'s guns and burned it, destroying its valuable stores and powder and saving only the ship's wine and liquor stocks.

The "gunboat" was in fact a large barge, camouflaged on Porter's orders so as to appear to be a formidable monitor and sent downriver to draw Confederate shore fire in the hopes of bursting some of their guns. The faux gunboat had drifted down the river, coming to rest at the perfect location. Ultimately the red-faced Confederates returned to salvage from the *Indianola* two Dahlgrens: an XI-inch and a IX-inch. Porter and Welles keenly felt the loss of the powerful *Indianola*. Rather than risk more ships to such an enterprise, Porter abandoned efforts to blockade the mouth of the Red River with detached ships.[9]

Learning of the loss of the *Indianola*, Farragut decided to send some of his own ships up the Mississippi to assist Porter. That would mean running past Port Hudson, 115 miles downriver from Vicksburg, where the river made a 150-degree bend to the southwest. Until August 1862, Port Hudson was not a formidable barrier, but in that month Union ship crews discovered that the Confederates had placed fifteen heavy guns on the river bluffs at the bend and south of the city on the east bank.

In early March, General Banks and Farragut agreed to mount a joint attack on Port Hudson, with Banks providing twenty-five thousand troops from Baton Rouge. At Prophet's Island, five miles south of Port Hudson, Farragut assembled a powerful force of the *Hartford*, *Richmond*, *Monongahela*, and *Mississippi*, as well as the gunboats *Albatross*, *Genesee*, and *Kineo*. Farragut planned to bring the shore batteries under fire from mortar boats and the ironclad *Essex* as the Union ships ran past them.

Farragut coupled each of his larger ships with a lighter gunboat lashed on the port aft quarter, the thought being that because the batteries were on the east bank the larger ships would protect the smaller ships, and should one of the two ships become disabled, the other could assist it. The exception was the side-wheeler *Mississippi*, bringing up the rear alone. To provide additional firepower, Farragut ordered boat howitzers mounted on the rigging platforms of the mizzenmasts of the sloops.

The Union ships made their run on the night of 14 March but discovered an unwelcome surprise in the form of a series of locomotive headlights that the Confederates had placed along the eastern bank. Turned on, these silhouetted the ships and allowed the shore gunners to deliver an accurate fire. Although the first two Union ships, the lashed-together *Hartford* and *Albatross*, made it past safely, the next two did not fare as well. A Confederate shot struck the *Richmond*, piercing its steam drum and causing it to drift back out of the battle. The *Kineo*, secured to the port side of the *Monongahela*, took a shot that lodged between its rudderpost and sternpost. The *Monongahela* also had its rudder damaged, and the two ships then went aground. Both ships got free but then drifted back downriver out of the battle. The last ship in line, Capt. Melancton Smith's *Mississippi*, ran aground while approaching Thomas Point. Unable to free his ship, which came under heavy Confederate fire, Smith ordered the crew to abandon ship. The men first spiked the guns, destroyed the engines, and then set the ship on fire. It finally drifted downstream completely ablaze before blowing up. Out of its 297 crewmen, 25 were killed and 64 were reported missing.

A good deal of the responsibility for the failure of this enterprise rested with the dilatory Banks. Although his forces probed the Confederate defenses, they failed to mount an attack in sufficient force and one timed to occupy the Confederate gunners. Learning of Farragut's failure, Banks then called off his own attack.[10]

With only two of his seven ships above Port Hudson, Farragut called on Porter to send some of his vessels south past Vicksburg to assist in patrolling the river between the two Confederate strongholds. Porter, however, was then involved in operations of his own in the bayous above Vicksburg and could not spare any ships. Ellet met with Farragut, however, and proposed that two of his own rams proceed downriver. Farragut protested that this would require Porter's consent. Assured by Ellet that Porter would consent if he were present, Farragut agreed, whereupon Ellet ordered the *Switzerland* and *Lancaster* south.

Early on 25 March 1863, Alfred Ellet set out. He led in the *Switzerland*, with the *Lancaster* under his brother John to starboard. Because of delays in their preparation, the rams did not get under way until near daybreak, and both were soon detected by the Vicksburg batteries, which opened an accurate fire. The *Lancaster* took several hits, including one in its steam drum that forced the crew to abandon ship. Before doing so, the men set the ship on fire, although it sank at the bow before being consumed. The *Switzerland*, which had sustained little damage, picked up the crew in the water. Porter was greatly displeased when he learned of Ellet's action, even briefly ordering his arrest, but *Lancaster*'s Farragut now had one more Union gunboat to patrol the river between Vicksburg and Port Hudson and was able to proceed again up the Red River, if need be.[11]

U.S. Navy rams Switzerland *and* Lancaster *running the Vicksburg batteries, 25 March 1863.*
NAVAL HISTORICAL CENTER (NH 59103)

Grant, meanwhile, rejected another frontal assault on Vicksburg, and heavy rain postponed any attempt down the Mississippi until spring. Grant and Porter then decided on a series of smaller operations that would position Union troops below Vicksburg without having to run the river batteries; these operations were to become known as the "water experiments." Although Porter said he thought the project ill-conceived, Grant also set four thousand men to work on the Young's Point peninsula canal abandoned the previous summer and begun anew by McClernand before Grant's arrival. This project proved more difficult than first thought, and on 8 March a sudden rise in the river caused a dam to give way, wiping out most of the work. Confederate snipers and artillery fire prevented reconstruction and led to the project's abandonment.[12]

Grant still hoped to find a means to send troops against Vicksburg and yet avoid the heights north of the city. Toward that end, he ordered McPherson's corps at Lake Providence in Louisiana to dig a canal and cut the levee at that point. Lake Providence had at one time been a channel for the Mississippi, and Grant hoped that, if the river could be diverted there, sizable Union forces might be moved by water into Bayou Baxter, thence into the Rensas River, the Ouachita, and finally into the Red. Although Porter ordered naval units to cooperate, a large number of trees barred the way. The swift river current also drove the steamers against the trees, damaging the ships and forcing the project's abandonment.[13]

During February to April, Grant and Porter tried again in the Yazoo Pass Expedition. Porter believed that his ships could work around east of Vicksburg by little-used waterways. Just below Helena, Arkansas, some 150 miles north of Vicksburg, Yazoo Pass led from the Mississippi to Moon Lake, which connected with the Coldwater River. The Coldwater in turn emptied into the Tallahachie River, which combined with the Yalobusha River to form the Yazoo, which joined the Mississippi just north of Vicksburg. Mississippi Delta farmers had used the Yazoo Pass route to trade with Memphis, but it had been closed off when the state of Mississippi ordered construction of a one-hundred-foot wide by twenty-eight-foot high levee at Yazoo Pass to prevent flooding. This levee had, then, considerably lowered water levels throughout the delta region.

Union engineers believed that cutting the Yazoo Pass levee would raise water levels to the point that shallow-draft gunboats and transports might navigate the delta waterways. Grant and Porter hoped that a flotilla of light-draft gunboats, transports, and auxiliaries could then move to somewhere above Haynes's Bluff. To implement this plan, on 2 February Union engineers blew up the levee with explosives.

The Union force set out the next day. Lt. Cdr. Watson Smith had charge of what was the largest such expedition of the war to date. It included the ironclads *Chillicothe* and *Baron de Kalb*; the gunboats *Rattler* (the flagship), *Marmora*, *Signal*, *Romeo*, and *Forest Rose*; the towboat *S. Bayard* with three barges of coal; and thirteen transports with some six thousand troops under Brig. Gen. Leonard F. Ross. The expedition got through the pass without much difficulty, but the Coldwater remained obstructed by a great many trees—some large ones having been deliberately felled by the Confederates—and widespread underwater growth, all of which the Union expeditionary force had to drag clear. The going was a bit easier when the expeditionary force reached the larger Tallahachie. At this point, it was joined by the light-draft gunboat *Petrel* with a 13-inch mortar as well as the rams *Lyoness* and *Fulton*.

The Confederates were well aware of Union intentions, and, at Greenwood at the confluence of the Tallahachie and Yalobusha rivers on a bend of the Tallahachie just west of the Yalobusha, they erected Fort Pemberton. Manned by fifteen hundred men under Maj. Gen. William W. Loring, the fort was constructed of cotton bales covered with earth and was in an almost impregnable position that commanded the river in either direction. Completely surrounded by water, the fort was thus not accessible by land. Most of its half dozen guns were small, but the works did contain an impressive 6.4-inch Whitworth rifle. The Confederates also sank as an obstruction in the channel the CSS *St. Philip*, the ex-*Star of the West* captured off Texas on 17 April 1861.

Smith relied primarily on his two ironclads, which he sent against the fort on 11, 13, and 16 March. Each time the ironclads received the worst of it. One Confederate shell penetrated the port side of the *Chillicothe*, exploding a Union shell and killing three men, mortally wounding another, and wounding ten. On the third attempt, the *Chillicothe* was rendered hors de combat, with twenty-two killed, drowned, or wounded in the three engagements. The *Baron de Kalb* was also "severely handled." Operations were also affected by the fact that Smith was quite ill, forcing him to yield command to a subordinate.

With Union troops unable to land, Ross decided to withdraw. The expeditionary force then encountered Union reinforcements under Brig. Gen. Isaac F. Quinby, who was senior to Ross and ordered a return to Fort Pemberton. Following other futile attacks, Quinby broke off the effort for good on 4 April, with Union forces retracing their steps north to the Mississippi.[14]

While the Yazoo force was encountering problems and Farragut was attempting to get his ships past Port Hudson, Porter launched his Steele's Bayou Expedition, hoping thereby to secure entrance to the Yazoo and land above Haynes's Bluff in order to turn the Confederate flank. On 14 March, Porter set out with the *Louisville, Cincinnati, Carondelet, Pittsburg,* and *Mound City,* four mortar schooners, and four tugs. In Black Bayou, progress was blocked by a dense forest of trees, which had to be pushed aside or dragged from the water. Nonetheless, in twenty-four hours the expedition had advanced four miles. Sherman and ten thousand men in transports followed.

The expedition reached the Yazoo on 16 March. There, progress was easy. This was not the case on the next stream, the smaller Rolling Fork. Trees and undergrowth there again impeded progress, and Union seamen were forced to employ boat howitzers loaded with grape and cannister to chase away Confederate sharpshooters. All manner of wildlife dropped from branches above as the ships brushed by, to be swept off the decks by crewmen with brooms.

As the flotilla approached the Sunflower River, a Confederate transport appeared, depositing both troops and light artillery on the levee. Porter estimated the Confederate force at four thousand men, and the Union transports with Sherman's men were then some distance off. The Union crews could hear the sound of axes felling trees behind the squadron, indicating that the Confederates were trying to trap the ships in place. Porter sent word via a local slave to Sherman requesting he come up immediately, and Sherman responded. As the Union troops struggled to reach Porter, the admiral attempted to deal with the Confederates ahead of him. Unable to elevate his ships' guns sufficiently to engage the Confederate artillery on the top of the levee, Porter blasted away at the troops on the shore.

With Porter contemplating scuttling his ships, the Union troops finally arrived. They drove the Confederates from both banks, allowing the Union ships to descend the river to safety. The 14–27 March expedition had covered 140 miles—70 each way—but, as with its predecessors, it ended in failure.[15]

On their return, Grant met with Sherman and Porter on board his headquarters steamer at Milliken's Bend to consider options. With winter past, additional land options were possible, including an earlier plan now rendered feasible by the receding waters. It involved marching Union troops down the Louisiana side of the river south of Vicksburg to New Carthage. Porter's ships would run past Vicksburg in order to ferry Grant's men across the river to Grand Gulf in Mississippi, allowing him to approach Vicksburg from the south. The plan was risky, but Grant was determined to try.

On 29 March, Grant left his base and moved his troops down the Louisiana shore. It was difficult going. Many areas were still flooded, necessitating the laying of log roads for the wagon trains. Meanwhile, Porter prepared for the dangerous run past the Vicksburg batteries. His crews did what they could, piling logs and baled hay around their ships' vitals. For additional protection, each ship had a coal barge lashed to its side. Porter ordered that the ships proceed fifty yards apart with no lights showing and the gunports covered until ready to fire. To muffle sound, when the ships approached the Vicksburg batteries, exhausts were to be vented into the wheel. Should a ship become disabled, it was to be scuttled and destroyed.

The squadron got under way at 7 PM on 16 April, Grant observing the scene from a navy tug. The flagship *Benton* led, the tug *Ivy* lashed to its side. The *Lafayette* followed with the *General Price* alongside, and then the *Louisville*, *Mound City*, *Pittsburg*, and *Carondelet*, three army transports, and the side-wheeler *Tuscumbia* placed in the van to make certain the army transports continued on course.

For a time it looked as if the ships might make it through unscathed, but Confederate pickets gave the alarm, and soon bonfires were blazing on shore. To provide additional illumination, the Confederates also fired some houses on the Louisiana shore, despite the presence there of Union troops. When the shore batteries opened up at 11:16 PM, the Union ships replied, maintaining a fierce fire. Two of the transports did attempt to return upriver, but the *Tuscumbia* blocked them. Although all Union ships were struck, some a half dozen or more times, only the transport *Henry Clay* suffered fatal injury. Soon a blazing wreck, it drifted downriver before sinking. Surprisingly, all its crew members were saved. The *Lafayette* was also hard hit, but the *Tuscumbia* took it in tow.

One by one, the Union ships arrived at New Carthage, Louisiana. Remarkably, in an action extending over two and a half hours, the total Union toll was only twelve men wounded. In the exchange, Vicksburg had suffered damage and one Confederate gun had burst, killing two men and wounding another six.[16]

Other Union ships subsequently also made the passage. A few days later, six transports with barges with supplies floated past Vicksburg, and only one, the *Tygress*, was lost. With New Carthage proving untenable, Grant consolidated his forces at Hard Times, Louisiana.

Porter and Grant hoped to overcome Confederate defenses at Grand Gulf on the east bank, twenty-five miles south of Vicksburg, and cross there. Grand Gulf boasted two batteries mounting thirteen heavy guns, including three rifled pieces, and on the morning of 29 April Porter mounted an effort to reduce the defenses. Porter got under way at 7 AM with the *Benton, Louisville, Carondelet, Mound City, Pittsburg, Tuscumbia*, and *Lafayette*. The *General Price* carried troops and towed transports past the batteries. The engagement lasted more than six hours, with the Union ships firing more than one thousand rounds.

Although Union shelling soon silenced the lower battery and caused upper-battery fire to slacken, most of the ships were damaged in turn. The *Benton* was struck forty-seven times. In all, Porter's ships sustained eighteen killed and fifty-six wounded, most of them in the *Benton* when a Confederate shell entered the ironclad's casemate and exploded. The *Tuscumbia* was also struck hard and badly damaged.

Grant, meanwhile, offloaded his men from the transports and marched them two miles past the batteries. At 6 PM the Union warships safely escorted all the transports past the batteries. Learning from an escaped slave of another landing site with a road to the interior, Grant ordered a crossing at that point, at Bruinsburg, Mississippi, six miles downriver. On 30 April, Porter's ships began ferrying McClernand's and McPherson's two corps across the river.[17]

To confuse Pemberton and prevent him from sending forces south, Grant and Porter mounted a diversion by Sherman's corps up the Yazoo in ships left behind for this purpose. During 29 April–1 May, Sherman employed the *Black Hawk, Baron de Kalb, Tyler, Choctaw, Signal, Romeo, Linden*, and *Petrel*, along with three tugs towing three mortar boats, and ten large transports. Commanded by Lt. Cdr. K. R. Breese, these ships proceeded up the Yazoo and disembarked the troops at Haynes's Bluff. The diversion had the desired effect. Pemberton recalled the men sent south to reinforce against Grant and sent them by forced march to Haynes's Bluff. Additionally, beginning on 17 April, Union Army Col. Henry Grierson had led seventeen hundred cavalry in a brilliant six-hundred-mile-long, two-week raid into Mississippi from La Grange, Tennessee, tearing up rails and destroying Confederate supply depots before ending up at Baton Rouge.[18]

Through 1 May, twenty-four thousand Union troops crossed the Mississippi at Bruinsburg in what was the largest U.S. amphibious operation to that point in history. Confederate Brig. Gen. John S. Brown with eight thousand men tried without success to destroy the lodgment. Grant recalled that with the landing,

> I felt a degree of relief scarcely ever equaled since. . . . I was now in the enemy's country, with a vast river and the stronghold of Vicksburg between me and my base of supplies. But I was on dry ground on the same side of the river with the enemy. All the campaigns, labors, hardships, and expenses from the month of December previous to this time that had been made and endured, were for the accomplishment of this one object.[19]

Meanwhile, on 4 May Porter proceeded up the Red River with the *Benton, Lafayette,* and *Pittsburg,* the rams *General Price* and *Switerland,* and the tug *Ivy.* He took Confederate Fort DeRussy, which had held seven guns but which the Confederates had already removed, including the two Dahlgrens from the *Indianola.* Porter then took Alexandria, where he confiscated and destroyed some Confederate property. Much of the latter had already been removed, including light-draft steamers sent upriver to Shreveport. After turning over the city to Union troops under General Banks, Porter dropped down the river to destroy the works at Fort DeRussy.[20]

Grant, meanwhile, defied Halleck's instructions that he await the arrival of reinforcements under Banks from Natchez. Even his friend Sherman urged delay, but Grant knew that this would give the Confederates time to both reinforce and fortify. Gambling boldly, he abandoned his river base and marched inland with twenty thousand men, carrying as much ammunition as possible along with five days' worth of food supplies in confiscated wagons, carts, and carriages. Grant ordered his men to forage and live off the land as much as possible.

Grant then conducted one of the most brilliant campaigns in American military history. Striking east, on 3 May he took Port Gibson, forcing the Confederates to abandon Grand Gulf to the north. Pemberton was largely ignorant of Grant's movements, the consequence of theater Cdr. Gen. Joseph Johnston having stripped away much of his cavalry. Advised by Johnston to join him in an effort to defeat Grant in open battle while at the same time ordered by President Davis to defend Vicksburg "at all cost," Pemberton obeyed Davis.

Grant, meanwhile, struck northeast to prevent a juncture of Johnston and Pemberton. On 12 May Grant was victorious in a battle at Raymond, and two days later he descended upon and took the city of Jackson, held by six thousand Confederates. Grant soon abandoned this important railhead, but not before having destroyed it as a transportation and logistics base for Vicksburg.

Grant then turned due west for Vicksburg. At Champion's Hill on 16 May, with twenty-nine thousand men, he defeated Pemberton, who had sallied from Vicksburg with twenty-two thousand men. Pemberton held the high ground and the fighting was heavy, with the Champion's Hill plantation changing hands three times before the Confederates retired westward into the Vicksburg defensive perimeter. Union casualties amounted to twenty-five hundred men, whereas the Confederates lost some four thousand.

By 18 May, Grant had invested Vicksburg. Following two unsuccessful assaults on 19 and 22 May, Grant went over to siege warfare, while at the same time releasing some of his steadily increasing manpower to Sherman to tear up the roads, destroy bridges, and carry out foraging, effectively countering Johnston's efforts to mount a relief operation.[21]

The Union Navy also played a key role in the siege of Vicksburg. It provided logistics support and landed some heavy guns and the crews to work them. It also provided naval gunfire, and mortar boats lobbed thousands of shells into the city. Porter's ships, divided into divisions above and below Vicksburg, also prevented any Confederate resupply from the west.

Porter followed Grant's operations closely, and on 18 May, with Sherman's troops having taken Snyder's Bluff, he sent ships up the Yazoo to open communications with them. This operation involved the ironclads *Baron de Kalb* (the flagship) and *Choctaw* and the tinclads *Forest Rose*,

Linden, Petrel, and *Romeo.* Porter then ordered Walke to Haynes's Bluff, where he discovered the shore batteries abandoned, including fourteen heavy guns and a large quantity of ammunition. Destroying these, the Union ships steamed farther upriver to Yazoo City. Here they found under construction the gunboats *Mobile* and *Republic,* and an as yet unnamed 310-foot-long "monster" (Porter's characterization) to be powered by six engines. The Confederates burned all three ships to prevent their capture.

The Union sailors then put to the torch the Yazoo City navy yard and its shops and sawmills. Farther upriver, they destroyed seven small steamers. On 13 July, in another foray up the Yazoo, the *Baron de Kalb* struck a torpedo under its bow. As the ship began to settle, a second torpedo went off under its stern, whereupon the ship sank in twenty feet of water, although no lives were lost.[22]

On 27 May, as the steady Union bombardment of Vicksburg continued from both land and water, Porter ordered Lt. George M. Bache to take the *Cincinnati* and destroy a Confederate battery on Fort Hill that threatened an impending move by Sherman's troops. As the ironclad worked into position, the river current turned the ship around, exposing its weak stern and allowing the Confederates ashore to rake it with shell fire. With his ship in a sinking condition, Bache tried to work back upriver close to shore. Using a hawser, the crew managed to secure the *Cincinnati* to a tree on shore, but the rope gave way, and the gunboat slipped into deeper water and sank. Forty sailors were casualties.[23]

The siege of Vicksburg was now drawing to a close. Grant's forces daily increased in strength, while Confederate soldiers and civilians in the city alike were driven into caves to escape the relentless Union shelling. With food stocks near exhaustion and even drinking water in scarce supply, on 3 July Pemberton met with Grant and the next day surrendered Vicksburg and 31,600 officers and men, along with 172 cannon and 60,000 small arms, including a considerable number of modern Enfield rifles imported from Britain that Grant then used to equip his volunteers, many of whom had been carrying smoothbore flintlocks. Union casualties in the campaign numbered some 17,000 dead.

Grant praised Porter and the navy for their role in the victory:

> The navy under Porter was all it could be, during the entire campaign. With its assistance the campaign could not have

been successfully made without twice the number of men engaged. It could not have been made at all, in the way it was, with any number of men without such assistance. The most perfect harmony reigned between the two arms of the service. There never was a request made, that I am aware of, either of the flag-officer or any of his subordinates, that was not promptly complied with.[24]

Port Hudson, the last Confederate bastion on the Great River, surrendered on 8 July, following a forty-seven-day siege by fourteen thousand Union troops under Banks. The entire Mississippi was now under Union control, and the Confederacy split. Lincoln summed it up: "The Father of Waters again goes unvexed to the sea." The president also paid praise to the navy, "Uncle Sam's Web-feet," who had made their tracks "wherever the ground was a little damp."[25]

Control of the mighty river greatly benefitted the Union. Significant resupply from the Trans-Mississippi West to the rest of the Confederacy were now largely cut off. Midwestern farmers could also export their goods via the river, ensuring the support of that important region for the Union war effort. The victory brought Grant's promotion to lieutenant general and his elevation to command of all Union armies, and Porter received the thanks of Congress and was made a permanent rear admiral. With the north south axis now secure, Grant was free to attempt to split the Confederacy from west to east.

The Union captures of Vicksburg and Port Hudson did not end Union riverine operations in the West. These continued for the duration of the war. Largely forgotten today, individual Union warships carried out aggressive patrolling activities, and frequent ship-shore confrontations occurred on the western rivers, usually when isolated Confederate units on shore opened fire on Union ships with small arms, field artillery, or both. The Confederates also conducted mine warfare. Proof that the navy's task in the West was not yet complete came in the largest Union riverine operation of the war, the spring 1864 Red River Expedition.

CHAPTER NINE

Union Operations against Charleston 1863

—⟶∿∿⟵—

W hile it was operating with the army along the western rivers, the greater part of the Union Navy's effort was concentrated in the blockade of the Confederate coasts. Ship by ship and cove by cove, the blockade steadily grew in effectiveness. Blockade running, meanwhile, became a major business operation in which specially built or converted ships, many of them constructed in British yards, operated out of Nassau in the Bahamas; Havana, Cuba; Bermuda; and Halifax, Nova Scotia. The two chief Southern ports utilized by the blockade runners were Wilmington, North Carolina, and Charleston, South Carolina.

Charleston was an especially powerful symbol to both sides. Northerners regarded it as the "Cradle of the Rebellion." The Ordinance of Secession had been signed there, and the first shots of the war had been fired in its harbor. Thus, quite apart from their continuing blockade running, Northern leaders had strong incentive to close or to take Charleston. Indeed, Union operations against that city developed into the longest campaign of the war. Taking Charleston would not end the war, but a Union success there would deliver a heavy blow to Southern morale. Unfortunately for them, Northern leaders seem not to have understood the effects on both North and South of a Union failure.[1]

Flag Officer Samuel Du Pont commanded the South Atlantic Blockading Squadron. Du Pont had joined the navy as a midshipman in 1815 and had been a captain since 1855. A leader in both naval reform and in advancing professionalism, Du Pont was a key figure in the creation of the Naval Academy at Annapolis. Du Pont had served with distinction in the Mexican-American War and was instrumental in the formation of the 1855 Naval Efficiency Board that had culled much deadwood from the officer corps. At the beginning of the Civil War he had chaired the Blockade Board, and in September 1861 he received command of the South Atlantic Blockading Squadron. Enjoying Welles's full confidence, Du Pont was, in July 1862, one of the first rear admirals in U.S Navy history.[2]

Du Pont's impressive success against Port Royal in November 1861 seemed to bode well for future aggressive operations along the south Atlantic coast. Indeed, immediately after the seizure of Port Royal, he had appealed for a joint army–navy operation against Charleston but had been rebuffed. That opportunity, if it had indeed existed, soon vanished.

Throughout the long operations against Charleston, Du Pont consistently held to the view that the city would only be taken through combined land and sea assault. Du Pont wrote to his friend Commo. Theodorus Bailey in late October 1862:

> I feel that very heavy work is before me, for there seems a morbid appetite in the land to have Charleston. . . . If a single tithe of that Potomac army had been sent to this region after the capture of the forts here, Savannah and Charleston would have fallen with scarcely any loss of life under a joint operation. The difficulties to be overcome have increased a thousandfold since then. . . . The Department thinks it can be done with a few monitors.[3]

At the end of 1861, operating from Port Royal, Du Pont had attempted to block the main channel at Charleston, or at least render it difficult for blockaders to navigate at night. On 20 December the blockaders had sunk the "stone fleet," a number of hulks filled with rocks. Powerful tides and storms soon washed this obstruction away.

Following this failure, Welles and others in Washington, including Lincoln, favored an assault by ships alone. They believed that a powerful force of ironclads might push past Fort Sumter, rather than attempt to batter it into submission, and force the Confederates to withdraw from the other forts and from James Island. Charleston would then simply surrender, just as New Orleans had yielded to Farragut. With the "panic" that would ensue following the fall of Charleston, the Union ironclads might then move against Savannah.

Assistant Secretary of the Navy Fox especially championed this view. A passionate believer in the new monitors, he saw in Charleston the opportunity for the navy to win glory, with the army largely a spectator. Certainly a joint operation would require many more men than the ten thousand troops under Maj. Gen. David Hunter at Hilton Head. Substantial land forces were simply not available given the requirements of the concurrent Vicksburg campaign. If Charleston was to be attacked and taken, the navy would have to do it alone. In December 1862 pressure was on the navy to reverse Union failures on land, including Grant's first attempt against Vicksburg and the bloody Union repulse at Fredericksburg.[4]

But Charleston was now well prepared to meet any attack. The Confederates had continually strengthened its works, to the point that by 1862 it was probably the best-defended port in the Western Hemisphere and certainly the Southern city best able to withstand a seaborne assault. Charleston boasted an integrated defensive system of some 385 land-based guns; the ironclad rams *Palmetto State* and *Chicora* (two others, the *Charleston* and *Columbia*, were building); obstructions blocking the river and harbor approaches; torpedoes; and prepared positions into which the relatively small numbers of Confederate troops available could be moved on short notice.

By 1863 Charleston's defenses were in three separate circles or defensive tiers: an outer layer on the Atlantic barrier islands astride the mouth of the harbor, along with the central position of Fort Sumter to cover the channel; a tier of artillery batteries in the inner harbor in order to take under fire any Federal ships that broke through; and a tier of land forts to protect the flanks and guard against an attack from that quarter similar to that mounted by the British when they captured the city in 1780 during the American Revolutionary War.

Not only man-made obstacles stood in the Union path. Strong tidal currents in the harbor could run three to five knots, posing a problem for the slow monitors, and the shallows of Charleston Bar blocked direct entrance to the harbor. A series of irregular breaks in the bar permitted deep-draft ships to utilize the Main Ship, Swash, and North Channels, but only light-draft vessels could use rightmost Maffitt's Channel (also known as Sullivan's Island Channel), which in any case ran hard against Fort

Sullivan. Navigation in and out of Charleston was difficult even in normal times; it was rendered much more perilous because the defenders removed buoys marking the channel, meaning that the wide and deep main ship channel was the only safe approach for an attacker.

The Confederate forts were particularly well sited for defensive purposes. Facing Charleston from the sea, to the left of the harbor entrance lay Morris Island, with Fort Wagner and Battery Gregg. Immediately ahead and just inside the harbor entrance was pentagon-shaped Fort Sumter; to the right of the main entrance was Sullivan's Island and its principal works of Fort Moultrie, along with Batteries Bee and Beauregard. Any attacking naval force reaching the harbor mouth would be subjected to fire from three sides: Battery Gregg, Fort Sumter, and Fort Multrie.

Charleston's inner defenses against attack from the sea were also impressive. They consisted of Fort Johnson and Battery Glover on James Island, Fort Ripley and Castle Pinckney in the harbor itself, and the White Point Battery (Battery Ramsay) in Charleston. Sumter, which was of brick, and Moultrie, of masonry-faced earth, were the two most powerful works in the defensive system. All save Sumter were earthworks or masonry-clad earthworks, low lying and difficult for naval gunfire to destroy.

Ironclads were the key to the Union plan. Welles, official Washington, and much of Northern public opinion believed that sufficient numbers of monitors and the *New Ironsides* could not fail to smash their way into the harbor, and in early October 1862 Welles summoned Du Pont to Washington to discuss the impending operation. The admiral was not impressed by the department's belief that ships alone would be successful. Du Pont wrote in January 1863, "I have never had but one opinion—that the capture of Charleston should be effected by a joint operation of Army & Navy—not that I am insensible to a *Naval* capture—but that *success* is a vital *necessity* now, and no means should be spared to secure this."[5]

If he was to have any chance at success, Du Pont wanted to have available the most powerful possible force. He wrote Fox, "Let there be no *stinting*, for *we* must not fail." Later, Du Pont wrote, "the limit of my wants in the need of ironclads is the capacity of the [Navy] Department to supply them." Fox and Welles ultimately sent Du Pont all but one of the navy's new monitors. By the spring of 1863, however, Welles was clearly impatient over his commander's failure to move.[6]

Du Pont's hesitance was not just over the number of ironclads he would have available in an assault, but rather their mechanical problems and growing doubts within the navy of their ability to destroy shore fortifications. He also wanted to give the new XV-inch Dahlgrens a combat test. For this he selected Fort McAllister on the Ogeechee River, Georgia, an earthwork fortification mounting eight or nine guns.

On 27 January 1863, Du Pont sent against McAllister a force under Cdr. John L. Worden and consisting of the newly arrived *Passaic*-class monitor *Montauk*; the gunboats *Seneca*, *Wissahickon*, and *Dawn*; and the mortar schooner *C. P. Williams*. The *Montauk* was unable to close with McAllister because of sunken obstacles that appeared to be protected by torpedoes. It nonetheless fired a total of fifty-two shells and shot with its XI-inch and XV-inch Dahlgrens over a period of four and a half hours but without noticeable effect. Worden reported that Confederate return fire was very accurate. His own ship was struck fourteen times but suffered no damage other than the loss of its cutter.

On 28 January a runaway slave provided information on the location of the torpedoes that had blocked the *Montauk*'s way the day before, and, after taking on a fresh supply of ammunition, Worden returned on 1 February with the *Montauk* and the same consorts. This time the monitor was able to close to only six hundred yards before opening fire. Each side opened accurate fire on the other, with the monitor taking forty-eight hits in the course of a four-hour engagement. Although the Union ironclad was not seriously damaged, the Confederate fort was also unbowed. Plainly worried over the *Montauk*'s unsatisfactory forays, Du Pont wrote a friend, "If one ironclad cannot take eight guns, how are five to take 147 guns in Charleston harbor?"[7]

As Du Pont was contemplating the situation, on the morning of 31 January Confederate Flag Officer Duncan N. Ingraham took advantage of morning fog to sortie from Charleston with the ironclad rams *Palmetto State* (Cdr. John Rutledge) and *Chicora* (Cdr. John R. Tucker) to attack ten wooden steamers of the Union blockading squadron lying off the harbor. The *Palmetto State* approached the side-wheeler *Mercedita* undetected. Before the alarm could be given, the *Palmetto State* had closed to a point where the *Mercedita* was unable to depress its own guns sufficiently to fire into the Confederate ship. Rammed and fired upon, the *Mercedita* lost seven men killed and wounded, most of them firemen and coal passers scalded when a Confederate shell passed through its steam chimney. "She being in a sinking and perfectly defenseless condition," Capt. Henry Stellwagen surrendered the ship and sent his executive officer, Lt. Cdr. Trevett Abbot, to the *Palmetto State*. A subsequent Union court of inquiry upheld Abbot's pledge, which the Confederates had demanded, that none of the *Mercedita*'s officers and crew again "take up arms" against the Confederacy, but the court also determined that this did not apply to the ship itself, which was recovered.

The *Chicora*, meanwhile, attacked the large side-wheeler *Keystone State*, hitting the Union ship ten times, disabling its machinery, and setting it on fire. The *Keystone State* suffered a quarter of its crew casualties: twenty dead and a like number wounded. Other Union warships—the *Augusta*, *Quaker City*, and *Memphis*—then arrived.

Although it had two feet of water in its hold and was leaking badly, the *Keystone State* survived. Lt. Cdr. Pendleton Watmough was able to bring the *Memphis* up in time and tow the *Keystone State* to safety. Meanwhile, the two other Union gunboats engaged the rams. Both the *Quaker City* and *Augusta* were damaged in the exchange of fire; the *Quaker State* took a shell amidships that exploded in the engine room, and the *Augusta* took a shell in the side that narrowly missed its boiler. Both ships survived. Capt. William R. Taylor's screw sloop *Housatonic* then arrived and took the rams under fire, chasing them back into Charleston Harbor.

Confederate commander at Charleston Maj. Gen. P. G. T. Beauregard praised Ingraham for a "brilliant achievement" and claimed that the engagement had broken the Federal blockade. Despite the damage wrought by the rams, that was not the case. Within hours of the engagement, however, the Confederates appealed to the British consul at Charleston, claiming that the Union ships had left their picket line, rendering the blockade ineffective and arguing that, in accordance with international law, the blockade should be lifted. Union Capt. William Rodgers Taylor of the *Housatonic*, however, proved by his ship's log and signed statement of his officers that his ship had fired on the two Confederate ships and indeed chased them back into the harbor. The blockade of Charleston continued, considerably strengthened by the arrival there on 1 February of the ironclad *New Ironsides*.[8]

On 18 February, Du Pont sent the *Montauk* back to Fort McAllister for a third time, this time to destroy the Confederate cruiser *Nashville*. Seized and converted from a passenger steamer at Charleston at the beginning of the war, the *Nashville* had been active in European waters during November 1861–February 1862 and had taken two prizes. In 1862 it had been converted into a blockade runner and, for nearly nine months, had been awaiting an opportunity to run the blockade, only to run aground in the Ogeechee River near Fort McAllister.

Taking up position about twelve hundred yards from the *Nashville*, the *Montauk* opened fire, setting the Confederate ship on fire and destroying it. Fort McAllister in turn fired on the monitor, hitting it five times without material result. In departing the area, however, the *Montauk* suffered damage from the explosion of a torpedo under its hull, which took several weeks to repair.[9]

Fort McAllister received additional Union attention on 3 March, when Du Pont ordered a fourth attack against it. This time he dispatched there the monitors *Passaic, Patapsco,* and *Nahant,* along with the gunboats *Seneca, Wissahickon,* and *Dawn,* as well as three mortar schooners. Du Pont informed Welles that he meant this and the earlier attacks against Fort McAllister as a test of the monitors rather than a serious attempt to take the fort. Capt. Percival Drayton of the *Passaic,* who led the fourth attack, reported that although, as before, the monitors were practically unscathed by the fort's fire, little or no damage had been done to the fort, certainly nothing that could not be repaired overnight.

The inconclusive nature of these engagements gave heart to Charleston's defenders, who now tended to denigrate the monitors. In spite of their ability to withstand punishment, it took nearly seven minutes to ready one of the giant XV-inch guns for firing, slowing the paired XI-incher to the same rate. This rate of fire rendered these ships simply incapable of inflicting in a short span of time the sort of damage necessary to reduce shore fortifications. This was especially true against Charleston, given the time necessary to work the ships into position.[10]

During the first week in April, the remaining monitors arrived. For the operation, Du Pont chose as his flagship the *New Ironsides,* certainly the most powerful ship in the U.S. Navy (it represented half the firepower of the Union fleet at Charleston) and the best suited of all its large ships for shore bombardment. Because the *New Ironside's* wooden spar deck was vulnerable to plunging fire, its crew protected it with green rawhides covered with sandbags. The men also erected similar barricades of sandbags below decks to protect against raking fire from bow or stern.

The monitors received additional deck plating against plunging fire, and vulnerable surfaces were liberally coated with tallow so that projectiles would be more likely to glance off.[11]

Du Pont understood the risks of mounting an attack inside Charleston Harbor. The attackers would have to navigate around numerous obstacles in the channel, and should one of the Union ships become hung up on one of these it would be easy prey for destruction by the shore batteries. Torpedoes also posed a significant threat. Du Pont hoped to partially deflect this threat with a new device, known from its appearance as a "boot-jack." Invented by Ericsson and the only countertorpedo device available, it consisted of a raft shaped to fit around the monitor's bows and pushed ahead by it. The boot-jack was equipped with grapnels to snare torpedoes. Ericsson also planned to place a torpedo at the end of each raft to be detonated when it came into contact with an obstacle, thereby destroying it. This part of the boot-jack was eliminated for fear that it would endanger other ships. The deep draft of the *New Ironsides* and its lack of maneuverability were also problems. Du Pont settled on an attack from inside the harbor. This would distance his ships from Fort Moultrie and provide deeper water for maneuvering. It would also place his ships where he believed certain of the Confederate forts could not fire on them.

The Confederate defenders, although mistaken in their expectation of a joint army–navy assault, nonetheless anticipated Du Pont's basic plan. They expected the Union monitors to run to several hundred yards from Fort Sumter, where they would be protected from the parapet and upper guns of the fort and then attempt to breach the fort. Du Pont's plan had the squadron running the outer Confederate defenses as well as Fort Sumter, and then destroying Sumter from the north and northwest.

British experiments suggested that ironclads were relatively safe from return fire at a range of twelve hundred to thirteen hundred yards, and Capt. John Rodgers of the *Weehawken* suggested the ships take up an arc formation and then anchor at that distance, both to improve their accuracy of fire and to keep them safe from torpedoes. Du Pont, however, preferred an attack at half that distance, even with the increased risk to his ships, in order to enhance the accuracy of his relatively small number of guns. Part of this had to do with his new XV-inch Dahlgrens. They fired 400-pound projectiles (as opposed to 170-pound balls for the XI-inch guns). The XV-inchers were so new that they had not been adequately tested, and

Chief of the Bureau of Ordnance Dahlgren had advised Du Pont that he thought their useful life would be about three hundred rounds. Given this and their slow rate of fire, Du Pont no doubt believed that accuracy of fire trumped all other considerations.[12]

Du Pont issued his orders on 4 April. Although attacking at night would have rendered the ironclads much more difficult to hit, the great difficulty of maneuvering them in the tricky current during hours of darkness precluded anything other than a daylight attack. Du Pont planned to employ nine ships, all ironclads: the seven monitors, the *New Ironsides*, and the hybrid *Keokuk*.

Once across the bar, Rodgers's *Weehawken* would lead the other ships up the main channel. The flagship *New Ironsides* would be fifth in the Union battle line. As the largest ship in the squadron, the *New Ironsides*'s signal flags could be more easily seen if the ship was in the middle of the formation. But its deep draft would force it to remain in the middle of the channel, preventing Du Pont from veering out of the line to take the lead as Farragut had done in the Mississippi before New Orleans. Du Pont would have to rely on Rodgers's judgment.

Du Pont ordered that the Union ships not return fire from the batteries on Morris Island. Instead they would steam into the harbor and then open fire against Sumter, without anchoring, six hundred to eight hundred yards from the northwest face of the fort. After Sumter had been reduced, Du Pont planned to have the ironclads, joined by the five wooden ships of his reserve squadron, concentrate on shelling Confederate batteries on Morris Island.[13]

If Du Pont and some of his captains were uncertain as to their prospects, the men seemed confident. One seaman wrote his hometown newspaper: "Your numerous readers may be prepared to hear the report of some loud Yankee thunder from this place. . . . All hands are wide awake and ready, and feel confident that a great and glorious victory will crown our efforts."[14]

On 5 April steamers towed the monitors to a point off the bar. The *Keokuk* then proceeded to mark the bar with buoys and report on the depth of water in order to cross it the next morning. This was accomplished, but delays and poor visibility from haze led Du Pont to reschedule the attack for 7 April. The Confederate defenders, meanwhile, were fully alerted.

Haze on the morning of 7 April soon burned off, but on the urging of his pilots, Du Pont agreed to delay the attempt until the ebb tide in order to facilitate spotting obstructions in the water. An additional two-hour delay occurred when the grapnels of the *Weehawken's* torpedo raft fouled its anchor chain. Finally, at 12:10 PM, Du Pont ordered signals hoisted for the squadron to get under way and steam at one cable length (two hundred yard) intervals. Despite difficulty maintaining position in the fast-moving current, by 1:15 PM the ships were all moving up the main channel. The *Weehawken*, however, continued to experience problems with its torpedo raft; in the rise and fall of the seaway, the two structures worked against each other. With the torpedo raft actually loosening the monitor's armor, Rodgers ordered it cast adrift. The boot-jack later washed ashore on Morris Island as a Confederate trophy.

At 2:10 PM the *Weehawken* encountered the first Confederate obstructions extending northeastward across the main channel from Fort Sumter to Fort Moultrie. These consisted of a series of buoys supporting a tangled mass of rope. Respected as a bold commander, Rodgers inspected the obstacles as best he could at close range through the narrow slits in the pilothouse. As he contemplated his next step, a torpedo exploded nearby or under the *Weehawken*, slightly lifting the ironclad but doing no damage. Wary of the torpedo raft, believing the obstructions too formidable, and fearful that his own ship or others following might become entangled in them and be held in place under the Confederate shore batteries, Rodgers turned his ship aside. This decision threw the remainder of the Union line into further confusion. It also ended Du Pont's plan of running past the point with the heaviest concentration of Confederate firepower. The obstacles had performed as intended, delaying the lead Union warship and thus the others to follow.

The battle began at about 3 PM, when a gun at Fort Moultrie opened up on the *Weehawken*, then about seven hundred yards from Fort Sumter. The shot struck the monitor's turret squarely but did no damage. Other guns at Fort Moultrie, as well as on Morris Island and at Fort Sumter, then joined in, and soon nearly one hundred guns and mortars had commenced firing. For a time the *Weehawken* disappeared in the spray from the projectiles, and it was assumed in the Union fleet that it had been sunk; however, the monitor soon reappeared. Shortly thereafter Du Pont signaled to return fire. The Union ships then opened up on the east and northeast faces of Fort Sumter, but they made no effort to pass the rope obstruction.

The battle continued at ranges of between 550 and 800 yards for nearly two hours. With only about a foot of water under its keel and swift current,

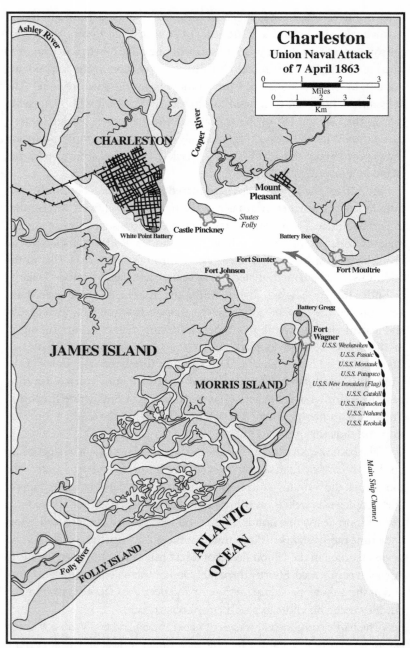

Charleston, Union Naval Attack of 7 April 1863

the *New Ironsides* had trouble holding the channel, and the monitors *Catskill* and *Nantucket*, which were astern, collided with the flagship. The *Keokuk*, the last Union ship in line, also ran past the flagship and was shortly in difficulty. The battle scene was obscured in smoke so thick that crews on the ships had difficulty seeing their target of Fort Sumter; visibility from the flagship was only about fifty yards.

Far from pounding the Confederate forts into submission, the ships themselves sustained some four hundred hits. These heavily damaged a number of the monitors. The *Keokuk* was the hardest hit. Protected by 4-inch iron armor laid on edgeways and an inch apart, with the intervening spaces filled with wood, it proved vulnerable to enemy fire. Running ahead of the crippled *Nahant* to avoid fouling it in the narrow channel, the *Keokuk* came within about six hundred yards of Fort Sumter's guns and remained there some thirty minutes. The ironclad was hit some ninety times, nineteen of these entering at or below the waterline. Having difficulty keeping his ship afloat, Rhind withdrew from the action and anchored overnight beyond the range of Confederate guns.

With the tide having turned and dusk approaching, Du Pont broke off the engagement at 4:30 PM. Because of their relatively small number of guns, the Union ships had fired only 139 rounds; the Confederates fired 2,229! Casualties were slight on both sides. The Confederates suffered four dead or mortally wounded and ten lesser injuries. The Union ships had one killed, in the *Nahant*, and twenty-two wounded (sixteen in the *Keokuk*, including Rhind, with the remainder in the *Nahant*). Nothing could conceal the fact that the Confederates had beaten back a major Union effort and gained a stunning victory.

Du Pont informed Welles that he had intended to resume the battle the next day but changed his mind on receiving damage reports from his captains. The *Keokuk*'s crew was struggling to keep their ship afloat. The *Passaic* had suffered the next most damage. Its XI-inch Dahlgren was disabled, and the top of the pilothouse was loosened and its armor bolt broken. The *Nantucket* had been hit fifty-one times and its XV-inch gun could not fire on account of a disabled port shutter. The *Nahant*'s turret was jammed, and the *Patapsco*'s heavy gun was out of action because of the fracturing of one of the bolts in a cap-square that held it on its mount. The *Weehawken* was struck fifty-three times, and some of its armor had been shattered, leaving the wood exposed. The carriage for its XI-inch gun was also disabled. Other monitors also had broken plates and additional problems. Interestingly, the only nonmonitor in the action, the *New Ironsides*, which had taken more than sixty hits, reported no serious damage, but it also had remained at some distance and only fired one broadside, at Fort Moultrie.[15]

Although Union engineers worked during the night to repair the monitors, Du Pont became convinced that another attack would have turned "a failure into a disaster." He reported to Welles that after listening to the reports of his commanders on the evening of 7 April, "without hesitation or consultation (for I never hold councils of war), I determined not to renew the attack, for in my judgment, it would have converted a failure into a disaster, and I will only add that Charleston can not be taken by a purely naval attack, and the army could give me no cooperation." Du Pont went on to note that, even had he been able to enter Charleston harbor, he would have had only twelve hundred men and thirty-two guns, "but five of the eight ironclads were wholly or partially disabled after a brief engagement." Du Pont's despair was reflected in these words to his wife Sophie, "We have failed as I felt sure we would."[16]

The crew of the *Keokuk* was able to keep their ship afloat that night only because the water was calm. Despite assistance from the tug *Dandelion*, the *Keokuk* sank the next morning when a wind came up. At 7:40 AM, Rhind ordered the crew to abandon ship, and the monitor went down a half hour later, only its funnels remaining visible. The Confederates later recovered its two XI-inch guns.[17]

Du Pont now declared that Charleston could not be taken by naval attack alone. He feared the Confederates might sink and then salvage one of his monitors, with the result being that the whole coast might be lost. Claiming that he had never advised the attack on Charleston, on 12 April Du Pont ordered the monitors to Port Royal, leaving the *New Ironsides* as the sole ironclad on Charleston station. This "guardian of the blockade," as the *New Ironsides* came to be known, performed yeoman service over the next months.

Du Pont's prudent position regarding another attack on Charleston became widely known in the North and was mistakenly perceived as defeatism. Although Welles assured Du Pont of the Navy Department's continued confidence in him, there were soon calls for his removal. Du Pont sensed the change in attitude from Washington and vigorously defended his actions in extensive correspondence; however, following some deliberation, Welles recalled the admiral on 3 June and replaced him with Andrew Foote. Welles gave as his reasons Du Pont's unwillingness to resume offensive operations against Charleston ("I do not find ... in any communication from you since the 7th of April any preparation for a renewed attack upon Charleston, or suggestions even for active operations against that place") and his "prolonged continuance on the blockade."[18]

It made little difference that Du Pont's assessment of the situation at Charleston was correct. Even had the attack by monitors been successful, there were no army plans in place. The effort had been an incredible waste of resources.

John Dahlgren had long sought to command operations against Charleston. Dahlgren had ruthlessly promoted his own advancement and exploited his friendship with Lincoln to achieve the rank of rear admiral in February 1863. Many in the navy resented the fact that this advancement had not been earned through demonstrated sea service. Whether to prove his critics wrong or from his own ambition, or both, Dahlgren actively lobbied for this command. Welles had serious reservations about Dahlgren, however, believing he was selfish and self-seeking. This opinion seemed confirmed when Welles asked Fox to sound out Dahlgren about going to Charleston as second in command, and Dahlgren refused to be subordinate to his old friend Foote. Fox reported that Dahlgren also said he would go to Charleston only if he had command of both naval and land forces. Welles wrote in his diary, "This precludes further thought of him.... It is one of the errors of a lifetime." Foote, however, offered to try to persuade Dahlgren.[19]

On 2 June Dahlgren proposed to Fox that the attack on Charleston be made a separate command from that of the blockade. Fox was enthusiastic and suggested that Dahlgren go to New York and propose it to Foote. The two men met in New York City the next day, with Foote agreeing that Dahlgren would command the ironclads in a new attack on Charleston. During the course of the meeting, however, Foote complained of a severe headache, and three weeks later he was dead of Bright's disease. Welles now reluctantly turned to Dahlgren, who became commander of the South Atlantic Blockading Squadron on 6 July.[20]

Before Dahlgren assumed command, another major ironclad battle occurred, this time in Wassaw Sound, Georgia. The Navy Department

U.S. Navy Rear Adm. John Dahlgren shown beside one of his rifled guns on a Marsilly broadside carriage. LIBRARY OF CONGRESS (B8171-3417)

learned that the ironclad *Atlanta* was about to come down from Savannah to attack the Union wooden blockaders and ordered the *Passaic*-class monitors *Weehawken* (Capt. John Rodgers) and *Nahant* (Cdr. John Downes) to the sound. For some days it appeared that it was a false alarm, but on 17 June Confederate Cdr. William A. Webb led the *Atlanta* and wooden steamers *Isondiga* and *Resolute* down the Wilmington River and into the sound. At about 4 AM Union lookouts spotted the Confederate ships, and Rodgers immediately ordered his monitors to get up steam and the crews beat to quarters. The casemated *Atlanta* mounted four Brooke rifled guns: two 6.4-inchers in broadsides and two 7 inchers in pivot mounts capable of firing to either side. It also had a bow-mounted percussion spar torpedo, which Webb hoped to explode against the *Weehawken*.

Exiting the river and making straight for the *Weehawken*, the *Atlanta* veered from the channel and grounded. Unaware of what had transpired, Rodgers advanced the *Weehawken* toward the Confederate ironclad, the *Nahant* following. The *Atlanta* opened fire, getting off six shots, all of which missed. Rodgers withheld fire until the *Weehawken* was only three hundred to four hundred yards distant, then loosed a 400-pound projectile from the *Weehawken*'s XV-inch Dahlgren that struck the Confederate ship's casemate. Although it did not penetrate, the shot crushed both the iron plate and its wooden backing. The Union monitor fired just five shots in fifteen minutes at relatively close range, four of them striking. Three of the projectiles did the damage. They smashed through the *Atlanta*'s armored casemate, disabled its guns, caused personnel casualties, and forced Webb to surrender.

Confederate ironclad Atlanta; *sepia wash drawing by R. G. Skerrett.*
NAVAL HISTORICAL CENTER (NH 57819)

Of the *Atlanta*'s 145-man crew, 16 were wounded, 1 mortally. The two other Confederate warships, which had kept their distance during the action, withdrew back up the Wilmington. His success earned Rodgers the thanks of Congress. The next year the repaired *Atlanta* was incorporated into the U.S. Navy and joined the South Atlantic Blockading Squadron.[21]

Within a week of taking up his command, Dahlgren ordered Cdr. Foxhall A. Parker to organize, "with as much dispatch as possible," a naval brigade of one battalion of marines and two of sailors. Dahlgren planned to employ them ashore.[22]

Dahlgren wasted little time in undertaking active operations against Charleston. From July to September 1863 he kept up a naval bombardment of the city's defenses, this time in cooperation with land attacks by troops under Maj. Gen. Quincy Adams Gillmore, who had made his reputation in the April 1862 bombardment and capture of Fort Pulaski, Georgia. Gillmore was convinced he could replicate this feat against both Forts Wagner and Sumter.

On 10 July Dahlgren's ships supported the landing of nearly three thousand of Gillmore's men on the south end of Morris Island and their advance to within a half mile of Fort Wagner. During this operation the monitors *Catskill, Nahant, Montauk,* and *Weehawken* dueled with Fort Wagner over nearly twelve hours. Meanwhile, the Union troops sapped their trenches forward, allowing them to position Parrott guns within range of the Confederate positions. For the next two months the navy supported the army ashore, mounting no fewer than twenty-five separate attacks to assist in taking the remainder of Morris Island. On 18 July, eleven of Dahlgren's ships, including six ironclads, as well as Gillmore's gunners subjected Wagner to one of the most intense bombardments of the entire war, firing some nine thousand projectiles over a dozen hours. Six thousand Union troops charged the Confederate positions, spearheaded by the 54th Massachusetts, a regiment of African-American troops commanded by Robert Gould Shaw.

Despite the furious Union bombardment, the Confederate defenders sustained only 8 men dead and 20 wounded, and they now came out of their bombproofs and repulsed the Union land assault in desperate fighting. Gillmore's men suffered 1,515 casualties that day, the defenders but 222. The 54th alone lost 272 men killed, wounded, or missing (Shaw was among the dead), but its heroism under fire vindicated the Union Army's decision to field African-American combat units.[23]

On 17 August, finally able to position a number of heavy guns to shell Fort Sumter, Gillmore began a week-long bombardment of the fort, again supported by the ironclads. On 21 August Dahlgren attempted a night attack on Sumter, which, however, failed when the *Passaic* grounded about a half mile from the fort. Although it was gotten off, this delay caused cancellation of the attack. Dahlgren hesitated between a daylight assault or another night attempt, but on 23 August he mounted another night attack against Sumter. He repeated this at close range on 1 September, the monitors suffering but little in the exchange. Still the fort held.[24]

Gillmore now prepared to shell Charleston itself. By the existing rules of warfare the city was a legitimate target. A fortified city, it was home to war industries and sheltered blockade runners. On 21 August Gillmore sent General Beauregard a demand for the evacuation of Fort Sumter and Morris Island within four hours, stating that if this was not carried out he would open fire on Charleston. With no immediate response forthcoming, at 1:30 AM on 22 August, Union shells began falling on the city. The chief weapon employed was the "Swamp Angel," a large 200-pounder Parrott rifled gun that, before it burst, sent three dozen shells five miles distant into the waterfront district, setting fires and causing panic. Gillmore claimed that the purpose of the shelling was to drive Confederate shipping from the city's wharfs, but the effort seems to have been largely an artillery exercise, and it only hardened Southern determination.[25]

Fort Wagner, the principal Union target, repulsed several attacks with heavy Union losses. Finally, on 6 September, as a result of Union sapping operations, the Confederates abandoned Fort Wagner, and Union troops occupied it. With the fort in Union hands, Charleston became far less desirable a haven for blockade runners.

U.S. Navy monitor Lehigh, *shown here in dock.* U.S. NAVAL INSTITUTE PHOTO ARCHIVE

On 7 September Dahlgren carried out a major attack on Fort Sumter, pummeling it with fire from the monitors *Passaic, Patapsco, Lehigh, Nahant, Montauk,* and *Weehawken.* The Union ships drew little response, save from Fort Moultrie on Sullivan's Island. The *Weehawken,* however, grounded in the pass between Fort Sumter and Cummings Point, and all the Union ships were subjected to a heavy attack at daybreak from the shore batteries. Dahlgren called in the *New Ironsides* to cover the stranded *Weehawken.* It anchored some twelve hundred yards from Fort Moultrie, engaging it and driving its gunners to cover. That day the *New Ironsides* fired 483 shells. The ship was struck at least seventy times in return, but it was not seriously damaged. The *New Ironsides* finally withdrew after having expended all its ammunition. That afternoon the *Weehawken* was refloated, and all the Union ships withdrew. In the exchange, the *Passaic* was hit fifty-one times. A number of these hits were on the turret ring, which disabled the turret.[26]

Dahlgren noted during these operations that Fort Sumter appeared to be partly evacuated, and he ordered a boat attack against it from Morris Island. On the night of 8–9 September, Cdr. Thomas H. Stevens led some four hundred sailors and marines in more than thirty boats. The Confederates were waiting. Alerted to the Union plan as a consequence of the recovery of a signal key from the wreck of the *Keokuk,* the defenders held their fire until the boats were nearly ashore, then opened up with cannon, small arms, and hand grenades. The *Chicora* provided enfilading fire. The attack began and ended so rapidly that the ironclads *New Ironsides, Lehigh,* and *Mohawk* were not able to get into position to provide covering fire. Union losses were 6 killed, 15 wounded, and 106 men taken prisoner, 11 of them officers.[27]

This failure ended Union offensive operations in Charleston Harbor. All the ironclads were now in need of extensive repairs at Port Royal, and it would be some weeks before these could be effected. The other forts continued to hold out, and the Confederates moved some of their heavy guns from Fort Sumter to the more powerful works of Forts Moultrie and Jackson.

Gillmore was increasingly frustrated that Dahlgren would not attempt to move his ships through the obstructions. Although the two men were cordial enough when together, Gillmore went so far as to send officers to complain to Welles. Believing that an effort to pass through the line of pilings that constituted the second obstruction would mean the loss of some ships, Dahlgren requested additional monitors from Washington. Welles demurred, having at last come around to Du Pont's position. The secretary wrote Dahlgren in October 1863, noting that with the capture of Morris Island, the port of Charleston was effectively closed. As a result,

> It is merely a point of honor whether you should go in and take position with your vessels in front of the city, with no cooperating army force to assist or sustain you. . . . The Department is disinclined to have its only ironclad squadron incur extreme risks when the substantial advantages have already been gained.[28]

Indeed, the Confederates provided additional incentive for the Union ships not to renew the assault as they attempted to dislodge the blockade with new defensive weapons of their own. Charleston did not fall to Union forces until February 1865, after Sherman's troops cut its land communications with the rest of the South.

CHAPTER TEN

Unconventional Weapons

—⟆⟆⟆—

The Torpedo and The Submarine

The Civil War saw considerable innovation in weaponry on land and sea. Among the notable changes at sea was the underwater mine. Known during the Civil War as the "torpedo," its name comes from the electric ray fish that shocks its prey. Because mines are principally defensive weapons, they have traditionally been a weapon of choice for weaker naval powers.[1]

America led the world in the development of underwater mine warfare. During the Revolutionary War, Yale University student David Bushnell built mines in his workshop near Saybrook, Connecticut, and deployed them against British warships in the Delaware River in January 1778. These devices were "contact" mines: floating kegs of powder triggered by a flintlock inside the keg. The shock of the mine striking an object released the hammer, which then set off the mine. Warned by the premature explosion of one of the mines, the British took the precaution of firing at anything in the water, which was referred to in the Patriot press as the "Battle of the Kegs."[2]

In 1801, American Robert Fulton attempted to interest Napoleon Bonaparte in France in mines of his invention to be employed in the Thames against the British. When Bonaparte rejected the plan, Fulton contracted with the British government to employ the mines against the

French! In October 1804 and in October 1805 Fulton made two attempts against French shipping at Boulogne. The mines were deployed from cutters and secured in pairs by means of long lines, with the plan that the line would catch on the cables of an enemy ship and the current would then cause them to rest against the sides of the ship. Although a number of Fulton's mines exploded, it was without significant effect.

In October 1805, Fulton demonstrated the power of mines by blowing up the 200-ton captured Danish brig *Dorothea*. The blast lifted the ship out of the water and broke it in two, the first time in history that such a large ship had been so destroyed. With the death in 1806 of Prime Minister William Pitt, Fulton's chief backer, however, Admiral the Earl St. Vincent dismissed the American inventor with the statement: "Pitt was the greatest fool that ever existed, to encourage a mode of war which they who commanded the seas did not want, and which, if successful, would deprive them of it."[3]

Fulton returned to America and presented his inventions to the U.S. government, which funded a test in New York Harbor in July 1807. Fulton blew up a 200-ton brig, but only after several attempts. In 1810 he carried out an experiment against a sloop, but it failed because the defenders were permitted to deploy a net. Nonetheless, Fulton continued to advocate moored mines as a means of closing American ports to an attacker. During the War of 1812, the Americans attempted without success to employ Fulton's mines against British ships off Norfolk and in Long Island Sound. Fulton also came up with an offensive system involving a harpoon and a mine.[4]

New means of detonation were also developed. As early as 1839 Russian Tsar Nicholas I funded experiments by Prussian emigré Moritz-Hermann Jacobi with a galvanic (electronic) mine. Americans Fulton and Samuel Colt, Russian Baron Pavel L'vovich Schilling von Cannstadt, and Jacobi all developed working mines by the time of the Crimean War (1854–56). The Russians subsequently deployed the mines to help prevent access by water to St. Petersburg. Jacobi's mines consisted of zinc canisters filled with gunpowder and set off by a detonator, a glass tube filled with acid, which when broken ignited the main charge of gunpowder. The Russians employed chemical, contact, and electrical command-detonated mines in both the Baltic Sea and the Black Sea. Mines of the Crimean War were, however, too small to inflict great damage.[5]

With this technology readily available, it is not surprising that the Confederacy utilized it. The Confederates employed land mines in the 1862 Peninsula Campaign. At first land mines and torpedoes were considered outside the bounds of civilized warfare, but as the fighting increased in destructiveness, such prohibitions fell by the wayside. The use of such weapons was justified by the need to deal with an enemy bent on "destroying" the South. Indeed, in April 1862 the Confederate Congress decreed a bounty of 50 percent of the value of all Union naval ships sunk or destroyed by "any new machine or engine."[6]

Southern strategists saw the mine as one means to reduce the Union naval advantage; influential Confederate Navy officer and scientist Matthew Fontaine Maury was an early proponent of torpedoes and conducted a number of experiments with them. The Confederate Torpedo Bureau was a highly secretive agency, with its officers required to take an oath not to reveal what they knew about the weapons and their means of explosion.[7]

Civil War torpedoes were of a variety of types. Either scratch-built or constructed from barrels as casings, they were essentially stationary weapons, a buoy held in place at an appropriate distance from the surface by a cable anchored to the sea bottom by a weight. The torpedoes were then positioned in rivers or harbors as a defense against Union warships.

By the Civil War there were two basic types of detonation: contact and electricity. In the former, the detonation occurred when "horns" surrounding the charge were broken, setting off a chemical reaction that ignited the charge. In the latter, the explosive charge was touched off by electrical current provided through wires connected to batteries on shore. The first type was more certain to explode, but contact torpedoes did not distinguish their victim and hence were a serious hazard for friend and foe alike. The second type of torpedo, which detonated on command by electricity, could only be employed close to shore. More often than not, early torpedoes failed to explode because of faulty detonating equipment, because the torpedoes themselves became waterlogged, or because they were swept away by the current.

Perhaps the first uses of torpedoes in the war came during the February 1862 Union assault on Fort Henry on the Tennessee River. As noted, the wife of a Confederate officer inadvertently revealed their presence, and Union sailors promptly swept the river for them and used cutters to bring eight of them to the surface. These torpedoes were sheet-iron cylinders some five and a half feet long, pointed at both ends, each containing about seventy-five pounds of gunpowder. They were fired by contact-type detonators. All of the torpedoes recovered were waterlogged and harmless.

The first victim of a torpedo was the Union ironclad *Cairo*. During the Vicksburg Campaign, on 12 December 1862 the 512-ton *Cairo* succumbed to a torpedo in the Yazoo River. The first loss of a warship in actual battle was the 2,100-ton *Tecumseh*, which went down to a torpedo on 5 August 1864 during the Battle of Mobile Bay. On 15 January 1865, only a month before the surrender of Charleston and despite picket and scout boats out with grapnels, the Union monitor *Patapsco* was sunk by a large mine or mines in the channel about seven hundred yards from Fort Sumter. It went down in only about fifteen seconds, taking down sixty-two officers and men. Only five officers and thirty-eight men were saved.[8]

Powder charges in Civil War torpedoes ranged from some fifty pounds to up to a ton. On 6 May 1864, one of the largest torpedoes, detonated electrically from on shore, sank the 542-ton Union gunboat *Commodore Jones* on the James River. The *Commodore Jones* and two other ships were sweeping for mines in the river when the explosion occurred. Its captain, Acting Lt. Thomas S. Wade, reported that the mine went off directly under the converted ferryboat and lifted it out of the water, paddle wheels still spinning, "absolutely blowing the ship to splinters." The explosion claimed some forty lives. The *Commodore Jones* was the first ship sunk by an electrically detonated mine in the history of warfare.

A landing party of marines and sailors from the *Mackinaw* promptly went ashore and found three Confederate positions, each with a Bunsen battery formed of nine zinc cups, with a wire leading from the battery to a torpedo in the river some two hundred yards distant. In one of the positions, the Union shore party captured two Confederates of the Submarine Battery Service commanded by Lt. Hunter Davidson, waiting to blow their mine should a Union ship venture over it. The shore party learned that there were many other mines in the river, and when Jeffries Johnson, one of the two Confederates, refused to divulge their location, the Union seamen placed him in the bow of the forward ships as a personal minesweeper, leading him to reveal the desired information.[9]

Mines were also employed offensively as so-called spar torpedoes, explosive devices placed at the end of a long pole or spar. General Beauregard, commanding at Charleston, advocated construction of small vessels mounting a spar torpedo in the bow to attack blockading warships. Such craft were designed to operate very low in the water. Encouraged by Beauregard, Confederate Army Capt. Francis D. Lee carried out a number of experiments and supervised construction of a torpedo boat, the *Torch*. Some 150 feet in length, it was launched in July 1863.

The Confederates regarded the *New Ironsides* as the principal threat of ships in the Union squadron, and Beauregard hoped to sink it by means of a spar torpedo. Not completed as Lee had intended from a want of iron armor and with an inadequate powerplant, the *Torch* nonetheless made an attempt. Shortly after midnight on 21 August 1863, James Carlin and a crew of eleven men sallied in the *Torch*, now armed with an unusual triple spar torpedo, with each warhead weighing one hundred pounds. The *New Ironsides* swung at anchor with the ebb tide, and this movement and its poor engine prevented the *Torch* from striking the Union ship broadsides. In his after-action report, Carlin recommended to Beauregard that the *Torch* be turned into a transport.[10]

The Confederates also built much smaller, 48-feet, 6-inch-long crafts, the prototype named the *David*. A half dozen others of this design, all known as Davids, were laid down, but only a few were actually completed. Operating low in the water, the *David* resembled a submarine but was in fact strictly a surface vessel propelled by a steam engine. The *David* and its sisters took in water as ballast to run on the surface awash, but the open hatch, necessary to provide air for the steam engine, invited disaster through swamping. With a crew of four, the *David* mounted a spar torpedo containing sixty pounds of powder inside a copper casing.

Commanded by Lt. William T. Glassell, the *David* set out on the night of 5 October 1863, approaching to within fifty yards of the *New Ironsides* before it was discovered. Hailed from the Union ship, the crew of the *David* responded with a shotgun blast and then placed their mine. Although the explosion of the spar torpedo next to its hull damaged the Union ironclad, the ship did not sink. A wave created by the blast also washed into the torpedo boat and put out the fire in its steam engine. Believing that the *David* was sinking, Glassell and two other members of her crew abandoned ship; one of them subsequently returned to the *David*, where Engineer James H. Tomb succeeded in restarting its furnace and escaping. Glassell and another crewman were captured.[11]

The Confederates carried out other subsequent attempts against Union ships at Charleston but without success. Spar torpedoes were also affixed to the bows of ironclad rams. Despite the failures, the threat of the torpedoes had a pronounced effect on the Union crews. Commander of the South Atlantic Blockading Squadron Admiral Dahlgren ordered a number of preventive measures, including picket duty by monitors, tugs, and boats; netting; and boat howitzers kept loaded with canister.[12]

The Union side also employed spar torpedoes. On 18 October 1864, the Union *Picket Boat No. 1* sank the Confederate ironclad ram *Albemarle* with such a device. This mine was affixed to the end of a 14-foot spar lowered by a windless. Once it was in position under the target's hull, a tug on a line released the mine, which floated up under the bottom of the ship. A second line activated the firing mechanism.[13]

The Confederates were particularly active in deploying both mines and spar torpedoes in the James River to prevent Federal ships passing upriver to Richmond. Acting Ens. John Grattan described a spar torpedo attack by a Confederate David, the *Squib*, against the Union flagship *Minnesota* near Newport News. One of four torpedo boats in the James River Squadron, the *Squib* mounted a single 53-pound torpedo on a 16-foot-long oak boom from the bow. Steaming as fast as ten miles per hour, it struck early on the morning of 9 April 1864. Gratton reported the result:

I can feel very thankful that I am alive to relate the narrow escape we have had from destruction. About 2:25 AM this morning, I was thrown out of my bunk by the concussion of an immense torpedo. I heard the sound and in a second afterwards the hatch gratings and gangway ladders came tumbling down the cock-pit. I immediately guessed what was the matter, as I could hear the ring of the torpedo striking the side of the ship, below the water line. The ship tottered and rolled like a small boat in the sea. The whole ship was lifted completely out of the water and came down with a tremendous jerk. As soon as the gratings and heavy hatch-braces had stopped tumbling down the hatch, I picked myself up, being pretty severely bruised, and managed to hobble to within a few feet of the cockpit ladder, when I struck my shin and had just got from under the hatch when a heavy iron bar from the spar deck came rattling down, just grazing my head. There was no light everything was dark as midnight, and I could hear the rush and heavy tread of five hundred men on the decks above. Every one thought the ship was sinking. In about five or ten seconds after the explosion I was on the deck with all the officers and men, not one in fifty being dressed. . . . I looked out towards the post quarter and could see a small sigar [sic] shaped steamer, about the size of the Captain's Gig, moving very rapidly toward the rebel shore. . . . I never saw such excitement and confusion before. . . . The torpedo went off within 10 feet of the magazine bulkhead. The Gunner says it is a miracle that the ship is not blown into a thousand atoms.[14]

Although the world's navies were slow to embrace the concept, the ideal delivery system for the torpedo was by a submersible. The concept was actually an old one. In the 1620s Charles von Drebbel, a Dutch physician living in London, had built a combination wood and greased leather craft that could submerge and was propelled by means of oars fitted in watertight sleeves.[15]

The first real submarine was invented during the American Revolutionary War by the same David Bushnell who had experimented with mines. He built at Saybrook on the Connecticut River a craft he called a "sub-marine." It consisted of two great tortoiselike shells made of oak staves similar to those of a barrel clamped together by iron hoops and coated with tar. Resembling an egg in its appearance, the 7.5- by 6-foot craft rode upright in the water with its smallest end facing down. An entry hatch at the top of the craft contained eight small windows to provide light for the operator below, and a 900-pound keel provided stability. Two brass pipes with check-valves to prevent flooding provided both fresh air and a means of exhaust. A foot-operated valve in the keel admitted water to submerge, and a pump expelled water to ascend. The craft was driven forward and up and down by means of two sets of screwlike paddles manually operated by cranks, one on top of the craft and the other in front of the operator. A rudder moved by a tiller steered the craft. In an emergency the operator could use a release chain to detach 200 pounds of the lead keel, which could also be let down to serve as an anchor. Bushnell even incorporated primitive navigation instruments, including a depth gauge and a compass. Its appearance caused the craft to be known as the Turtle.

The *Turtle*'s destructive power came in the form of a cask containing 150 pounds of gunpowder, attached by a long bolt to the submarine. When withdrawn, the bolt released the mine and activated the timer, a clockwork device set to explode the mine after about an hour by means of a flint lock.

Bushnell installed a long auger in a socket in the top of the *Turtle*. The submarine was to dive beneath its target and the operator would screw the auger, attached to the mine, into the target ship's hull. Once this was accomplished the auger was released and the mine floated free against the target ship.

The *Turtle*'s chief drawback was that the operator had merely thirty minutes of air once the craft was submerged. This meant that any attack would have to be carried out at night or in a period of poor visibility in order for the *Turtle* to get as close as possible before it submerged for the final run to its target.

An effort at New York on the night of 7 September 1776 against Adm. Lord Richard Howe's flagship, the sixty-four-gun *Eagle*, miscarried when a poorly trained replacement operator was unable to get the auger to enter the *Eagle*'s hull. Several other attempts were made to sink British ships in the Hudson without success, and the *Turtle* was later destroyed, probably to prevent it from falling into British hands.[16]

In 1797 Robert Fulton submitted plans to the French Directory for a "plunging boat." Fulton's submarine, the *Nautilus*, was built at a workshop near the Seine River and was completed in June 1800. A considerable advance over the *Turtle*, it was some 21 feet long and cigar shaped, with a double hull of copper over an iron frame and sporting a sail and collapsible mast, along with a 20- by 6-foot deck for its three-man crew when the submarine was on the surface. The *Nautilus* was powered by hand cranks driving a propeller and had a system to control ballast.

Successfully tested on the surface and underwater on the Seine at Paris, the *Nautilus* was then sent to Le Havre, and that August Fulton took the *Nautilus* to a depth of fifteen feet and remained underwater for an hour. Fulton also successfully tested a contact mine against a barrel target. During 12–15 September, Fulton took the submarine to sea, and on two separate occasions tried to approach English brigs near the Marcou Islands, but each time they got under way before he could close the range. Poor weather and approaching winter forced Fulton to end his tests and return to Paris.

Fulton conducted further tests on the *Nautilus* at Brest in late July 1801, and at one point he took the submarine down to a depth of twenty-five feet. He also added a window topside at the bow. In addition to work on the submarine, Fulton developed copper "submarine bombs" containing ten to two hundred pounds of gunpowder each. Apparently warned, the British posted extra lookouts on their ships in the Channel and used ships' boats to circle the warships as an additional precaution. In any case, Fulton declared himself displeased with the submarine and dismantled it, whereupon Bonaparte removed his support. Fulton then went to Britain, but his work there was in torpedoes rather than submarines.[17]

Other submarines followed. During the War of 1812 a resident of Norwich, Connecticut, built a submarine and made several attempts in it to attach a mine to the hull of the British seventy-four-gun *Ramilles* at New London.[18]

In 1850 during fighting between the German states and Denmark, Bavarian artilleryman and inventor Wilhelm Bauer built a 26.5-foot-long submarine, *Le Plongeur Marin*. Powered by an internal handwheel turning a screw propeller, the submarine submerged by letting water into a double bottom; to rise, the water was expelled by means of a pump. In 1856 Bauer constructed a 56-foot-long submarine in Russia. This *Diable-Marin* was powered by a treadmill and was capable of transporting a five-hundred-pound mine. We know little else about Bauer's invention, but during coronation ceremonies for Tsar Alexander II (1855–81) Bauer reportedly transported underwater a small orchestra that played the Russian national anthem. The reaction of the musicians to the experience is unknown.[19]

Given these experiments, it was no surprise that enterprising Southerners would attempt to build such craft during the Civil War. In March 1862 at New Orleans, Robert R. Barrow, James R. McClintock, and Baxter Watson applied for a letter of marque for a submarine craft they named the *Pioneer*. Only about 20 feet long, it was propelled by means of a crankshaft turned by its two-man crew. It was sunk to avoid capture when Union forces took the city.

Horace L. Hunley, one of the sureties on the *Pioneer*, as well as McClintock and Watson continued experiments at Mobile, Alabama. There in mid-February 1863 they tested another submarine along the same lines, this one designed for five men and to deliver a spar torpedo. It sank in rough water off Fort Morgan in Mobile Bay, but no lives were lost.

Confederate submarine Pioneer. NAVAL HISTORICAL CENTER (NH 42854)

Undaunted, Hunley and his friends built a third submarine. In early August 1863, with Charleston under Union naval assault, General Beauregard requested that it be sent there, with the inducement of large rewards for the destruction of Union blockaders. The submarine arrived at Charleston on 15 August, transported on two covered railroad flatcars.

The *H. L. Hunley* was built from an iron steam boiler with the addition of tapered bow and stern sections. Some 40 feet in length, 3.5 feet in breadth at its widest point, and 4 feet in depth, the *H. L. Hunley* resembled a long thin cigar. It was designed for a crew of nine men: one to steer and eight positioned along the length of the center section to provide the power, turning by hand a crankshaft that moved the propeller and drove the craft forward at about four knots. The *H. L. Hunley* was to run awash until close to its target and then use its rudders to submerge. The submarine suffered from serious limitations; it was difficult to control, and fresh air was available only when it was awash.

On 29 August, following several practice dives in Charleston Harbor, the submarine sank at the dock. Its commander, Lt. John J. Payne, had ordered the *H. L. Hunley* to get under way while at the same time he was climbing into the forward hatchway. Apparently he became fouled in a hawser and got his foot on the lever that controlled the fins. The submarine

Confederate submarine H. L. Hunley; *sepia wash drawing by R. G. Skerrett.*
Naval Historical Center (NH 999)

moved from the dock and dived; because its hatches were open, it rapidly filled with water. Five men drowned but three others, including Payne, escaped. The submarine was raised and refitted. Another crew volunteered, with Hunley in charge.

On 15 October the *H. L. Hunley* sank in Charleston Harbor, once again apparently because of human error. Hunley had evidently left the valve to the front ballast tank open. He and seven others perished. The submarine was again recovered, and, somewhat remarkably given the submarine's track record, a third crew, commanded by infantry Lt. George Dixon, volunteered.

The *H. L. Hunley*'s destructive force came from a spar torpedo, possibly designed by General Beauregard. Secured to the bow, the spar held the 130-pound torpedo, which terminated in a barbed lance-head. When the submarine drove toward its victim, the spar's barb would lodge in the timbers below the waterline. The submarine would then back off and explode the torpedo by means of a long lanyard.

Following additional training, the *H. L. Hunley* set out on the night of 17 February 1864 approaching the 1,934-ton Union screw sloop *Housatonic*. The sloop was prepared for an attack; Capt. Charles Pickering had six lookouts posted, steam in the engine room was up, and crewmen stood ready to slip the ship's cable at a moment's notice. At about 9 PM lookouts on the *Housatonic* spotted the *H. L. Hunley*'s two hatches above water, along with its slight wake, but when the submarine was only about seventy-five to one hundred yards from the ship and too late for anything save small-arms fire. About three minutes after the submarine was first detected, and as the sloop was getting under way, the spar torpedo exploded, tearing a large hole in the Union ship, which then sank. Only five Union sailors were lost. The sloop went down in shallow water and most of the crew members simply climbed into the rigging to await rescue.

The *Housatonic* enjoyed the dubious distinction of being the first ship in history to be sunk by a submarine. The unstable *H. L. Hunley* survived long enough to signal by lantern that it was returning to land, but, probably damaged in the blast, it sank shortly thereafter with all hands. Located in 1995 and raised in August 2000, The *H. L. Hunley* is now undergoing preservation.[20]

The last Confederate submersible to see service in the war was the *St. Patrick.* Built privately at Mobile by John P. Halligan and completed at the beginning of 1864, this 30-foot-long craft had a crew of six and reportedly could "be sunk and raised as desired." Transferred to the Confederate Navy on 25 January and commanded by Lt. J. T. Walker, at 1 AM on 28 January it attacked the Federal side-wheel sloop *Octorara.* The *St. Patrick*'s spar torpedo struck the side of the Union warship but failed to explode. The *St. Patrick* then managed to escape a hail of Union fire and return to Mobile.[21]

The Union also experimented with submarines. One of these, the *Alligator,* predated the *H. L. Hunley* and was the first U.S. Navy working submarine. Developed beginning in 1861, it was 47 feet long with a beam of 6 feet. It was conically shaped with a long pointed bow. Flush-mounted canisters on the top of the submarine could be raised or lowered to control its buoyancy. The *Alligator* also had a diver lockout chamber, an air compressor for diver operations, and an air purification system that consisted of a woolen blanket soaked in lime water stretched over a roller with a fan blowing over it.

Originally propelled by oars, the *Alligator* later received a hand-cranked propeller. In June 1862 it was towed from Philadelphia to Hampton Roads to take part in the Peninsula Campaign, probably with a view toward clearing obstructions in the James, but it arrived with Union forces already withdrawing. In any case, the long *Alligator* was designed to operate in deep harbors and would have been of little use in the twisting, shallow James. Ordered to Port Royal in the spring of 1863, where it could hardly have been of much service to Du Pont and the Union Blockading Squadron in the attack on Charleston, the *Alligator* was under tow by the *Sumter* off Cape Hatteras on 2 April 1863 when a severe storm led the *Sumter*'s crew to cut the tow lines and the *Alligator* to sink.

Maj. Edward B. Hunt of the Army Corps of Engineers also designed a one-man submarine. While testing his "submarine battery" on 2 October 1863 at the Brooklyn Navy Yard, Hunt succumbed to carbon dioxide poisoning.[22]

Defenses against torpedoes and spar torpedo attacks included keeping ships in motion and deploying their boats on patrol when the ships were stationary; putting out outriggers and hawsers with rope netting dropped into the water (such "torpedo nets" continued to be employed into World War II) as well as other barriers around stationary ships; anchoring ships in water sufficiently shallow that a submarine could not pass underneath them; and posting additional lookouts.

Regardless of these precautions, during the war some fifty ships were sunk or damaged by torpedoes or spar torpedoes, four-fifths of them belonging to the Union. Indeed, torpedoes sank more Union warships during the war than any other means employed by the South. Of Confederate ships only the *Albemarle* was lost to a Union torpedo. The other Confederate ships that succumbed were the mistaken victims of Southern torpedoes. Despite limitations, such explosive devices had a profound psychological effect on sailors on board ship, producing what became known as "torpedo fever" among Union crews.[23]

Finally, mention should be made of another unconventional weapon, the Courtenay or coal torpedo. Designed by Thomas E. Courtenay, this iron explosive device was cast in the shape of a lump of coal and was designed to be placed in a pile of that fuel so that it would be ultimately shoveled into a steamship's furnace and there explode. Among the apparent successes for the Confederates in this regard was the sinking of Gen. Benjamin Butler's headquarters ship the *Greyhound* on the James River. "Horological torpedoes," set off by means of a timing device, also reportedly caused the August 1864 explosion in the Union Army's City Point supply depot that killed 160 men and caused $4 million in damage.[24]

CHAPTER ELEVEN

The Commerce Raiders

———~/\/\~———

D estruction of Union commerce was a major Confederate goal at sea. Secretary of the Navy Mallory and other Southern leaders hoped that a *guerre de course* would create serious economic dislocation in the North and lead business interests there to demand a negotiated end to the war that would result in Southern independence. Mallory had no confidence in privateers. What he sought were regular commissioned naval warships operating in accordance with established international law. Although only a handful of such ships took to the seas during the war, they were nonetheless effective.

International law favored Mallory's plan, for enemy commerce at sea was subject to capture and confiscation. The United States was a major maritime power, and its commerce was vulnerable to seagoing predators. Nonetheless, Confederate cruisers would face daunting problems. The blockade would make it very difficult for prizes to be brought to a Confederate port. Secure bases were another problem, although Matthew Fontaine Maury's gloomy predictions that the raiders would not have "a friendly port in the wide world" proved unfounded.[1]

Obtaining the raiding ships themselves was the most difficult problem. The Confederacy lacked modern shipbuilding facilities, and its ports were under blockade. Great Britain, the world's most advanced and largest shipbuilder, was the logical source, especially as its leadership was sympathetic to the South. As early as 9 May 1861, Mallory decided to send two agents to Europe. He ordered serving naval officer Lt. James H. North to purchase or contract for the construction of ironclad warships suitable for breaking the blockade, while former U.S. Navy officer James D. Bulloch (later made a commander in the Confederate Navy) was to procure ships, guns, and ammunition and "get cruising ships . . . afloat with the quickest possible dispatch."[2]

Mallory had decided views on the types of ships required. Such ships should be

> enabled to keep the sea, and to make extended cruises, propellers fast under both steam and canvas suggest themselves to us with special favor. Large ships are unnecessary for this service; our policy demands that they shall be no larger than may be sufficient to combine the requisite speed and power, a battery of one or two heavy pivot guns and two or more broadside guns, being sufficient against commerce. By getting small ships we can afford a greater number, an important consideration. The character of our coasts and harbors indicate attention to the draft of water of our vessels. Speed in propeller and the protection of her machinery cannot be obtained upon a very light draft, but they should draw as little water as may be compatible with their efficiency otherwise.[3]

Pending foreign construction, Mallory sought to outfit some ships at home. On 17 April he met with Cdr. Raphael Semmes, a kindred spirit on the subject of commerce raiding.[4]

Born in Maryland in 1809, Semmes joined the U.S. Navy as a midshipman at age sixteen and spent much time in survey work along the southern coast and Gulf of Mexico. During leaves of absence ashore, he studied law, was admitted to the bar, and established his residence in Alabama. Semmes distinguished himself during the Mexican-American War, despite having been captain of the brig *Somers* when it went down with half its crew in a sudden squall off the Mexican coast in December 1846. Interestingly, in his 1852 book, *Service Afloat and Ashore During the Mexican War*, Semmes argued that if Mexico had fitted out privateers against U.S. shipping during that war, Washington should have treated them as pirates.

At the time Alabama seceded, Cdr. Semmes was serving on the Light-House Board. Resigning his commission in February 1861, he traveled to Montgomery to present his views to the Confederacy's Committee on

Naval Affairs. Shortly thereafter President Davis sent Semmes into the North to purchase military and naval supplies along with equipment for the Tredegar Iron Works. In March, Semmes became a commander in the Confederate Navy and, on his return to Montgomery, he became chief of the Light-House Bureau.[5]

Mallory shared with Semmes information on available ships, and on 18 April he gave him command of the former steamer packet *Habana* at New Orleans. Launched in 1857, this 437-ton ship had been employed on the New Orleans to Havana route. Renamed the *Sumter* and commissioned on 3 June, it was the first Confederate Navy commerce raider. Semmes wrote that it was as "unlike a ship of war as possible. Still, I was pleased with her general appearance. Her lines were easy and graceful, and she had a sort of saucy air about her which seemed to say that she was not averse to the service of which she was about to be employed."[6]

Workmen stripped the *Sumter* down to what became the gun deck, which was then reinforced. The ship also received additional coal bunkers and was rerigged as a barkantine. With its retractable funnel and screw propeller, there would be no outward means to identify it as a steamer. Its armament consisted of an IX-inch gun in pivot mount and four 32-pounders in broadside, all shipped by rail from the Norfolk Navy Yard.

Semmes signed on 114 officers and men. Although their pay was only slightly higher than that of navy seamen, the men were to receive gold rather than inflated Confederate script. Their chief incentive, however, was the possibility of prize money.

With the *Sumter* ready for sea, on 18 June 1861 Semmes ran his ship down to the Mississippi River mouth to await the right moment to escape the blockading *Powhatan* and *Brooklyn*. Mallory's orders called on Semmes to "do the enemy's commerce the greatest injury in the shortest time."[7]

On 30 June 1861, taking advantage of word that the twenty-one-gun *Brooklyn* was off station, Semmes made for the sea, but the Union warship turned about on spotting the *Sumter*'s tell-tale black smoke. Making eleven and a half knots to only nine for its prey, the *Brooklyn* steadily gained. The gap closed to only four miles as Semmes called for all possible speed and drove steam pressure to dangerous levels. Semmes also ordered his men to throw overboard water casks and even a howitzer. A fresh wind and sloop rig that enabled the *Sumter* to sail close to the wind and yet also use its engine worked to the raider's advantage, and gradually it pulled away.

The Confederate commerce raider Sumter *running past the blockading U.S. Navy steam sloop* Brooklyn *into the Gulf of Mexico, 30 June 1861.* NAVAL HISTORICAL CENTER (NH 51797)

Finally, after a three-and-a-half-hour pursuit, the *Brooklyn* gave up. Porter later acknowledged it to be "one of the most exciting chases of the war."[8]

On 3 July the *Sumter* took its first prize, the merchant bark *Golden Rocket.* Semmes's memoirs reveal a great hostility toward the North and contempt for the U.S. Navy. He wrote in his journal: "Our first prize made a beautiful bonfire and we did not enjoy the spectacle the less because she was from the black Republican State of Maine." Porter called it "the first illegal prize made by a Confederate vessel-of-war."[9]

Semmes and other Confederate raider captains found themselves handicapped by the British government's 14 May neutrality proclamation. Other leading maritime powers followed suit. This meant there were very few places to which captured ships might be sailed and sold. Semmes tried to talk Spanish officials in Cuba into adjudicating five of his prizes there, but they refused, and these ships were eventually returned to their U.S. owners.

As a result, Confederate captains routinely burned the Northern merchant ships they captured. Occasionally a ship would be let go on bond simply to carry passengers or because its cargo belonged to a neutral nation. Bonding meant that a captain signed a paper guaranteeing to pay a set sum to the Confederate government at the end of the war, the amount decided in condemnation procedures.

Semmes also discovered that neutrality laws limited the time that cruisers might spend in port and repairs that might be effected to them. Large numbers of captured seamen and passengers were both a problem and a danger to a commerce raider. Those captured were routinely sent ashore in their own boats or, if no land was in sight, transferred to neutral ships or to Union merchant ships carrying a cargo belonging to a neutral nation.

Over the next six months, Semmes cruised the Caribbean and captured nine other ships. He then sailed along the South American coast to Brazil and back to the West Indies but found only two U.S. registered ships, both of which he burned. The absence of other U.S. ships convinced Semmes that he would be more successful in European waters, and he headed into the Atlantic. Late in November the *Sumter* narrowly escaped an encounter with the powerful U.S. Navy screw sloop *Iroquois*. During the crossing, Semmes took six Union prizes.

On 3 January the *Sumter*, now in poor repair, put into Cádiz, but Spanish authorities there would not permit an overhaul of the *Sumter*'s engine and ordered him to depart. On 18 January, Semmes took two prizes, and a day later he put into Gibraltar. British authorities there were much more accommodating, although the U.S. consul managed to block the sale of coal. In the meantime, U.S. Navy warships, including the screw sloop *Kearsarge*, arrived. Since his ship needed repairs that could not be effected at Gibraltar, Semmes bowed to the inevitable. Under authorization from Confederate commissioner James M. Mason in London, in April Semmes laid up the *Sumter*, paid off most of its crew, and departed for London. In December 1862 the *Sumter* was sold at auction to a British firm and put back into commercial service as the *Gibraltar*. John M. Kell, first lieutenant on the *Sumter*, effectively summed up its role when he wrote, "I have always felt that the little *Sumter* has never had full justice done her. . . . No ship of her size, her frailness, and her armament ever played such havoc on a powerful foe."[10]

Despite the *Sumter* being both too small and slow to be an effective commerce raider, Semmes had made his reputation in it by taking seventeen prizes in just six months. Semmes burned seven ships, and another seven were seized by Cuban authorities to return to their Union owners. The cost to the Confederate government of running the *Sumter* was only $28,000, a figure less than the least valuable of its prizes.

Semmes was advanced to captain in August 1862. He had arrived in Nassau two months before, hoping to catch a blockade runner to the

South. There, however, orders arrived from Mallory sending him back to England to take command of a ship nearing completion at Liverpool.[11]

Although Lieutenant North proved a failure, Bulloch achieved considerable success. He had arrived in Liverpool in early June 1861 and other Confederate agents ultimately contracted for eighteen ships abroad. The most successful of these were secured in Britain: the *Alabama, Florida, Shenandoah, Chickamauga, Georgia, Rappahannock,* and *Tallahassee.* The other eleven ships became blockade runners, were sequestered by the British and French governments, or were not completed by the end of the war.

Bulloch was able to skirt the Foreign Enlistment Act of 1819 that prohibited British citizens from equipping, furnishing, fitting out, or arming any ship intended for service by foreign belligerent navies. Eminent Liverpool lawyer F. S. Hull advised Bulloch that construction of such a ship was not illegal in itself, whatever the intent, and that the offense lay only in the equipping. Bulloch thus took care to see that none of his cruisers went to sea with ordnance, small arms, or warlike stores of any kind. These he obtained and shipped in other ships, and the cruisers were outfitted in international waters at sea.[12]

THE *FLORIDA*

Three of the Confederate raiders invite particular mention. In order of commissioning, they are the *Florida, Alabama,* and *Shenandoah.* In late June, William A. Miller & Sons of Liverpool, builder of a number of ships for the Royal Navy, began construction of the first. Supposedly a ship for an Italian buyer, it was known as the *Otero.*

Bulloch also worked to secure war supplies and ships to transport these to the Confederacy. On 15 October he himself departed Holyhead in the *Fingal* for Bermuda, and on 22 November he ran that ship into Savannah with the most important cargo to reach that city by sea during the war: fourteen thousand Enfield rifles; one million cartridges; two million percussion caps; thousands of sabers, bayonets, rifles, and revolvers; ten rifled cannon and ammunition; four hundred barrels of powder; and medical supplies. With Savannah too tightly blockaded, Bulloch was unable to return the *Fingal* to England; later it became the ram *Atlanta.*[13]

Bulloch returned to Liverpool on 10 March aboard a blockade runner out of Wilmington just as the *Otero* was nearing completion. Patterned after a Royal Navy dispatch boat, the *Otero* was lengthened to 191 feet to provide additional storage space and to allow greater rigging and an increase in sail area. Displacing some 700 tons and powered by a single screw, the ship could make nine and a half knots under steam and twelve under sail.[14]

In January 1862 the U.S. consul at Liverpool uncovered information as to the ship's true identity, but Bulloch was able to get the ship to sea before any action might be taken. The *Otero* departed Liverpool for Nassau on 22 March. At the same time, Bulloch sent out the cargo ship *Bahama* from Scotland with guns, ammunition, and provisions.

At Nassau Lt. John N. Maffitt took command. Under pressure from the Americans, British officials detained the ship, but a decision by the British Vice-Admiralty Court released it. Meanwhile, supplies from the *Bahama* were shifted to a local schooner that then followed the raider to sea. During 9–16 August off the uninhabited island of Green Cay in the Bahamas, Maffitt oversaw the arming and outfitting of the *Otero*. It mounted two 7-inch and six 6-inch rifled guns and a 12-pounder howitzer.[15]

On 17 August, Maffitt officially commissioned his ship the *Florida*. Unfortunately, much of the crew had contracted yellow fever, and Maffitt soon had to put into Cardenas, Cuba, for medical assistance. Five men subsequently died, including Maffitt's stepson, and were buried at sea; Maffitt himself was near death for a time. The *Florida* then put into Havana, where Maffitt engaged a pilot who was familiar with the Confederate port of Mobile.

Getting to sea and keeping close to the Cuban coast, Maffitt managed to avoid Union warships searching for his ship. He then made a desperate dash across the Caribbean, and on 4 September, with only a skeleton crew able to work the ship, the *Florida* arrived off Mobile Bay, then blockaded by U.S. Navy Cdr. George Preble's squadron of the screw sloop *Oneida*, the screw gunboat *Winona*, and the schooner *Rachel Seaman*. Without hesitation, Maffitt ran the *Florida* for the bay. The *Florida* flew an English ensign, and Preble hesitated, wary of a repeat of the *Trent* affair that might bring war with Britain. With the *Florida* about a mile away and bearing down full steam on the *Oneida*, Preble ordered engines reversed to avoid being rammed by what he still believed to be an English ship. Maffitt closed to within eighty yards of the *Oneida* before Preble got into position to fire a warning shot across the *Florida*'s bow.

Expecting Preble to handle the situation, the captains of the *Winona* and *Rachel Seaman* held back. Preble then ordered a second warning shot before firing a full broadside at point-blank range. The shot went too high to inflict major damage. Maffitt believed that, had the guns been depressed, "the career of the *Florida* would have ended then and there." With all three Union ships now firing on the *Florida*, Maffitt ended any question as to his ship's identity by replacing the English ensign with the Stars and Bars.[16]

The *Florida* narrowly escaped destruction. One 11-inch shell pierced its hull close to the waterline starboard, decapitating a fireman and wounding nine others before it tore through the port side and exploded. Had the shell been set to explode a second sooner, it probably would have brought the end of the *Florida*.

To increase speed, Maffitt ordered all sails set, but Preble ordered grape shot fired into the raider's rigging, and Maffitt sent his men below. The *Oneida* and *Florida* were sufficiently close for marines on the Union ship to fire their muskets. Maffitt recalled, "The loud explosions, roar of shot and shell, crashing spars and rigging, mingled with the moans of our sick and wounded, only increased our determination to enter our destined harbor."[17]

Although damaged by the Union cannonade, the *Florida* gained the bay and soon anchored under the protecting guns of Fort Morgan. The ship's fore-topmast and fore-gaff were both gone, and the main rigging was set adrift. Maffitt reported fourteen hundred shrapnel shot in the ship's hull. The ship looked, he wrote, "like a case of smallpox. . . . We were torn to pieces."[18]

Only after expiration of the quarantine period on 3 October could Maffitt begin repairs. A shortage of skilled workers and lack of facilities delayed the work, as did the *Florida*'s deep draft, which forced it to remain in the bay and necessitated shuttling both workers and machinery back and forth from Mobile. Equipment, even rigging, was in short supply, and bad weather also intervened.

Not until 10 January 1863 was the *Florida* ready for sea, and by then a dozen Union blockaders were off Mobile. Maffitt waited until a dark night for the attempt, but the *Florida* ran aground in the bay. It took two days and removal of its coal and ordnance before the ship could be freed. The *Florida* grounded a second time and the process was repeated. These delays, however, brought a storm from the northeast and with it ideal conditions for an escape attempt.

At 2 AM on 17 January in a thick mist, the *Florida* passed two Union blockaders without being detected. Lookouts on a third ship sighted the raider as a consequence of sparks from its funnel, and Maffitt ordered full steam and all sails set. At fourteen and a half knots, it easily outran its pursuers. Only one threat remained, the *R. R. Culyer*, the sole blockader capable of overtaking the *Florida*. This Union ship was sighted about 5 AM only three miles away. Maffitt ordered all sails stricken and the engines stopped. The sea was rough, and the waves hid the low-lying raider, enabling it to escape. Both passages of the *Florida* through the blockade were major embarrassments for the U.S. Navy.[19]

The *Florida* then cruised the North Atlantic, taking twenty-two merchant ships. Among these were the barks *Coquette* and *Lapwing*. Maffitt seized the *Lapwing* on 28 March 1863, transferring a howitzer to it and employing it as a tender. The *Florida* took the *Coquette* on 6 May 1863, and twenty-three-year-old Lt. Charles Read secured permission to sail this prize, renamed the *Clarence*, on a daring mission to Hampton Roads to cut out a Union gunboat or a steamer.

Read set out that same day with twenty men, his ship armed with a single 12-pounder howitzer, to sail the thirty-four hundred miles from Brazil to Norfolk. A month later he took and burned his first prize. Others followed, but from the prisoners he learned that Union security precautions would make it impossible to enter Hampton Roads. Having taken six prizes in the *Clarence*, on 12 June Read shifted operations to one of them, the *Tacony*, which was faster than the *Clarence*, which he then burned. Taking other prizes in the *Tacony* (sometimes known as the *Florida No. 2*), Read was soon forced to release his growing number of prisoners, which meant his presence was no longer a secret. Continuing north, Read reached the New England fishing grounds in late June, where he took and burned a half dozen schooners and captured a large clipper ship. By now Read had exhausted his ammunition and there were some forty U.S. warships searching for him. Read, however, took fifteen prizes in the *Tacony* before he burned that ship on 15 June after transferring to yet another prize, the small *Archer*.

On 26 June Read boldly sailed the *Archer* into Portland, Maine, where he captured the U.S. revenue cutter *Caleb Cushing* and managed to sail it out of the harbor. Federal officials armed two steamers and set out in pursuit. Unfortunately for Read, he was unaware of the location of the cutter's ample ammunition supply, and, following a brief gunfight, he scuttled the ship and surrendered. Read and his small band had taken twenty-one prizes, burning fifteen of them and causing widespread panic along the North Atlantic seaboard. Exchanged in 1864, Read then distinguished himself in the Red River Campaign.[20]

The *Florida*, meanwhile, arrived at Brest, France, in August 1863 to undergo repairs. There Maffitt fell ill, as did his replacement, Cdr. J. N. Barney. In January 1864 Lt. Charles Morris assumed command, and the next month he took the Florida out on its second cruise, principally off South America, during which the raider took another eleven Union merchant ships.[21]

On 4 October, the *Florida* put in at Bahia, Brazil, to take on coal and undergo repairs to its boilers. U.S. Navy Cdr. Napoleon Collins's screw sloop *Wachusett* had arrived in the port a week before, and Collins soon learned the *Florida's* identity. Having given reassurances that he would respect Brazilian neutrality and being confident that Collins would do the same, Morris permitted most of his crew shore leave. However, because the Confederate ship was so much faster than the *Wachusett*, the American consul at Bahia urged Collins to attack the raider in the harbor. Collins was opposed to this violation of international law but put it to vote of his officers, and the vast majority of them approved.

Early on the morning of 7 October the *Wachusett* steamed to where the *Florida* was anchored and rammed it. The *Florida*, although damaged, did not sink. Following pistol shots from the *Florida*, the *Wachusett* opened up with both a broadside and small-arms fire, and Collins demanded the *Florida* surrender or be blown out of the water. Lt. T. K. Porter, commanding in Morris's absence, had no choice but to comply. He had aboard only twelve officers and fifty-eight men, and none of the guns were loaded.

The *Wachusett* towed the *Florida* to sea as Brazilian guns ashore opened fire on the Union ship without effect. Collins then paroled the Confederate officers and placed the men in double irons. A prize crew then sailed the *Florida* to the United States. In its two years of operations, the *Florida* had captured thirty-three Union merchant ships and caused an estimated $4,051,000 in damages. Expenses of the raider's construction and cruises probably ran only $400,000.

Anchored at Newport News, Virginia, the *Florida* was accidentally rammed by the army transport *Alliance* and sprang a leak. Nine days later, on 28 November 1864, the *Florida* sank at anchor, its pumps having mysteriously stopped. The Brazilian government had registered strong protests over the seizure, and there was also general condemnation from other foreign governments, leading to the decision by Washington to return the ship. The U.S. government subsequently officially apologized to the Brazilian government and promised to punish those guilty of the violation of Brazilian neutrality. Nonetheless, Collins won promotion to captain in 1866 and retired from the navy as a rear admiral in 1874.[22]

THE *ALABAMA*

The *Alabama* was the second English-built raider. On 1 August 1861, Bulloch placed an order for a ship with the Birkenhead Ironworks, owned by the firm of John Laird and Sons. Identified in the dockyard as Hull No. 290, the ship was launched on 15 May under the name *Enrica*. Bulloch expected to command it. Mallory had in fact promised him the first ship completed in Britain but, in his absence, that had gone to Maffitt. However, with Semmes now without a ship, Mallory decided that he would get the *Enrica* while Bulloch continued his other important work.[23]

Any trained observer could see that Hull No. 290 was designed for easy conversion into an armed cruiser, and the U.S. consul at Liverpool hired a private detective to discover more about the ship. In a series of notes beginning on 23 June, U.S. Minister to Britain Charles Francis Adams complained to London about the *Enrica* and furnished evidence as to its true nature. Adams also ordered Capt. T. A. Craven of the U.S. Navy screw sloop *Tuscarora* at Southampton to intercept the *Enrica* if it put to sea.

On 26 July Bulloch received a warning that the *Enrica* was about to be impounded. The British cabinet took that decision the same day, but the order was held up. Bulloch immediately informed the Lairds that he wanted to carry out an additional trial and brought on board a British master, Capt. Matthew J. Butcher, and a skeleton crew. On the morning of 29 July, Bulloch and invited guests set out in the *Enrica*, with the steam tug *Hercules* as tender. After lunch, Bulloch informed his guests that the ship would be out that night, and he took them back to Liverpool in the tug. Early the next morning Bulloch returned on the *Hercules* with additional crewmen. Learning that the *Tuscarora* was at sea searching for the *Enrica* toward Queenstown on the south Irish coast, Bulloch ordered Butcher to proceed north around Ireland and on to Terceira Island in the Azores.[24]

Bulloch, meanwhile, sent out the *Agrippina* with stores, ordnance, ammunition, and 250 tons of coal. On 13 August Bulloch and Semmes, who had only just arrived, departed Liverpool aboard the *Bahama*. The *Enrica* arrived at Porto Praia da Vitória, Terceira, on 9 August, the *Agrippina* on the 18th, and the *Bahama* on the 20th. Semmes ordered the three ships to Angra Bay on the sheltered lee side of the island in order to fit out the *Enrica*.[25]

On 24 August in international waters, Semmes commissioned his ship the *Alabama*. He also persuaded some eighty seamen from the other ships to sign on, promising them double standard wages in gold along with prize money for any ships destroyed. Bulloch, meanwhile, returned to Liverpool in the *Bahama*.[26]

The *Alabama* was a sleek, three-masted, barkantine-rigged wooden ship. Semmes described it as "a very perfect ship of her class." Some 230 feet long and 900 tons burden, it had a single screw propeller powered by two 300-horsepower engines and four boilers. As with the *Sumter*, it had a retractable funnel.

The propeller could be detached from the shaft and lifted into a special well so that the ship could make faster speed under sail alone. The *Alabama* was capable of thirteen knots under steam and sail and ten knots under sail alone. It mounted eight guns: two pivot-mounted heavy guns—a rifled seven-inch (110-pounder) Blakeley on the forecastle and a smoothbore 68-pounder (8-inch) abaft the main mast—and six heavy 32-pounders. The average crew size was 24 officers and 120 men. Designed to be able to keep at sea for long periods, the *Alabama* boasted a fully equipped machine shop so that the crew might make all ordinary repairs themselves. It carried sufficient coal for eighteen days continuous steaming. Semmes used the coal sparingly, with most of the captures made under sail alone. The entire cost of the ship, including outfitting, came to $250,000.[27]

The *Alabama* took its first prizes, all American whalers, in the vicinity of the Azores. The first, taken on 5 September, was the *Ocmulgee* of Massachusetts. The *Alabama* approached under a U.S. flag. Flying a false flag remained standard practice, and Semmes regularly presented his ship as a British or Dutch ship and even as a U.S. Navy warship.[28]

Semmes's officers were able, and his first three lieutenants had served with him on the *Sumter*. First Lieutenant Kell later wrote a book about his experiences, as did Fourth Lt. Arthur F. Sinclair. Semmes did have problems with his crew, the vast majority of whom were British seamen, many of them castoffs from Liverpool. Difficulties were especially pronounced in port with the availability of alcohol. Partly for this reason, Semmes rarely allowed his men ashore, which in turn created morale problems. The large number of foreigners in the crew also made it more difficult to enforce discipline, which grew lax in the course of cruising. The same problems affected other raiders, including the *Florida*, where Spanish and Italian seamen in the crew did not get on well together and had problems with the English language.[29]

In two weeks, Semmes decimated the Union whaling fleet in the Azores. Weathering a severe storm unscathed, the *Alabama* then headed west to the sea-lanes off Newfoundland and New England, plied by many Northern ships transporting grain to Europe. Ironically, destroying ships laden with wheat for Britain and France was not in the interest of the Confederacy. Britain was a net importer of food, and "King Corn" was far more important to political stability than "King Cotton." Driving up grain prices when there was a European wheat shortage served to remind both London and Paris of the importance of good relations with the North.

That October Semmes took eleven vessels, destroying eight and releasing three on bond. Nature then again intruded in the form of a hurricane, which reached its height on 16 October. Sails were split and the main yard snapped, but the *Alabama* again proved its ability to withstand heavy weather.[30]

More than a dozen Union warships were now searching for the *Alabama* and the other raiders, but they were always a little late or in the wrong location. Semmes sailed to Fort de France, Martinique, to take on coal from the *Agrippina*. The tender was already in port when the *Alabama* arrived there on 18 November. Apprehensive over the possible appearance of a U.S. warship, Semmes ordered the *Agrippina* to Blanquilla Island off Venezuela. The tender was hardly clear of the harbor when the heavily armed U.S. Navy screw frigate *San Jacinto* arrived and took up position off the harbor. The *San Jacinto* had double the *Alabama*'s armament and crew, but it was also old and slow (only seven knots under steam), and that same night, Semmes took advantage of a rain squall to escape to Blanquilla.[31]

Newspapers from a British ship brought word that U.S. forces had taken Galveston, Texas, with a Union expeditionary force there expected to invade the state in January. Semmes knew Galveston Harbor was shallow, forcing the Union transports to anchor offshore. He developed a daring plan to sail to Galveston and attack the transports. En route to Galveston, he hoped to take a steamer from Panama carrying gold transshipped from California.

On 29 November the *Alabama* stood for the passage between San Domingo and Puerto Rico, the usual route for mail steamers on their way north. There, Semmes took several prizes, among them the large bark-rigged steamer *Ariel* of the Aspinwall Line. Although outward bound, it was Semmes's most important prize. The *Ariel* had on board more than 700 people, including some 500 passengers and 140 U.S. marines on their way to Pacific Squadron assignments. Semmes disarmed and paroled the marines, but the large number of prisoners forced him to let the *Ariel* proceed under bond.[32]

Semmes then headed into the Gulf. On 23 December he rendezvoused with the *Agrippina* at the Arcas Islands off the coast of Yucatan and passed a week taking on supplies and coal and preparing for the Galveston raid. He planned to arrive during daylight, note the disposition of the transports, and return for a night attack. Semmes expected to be able to use the *Alabama*'s superior speed to run or fight on his choosing.

The *Alabama* arrived off Galveston late in the afternoon of 11 January 1863. Instead of a fleet of Federal transports, the lookouts spotted only five Union warships lobbing shells into Galveston. Semmes correctly concluded that the Confederates had retaken the port. Indeed, Galveston had fallen eleven days before, and Banks and his troops had been diverted to New Orleans.

Lookouts on the Union warships soon spied the *Alabama* about a dozen miles offshore, although they did not identify it. The Union squadron commander, Commo. Henry H. Bell, flew his flag in the twenty-one-gun steam sloop *Brooklyn*, the same ship that had chased the *Sumter* without success. His ship's steam engine not functioning, Bell dispatched Lt. Cdr. Homer C. Blake in the *Hatteras* to investigate. A former Delaware River excursion side-wheeler, the *Hatteras* mounted only four 32-pounders and a 3.67-inch rifle.

Under topsails only, the *Alabama* moved slowly along the coast, drawing the Union ship away from the rest of the squadron. As soon as it was dark and with the two ships about twenty miles from the other Federal ships, the *Alabama* lay to and turned toward the *Hatteras* under steam.

With the *Alabama* within hailing distance, Blake demanded its identity, only to be told that it was an English ship. Reassured, Blake demanded, and received permission, to inspect the ship's registry. After a boat had been lowered and was under way from the *Hatteras*, Kell called out, "This is the Confederate States steamer *Alabama* . . . , Fire."

The *Alabama*'s broadside ripped into the hull of the *Hatteras* and was decisive. The two ships were at short range, and both crews fired small arms as well as their main guns. Knowing the weakness of his own ship, Blake tried to ram, but the faster *Alabama* avoided it. After thirteen minutes, his ship on fire and sinking, Blake surrendered. Two of his crewmen were dead and five were wounded. The *Alabama* had been hit only five times and had two men wounded.

Semmes took the Union crew on board, then sailed for Port Royal, Jamaica, where on 20 January he paroled his prisoners. The Union boat crew escaped, the men rowing back to the squadron. Porter acknowledged the audaciousness of the deed. "No one can deny," he wrote, "that Semmes displayed great daring in this bearding the lion in his den, and entering waters he knew to be full of his enemy's gunboats."[33]

In late January the *Alabama* sailed from Jamaica east through the West Indies to Brazil, arriving on 10 April at Fernando de Noronha, where Semmes took on coal from a prize. This was fortuitous because the *Agrippina* had been delayed. Semmes then made for Bahia, taking several more prizes en route. There in mid-May, the *Georgia* came in, and the *Florida* was only one hundred miles to the north. The only Union warship then in the South Atlantic was the screw sloop *Mohican*. Acting Rear Admiral Wilkes, commander of the West Indian Squadron created specifically to track down the *Alabama* and *Florida*, had detained in the West Indies as his own flagship the powerful fast steamer *Vanderbilt*. The *Mohican* itself missed the Confederate cruisers in several locations by only a few days. Had the *Vanderbilt* been in concert, the career of the *Alabama* might have been ended. Wilkes was more interested in capturing blockade runners for prize money than in hunting the *Alabama*, and Secretary Welles later relieved him of command for "wholly inexcusable" misconduct in misusing the *Vanderbilt*.[34]

On 21 May 1863, the *Alabama* sailed from Bahia to cruise off the Brazilian coast. The *Agrippina* did not arrive at Bahia until 1 June, only to discover the U.S. Navy warships *Mohican* and *Onward* there. Fearful that his ship and its contents might be seized by the Federal ships when he left port, Capt. Alexander McQueen sold the coal and took on cargo for Britain. The tender never again encountered the *Alabama*.[35]

Between Bahia and Rio, the *Alabama* took eight prizes: five were burned and two were bonded. The remaining prize was the 500-ton *Conrad*, a fast bark-rigged clipper taken on 20 June. Semmes armed it with two 12-pounders from one of his prizes, commissioning it as the auxiliary cruiser *Tuscaloosa* under Lt. John Low. Semmes ordered Low to proceed on his own and then rendezvous at Cape Town. Low subsequently took two prizes. When the *Tuscaloosa* arrived at Cape Town, however, British authorities debated whether it was a legal warship; in December 1863 they seized the *Tuscaloosa* as an uncondemned prize. Eventually it was turned over to the U.S. consul.[36]

Semmes, meanwhile, sailed to the Cape of Good Hope to intercept ships homeward bound from the East Indies, but in two months off South Africa he took only one prize. Indeed, of its eventual total of sixty-four prizes, the *Alabama* took fifty-two of them in its first ten months at sea. In its last twelve months the *Alabama* averaged only one capture a month. There are three reasons for this: the "flight from the flag" of U.S. merchant ships shifting to foreign registry, U.S. merchants turning to foreign ships to transport their goods, and merchant skippers utilizing less-frequented trading routes.

Semmes now learned that the *Vanderbilt* was searching for him, and for a time the two ships played a game of cat and mouse. On 24 September Semmes departed Cape Town for the Far East, taking his ship far to the south of Mauritius. Engine problems forced the *Vanderbilt* to return home.[37]

Semmes hoped to cripple the U.S. Orient trade. During the first half of November, he took four merchant ships. But on 21 December, when the *Alabama* put in at Singapore, Semmes found twenty-two U.S. merchant ships safely in that harbor. He also learned that other Northern ships had been warned and were in refuge at Bangkok, Canton, Shanghai, and Manila. By now Semmes was having problems with his crew, and at almost every port some men deserted, although other men signed on.

The *Alabama* was now in need of a major overhaul. Its copper plating was coming loose from the wooden hull and its boilers were so corroded that it was dangerous to use full steam. Learning that the weaker Union screw sloop *Wyoming* (six guns) was patrolling Sunda Strait between Sumatra and

Confederate Capt. Raphael Semmes, shown here leaning against one of the pivot guns on the Confederate commerce raider Alabama *at Cape Town, South Africa, in August 1864. First Lt. John M. Kell, the ship's execuive officer, is in the background.*
NAVAL HISTORICAL CENTER (NH 57256)

Java, Semmes resolved to do battle. The two ships did not meet, however, because the *Wyoming* had steamed to Batavia for repairs to its boilers.[38]

Semmes sailed through the Straits of Malacca and took two more U.S. merchant ships before entering the Indian Ocean, briefly calling at Anjenga on the southwestern Indian coast, and sailing west to the Comoro Islands for provisions. The ship departed there on 12 February, retracing its course back to Cape Town, where it arrived on 20 March. On the return trip, Semmes took only one prize, and at Cape Town he learned that the British had seized the *Tuscaloosa*.

On 25 March 1864, the *Alabama* departed for Europe. In the Atlantic, Semmes took his last two prizes, the crew conducting target practice on one. Semmes noted in his journal "reasonable success," and Lieutenant Sinclair recorded "considerable damage" to the target ship in "fine execution." Nonetheless, extremes of temperature and dampness had accelerated the normal deterioration in the cannon powder that would have occurred from long storage, causing it to lose some of its force in projecting shot. Semmes ordered defective powder thrown overboard. Some caps and fuzes were also found defective, with only one shell in three exploding, and Semmes had new fuzes installed on all the shells aboard ship. Semmes believed that powder made up in cartridges and kept in sealed copper canisters was satisfactory; only after the engagement with the *Kearsarge* did he claim that it was only at two-third's strength.[39]

On 10 June 1864, the *Alabama* reached Cap de la Hague on the Normandy coast, and the next day it dropped anchor at Cherbourg. Since its commissioning, the raider had sailed seventy-five thousand miles, taken sixty-four prizes, and sent to the bottom a Union warship worth $160,000. In the *Sumter* and the *Alabama*, Semmes had taken eighty-one Union ships. He estimated he had burned $4,613,914 worth of Union shipping and cargoes and bonded others worth $562,250. Another estimate places the total Union loss at nearly $6 million. Twenty-five Union warships had been engaged in searching for the *Alabama*, another hefty expense. Beyond this, the raider's exploits had been a considerable boost to Southern morale.[40]

Immediately on his arrival at Cherbourg, Semmes requested permission to place his ship in dry dock for repair. French officials refused, pointing out, as Semmes knew, that the facilities were reserved for the French Navy and that only Emperor Napoleon III could grant permission. The authorities suggested that Semmes move his ship to Le Havre or another port with private dockyard facilities, but Semmes expressed confidence that the emperor would approve his request.

Events now moved swiftly. On 12 July U.S. Minister to Paris William Dayton telegraphed news of the *Alabama*'s arrival to the Dutch port of Flushing, where Capt. John A. Winslow's screw steam sloop *Kearsarge* was monitoring the CSS *Georgia* and *Rappahannock* at Calais. Only two months out of a Dutch dockyard, the *Kearsarge* was in excellent condition with a well-trained crew.

Winslow had spent a year looking for the *Alabama*, and he was determined that this time it would not elude him. Winslow quickly got under way, arriving at Cherbourg on 14 June and positioning his ship off the breakwater, although without anchoring. International law required that if the *Kearsarge* anchored in the harbor, the *Alabama* would receive a twenty-four-hour head start on departure.

Semmes might have attempted escape. Cherbourg had two channels, and it would be difficult for the *Kearsarge* to cover both, especially at night. But the *Alabama* was in poor condition, and it would have been hard to have kept the ship at sea for much longer. Semmes might have laid up his ship, as with the *Sumter* at Gibraltar, but he did not hesitate to do battle. This was an affair of honor and defense of the flag. Delay would only bring more Union warships. Indeed, Winslow had already telegraphed Lisbon to request that the heavily armed sailing sloop *St. Louis* join him.

Semmes ordered one hundred tons of coal brought on board and set his crew to work preparing for battle. Sailors filled the coal bunkers to help protect the ship's machinery from shot; they also landed nonessential spars and rigging, holystoned the deck, cleaned small arms and swords, and practiced gunnery drill. Semmes took the precaution of sending ashore his treasury of some forty-seven hundred gold sovereigns, the ten ransom bonds on ships he had released, and his collection of chronometers from each of his captures. As a point of pride, he kept on board his collection of flags from his prizes.[41]

Semmes informed French authorities that he would be fighting the next day, and then attended mass. That night there were farewell parties in Cherbourg cafes, although the crew members apparently behaved themselves and turned in early. At 9 AM on Sunday, 19 June 1864, the boilers were lit and Semmes called the men aft and addressed them for the last time. As the *Alabama* steamed out of the harbor, it passed the French ship of the line *Napoleon*, the band of which struck up "Dixie" and its sailors cheered. It was a perfect day, partly hazy, with a calm sea and light wind from the west. The French broadside ironclad *Couronne* accompanied the *Alabama*, followed by several other craft, including the yacht *Deerhound*, owned by John Lancaster, a pro-Southern Englishman.[42]

The battle between the *Kearsarge* and the *Alabama* was one of the most spectacular naval engagements of the war. An estimated fifteen thousand people watched from the cliffs and windows of houses ashore, although most saw only smoky smudges on the horizon. Numerous etchings and paintings of the battle exist, including one by impressionist master Edouard Manet, who may have been on a French pilot boat that day.

Despite Semmes's later claim that the *Kearsarge* had the advantage in size, weight of ordnance, number of guns, and crew, the two ships were closely matched. Semmes admitted as much in his journal. Commissioned in January 1862, the *Kearsarge* displaced 1,550 tons. At eleven knots maximum speed, it was slightly faster than its opponent. Its crew complement was 160 men. It mounted in broadside four 32-pounder guns and also had a 4.2-inch rifled gun and a small 12-pounder howitzer. Its strength, however, was in two XI-inch pivot-mounted Dahlgrens, throwing 135-pound shell. The *Alabama*, with its Blakeley rifle, would have the edge at long range, but the *Kearsarge* would have the advantage in medium- to short-range fire. Both ships could fight only five guns on one side, but the *Kearsarge* threw a heavier broadside weight of metal: 364 pounds to 274.

At 10:20 AM, a lookout on the *Kearsarge* spotted the *Alabama* coming out. Winslow, who had just begun reading Sunday service to the crew, closed his prayer book and ordered the men beat to quarters. The *Kearsarge* steamed to the northeast, not only to ensure that the battle would occur in international waters but also so as to be able to prevent the *Alabama* from running back to the French shore should it try to do so. Semmes and the *Alabama* followed, while the *Couronne* took up position at the three-mile French territorial limit.

Semmes expected to use his starboard guns in broadside and shifted one 32-pounder from port to strengthen that side. The added weight caused the ship to list about two feet to starboard, but this exposed less of that side to enemy fire.

When the two ships were about a mile and a quarter apart, Winslow reversed course and headed for the *Alabama*. He too planned to use his starboard battery, so the two ships met going in opposite directions. The battle began at 10:57 AM, some six or seven miles offshore, and lasted slightly more than one hour. It opened with a Confederate broadside at somewhat less than a mile. Only after several minutes, two or three Confederate broadsides (all of which passed high), and at a range of about a half mile did the *Kearsarge* reply.

Winslow ordered a port turn to try to place his own ship in position to rake his opponent, but Semmes veered to port to prevent this, which nonetheless allowed Winslow to close the range. When the *Alabama* turned back to starboard, the *Kearsarge* mirrored its movement. Because the *Kearsarge* was faster and Winslow sought to narrow the range, the circles grew progressively smaller, from one-half to one-quarter of a mile in diameter, with each ship firing its starboard battery only, the current gradually carrying the ships westward. The Federals were fortunate in that one Blakeley shell that lodged in the *Kearsarge*'s wooden sternpost failed to explode. Had it done so, it could have destroyed the ship's steering.

The *Kearsarge* had long lengths of chain strung over the vital middle parts of the ship to protect the engines, boilers, and magazines. This had proven effective in fighting along the Mississippi, and the chain had been in place on the *Kearsarge* for some time. An outward sheathing of 1-inch wood painted the same color as the rest of the hull concealed this from observation, but the French had informed Semmes of it.

The *Alabama* had chain in its lockers that might have been used for the same purpose. Semmes later claimed the *Kearsarge* had an unfair advantage as a "concealed ironclad." In his after-action report to Commo. Samuel Barron, he wrote, "The enemy was heavier than myself in ship, battery, and crew, and I did not know until the action was over that she was also iron-clad."[43] Semmes convinced himself that he was tricked into battle and that the chain was the only reason the *Alabama* lost. Historian George Dalzell observed, "This is a curious misconception of the character of warfare to take possession of the mind of a professional naval officer of life-long training, whose own vessel was born in deception and who for nearly two years had been disguising her with false colors to decoy unarmed merchantmen." Even had Semmes not known of the chain, Winslow did nothing untoward. James Bulloch observed, "It has never been considered an unworthy ruse for a commander . . . to disguise his strength and to entice a weaker opponent within his reach."[44]

Lieutenant Sinclair later criticized Semmes for this very failure. Sinclair noted that Semmes "knew all about it and could have adopted the same scheme. It was not his election to do so."[45]

Observing by spyglass that shot striking the *Kearsarge* were having no effect, Semmes ordered his gun crews to fire higher. One shell then tore through the Union ship's smokestack and another sheared off the top of the engine-room hatch. As the range narrowed, both sides substituted explosive shell for solid shot. Semmes hoped to close and attempt to board, but Winslow kept to the most effective range for his own guns, able to do so because his ship was both faster and more maneuverable than that of his opponent.

Repeated hits from the two Dahlgrens on the *Kearsarge* tore large holes in the *Alabama*'s hull. With the *Alabama* taking on water, an 11-inch shell struck at the waterline and exploded in the engine room, extinguishing the boiler fires. Water then entered the hull beyond the ability of the pumps to remove it. During the seventh circle Semmes was slightly wounded in the right hand by a shell fragment, but a quartermaster bandaged the wound and rigged a sling.

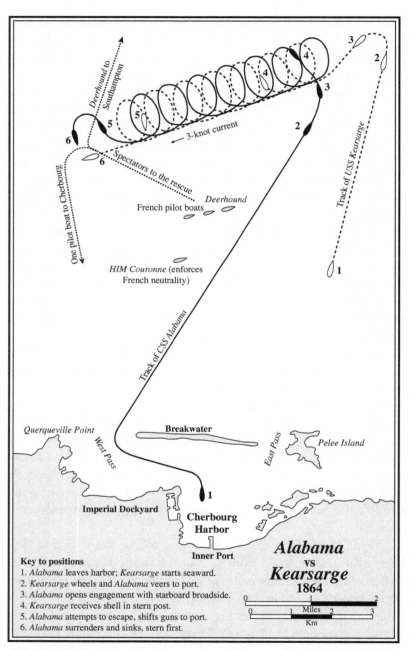

Deerhound to Southampton

5

6

6

One pilot boat to Cherbourg

Spectators to the rescue

← 3-knot current

Track of USS Kearsarge

3

2

3

2

1

4

4

5

2

Deerhound

French pilot boats

HIM *Couronne* (enforces
French neutrality)

Track of CSS Alabama

Querqueville Point

West Pass

Breakwater

East Pass

Pelee Island

1

Imperial Dockyard

**Cherbourg
Harbor**

Inner Port

Alabama
vs
Kearsarge
1864

Key to positions
1. *Alabama* leaves harbor; *Kearsarge* starts seaward.
2. *Kearsarge* wheels and *Alabama* veers to port.
3. *Alabama* opens engagement with starboard broadside.
4. *Kearsarge* receives shell in stern post.
5. *Alabama* attempts to escape, shifts guns to port.
6. *Alabama* surrenders and sinks, stern first.

0   1   2
Miles
0   1   2   3
Km

Alabama vs Kearsarge, 19 June 1864

Engagement between the U.S. Navy screw sloop Kearsarge *and the Confederate raider* Alabama, *off Cherbourg, France, 19 June 1864; contemporary engraving.*
NAVAL HISTORICAL CENTER (NH 59354)

At the beginning of the eighth circle, when the two ships were about four hundred yards apart, Semmes turned the *Alabama* out of the circle, ordering Lieutenant Kell to set all sail in hopes of making the French shore. Semmes also opened fire with his port battery. But the *Alabama* was taking on too much water and was completely at the mercy of the *Kearsarge*, the guns of which were ever more accurate. Winslow was then preparing to fire grape shot.

Kell, returning from below and a check on conditions, reported to Semmes that the *Alabama* could not last ten minutes, whereupon Semmes ordered him to cease firing, shorten sail, and haul down the colors. Semmes then sent a dinghy to the *Kearsarge* to notify Winslow that he was ready to surrender. Semmes and Sinclair both later claimed that the *Kearsarge* continued to fire after the colors were struck and a white flag displayed; Winslow asserted that he had ordered fire halted when the *Alabama*'s colors came down and a white flag was raised at its stern, but that shortly afterward the Confederate ship had fired from its two port guns and that he had then moved his ship into position to rake his antagonist but, seeing the white flag still flying, had again held fire.

Semmes ordered all hands to try to save themselves, but only two boats could be used, and most of the crew simply leaped into the sea. Semmes gave his papers to a sailor who was a good swimmer, hurled his sword into the water, and then jumped in himself.[46]

The *Alabama* went down in about fifteen minutes, at 12:24 PM. One *Kearsarge* eyewitness recalled: "Suddenly assuming a perpendicular position caused by the falling aft of the battery and the stores, she went down. . . . As she disappeared to her last resting place, there was no cheer; all was silent."[47]

Surprisingly, the *Alabama* got off twice as many shots as its opponent, 370 rounds to 173, but crewmen on the *Kearsarge* later counted only thirteen hull hits and sixteen in the masts and rigging. Only one shot from the Confederate ship caused personnel casualties: a Blakeley shell explosion on the quarterdeck that wounded three men at the after pivot gun, one mortally.[48]

A high percentage of the Union shots struck. Semmes later said one Union shot alone killed or wounded eighteen men at the after pivot gun. In all, the *Alabama* suffered forty-one casualties: nine dead and twenty wounded in action and twelve men drowned. The superior Union gunnery was probably attributable to excellent training by *Kearsarge* executive officer Lt. Cdr. James S. Thornton.[49]

Winslow was slow to order his men to pick up survivors, partly because most of his own boats had been badly damaged in the exchange of fire. As a result, many of those in the water were taken aboard other ships, especially the *Deerhound*, which rescued and transported to Southampton forty-two men, including Semmes and Kell. The British government rejected a demand from Minister Adams to turn them over to U.S. authorities. The *Kearsarge* took aboard six officers and sixty-four men, including twenty wounded. Winslow paroled them at Cherbourg. Unfairly, Semmes blamed Winslow for not doing enough to save those in the water, writing "Ten of my men were permitted to drown."[50]

Semmes was lionized in Britain. After a brief trip to the Continent, in October he took passage in steamers to St. Thomas and then to Havana, where he traveled by a British ship to Bagdad at the mouth of the Rio Grande on the Mexican side of the Texas border before making his way overland to Richmond. Promoted to rear admiral in February 1865 (and thus second in seniority in the Confederate service only to Franklin Buchanan), Semmes assumed command of the James River Squadron. This lasted barely three months, Semmes being forced to destroy his ships on the night of 2 April 1865, when Confederate forces abandoned Richmond. He then formed the men into a naval brigade under his command as a brigadier general. Semmes was in fact the only Confederate to hold flag rank (or its equivalent) in both the navy and army. The brigade withdrew to Greensboro, North Carolina, where it joined Gen. Joseph E. Johnston's army and surrendered with it.[51]

On Lincoln's recommendation, Congress extended a vote of thanks to Winslow and approved his promotion to commodore. Welles, however, unfairly blamed Winslow both for Semmes's escape and for paroling the prisoners, which he believed implied recognition of belligerent status for the *Alabama*, but Winslow pointed out that he had no room aboard his ship for prisoners. Winslow later retired from the navy a rear admiral.[52]

THE *TALLAHASSEE*

The *Tallahassee* was another successful raider. Originally the English fast cross-Channel steamer *Atalanta*, it was converted into a blockade runner and made four successful trips to the South in 1864. The Confederate government purchased the ship at Wilmington that summer and turned it into a commerce raider mounting three guns under Cdr. John Taylor Wood. Passing through the Union blockade on 4 August, the *Tallahassee*, probably the fastest of all Confederate commerce raiders, steamed up the East Coast and took a number of prizes. Evading Union warships but short of coal, Wood put into Halifax, Nova Scotia. When the raider returned to Wilmington on 26 August, it had taken thirty-three Union ships.

Renamed the *Olustee*, the ship made a second cruise under Lt. William Ward during which it captured six more prizes. Damaged by Union gunboats on the return run through the blockade to Wilmington, it was then disarmed, converted back into a blockade runner under the name *Chameleon*, and sent to Bermuda to secure badly needed military supplies. Unable to pass back through the blockade, Capt. John Wilkinson reluctantly sailed the ship to Liverpool, where he turned it over to Bulloch in April 1865 to be sold.[53]

THE *SHENANDOAH*

The defeat of the *Alabama* signaled the beginning of the end for Confederate commerce raiders, but Mallory continued to press the war against commerce and instructed Bulloch to locate a ship that might be easily converted to operate in the Pacific against U.S. whalers. Because tightened English neutrality laws precluded building such a ship in England, it would have to be a conversion.

In September 1864 Bulloch located and purchased the 1,160-ton *Sea King*. The first composite auxiliary screw steamship in the world, it was built in Glasgow in August 1863. Designed to transport troops to India, the *Sea King* was 230 feet long, capable of nine knots under steam, and had one screw, two boilers, and direct-acting engines. Flag Officer Samuel Barron, ranking Confederate officer in Europe, named Lt. Cdr. James I. Waddell its captain, ordering him to destroy the Union whaling fleet in the Pacific.[54]

On 8 October the *Sea King* slipped out of the Thames estuary. It was the last cruiser Bulloch got to sea. Commanded by British Capt. G. H. Corbet, it appeared to be on a merchant voyage, but it proceeded to Funchal, Madeira, to rendezvous with the supply ship *Laurel*, which carried Waddell, the remainder of the crew, armament, and stores. Its crew complement was seventy-three officers and men, and the ship was armed with four 8-inch and two 12-pounder smoothbore cannon and two 32-pounder rifled guns. On 19 October 1864 Waddell officially commissioned it the CSS *Shenandoah* and began his cruise for Union ships.

Waddell had hoped to secure the vast majority of the original crew, but only twenty-three signed on. He collected other volunteers en route, some of them from prizes. The *Shenandoah* took six Union merchant ships in the Atlantic, then in mid-December it rounded the Cape of Good Hope. Arriving at Melbourne, Australia, at the end of January, it underwent major repairs, including work on the propeller. Although a number of crewmen deserted at Melbourne, others took their places.

The *Shenandoah* sailed again on 18 February and cruised the whaling grounds in the Pacific Ocean and off Alaska. Its long stay at Melbourne allowed U.S. whaling ships in the South Pacific to disperse, but Waddell took the *Shenandoah* to the Bering Sea. Reaching there on 16 June, in six days Waddell took twenty-four New England whaling ships, burning all but those necessary to ship his prisoners.

One of his captives informed Waddell that the war was over, but there was no newspaper clipping or other evidence to substantiate the claim. Later Waddell secured newspapers recounting the Confederate government relocation from Richmond and President Davis's proclamation that the war would continue. Fortified with this information, Waddell took nineteen additional prizes in four days, sparing only those necessary for his prisoners. The *Shenandoah* then sailed south along the coast, Waddell planning a daring night raid into San Francisco Bay to seize the Union monitor *Comanche*.

Finally, on 2 August 1865, Waddell accepted as proof of the end of the war a report from an English captain. Waddell struck its guns below and sailed the *Shenandoah* seventeen thousand miles to Liverpool. The voyage was made almost exclusively under sail and without stopping at any port. Arriving on 6 November, Waddell turned over the ship to British authorities. The *Shenandoah* thus became the only Confederate warship to sail around the world. It had taken thirty-eight Union ships, of which Waddell burned thirty-two. The remainder he had sent under cartel to San Francisco. Damage to Union shipping was estimated at some $1.36 million. In 1866 the *Shenandoah* was sold to the Sultan of Zanzibar. It sank in the Indian Ocean in September 1872.[55]

During the Civil War, Confederate commerce raiders took 257 U.S. merchant ships, or only about 5 percent of the total. They hardly disrupted U.S. trade, and Welles staunchly resisted demands that he release ships from blockade duty to hunt them down, thus thwarting Mallory's hopes. Nonetheless, cruisers deployed by the U.S. Navy to hunt down the raiders cost the government some $3.325 million. In fourteen months from January 1863, a total of seventy-seven Union warships and twenty-three chartered ships were employed in this effort.

The raiders did drive up insurance rates substantially, but their major effect was to force a large number of U.S. ships into permanent foreign registry. More than half of the total U.S. merchant fleet was permanently lost to the flag during the Civil War. The cruisers burned or sank 110,000 tons of shipping but 800,000 tons were sold to foreign owners (seven hundred ships to British interests alone), and these were the best ships. Legal impediments prevented this tonnage from returning.[56]

After the war the matter of the British government having allowed the fitting out of a number of the Confederate cruisers became a major thorn in Anglo-American relations. U.S. government leaders believed, rightly or wrongly, that London's early proclamation of neutrality and then persistent disregard of this in the early part of the war had heartened the South

296 | CHAPTER ELEVEN

and prolonged the conflict. There were those in the U.S. government who proposed taking British Western Hemisphere possessions, including Canada, as compensation.

In 1871, when the Continental balance of power decisively changed with Prussia's defeat of France, British statesmen concluded that it might be wise to reach some accommodation with the United States against the possibility of a German drive for world hegemony. An international tribunal met in Geneva beginning that December to discuss what became known as the "Alabama claims," and in September 1872 it awarded the United States Government $15,500,500 in damages. This settlement came to be regarded as an important step in the peaceful settlement of international disputes and a victory for the world rule of law.[57]

CHAPTER TWELVE

The Red River Campaign

C ombat continued on the western rivers following the Union capture of Vicksburg, although mostly on a small scale. The great
exception to this was the last major Union riverine operation of
the war, the Red River Expedition of March–May 1864. The largest combined operation to that point in U.S. military history, it was also one of the
war's major military fiascoes.

Following the capture of Vicksburg, General Grant favored operations to capture Mobile, Alabama. He recalled in his memoirs that as early
as 1862 he had urged that Sherman's troops, "frittering away their time in
the trans-Mississippi, should move against Mobile," and that he had continued to counsel such a course from "time to time" until he took command of the Union armies in March 1864.[1]

Mobile was an important strategic center. It was the last deepwater
Confederate port on the Gulf, and Confederate forces there were a threat
to Union lines of communication west in the Gulf of Mexico. Taking
Mobile would free up a number of Union blockaders and secure the
Union right flank in the drive against Atlanta.

With the sizable force he had available, Grant might easily have
moved on Mobile after taking Vicksburg. Unfortunately for the Union
war effort, President Lincoln and General-in-Chief Halleck had other priorities. Not until he took over direction of all Union armies as a lieutenant

general on 12 March 1864 with Halleck as his chief of staff was Grant able to dictate strategy and plan an effort against Mobile.

Before Grant assumed his post, Lincoln, long an advocate for operations against Texas, approved Halleck's plan for an expedition up the Red River against Shreveport, Louisiana. Although Grant opposed siphoning off critical resources against an objective so far removed from the decisive theaters of war, Halleck had been able to set the campaign in motion before Grant could interfere. When Grant formally assumed command of the Union armies, the campaign was already under way, although Grant was able to limit the involvement of troops from Sherman's command who were committed to it.

Located in extreme northwestern Louisiana on the west bank of the Red River, Shreveport had long been on the short list of important Union military objectives. A city of twelve thousand people, Shreveport served both as the capital of Confederate Louisiana and as the headquarters of Lt. Gen. Kirby Smith's Army of the Trans-Mississippi. By 1864 it was also a thriving manufacturing center and supply depot, and it boasted a naval yard for the construction of the ironclad *Missouri* and a secret project of five river-defense submarines.

Shreveport also served as an important communications point and hub for other war-related industries in east Texas. The city marked the terminus of the "Texas Trail," the cattle road that led west into Texas, and it also served as the principal conduit for goods and supplies shipped from Mexico.

Union forces had tried to gain a toehold in Texas. In September 1863 efforts to take Sabine City had failed, although a second Union joint naval and army attempt at Brownsburg near the Mexican border was successful. The Red River appeared to be the ideal avenue into the interior of the Confederate Trans-Mississippi West.[2]

Despite sound military reasons for taking Shreveport, the chief Union motivations were economic and political. A shortage of cotton sharply drove up its price for New England textile manufacturers and forced thousands of workers from their jobs. The Red River Valley was the greatest cotton production area in the Confederacy. In normal times, cotton was shipped down the Red River to the Mississippi and New Orleans for export abroad. Reportedly, in the spring of 1864, upwards of two million bales were stored along the Red and its tributaries.

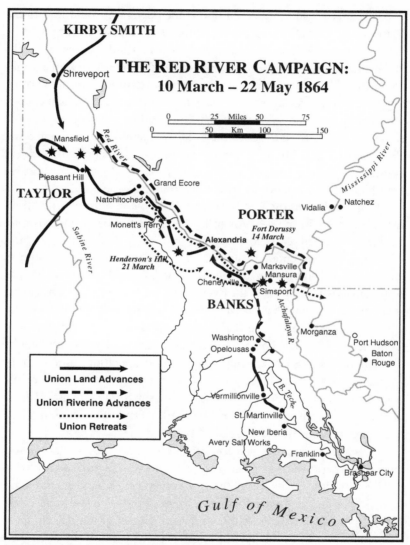

Red River Campaign, 10 March–22 May 1864

Policymakers in Washington hoped the operation would lead to the confiscation of significant stocks of cotton. To win the November presidential election, Lincoln would need to carry New England, and restoring jobs in the mills would go a long way toward that end. Of course, any major military triumph would resonate with the broad spectrum of Northern voters. Supporters of the plan also hoped that Union success in Arkansas and Texas would bring to an end Southern resistance in Louisiana. Diplomatic considerations also figured in the decision. Emperor Napoleon III had sent a sizable French expeditionary force to Mexico, and policymakers in Washington came to favor operations against Texas to forestall any possible French designs on that border state and former Mexican province.[3]

In normal times the Red River was navigable to Shreveport without major difficulty. Rising near Amarillo, Texas, the thirteen-hundred-mile-long river flowed east, forming the boundary between Texas and Oklahoma. It then entered southwestern Arkansas and turned south to Shreveport, continuing on to join the Mississippi above Baton Rouge. Although twisting, normally the river was broad and deep and naval operations on it would not have been difficult. Unfortunately for Union plans, when the operation up the Red began, exceptionally dry weather and Confederate defensive schemes had reduced its water levels considerably.

The navy's role was to support the Union operations ashore. Ships would proceed up the Red, providing transportation for some of the troops part of the way and furnishing gunfire support and logistical assistance. To carry out these missions, Rear Adm. David Porter assembled a large force of some ninety ships of all types.

On paper at least, the plan appeared to promise success. Union forces enjoyed numerical advantage in every area, and Washington committed to it 42,900 troops, organized in three major bodies. Maj. Gen. Nathaniel P. Banks commanded the largest contingent. Handsome and vain, Banks hailed from Massachusetts and was a former speaker of the U.S. House of Representatives and probably the most popular political figure in New England. Banks's political standing had secured him a major generalcy of volunteers, but although he was a political heavyweight, Banks was also a military flyweight. Despite his lack of military training and experience, he followed his own counsel and refused sound military advice offered by his professional officer subordinates. He had already demonstrated his incompetence in a combined operation with Farragut against Port Hudson.

Reportedly Banks agreed with Grant on the primacy of Mobile over Shreveport, and he later charged that Halleck had pressured him into the Red River Campaign. There were strong indications that Banks was considering a run for the presidency in 1864 on the Republican ticket. Lincoln reasoned that keeping Banks occupied in the West would mean that he was less likely to stir up trouble for his own effort to secure his party's nomination for another run for the White House.[4]

Banks exuded confidence, glossed over the difficulties facing him, and failed to insist on the detailed staff work essential for success. He would command some 19,000 infantry and cavalry of the Department of the Gulf. This force included four divisions of infantry and 3,900 cavalry. They would march southwest from New Orleans to Brashear City, and then northwest to Opelousas and the main north–south road that would carry them to Alexandria. There they were to be joined by some 2,500 men of the U.S. Colored Corps and also link up with the second Union prong of 10,000 men of Sherman's Army of the Tennessee, commanded by Brig. Gen. Andrew Jackson Smith. The combined southern force would number 32,500 men and ninety artillery pieces. It would press on to Shreveport, accompanied by Porter's ships providing logistical and gunfire support.

Sherman had great disdain for the grandstanding Banks. In any case, with the upcoming Atlanta campaign, Grant demanded that Sherman not command in person and that he attach conditions on the employment of those of his men who would serve under Banks. Thus Sherman insisted that Smith's men accompany Porter rather than Banks and that they move in transports up the Red. Smith's veterans, however, were under orders not to proceed beyond Shreveport and were detailed to the campaign for one month only, until mid-April.

Sherman warned his friend Porter that if things went badly and Banks had a chance to save his own force, he would sacrifice Porter's ships to do it. Although Banks chafed at Sherman's strictures, he was not overly concerned by them. Banks believed that the Confederates would make a stand before Shreveport and that the big battles would take place in Texas, after Shreveport had been taken.[5]

As the combined Union land and naval force under Banks, Smith, and Porter drove on Shreveport from the south, a third Union pincer of Maj. Gen. Frederick Steele's Department of Arkansas, or VII Corps, would move in from the north. Some 3,600 men were to proceed south from Fort

Smith to Arkadelphia and there join another 6,800 men moving southwest from Little Rock. This combined force of 10,400 was to proceed to Washington in southwest Arkansas, then move due south to close on Shreveport, trapping the city's defenders from that direction. To accomplish this, Steele's men would have to cross the Red River, which would not be an easy task because the Red was both broad and fast at this point.

Steele was not enthusiastic about the plan and tried to minimize his participation. He sought to make his role a demonstration only, one that would prevent Confederate forces in southern Arkansas from joining those opposing Banks. First Halleck and then Grant insisted, however, that Steele's men participate fully and actually link up with Banks at Shreveport.

As is the case in all such polycentric military plans, success depended on the three prongs coming together at precisely the same time. Failure of any one of the three would place the whole operation in jeopardy. Adhering to schedule would be essential because in mid-April the best ten thousand Union troops, the hardened veterans provided by Sherman, would be lost to the operation. Maintaining a tight schedule, however, would be extraordinarily difficult given Banks's inattention to detailed staff work, the lack of direct communication between the different commands, and the suspicion—even animosity—between the commanders. Only Porter and Smith cooperated effectively, and both despised Banks. Another danger lie in the possibility of Confederate Gen. Kirby Smith concentrating his entire command in order to overwhelm each of the three Union prongs piecemeal.

Banks presented himself as the expedition's overall commander, but in fact there was none, another serious shortcoming. Although Banks bombarded Halleck in Washington with demands for clarification as to his full authority, Halleck did not trust him as a military commander. Indeed, Halleck proceeded to orchestrate the component commands himself from Washington even as Banks embarked on his letter-writing campaign with the other generals in an effort to effect his own ends. The entire planning process was also rendered more difficult by Halleck's tendency to issue vague orders so that he would not be blamed if things went awry.[6]

Confederate General Smith was well aware of Union preparations, having been kept informed through spies. He and Maj. Gen. Richard Taylor, commander of the Western District of Louisiana, constantly haggled over where to position their limited resources, but in early March 1864, with

Union forces clearly preparing to move, Smith called on his scattered legions to concentrate in order to meet the expected Union offensive.

The Red River Campaign began on 10 March 1864, when, three days behind schedule, Sherman's troops and their equipment boarded twenty-one army Quartermaster Corps steamer transports at Vicksburg. Commanded by Brig. Gen. A. J. Smith, these ten thousand veterans included two divisions from XVI Corps and one division from XVII Corps. On the evening of 11 March, the Union transports rendezvoused with Porter's warships already off the mouth of the Red River.

Union spies provided Porter with exaggerated reports of the strength of probable Confederate forces in the river and the ironclads and submarines building at Shreveport. Not wishing to be caught short, Porter brought with him all the ships that he could secure, in what was the most powerful assembly of naval strength on inland waters of the entire war. In addition to his command ship, the tinclad *Black Hawk*, Porter could draw on the ironclads *Benton, Carondelet, Chillicothe, Choctaw, Eastport, Essex, Lafayette, Louisville, Mound City, Neosho, Osage, Ozark,* and *Pittsburg.* Porter also had the lighter-draft gunboats *Covington, Cricket, Forest Rose, Fort Hindman, Gazelle, Juliet, Lexington, Ouachita, St. Clair, Signal,* and *Tallahatchee,* along with the ram *Sterling Price.*

Accompanying the warships was a host of smaller vessels, including tugs, tenders, dispatch boats, and supply ships. The Mississippi Marine Brigade had its own ships, and there was also a hospital boat. Porter and his officers were, however, greatly concerned about the depth of the river and the effect this might have on their bigger ships and overall operations.

On 12 March the Union warships and transports entered the Red River and began their progress upriver, led by the *Eastport,* under Lt. Cdr. Seth Ledyard Phelps. The largest ship in the expeditionary force, the 570-ton *Eastport* promptly grounded on the sandbar at the mouth of the Red but was subsequently hauled across. The other ironclads then followed.

The mouth of the Red was in fact a complex of different streams, with both the Ouachita/Black River joining it nearby and the Atchafalaya River, a former course of the Mississippi, exiting that river near the mouth of the Red. Porter sent some of his ships up the Ouachita to neutralize the Confederate fortification at Trinity, and on 13 March Smith's men disembarked at Simmesport on the Atchafalaya River to march north overland on the Marksville Road west of the Red River against Confederate Fort

DeRussy upstream. After the Union troops and their equipment were ashore, the transports rejoined Porter's warships.

Over the preceding months, Confederate Brig. Gen. William R. Boggs, a graduate of West Point and Kirby Smith's chief of staff, had supervised construction of an extensive defensive system of works and obstacles to protect Shreveport against the expected Union advance. These included Fort DeRussy, the only real defensible position in the river south of Alexandria. Located on the western bank of a U-turn in the river midway between the river's mouth and Alexandria, it was named for Col. L. G. DeRussy, who supervised the construction.

These works had been briefly held by Porter in May 1863 during his foray up the Red. Boggs now strengthened DeRussy with forty-foot-thick, twelve-foot-high earthen walls, surrounded by a deep, wide ditch. Later the works were reinforced by railroad iron. In March 1864 DeRussy mounted eight heavy guns and two field pieces. Headquarters at Shreveport referred to the works as the "Confederate Gibraltar," but its strength faced the water approaches. Boggs hoped, however, that Fort DeRussy and Taylor's troops would be sufficient to defend Alexandria.

About eight miles below DeRussy, at another hairpin turn in the Red at a place known as the Bend of the Rappiones, the Confederates erected an additional barrier in the form of a major river obstruction. They drove two rows of heavy pilings into the riverbed completely across the stream. Confederate engineers then built a raft of wood and iron across its top and cut down a large number of trees upriver, allowing them to collect against it.[7]

Porter and Smith worked out a plan in which Smith's troops would assault Fort DeRussy from the land, while Porter's men removed the river obstructions and attacked the fort with ironclads from the water. Maj. Gen. John Walker's division of Texas troops—thirty-three hundred men and twelve artillery pieces—defended the lower Red River area. As the Union troops moved through Simmesport, Walker sent word to General Taylor. Estimating Union strength at fifteen to seventeen thousand men, Walker hastily evacuated his troops, a decision that doomed Fort DeRussy but saved the bulk of the Texans for the much more important battles to come.

General Smith's men soon arrived at Marksville, three miles from Fort DeRussy. Smith deployed his troops on either side of the road and advanced them overland the twenty-eight miles to DeRussy, arriving there on the afternoon of 14 March, whereupon the Confederates opened up on the Union soldiers with field pieces.

Meanwhile, Porter sent Lt. Cdr. Seth Phelps with the *Eastport, Osage, Fort Hindman,* and *Cricket* ahead to clear the water obstructions known to be located below Fort DeRussy. Phelps's ships reached these in mid-morning on 14 March and immediately began removing them. Phelps employed the powerful *Eastport* to ram the pilings and loosen them. Sailors then secured hawsers to the pilings and pulled them free when the *Eastport* backed away. Thanks to this steam power, by late afternoon Phelps and his men had opened a path. They then proceeded to Fort DeRussy, arriving there at dusk on 14 March, just as the Union troops were beginning their land assault.

The *Eastport, Osage, Fort Hindman,* and *Cricket* immediately opened a brisk fire on the fort. However, Phelps soon ordered this halted for fear of hitting friendly troops, but not before a 100-pounder Parrott shell exploded over the water battery, scattering its defenders.

At 6 PM on 14 March, Union Brig. Gen. Joseph A. Mower personally led his 3rd Division in charging the fort, which soon surrendered. Of 300 Confederates at the time of the action, 185 surrendered; the remainder escaped. Union forces also captured all the Confederate guns and stocks of ammunition. Union casualties in the land operation were 38 dead and wounded.[8]

The men of Mower's 3rd Division then rejoined the transports to proceed upriver. Porter, who had abandoned his own effort up the Atchafalaya River, then employed both the *Benton* and *Eastport* to assist in destroying Fort DeRussy. The *Benton* even fired its heavy guns into the fort at point-blank range but was unable to destroy the well-constructed Confederate casemates. Indeed, the firing of its heavy guns opened up leaks in the *Benton,* necessitating repairs.

Porter had sent word to Phelps via the steam tug *Dahlia* to proceed to Alexandria, but the *Dahlia* was delayed at the obstruction, where a number of trees cut down for it had floated out and blocked its passage. The *Dahlia* did not arrive at Fort DeRussy until near midnight, but Phelps had, at about 9 PM, already sent the *Fort Hindman* and *Cricket* ahead. On receipt of Porter's orders, Phelps followed with the *Easport* and two river monitors.

On the morning of 16 March, Phelps had nine gunboats at Alexandria, from which he landed 180 men under *Osage* captain Lt. Cdr. Thomas Selfridge to take possession of the city, which was subsequently secured by Mower's troops. Porter had hoped to be able to capture Confederate shipping there, but news of the surrender of DeRussy caused General Taylor to order the immediate evacuation of all vessels and Confederate ground units. Six steamers got away upriver just ahead of the Union ships and all escaped, save for the *Countess*, which went aground in the falls and was burned to prevent capture. In their haste to escape the city, however, the Confederates did abandon three field pieces. Arriving at Alexandria, Porter settled down to await the arrival of Banks.

Porter was completely in the dark as to how Banks and Steele might be faring. In fact, both commands were behind schedule. Banks was to have been at Alexandria on 17 March, but his entire force did not arrive there until 26 March, and Steele did not set out until the very day that Porter and Smith took Alexandria. Steele had been spurred into action by a letter from Grant ordering "full cooperation" rather than a "demonstration."[9]

These delays assisted the Confederates, who were building up their strength. With the addition of Walker's Texans, General Taylor now commanded some seven thousand men, and he made skillful use of his inferior resources. Taylor's plan was to conduct delaying actions that would mask his actual strength and to engage Banks in pitched battle only at a time and place of his own choosing. Taylor soon found himself without his "eyes," however, when Union Brig. Gen. Albert Lee's cavalry advance of Banks's force arrived at Alexandria on 21 March. Although both men and horses were exhausted, they went into action that night in stormy conditions. Securing the Confederate password, the Union troopers caught the Southern cavalrymen in bivouac without proper defensive preparations and captured 350 of them, along with 400 mounts, for no losses of their own.

Banks and the main body of his XIX Corps were, however, well behind schedule. Banks had dallied in New Orleans, and his men were already five days late when they moved west eighty miles by railroad and twenty-five miles by river transport to arrive at their assembly point of Franklin for the march north. Fortunately, Banks had the presence of mind to send Lee on ahead along the roads that the XIX would use to move to Alexandria. The long Union infantry column then snaked north, stretched out over a span of some twenty miles, a day's march between its head and tail. Banks never considered parallel lines of advance, which, however, would have been difficult in the bayou country of southern Louisiana; nor did he take steps to shorten the column. Heavy rain and knee-deep mud also served to impose delay. The head of the column did not arrive in Alexandria until 25 March. The rest of the men came in the next day. The expeditionary force was now eight days behind schedule. Banks did not share the march with his men. He arrived in Alexandria on 24 March on the army transport *Black Hawk*. This ship bore the same name as Porter's own flagship, which was considered an affront by Porter and his officers. [10]

Banks was upset to find on his arrival at Alexandria that navy personnel were busily engaged in seizing and transshipping cotton. Indeed, the sailors expanded their efforts, locating stocks as far as ten miles from the city. Under naval prize law, Porter was legally entitled to seize belligerent property, which would then be turned over to a prize court (in this case, at Cairo) for adjudication. The personnel involved stood to receive half of the proceeds, with the remainder going to a fund for disabled seamen. Private property was, of course, exempt from seizure, but because it was virtually impossible to prove which was government and which was private cotton, naval officers soon had stencils and branding irons made with "CSA" on them to ensure that the seized cotton would be identified as legitimate booty.

With four-hundred-pound bales of cotton difficult to move, the navy commandeered wagons and mules, stenciling them with "USA." On 24 March, Porter reported having seized 2,129 bales of cotton, 28 barrels of molasses, and 18 bales of wool, "all belonging to the Confederate government." In response to these confiscations, General Taylor ordered his men to burn all the cotton they could locate that might be liable to Union seizure.

The Union Army had no similar system to allow its personnel to profit from confiscated property, and thus there was immediate animosity between the two services over this. More important to Banks, he had brought with him a number of cotton speculators and now saw his own role as savior of the New England cotton mills fast disappearing. Porter can hardly be blamed for taking advantage of the situation with Banks absent, and the general had only himself to blame for the tardiness of his arrival. On 2 April, however, Banks drafted an order that allowed Louisiana citizens to sell their cotton rather than see it lost, but this came too late for most of the stocks at hand. [11]

With the arrival of the last of his force on 26 March, Banks had 32,500 men in and around Alexandria. These included the 2,500 U.S. Colored troops of the Corps d'Afrique, who had arrived by boat. The navy and army together had some 90 vessels at Alexandria. Porter's ships mounted 210 heavy guns, and Banks had 90 artillery pieces ashore. With such powerful resources available, few doubted that taking Shreveport would be an easy matter.

On 26 March a letter arrived for Banks from Grant dated eleven days before. Grant informed Banks of his appointment as Union Army general-in-chief and then outlined his minimal expectations for the campaign. Little knowing that Banks was already well behind schedule, Grant laid down a strict timetable that he expected to be followed. He told Banks that Shreveport had to be taken as soon as possible but, regardless of circumstance, Smith's troops would have to be returned to Sherman by mid-April. If Banks could take Shreveport, he was to garrison it, maintain navigation on the Red River, and remove the bulk of his forces to New Orleans to prepare for operations against Mobile.

Orders also arrived at Alexandria on 26 March recalling Ellet's Mississippi Marine Brigade. Porter was glad to see them depart. These poorly disciplined marauders had looted and burned their way to Alexandria but were recalled to provide security on the Mississippi in the absence of Porter's ships. The brigade left on 27 March.

Grant's orders exploded Banks's plan for a leisurely advance on Shreveport but did not prevent him from neglecting his military duties in order to supervise new elections for local officials at Alexandria on 1 April. Porter, meanwhile, was very concerned about the dropping water in the Red and decided that he could wait no longer if he was to proceed upriver. Experienced river pilot Wellington W. Withenbury advised Porter to take only his light-draft ships and leave the heavy ironclads behind. He also warned Porter about the "falls" at Alexandria, sandstone boulders in the river that usually were well below the surface but would be treacherous in low water. The twisting course of the river through these rapids was known to locals as the "chute."

Porter listened to this sound advice, and then proceeded to order Withenbury to take the large *Eastport* over the falls. Withenbury protested, but Porter insisted that he follow orders. It is uncertain exactly what Porter expected to find upriver, but there was a Union spy at Shreveport who may have been providing him with information at this time. In any case, Porter had to assume there might be as many as five Confederate ironclads in the river, which is no doubt why he believed he needed the *Eastport* with him. Its large ram and powerful armament made it Porter's most effective warship against ironclads. But Porter also assured anyone who would listen that he could take his ships "wherever the sand was damp," and he informed Banks that he would accompany his men even if "I should lose all my boats," which indeed came close to realization. Later Porter expressed his motivation to Sherman differently, noting that Banks "deemed the cooperation of the gunboats so essential that I had to run some risks and make unusual exertions to get them over the falls."[12]

The falling water in the Red resulted largely from deliberate Confederate actions to impede Union naval movements. The first of these was Kirby Smith's order to carry out the plan to place a large steamer, the *New Falls City*, athwart the river channel near Tone's Bayou. Its bow and stern rested as much as fifteen feet up on each bank and rapidly formed a sandbar upriver of it. Confederate engineers then broke the ship open and poured mud into the steamer's hold, creating an instant large dam on the river itself. The engineers next blew up another dam, diverting the Red into old Tone's Bayou channel and thence into Bayou Pierre. Although much of the water flowed back into the Red River a few miles above Grand Ecore, a large amount of it remained to form a nineteen-mile-wide collection lake in the bayou, dropping the water level in the Red considerably.

On 29 March, Porter set out with a dozen ships, the *Eastport* and *Osage* leading. Withenbury's concerns over the water depth proved correct, for when he guided the *Eastport* into the chute it immediately grounded, and it took three days to get it through. Meanwhile, Porter managed to pass some of his lighter warships upriver, aided by the *Eastport*'s deflection of water to its sides. Although the hospital ship *Woodford* was wrecked in the falls, Porter did get past Alexandria the *Eastport*, *Cricket*, *Mound City*, *Chillicothe*, *Carondelet*, *Pittsburg*, *Ozark*, *Nwosho*, *Osage*, *Lexington*, *Fort Hindman*, and *Louisville*. Thirty transport steamers accompanied them.

Because the only communication with the ships above Alexandria was by road, supplies had to be landed, moved by wagon around the falls, and then reloaded on board ship. In order to protect this vital supply line and the city itself, Banks left behind at Alexandria an entire division of four thousand men.

From Alexandria on, everything seemed to go wrong. It took the Union ships four days to cover the one hundred miles to Grand Ecore, in consequence of the lighter ships having to wait for the heavier ones and the occasional exchange with Confederates along the riverbanks. One Southern sharpshooter claimed the commanding officer of the *Chillicothe*.

Porter's ships were also short of coal, and each night when they tied up along the shore, crewmen were sent out to scavenge all wooden fence posts in the immediate vicinity for fuel. As they moved up the Red, the Union sailors could see near the river smoke from thousands of bales of cotton that the Confederates had deliberately torched rather than see it fall into Union hands. One planter told Selfridge that Confederate troops had burnt five thousand bales of his cotton (at $400 a bale at New Orleans, these stocks were worth $2 million) and his $30,000 gin house, making him penniless overnight.[13]

Lee's Union cavalry had departed Alexandria on 26 March, and Smith's men followed the next evening over the morning of 28 March. Reaching the steamboat landing at Cotile, twenty-two miles north of Alexandria, Smith's troops boarded the transports to accompany the fleet to Shreveport. Maj. Gen. William B. Franklin left Alexandria with the bulk of Banks's men on 29 March.

Lee's cavalry took Natchitoches on 30 March, and Franklin's men arrived there on 1 April, having covered the eighty miles from Alexandria in four days of hard marching. They bivouacked between Natchitoches and Grand Ecore four miles north on the Red River. That same day Banks wrote Halleck from Alexandria that he expected little or no Confederate resistance and that he would be in Shreveport by 10 April and would then pursue Confederate forces into Texas. A concerned Halleck showed the overconfident message to Lincoln, who commented prophetically, "I am sorry to see this tone of confidence; the next news we shall hear from there will be of a defeat."[14]

Not until 2 April did Banks depart Alexandria in the steamer *Black Hawk* for Grand Ecore. Arriving there the following day, he was faced with deciding the next stage in the progression to Shreveport. Smith's ten thousand troops were scheduled to leave in only twelve days.

At Grand Ecore each part of the operation went its own way. The Arkansas portion remained completely separate from that in Louisiana, but the Louisiana portion now divided as well. Confronted by plethora of very different maps (the army was using a single-sheet map of the state of Louisiana published in 1853 that provided very little detail) indicating towns, roads, and bayous for a route to Shreveport, Banks consulted Withenbury. The river pilot had a considerable financial investment in cotton grown near the river upstream. Knowing it would be safe only if the army did not proceed upriver with the navy, he thus presented to Banks the option of two interior roads, one to the east (actually a better route, but it would take three additional days to traverse), and one far inland to the west. Withenbury was much more specific in information on the western route. Porter asked Banks for time to make a reconnaissance upriver, but the general was well aware of the pressing time constraints on a third of his force, and he made the decision to move north along the westerly road some twenty miles inland and well away from the support afforded by Porter's ships. Banks and Porter agreed to meet at a point opposite Springfield Landing about 30 miles south of Shreveport (110 miles by the river) on 10 April.

Between Grand Ecore and Shreveport, the river was narrow and winding. Fearful that the *Eastport* might ground in these conditions, Porter decided to leave it behind at Grand Ecore and proceed with the monitors *Osage* and *Neosho*, the ironclad *Chillicothe*, the timberclad *Lexington*, and the tinclads *Cricket* (the flagship) and *Fort Hindman*. Accompanying the gunboats were twenty army transports and 2,300 men of Smith's XVII Corps.[15]

U.S. Navy Mississippi Squadron sidewheel tinclad Fort Hindman. U.S. NAVAL INSTITUTE PHOTO ARCHIVE

Porter's ships set out on 7 April. As they proceeded north up the twisting river, Porter quickly concluded that marching along the Red would have been the best route by far for Banks's troops. The roads there were in good repair and flanked by wide fields. The troops would also have been able to move without the large supply train transporting ten days of rations specified by Banks, and the gunboats could have supported the Union right flank.[16]

Banks's men, meanwhile, resumed their march north beginning on 6 April, Lee's cavalry leading. Banks arranged the order of march with the cavalry in front, followed by three hundred supply wagons protected by the twenty-five hundred U.S. Colored Troops of the Corps d'Afrique, then the main body of fifteen thousand men under General Franklin (with Banks at their head), its seven hundred wagons, and finally the bulk of General Smith's force, some seventy-five hundred men of XVI Corps bringing up the rear, protected by a screen of one brigade of cavalry, which, however, did not provide flank security. The artillery was split among the components. This march order in effect hemmed in the main force of Franklin's infantry between wagons to front and rear, making it impossible for Banks to deploy that force rapidly in either direction.

On 7 April about three miles north of Pleasant Hill, Lee's cavalry encountered Confederate cavalry under Brig. Gen. Thomas Green and there fought a sharp battle. The Confederates withdrew but nonetheless purchased time for their infantry to come up. The next day, the Union column reached Sabine Crossroads just south of the small town of Mansfield and about forty miles as the crow flies south-southwest of Shreveport. The resulting battle is known either as Mansfield or Sabine Crossroads. The closest point Banks got to Shreveport, it was also the decisive clash of the Red River Campaign and one of the last major Confederate victories of the war.

On 8 April, with the Federal column snaking back over twenty miles of road, Taylor and about 8,800 Confederates struck its head. Taylor ordered the battle begun, even though 5,000 Southern reinforcements under Brig. Gen. Thomas Churchill had not yet arrived. The battle started with cavalry skirmishes and artillery duels. Because Banks's men were spread out and handicapped by the poor march arrangements, their superior numbers never came into play; only about 12,000 men, or some half of the Union force, actually participated.

Following preliminary dueling, at about 4 PM on 8 April Taylor ordered his men to advance. In hard-fought, hand-to-hand combat, the Confederates drove the Union troops back. When the attackers mounted a double envelopment, Union resistance collapsed, and the panicked Federals fled to the rear. Only a stand by Brig. Gen. William Emory's division three miles back prevented complete disaster. Banks's force suffered 2,235 casualties (113 killed, 581 wounded, and 1,541 missing). The Confederates also captured 20 guns, 250 wagons, and nearly 1,000 draft animals, as well as thousands of small arms. Taylor's own losses of 1,500 men were actually heavier in terms of numbers of men engaged, but he had ended the Union drive on Shreveport.

Banks withdrew his men to Pleasant Hill, fourteen miles south, where the last major battle of the campaign occurred. The Union troops marched all night, with the head of the column arriving at Pleasant Hill at 8:30 AM on 9 April. There they set up strong defensive positions. Although still badly outnumbered, Taylor pursued and, with Churchill's reinforcements, prepared to attack again in hopes of destroying the Federal force. The Confederates struck at 4:30 PM, but Union counterattacks nullified the initial Southern success.

Nightfall ended the fighting. Federal losses amounted to 152 killed, 859 wounded, and 495 captured. Taylor estimated his own total casualties in the two days of fighting at 2,200 men, or about 700 in this engagement. Despite having won a tactical victory in the battle of Pleasant Hill, Banks believed his army was threatened with destruction and, following a conference with his subordinate commanders, decided to withdraw completely. All Union troops retired at night to Grand Ecore and from there to Alexandria. Although he had not destroyed Banks's force as he had hoped, Taylor had saved Shreveport and driven Federal forces from eastern Louisiana.[17]

Porter was at Springfield Landing, having arrived there on 10 April to await Banks for the final push to Shreveport. Porter was already contemplating how best to dispose of the major obstruction in the river caused by the sunken *New Falls City* when he learned via courier of the battle of Pleasant Hill, actually south of his own force. Banks's decision to withdraw forced an already skeptical Porter to act. Distributing the warships among the troop transports with the *Osage* bringing up the rear, Porter gave the order to descend the river.

Banks's precipitous withdrawal freed up thousands of Confederates, and a number took up position on the bluffs along the river. In some places the bluffs were actually higher than the pilothouses of the ships so that Confederate snipers could easily fire down on the decks of the Union ships. Although the Union ships could use their heavy guns to drive the Confederates away, the task of descending the river was now much more difficult. The falling river also contributed to problems.

On 12 April at Blair's Landing the *Osage*, which was lashed to the steamer *Black Hawk*, grounded. As the Union seamen were working to free the ship, lookouts detected troops and some artillery pieces gathering several miles away in a wood. Employing a spyglass from atop the pilothouse of the *Osage*, Selfridge identified them as Confederates and ordered the *Lexington* to move downriver and open an enfilading fire.

Nonetheless, the Confederate infantry advanced to the river and opened up with small arms. The *Osage* responded with grape and cannister, and finally with shrapnel and fuzes cut to only one second. In the exchange, the Union ships were riddled with bullets. Selfridge later counted fifty bullet holes in the *Osage*'s pilothouse alone. The fight lasted about an hour and a half, until the Confederates withdrew. The Confederates reportedly sustained some three hundred casualties and the Union side but seven wounded. Among the Confederate dead was cavalry Brig. Gen. Thomas Green, an exceptionally able field commander who nonetheless had led the impetuous advance.[18]

Porter now requested, and received, troops from Banks to keep Confederate soldiers away from the river where the crews on his gunboats frequently had to free Union transports that had gone aground on sandbars. The large transports were a constant problem and limited the progress of Porter's ships to about twenty miles a day. Nonetheless, the Union flotilla was never in any immediate danger from the Confederates. A far more serious threat loomed in the falling water level.[19]

At the same time he had ascended the Red, Porter had also dispatched ships up the Ouachita River. These reached as far as Monroe, Louisiana. This expedition confiscated three thousand bales of cotton, brought off about eight hundred slaves, and "destroyed much rebel property."[20]

On 15 April, Porter's ships reached Grand Ecore. That same day, however, the *Eastport* struck a mine about eight miles below Grand Ecore and slowly settled in the river. Porter immediately ordered two steam pump boats up from Alexandria, and they succeeded in raising the badly damaged ship. Commander Phelps took charge of operations, including the offload-ing of the *Eastport*'s guns and ammunition. But the leak at the bow could not be found and was only contained by construction of a bulkhead.

Banks remained at Grand Ecore while efforts were in progress to refloat the *Eastport*, but Franklin and others warned Porter that Banks intended to depart soon. Informed on the afternoon of 21 April that Porter was ready to move, Banks ordered an immediate withdrawal, leav-ing the fleet to its own devices.

That same day Porter set out from Grand Ecore with the *Eastport* and his other ships, the transports proceeding on ahead under escort to Alexandria. The *Champion No. 3* pump boat remained alongside it, and the *Champion No. 5* took the *Eastport* under tow. The *Eastport* was long (260 feet) and down at the bow, and thus difficult to control. It had pro-gressed about twenty miles when it got out of the channel and grounded. Pickets were immediately sent ashore to watch for Confederates, for the fleet was now without army support.

Working day and night, the two pump boats and the *Fort Hindman* finally managed to pull the *Eastport* free on 23 April. Again under tow, the *Eastport* made it five more miles before grounding again. Gotten off only after great effort, the ship continued to ground in the river. On 25 April, it grounded several more times, and finally could not be moved. Porter had thus far been lucky for the Confederates had been following Banks, attack-ing his rear guard and taking little notice of the gunboats, but this could not last forever. Bloodied in an attack on Banks's rear guard at Monett's Ferry on the Cane River, the Confederates turned their attention to Porter's ships.

Porter was determined not to abandon the *Eastport* as long as Phelps thought there was hope of reaching Alexandria. Indeed, Porter later reported to Welles, "I must say that, mentally, I never went through such anxiety in my life." But, following five days of near-unceasing effort and the repeated groundings, the Union crews were utterly exhausted, and the *Eastport* and its consorts had covered only sixty miles, with a like distance to go before friendly lines. This, coupled with the fact that the river con-tinued to drop and the belief that the Confederates would soon make an attempt to capture the defenseless *Eastport* and the three ships accompa-nying it, led Porter to bow to the inevitable.

The Union seamen made one last attempt to lighten the *Eastport* by removing its iron plating, but they lacked the proper tools for such work, which in any case would clearly take too much time. On 26 April Porter ordered the ship to be destroyed. Union seamen then placed a ton of powder in various locations on it, and Phelps then touched off a powder train and leapt into the waiting cutter. At 1:45 PM, seven separate explosions destroyed the *Eastport*, "as perfect a wreck as ever was made by powder." What was left blocked the channel for some time afterward.[21]

Phelps was the last to leave the ship, leaping into the cutter only as the explosions began. An eyewitness reported:

> Hidden by the smoke, the captain had not been seen to escape the boat and but four could be distinctly made out in her, and for a moment intense anxiety was felt on board the *Fort Hindman*. Then a little veer of the boat showed to the watchers with glasses that five sitters were in her. He is there! All could see that the fragments had fallen and the boat still pulled for the ship. That she passed through those falling timbers and plates of iron untouched, was one of those mysterious happenings which we ascribe to the especial providence of God.[22]

Porter hoped to salvage the *Eastport's* plating to keep it out of Confederate hands, but this proved impossible. Troops were already gathering in the vicinity and had opened up on the ships even as the *Eastport* was being readied for destruction, leading Porter to order the *Cricket* to return fire with grape and cannister.

Following the destruction of the *Eastport*, the *Cricket*, *Fort Hindman*, *Juliet*, and two pump boats got under way. They proceeded about twenty miles without incident until they reached a bend in the river about five miles above the juncture of the Cane River with the Red. There they come under attack from a sizable force ashore that Porter estimated at twelve hundred men, supported by eighteen 12-pounder and 24-pounder artillery pieces.

The *Cricket* was leading and was separated from the other ships when the Confederates attempted to rush it from along the bank. The flagship repulsed the attack with grape and cannister, whereupon the Southerners opened up with their artillery, every shot of which told and immediately cleared the gunboat's decks. One shot hit the *Cricket's* after gun, disabling it and killing or wounding its entire crew. At the same time a shell exploded near the forward gun, sweeping away its crew and wounding men in the fireroom. Nonetheless, Porter managed to pass his ship through the Confederate gauntlet to a point where he could open up an enfilading fire. Meanwhile, the *Champion No. 3* took a 12-pounder shell in its starboard boiler, releasing clouds of steam and killing three men and wounding a fourth. Of 150 to 200 escaped slaves on board, only 15 survived. The abandoned *Champion No. 3* was subsequently captured by the Confederates and repaired. Both the *Juliet* and *Champion No. 5* were also struck. The *Juliet* had its steering crippled and steam pipes cut and was disabled, but the *Champion No. 5* towed it to safety.

It was too risky to attempt to pass the Confederate shore position at night for fear of grounding, so it was not until the next morning, 27 April, that the *Champion No. 5* and the *Fort Hindman* towing the *Juliet* made the attempt. All soon came under heavy Confederate artillery and rifle fire. The *Champion No. 5* took a shot in its pilothouse and soon sank. Other Union gunboats came up to assist. The *Osage* and *Lexington* joined the fray, but the *Neosho* arrived too late to participate.

The thin-skinned Union gunboats took such a beating that it was a wonder they survived. In the battle the *Cricket* was hit thirty-eight times with solid shot and shell. It suffered twenty-five killed and wounded, half its crew. The *Juliet* lost two killed, thirteen wounded, and one missing; the *Fort Hindman* was struck nineteen times by artillery rounds and suffered two men killed.[23]

The engagement over, Porter's remaining ships limped down to the rapids above Alexandria. By 27 April, he had twelve ships there. Banks's men had arrived during 25–26 April and could now provide protection, but Porter's worries were by no means over. Indeed, the situation facing the squadron appeared desperate. Porter wrote Welles that the Confederates were

> [T]urning the source of water supply off into the lakes, which would have been remedied had the army succeeded in getting to Shreveport. I can not blame myself for coming up [the river] at the only season when the water rises. All the rivers are full and rising, but the Red River is falling at the rate of 2 inches a day, a most unusual occurrence, this river always being full until the middle of June. Whether we will yet have a rise it would be impossible for any one to foresee. It seems like an impossibility

that we could be caught in such a predicament in a time of rising water, but such may be the case.

If General Banks should determine to evacuate this country, the gunboats will be cut off from all communication with the Mississippi. It can not be possible that our country would be willing to have eight ironclads, three or four other gunboats, and many transports sacrificed without an effort to save them. It would be the worst thing that has happened this war.[24]

On 28 April Porter reported a water depth of only three feet, four inches at the falls, with seven feet required to pass his ships over. Porter was thus in the position of perhaps having to destroy all the ships or see them fall into the hands of the Confederates. He complained bitterly to Welles about what he believed to be Banks's precipitous retreat (confirmed by Brig. Gen. Thomas K. Smith in a letter) in which "little consideration was paid to the situation of myself and little squadron when exposed to all the power of the enemy's forces." Porter reported that sizable Confederate forces were approaching Alexandria, and their heavy artillery could be positioned in the hills opposite the city. Of Union ground commanders in the area, only Gen. A. J. Smith enjoyed the men's confidence.[25]

Despite Porter's concern, Banks did provide the requisite security and, most importantly, Lt. Col. Joseph Bailey, acting engineer of XIX Corps, arrived on the scene. The situation then appeared ominous. The rocks in the river were visible for more than a mile, the total fall of the river being 13 feet. Bailey, however, proposed constructing a dam across the river at the rapids to raise the water level and allow the ships to pass over. At the point just above the lower chute, where the dam would be built, the river was nearly 760 feet wide, and the fall would be 6 feet below the dam. To get the ships over the upper fall, the river would have to be raised 7 feet above the dam.

Bailey's plan seemed like madness, and a number of other engineers ridiculed it. Porter reported, "perhaps not one in fifty believed in the success of the undertaking." Certain it would work, Bailey convinced a skeptical Porter, who then requested and received the requisite manpower from Banks: some thirty-five hundred troops and two hundred to three hundred wagons.[26]

The troops tore down all nearby mills for materials, and several regiments from Maine were also soon hard at work felling trees in the vicinity. Wagon teams transported to the river the felled lumber as well as stone and bricks. Bailey oversaw the construction, which consisted of a series of wing dams of large trees and cribs of rocks, bricks, and heavy pieces of machinery taken from nearby sugar houses and cotton gins. These cribs extended outward on either side and then into the river. Bailey connected the space between the wings with four large navy coal barges filled with bricks, sunk in the main channel. All this was accomplished notwithstanding a strong river current of nine knots.

The work began on 30 April, and by 8 May the project was essentially complete with the water having risen 5 feet, 4.4 inches. One more day would have been sufficient for Porter to be able to move all his ships over the falls, and he brought the *Fort Hindman, Osage,* and *Neosho* over the upper falls and positioned them to pass through the dam. Then disaster struck. The pressure of the water was such that on the morning of 9 May it swept away two of the barges. Seeing what had happened, Porter immediately jumped on a horse and rode to where the *Lexington* was anchored, ordering it to proceed immediately. Porter reported that everyone on shore held their breath as the *Lexington* moved into position and then passed safely through, when "Thirty thousand voices rose in one deafening cheer."[27]

Fortunately, the water was sufficiently deep to enable all of the shallow-draft ships, their hatches battened down, to pass over the falls. The *Lexington* was followed by the *Neosho* (which sustained some damage because the pilot lost his nerve and disobeyed Porter's instructions to proceed at full steam), the *Osage,* and the *Fort Hamilton.*

Six of the ironclads and two tugs were still stranded, but Bailey immediately went to work supervising construction of three wing dams upstream at the upper falls to force the water into one channel some 55 feet across. The earlier work had taken eight days; this new project took only three. The water rose in the channel, making 6 feet, 6.5 inches depth and allowing Porter to send through the upper falls the *Mound City, Carondelet,* and *Pittsburg.* Men on shore assisted by pulling on hawsers secured to the ships. The next day, the *Ozark, Louisville,* and *Chillicothe,* along with two tugs, were also gotten through the upper falls. The first three ships went through the dam on 12 May, with the remaining five reaching safety the next morning.

As it worked out, it was fortunate that the two barges had given way, as they swung around on some rocks and formed a cushion for the ships passing through, preventing the latter from dashing into these rocks and being destroyed. Porter took pains to praise the army troops involved, but most especially Bailey. Porter said Bailey had saved the Federal government "a valuable fleet, worth nearly $2,000,000; more, he has deprived the enemy of a triumph that would have emboldened them to carry on this war a year or two longer."[28]

As soon as the Union ships had passed through, Banks's men also departed Alexandria on foot. They arrived at Simmesport on 16 May without significant Confederate harassment. Bailey then supervised construction of an improvised bridge of steamboats across the Atchafalaya, and by 19 May the entire command was over that river. A. J. Smith's troops immediately departed for Vicksburg. Washington deemed it was too late to try to employ Banks's forces against Mobile, and the XIX Corps and part of the XIII Corps were ordered to join the Army of the Potomac.[29]

While work on the dam was going forward at Alexandria, on 5 May the small light-draft gunboats *Signal* and *Covington* were convoying the Quartermaster Corps steamer *Warner* down the Red when they got into a fierce fire fight with Confederate infantry and artillery positioned at Dunn's Bayou below Alexandria. Only about one hundred yards from the Confederate guns, all three Union ships suffered heavily. When the *Warner* hoisted a white flag and Lt. George Lord of the *Covington* sent a party of men to burn that ship, the army colonel in charge begged him not to do so because he had 125 wounded aboard. Lord then agreed to allow the *Warner* to surrender.

Informed that the *Signal* had its steam pipe cut and was disabled, Lord took it in tow and headed upriver when the rudder of his own ship became disabled. Lord then had the *Signal* anchor and, with the steam pipe soon cut on his own ship, ran it ashore on the opposite bank. He continued to fire on the Confederates until he had exhausted his ammunition and his boat howitzers were disabled. With many of his crew killed or wounded, Lord spiked the guns, landed his men, and set fire to his ship. He and his crew managed to make it by land back to Alexandria. The *Signal* had too many wounded for its commander to follow suit, and it was captured. The Confederates then removed its guns and sank the *Signal* as a river obstruction. The entire engagement had lasted about five hours.[30]

Porter's squadron reentered the Mississippi River on 21 April. This last major Union riverine operation of the war was over. It had nearly brought the destruction of the entire Union flotilla, and it had indeed cost five ships. In addition to the powerful *Eastport*, the lost ships were the *Champion No. 3* and *Champion No. 5*, the *Covington*, and the *Signal*. The navy sustained about 120 casualties, killed, wounded, and captured; this did not count nearly 200 non-combatant African-Americans lost on the two pump boats. It could have been much worse, yet Selfridge referred to the expedition as "one of the most humiliating and disastrous that had to be recorded during the war."[31]

A day later, on 30 April the Arkansas prong of the ground effort, the so-called Camden Expedition, met defeat. On 26 April, with his force having reached Camden, General Steele learned that the Confederates had captured and destroyed a Union wagon train on its way from Camden to Pine Bluff. Steele also discovered that Gen. Kirby Smith and Gen. Sterling Price had joined forces and were driving against him. The next day Steele ordered a retreat toward Little Rock, and the Confederates retook Camden. The Southerners vigorously pursued the retreating Union troops but were too late. At Jenkins' Ferry, Arkansas, on 29 April the Confederates made contact as Steele's men waited to cross the Sabine River. Steele had 4,000 men in prepared defensive positions to protect the crossing site. Fighting continued for most of the day, but Steele was able to get the majority of his men across the river on a pontoon bridge. Union casualties totaled 700 men, whereas the Confederates lost between 800 and 1,000 of 6,000 committed. In the entire campaign, Union losses were 2,750, whereas the Confederate suffered 2,300, but the Union material losses in guns, wagons, and pack animals were far heavier. The battle of Jenkins' Ferry also opened the way for the Confederates to invade Missouri.[32]

Recriminations over the Red River Campaign began almost immediately. Ultimately Congress investigated and issued a formal report. Most of the blame fell on Banks, whereas those whom he accused of incompetence were exonerated. Banks never again held a field command, and the Battle of Mansfield ended any possibility of him securing the 1864 presidential nomination. Lincoln removed Banks from his post, his place taken by Maj. Gen. E. R. S. Canby. Banks subsequently left the army altogether.[33]

Union riverine warfare, begun with such great effect more than two years before at Fort Henry, thus ended on a sour note. Aside from the destruction of considerable Confederate property, much of this self-inflicted, the Red River Campaign had been an embarrassing fiasco. Sherman, then preparing to move against Atlanta, when asked what he thought of the campaign, best summed it up with, "One damn blunder from beginning to end."[34]

Chapter Thirteen

The End of the War

~~~

Coastal Operations

As more Union steam warships entered service, the blockade grew increasingly effective. The Texas coast, however, remained a porous location for blockade runners early in the war, and, following his failure against Vicksburg in mid-1862, Admiral Farragut attempted to close it. The first major step was to establish bases on the Gulf, and by mid-October 1862, the navy had secured Pensacola, Corpus Christi, Sabine Pass, Port Lavaca, and Galveston.

Galveston was of great interest to both sides. The largest prewar Texas seaport, it had a population of some seven thousand people and was that state's second-largest city. Galveston shipped much of the state's cotton (two hundred thousand bales in 1860) and sugar, and also boasted some war industries. In Union hands, it would be an excellent westernmost blockading base and could serve as a staging area for an invasion into the interior to secure Texas cotton and the border with Mexico.

The U.S. Navy initiated a blockade of Galveston in July 1861, but it was not until 4 October 1862 that Union forces attempted to take the city. On that date Cdr. William B. Renshaw arrived with the steamers *Westfield* (the flagship), *Harriet Lane, Owasco,* and *Clifton,* and the mortar schooner *Henry James.* Renshaw sent the *Harriet Lane* over the bar under a flag of truce with a demand for surrender. When the Confederates delayed in responding, Renshaw ordered all his ships in.

A brief exchange of fire followed, but inadequate shore defenses (the guns of what appeared to be a formidable battery on Pelican Island north of the waterfront turned out to be "quakers" or dummies) led Confederate commander Col. Joseph J. Cook to accede to Renshaw's demands on condition of a four-day truce. Renshaw reluctantly agreed in order to prevent civilian casualties, but much to his chagrin, the Confederates used the truce to remove personnel, artillery, and equipment.[1]

To strengthen U.S. forces at Galveston, the small gunboats *Corypheus* and *Sachem* arrived there from New Orleans, along with three companies of the 54th Massachusetts Infantry. To ensure themselves of naval gunfire support, the Union troops took up position in large warehouses at the end of Kuhn's Wharf, which projected north into Galveston Bay from the waterfront. Strong barricades denied access to the wharf from the waterfront. The troops also removed portions of the wharf in front of the barricades and only a single plank connected to the waterfront.

At the end of November, Confederate Army Maj. Gen. John B. Magruder assumed command of Southern military forces in Texas. He immediately made the recapture of Galveston a priority. Toward that end, Magruder planned a joint army–navy operation to prevent the Union ships from supporting the small land force. He planned his attack for 1 AM on 1 January 1863.

Magruder assembled his land force at Virginia Point at the northern end of the still intact railroad bridge to Galveston Island. To get at the Union troops on the wharf, Magruder planned to send some five hundred men through the shallow water with fifty scaling ladders. Twenty guns would provide artillery support: six siege pieces (including an 8-inch gun on a railroad flat car, the largest weapon on the Texas coast, and fourteen field guns). The Confederates moved this artillery into position on the night of 31 December.

Meanwhile, Confederate Maj. Leon Smith was to lead a small flotilla of improvised warships against the Union gunboats. Assembled at Harrisburg on Buffalo Bayou, these ships would proceed east to the upper part of the bay, thence south to Galveston. Cotton bales piled high aboard the ships provided some protection against small-arms fire. The ships included the "cottonclads" *Bayou City* and *Neptune* and the armed tenders *John F. Carr* and *Lucy Gwin.* Three of them carried sizable contingents of "horse marines" from the 5th and 7th Texas cavalry: some 150 on the *Bayou City,* 100 on the *Neptune,* and 50 on board the *John F. Carr.* These troopers were armed mostly with Enfield rifles and some double-barreled shotguns.[2]

Magruder wanted his land forces to initiate the battle. He ordered

Smith to bring his ships in as close as possible to the Union warships without being detected, then wait for the land attack to begin at 1 AM on 1 January. Magruder planned to carry out the land assault with or without the flotilla, but on no condition did he want the ships to begin the fight. Without the distraction of the land battle, the Confederate ships would have no chance against the far more powerful Union squadron.

Renshaw had at his disposal the *Westfield* (the flagship), *Harriet Lane*, *Owasco*, *Corypheus*, *Sachem*, and *Clifton*. Five supply ships were also anchored offshore. In all, the Union warships mounted thirty guns, and these were generally larger than the half dozen cannon on board the Confederate ships.

The battle did not unfold as Magruder had planned. At about 1 AM Union lookouts spotted the approach of the Confederate ships west of Pelican Island in the bay and sent signal rockets up to alert the ships and the troops ashore. Obeying Magruder's orders, Smith then ordered his ships to withdraw some distance.

Renshaw, meanwhile, tried to position the *Westfield* to cut off the Confederate ships, but the Union flagship promptly grounded in shallow water near Pelican Island. Unable to free itself, the *Westfield* signaled to the *Clifton* for assistance, but despite efforts by sailors on both ships, the flagship remained hard aground. This mishap was a great aid to the Confederates, as it rendered hors de combat at the beginning of the battle the two most powerful Union ships.

As events unfolded in the bay, Magruder brought his land troops across the railroad bridge to Galveston Island, with the fighting beginning about 4 AM. Assisted by grape from the heavy guns of the *Harriet Lane* under Cdr. Jonathan M. Wainwright, the Union troops easily turned back the Confederate attack. Later the *Corypheus* and *Sachem* joined in, firing into the Confederate shore positions with considerable effect. By dawn the attack appeared a failure.

As soon as the fighting on land began, the Confederate squadron turned about and made full steam down the bay toward the wharf. Soon they were bearing down on the *Harriet Lane*, the nearest Union ship. Capt. Henry Lubbock's *Bayou City* was slightly in the lead, and one of its shells tore a large hole in the *Harriet Lane* just aft of its port paddle wheel, but then the 32-pounder on the *Bayou City* burst, killing several members of the crew. The *Bayou City* continued on, however. Lubbock hoped to ram the

Harriet Lane and take it by boarding, but the Confederate ship struck the iron-hulled Union ship only a glancing bow and lost most of its own port wheelhouse in the exchange.

Meanwhile, riflemen on the *Bayou City* and *Neptune* poured a steady hail of small-arms fire into the *Harriet Lane*. A portion of the Union ship's anchoring apparatus was sheered off, causing a length of cable and anchor to fall into the water, and, in the frenzied maneuvering, the ship ran aground at the bow. Capt. William Sangster of the *Neptune* then maneuvered his own ship to ram the stationary Union ship. The *Neptune* took a shell from the *Harriet Lane* as it smashed into it aft of the starboard paddle wheel. As the men of the *Neptune* attempted to grapple the *Harriet Lane* and board it, the *Owasco* and other Union ships took the *Neptune* under fire, forcing it to back off in sinking condition. The explosion of an IX-inch shell from the *Harriet Lane* hastened the *Neptune*'s demise, but fortunately for its crew, the water was only eight feet deep.

Thinking the battle won, sailors on the *Harriet Lane* let out a cheer. The celebration was premature, for the *Bayou City* came about and crashed into the *Harriet Lane*'s port paddle wheel. With the two ships locked together, the far more numerous Confederates aboard the *Bayou City* stormed the Union ship and quickly captured it. Wainwright and his executive officer were among the Union dead.

Realizing what had happened, the remaining Union ships attempted to recapture the *Harriet Lane*. The *Owasco* led the attack, sending a shell into the *Harriet Lane*'s stern, but riflemen on the *Bayou City* exacted such a toll of Union personnel that the *Owasco* soon backed off. Both sides then regrouped, and a temporary calm descended over the bay.

Lubbock then boldly set out under a flag of truce in a boat for the Union ships. Taken aboard the *Owasco*, he brazenly demanded that the Union ships surrender, allowing three hours for the decision. If Renshaw agreed, he would be allowed to depart with his men in one of his ships. Convinced that the battle was now lost, the men of the 54th Massachusetts, whose requests to be taken off by the Union ships had not been answered, surrendered.

Renshaw ordered Lt. Cdr. Richard L. Law, captain of the *Clifton*, to withdraw the remaining Union ships from the harbor and escape while he scuttled the *Westfield*. Renshaw ordered his men into the ship's boats and spread turpentine over the forward magazine, setting it alight. But as Renshaw stepped into the ship's cutter, the magazine exploded with a great roar, killing him and the boat crew. Law, meanwhile, escaped to sea with the remaining four Union ships, all still flying white flags. Law later faced a court-martial and was suspended from duty.

The Battle of Galveston was over. Their daring combined arms foray had brought the Confederates an impressive victory. At a cost of one ship lost and 26 men dead and another 117 wounded, they had retaken Galveston and reopened it to blockade runners. They had also destroyed two Union warships, captured two barks loaded with coal and a small schooner, and taken substantial stores and at least twenty-five thousand rounds of small-arms ammunition. They had also killed several dozen Union sailors and soldiers and taken prisoner more than 350 others, some of them wounded.

Magruder ordered the *Harriet Lane* repaired and its U.S. flags kept flying, hoping to decoy other Union ships into the harbor where they might be captured. The *Harriet Lane* was too badly damaged to get to sea readily, but on 3 January the U.S. transport steamer *Cambria* arrived off the bar with the Federal 1st Texas Cavalry Regiment and equipment for an additional regiment that was to have been raised locally. The *Cambria* sent in a boat to request a pilot, and Magruder responded with a bogus pilot boat. The Union captain detected the ruse and steamed back to sea.[3]

Although Farragut quickly reestablished the blockade off Galveston, on 11 January the Union side suffered an additional embarrassment when the *Alabama* arrived off the port and sank the *Hatteras*. Meanwhile, Magruder worked to strengthen Galveston's defenses. During the course of the year he added railroad spurs and a dozen forts and redoubts mounting thirty-one cannon. Galveston remained in Confederate hands the remainder of the war.[4]

On 21 January at Sabine Pass, the Confederates replicated their Galveston success. On Magruder's orders, Confederate Maj. O. M. Watkins attacked two Union blockaders with the paltry force of the cottonclad steamers *Josiah A. Bell* (one 8-inch Columbiad bored out as a 6-inch rifled gun) and *Uncle Ben* (two 12-pounders, for which, however, there was no ammunition, the guns kept there merely to inspire confidence in those on board). Both Confederate ships had large numbers of riflemen on board. The Union ships were two sailing ships: the ship-rigged, heavily armed *Morning Light* (eight 32-pounders and one 2-inch breechloading rifled gun) and the small schooner *Velocity* (two 12-pounder boat howitzers).

The Confederates opened the battle at two and a half miles with their rifled gun. At a thousand yards' range, their sharpshooters initiated rifle fire, sweeping free the decks of the Union ships. The absence of any appreciable wind proved decisive. The Confederate steamers were able to maneuver at will and take up a raking position at close range, riddling the *Morning Light* and forcing its surrender after a ninety-minute fight, whereupon the *Velocity* also struck. Without the loss of a single man and with virtually no damage to their own ships, the Confederates had captured two Union ships mounting 11 guns and 150 small arms. One Union sailor was killed and 2 mortally wounded; 109 were captured.[5]

Thanks to the French military intervention in Mexico, Texas assumed increasing importance to the Union war effort. In June 1863 French troops took Mexico City, and fears grew in Washington over the impact of this on Texas. Union leaders then planned a major two-pronged operation against the upper Texas coast. A land expedition was to move from Bayou Teche in Louisiana against Maj. Gen. Richard Taylor's Confederates in east Texas, while an amphibious operation would take Sabine Pass and cut the Houston to Beaumont rail line to prevent Magruder from sending assistance to Taylor.

On the morning of 8 September 1863, Lt. Frederick Crocker proceeded up Sabine Pass with the shallow-draft gunboats *Clifton* (the flagship), *Sachem*, *Arizona*, and *Granite City* convoying eighteen transports with four thousand ground troops under Maj. Gen. William B. Franklin. The *Clifton* (two IX-inch Dahlgrens and four 32-pounders) was the largest Union ship, with the four ships mounting a total of twenty-seven guns. This was to have been a joint operation, with troops assaulting the fort from the land, but Franklin did not send any men ashore, and the navy proceeded alone. This is unfortunate, because there were only some three hundred Confederates in the fort and its vicinity. As several Confederate ships steamed down Sabine Lake to join the fray, the Union gunboats began shelling Fort Griffin, located about two miles from the Gulf on the west side of the pass. Thanks to markers in the water, the Confederate gunners, Irish immigrants of Company F of the 1st Texas Heavy Artillery Regiment, had the range, and they responded with accurate and very rapid fire from four 32-pounders and two 24-pounders.

Two Confederate hits decided the battle. One severed a steam pipe on the *Sachem* and the other ruptured the boiler on the *Clifton*. Both ships

329 THE END OF THE WAR | 329

surrendered, and Franklin then called off further operations. Subsequently, two of the transports grounded while recrossing the bar but were protected by the *Arizona*, the engine of which had failed. Scores of hobbled horses and mules, along with 250,000 rations, were simply pushed overboard in order to float the ships free the next day. The expedition then returned to New Orleans. It had cost the Federal side two gunboats and thirteen guns, as well as 28 men killed and 340 taken prisoner.[6]

This string of defeats along the Texas coast claimed seven Union ships in only nine months. The skein was not broken until 2 November 1863, when twenty-five hundred troops under Maj. Gen. Nathaniel Banks, supported by a naval force under Capt. J. H. Strong consisting of the screw sloop *Monongehela* (the flagship) and the screw gunboats *Owasco* and *Virginia* (the ex-blockade runner *Virginia*) took Brazos Island near the mouth of the Rio Grande. The Union ships also captured four British blockade runners in the vicinity. Federal forces then went on to secure Brownsville, which they held until July 1864. Then on 16–17 November, they took Corpus Christi and Mustang Island, securing the south Texas coast. The Red River Expedition, which had as its ultimate goal the invasion of Texas from the east, led to the abandonment of any new effort against Galveston.[7]

Union joint operations were ongoing in the East. Typical of the large number of such efforts was Cdr. Foxhall A. Parker's 7–9 January 1863 foray up the Pamunkey, a tributary of the York River in Virginia. The *Mahaska* and *Commodore Morris* supported the troop movement and convoyed the transport *May Queen*. Before withdrawing because of low water and obstructions, the expedition destroyed a dozen Confederate river craft and stores at West Point and White Horse.[8]

THE BATTLE OF MOBILE BAY

In 1864 the war entered its third year. In the East, Richmond remained defiant, while in the West, most of the Confederate heartland lay unconquered. Death tolls continued to climb, and it seemed to many as if the conflict might continue indefinitely. Lincoln's reelection even appeared in jeopardy. The Democrats nominated General McClellan to oppose him, adopting a plank that called for immediate cessation of hostilities and the restoration of peace "on the basis of the Federated Union of the States." Although McClellan repudiated this position, he clearly sought to capitalize on war weariness. Most people assumed that, were McClellan to win the election, the war would be brought to a negotiated end.

General Grant, Lincoln's new general-in-chief since March, was keenly aware of this situation, and in the spring of 1864 he developed a plan to smash Confederate resistance in both the East and West, which would have the salutary side effect of bringing about Lincoln's reelection. Grant planned simultaneous offensives to commence in May. The eastern strategy relied on superior Union numbers. Its centerpiece was a massive push south to take Richmond, supported by secondary operations up the James, up the Shenandoah Valley, and from West Virginia. The latter three operations were to present General Lee with a multiplicity of fronts and prevent reinforcements from reaching his Army of Northern Virginia that would face the Army of the Potomac driving on Richmond.

In the Western Theater, Grant's plan centered on the destruction of Confederate Gen. Joseph E. Johnston's Army of Tennessee. Utilizing the key railhead of Chattanooga, Tennessee, Maj. Gen. William T. Sherman would drive into Georgia. At the same time a Union naval force would secure Mobile Bay, allowing another Union land army to drive north from Mobile, Alabama, and drawing off other Southern resources away from Sherman.

Grant had long sought to take Mobile. The city was a major industrial center, second only to the Tredegar at Richmond in manufacturing heavy guns and rolling heavy iron plate. The Confederacy had also established at Selma a second cannon foundry capable of producing the heaviest guns. Mobile was also the last deep-water port on the Gulf available to the Confederacy, and the city of Mobile itself, only thirty miles from the Gulf, was an important transshipment point for goods brought in by blockade runners and sent upriver to the interior.

Mobile Bay was also on Farragut's mind. His orders of late January 1862 had directed him to take not only New Orleans but also Mobile Bay, the forts of which he was to turn over to the army to hold. Farragut had wanted to move against Mobile immediately upon securing New Orleans in the spring of 1862 but had been directed to operate on the Mississippi. The resulting delay gave the Confederates time to strengthen Mobile.

Grant favored a move against Mobile on his capture of Vicksburg and had conferred with Farragut about the possibility, but Lincoln and

Halleck, then Union general-in-chief, had shifted priority to the disastrous Red River Expedition. Now Grant was at last able to dictate strategy.

Following the Red River fiasco, Maj. Gen. Edward R. S. Canby replaced Banks in command of the Military Division of West Mississippi. Canby proved to be a capable commander. While en route to his New Orleans headquarters, on 4 June he received a telegram from Sherman requesting that he carry out a strong feint or real attack against Mobile. Sherman had a sizable numerical advantage over the forces opposing him and was then closing in on Atlanta, but he wanted to make certain that the Confederates were not reinforced. Sherman urged Canby to attack from Pascagoula, Mississippi, in conjunction with naval units under Farragut.

Two weeks later, on 17 June, Canby arrived off Mobile Bay from New Orleans by ship to meet with Farragut on the *Hartford*, the flagship of the West Gulf Coast Blockading Squadron. The two men got on well and developed a plan whereby Farragut's ships would run past the forts guarding the mouth of the bay and destroy the Confederate squadron. After this a joint army–navy assault was to take Forts Morgan and Gaines at the entrance to the bay. A land force would then advance on Mobile from Pascagoula, while the navy secured the earthen fortification of Fort Powell at Grant's Pass in Mississippi Sound. Canby anticipated no problem in obtaining the twenty thousand land troops he thought necessary for the operation. Farragut, however, was concerned about obtaining two or three ironclads, which he deemed essential to deal with the Confederate ram *Tennessee*.[9]

The Confederates anticipated a Union attack against Mobile and had pushed development of their defenses. In March 1864, Confederate Brig. Gen. Richard L. Page, a long-serving U.S. Navy officer before the war, assumed command of the outer defenses of Mobile Bay. He supervised the construction or reinforcement of forts to cover the channel into the bay and approaches to Mobile itself.

Fort Morgan was the principal Confederate position and by far the most powerful of the three forts. An old pentagonal casemated masonry structure begun in 1818, it was situated at the tip of Mobile Point, a long neck of land that jutted out into the bay and controlled its entrance from the east. The fort mounted forty guns, including seven 10-inch Columbiads, and another twenty-nine guns were located in exterior batteries.

Two other forts were located up the channel. Fort Gaines on the eastern tip of Dauphin Island to the west of the channel mounted twenty-seven guns, three of which were 10-inch Columbiads. In the bay, unfinished Fort Powell at Cedar Point guarded the shallow Grant's Pass. It mounted only six guns, one a 10-inch Columbiad.[10]

The defenders also placed obstructions in the form of pilings in the channel between Forts Morgan and Gaines and on both sides of Fort Powell. The channel between the pilings and Fort Morgan was further narrowed by 180 submerged torpedoes. Fitted with percussion caps or fulminate of mercury fuzes, they were rigged to explode when struck by a passing ship. The torpedoes were in three parallel rows, but most of them had been in the water for some time, and a number were defective. The remaining channel for shipping was, however, only about 150 to 200 yards wide.[11]

Confederate Rear Adm. Franklin Buchanan commanded Confederate naval forces in the bay and was determined to contest any Union attack. In August 1862, following recovery from the wound received aboard the *Virginia*, Buchanan received promotion as the South's first admiral and was assigned to Mobile. When he arrived there at the end of 1862, the Confederates had seven ironclads under construction or about to be laid down on the Alabama and Tombigbee rivers. Buchanan hoped he might have eight ironclads with which to defend the bay, but by the time of the battle with Farragut, he had only five: the rams *Tennessee II*, *Huntsville*, and *Tuscaloosa*, and the *Baltic* and *Nashville*. Three other rams were still under construction on the Tombigbee. However, the *Huntsville* and *Tuscaloosa* could make only two and a half knots, barely enough to steam against the current in the bay, and were thus relegated to the status of floating batteries. The Confederacy lacked sufficient plate for its ironclads, and the *Nashville* was sacrificed to complete the *Tennessee II*. The *Baltic* was too unwieldy. Thus, Buchanan actually had only four ships available: the ram *Tennessee II* and the wooden side-wheeler gunboats *Gaines*, *Morgan*, and *Selma*.[12]

The *Tennessee II*, usually referred to as the *Tennessee*, served as Buchanan's flagship and was by far his most powerful warship. Laid down at Selma some 150 miles upriver from Mobile in October 1862, it was launched in February 1863 and completed at Mobile. Commissioned in February 1864, this modified *Columbia*-class ironclad measured 209 feet in length with the distinctive shorter 79-foot casemate. It was protected by 6 inches of iron on the casemate, 5 inches on the sides, and 2 inches on the deck. The 1,276-ton *Tennessee* mounted six Brooke rifles: two 7-inch pivot-mounted fore and aft and four 6.4-inch in broadsides. Inadequately powered, it was difficult to maneuver, but its principal defect was its relatively exposed rudder chains that ran in channels in the after deck. The *Gaines* and *Morgan* were built in 1862. They were of 863 tons and armed with five guns each (one 7-inch and one 6-inch rifled gun, two 32-pounder rifles, and one 32-pounder smoothbore). The 320-ton *Selma* was a converted coastal packet mounting three rifled guns (one IX-inch, one 8-inch, and one 6-inch).[13]

Meanwhile, over several weeks from late February to mid-March, Farragut subjected Fort Powell to prolonged bombardments by mortar schooners and other light-draft ships brought from the Mississippi River. This was a feint intended to convince the Confederates that a Federal descent on Mobile was in the offing in order to keep them from sending troops north against General Sherman's incursion into Mississippi. The bombardment was conducted at extremely long range, four thousand yards, and Fort Powell replied to it. Neither side inflicted damage on the other, although a 7-inch Brooke at Fort Powell burst in the exchange. The *Morgan*, *Gaines*, and *Selma* hovered on the other side of the fort, ready if necessary to extract the defenders. The *Tennessee* came down the bay but remained in the vicinity of Fort Morgan. The exchange helped convince Farragut of the absolute necessity of a combined arms operation against the Confederate forts.[14]

Buchanan did not wish to wait until he was attacked. He hoped to employ the *Tennessee* and his little squadron to raise the blockade. Shortly after midnight on 23 May, when the ironclad had steam up, the crew found it had run aground. The tide refloated the *Tennessee* four hours later, and Buchanan hoped to continue his plan. However, on seeing that the Union ships off the bar were fully alerted, he called off a daylight attack.[15]

Once again Farragut appealed to Washington for ironclads to counter the threat posed by the *Tennessee*. This time the department agreed, ordering to Mobile Bay two single-turreted *Cononicus*-class monitors: the *Manhattan* from New York and the *Tecumseh* from the James. Each mounted two XV-inch Dahlgrens. The department also detached from Porter's Mississippi fleet the double-turreted river monitors *Chickasaw* and *Winnebago*, each with four XI-inch Dahlgrens.

The Union plan called for Farragut's ships to run past the Confederate forts while Union Maj. Gen. Gordon Granger's IV Corps from New

Orleans went ashore. Once Farragut had neutralized Buchanan's force, the Union ships and Granger's men would assault and take the forts. Pending the arrival of the four ironclads, Farragut counted fourteen warships, all wooden: the big screw sloops *Brooklyn, Hartford, Richmond, Lackawanna,* and *Monongahela;* the smaller screw sloops *Ossipee, Oneida,* and *Seminole;* the screw gunboats *Kennebec* and *Itasca;* the side-wheeler gunboats *Octorara, Metacomet,* and *Port Royal;* and the ex-ironclad *Galena,* now an unarmored screw sloop.

As preparations went forward off Mobile Bay, some of the heaviest fighting of the war was occurring in the East. Grant took the field with Maj. Gen. George Gordon Meade's Army of the Potomac for the drive on Richmond. Lee parried Grant's blows and inflicted Federal casualties equivalent to the size of his own force, but his own Army of Northern Virginia never recovered from Grant's relentless attacks. General Butler allowed his Army of the James to be bottled up and then defeated by the Confederates under General Beauregard, ensuring the failure of Grant's effort to get in behind Lee at the Petersburg railhead south of Richmond. Grant then settled down to what became the longest siege of the entire war.

Grant's operations in the East affected those in the West, for on 1 July Canby received a dispatch from General Halleck in Washington requesting that he detach as many men as he could spare and send them to Fortress Monroe. Halleck suggested that the twenty-thousand-man XIX Corps or its equivalent in numbers be sent. Grant was then trying to increase his force at Petersburg to avoid a protracted siege. Complying with this request, Canby informed Farragut that the attack on Mobile had been canceled.[16]

Farragut was not pleased with this news, but he was somewhat mollified that Canby was working to revive at least part of the operation. Farragut was also heartened to learn of the arrival of the *Manhattan* at Pensacola on 7 July. Two days later, Canby again met with Farragut and told him that he could make available perhaps four thousand men to operate against the Confederate forts. Although insufficient in numbers to take Mobile, this force would be sufficient to enable Farragut to proceed with his plan to secure Mobile Bay.

The revised plan called for some three thousand Union troops with artillery to come ashore on the Gulf beach about three miles behind Fort Morgan at the same time that the fleet passed into the bay through the main channel. The soldiers would then work their way to within a mile of the fort and entrench. As Farragut's ships entered the bay, the troops would open up artillery fire against the fort from that direction. A reserve of fifteen hundred men would remain in Mississippi Sound. After the fleet had entered the bay, part of this body would land on Dauphin Island to attack Fort Gaines in conjunction with the navy.[17]

On 12 July, Farragut issued orders to the crews to prepare for battle. The men were soon at work removing unnecessary spars and rigging and protecting valuable machinery with sandbags and chain. Six days later, however, Canby sent word that there would be a delay in assembling the troops. Farragut replied that time was running out and that the weather would not hold much longer. He was willing to proceed if the army would provide as few as one thousand men against Fort Gaines. These men could then proceed to Fort Morgan after Gaines had been taken. The arrival of the *Manhattan* from Pensacola, along with word that two of the other monitors would also soon be available, emboldened Farragut.

On 26 July Canby reported that he had two thousand men ready to act against Fort Gaines. Another three thousand would be available as reinforcements following the evacuation of Union garrisons in Texas. Three days later, Canby informed Farragut that although the men from Texas had not yet arrived, he was that day embarking twenty-four hundred men to operate against Dauphin Island in cooperation with the navy. General Granger had command.[18]

On 29 July Farragut issued General Order No. 11, spelling out the plan. All ships would pass to the east of the easternmost buoy, in the area clear of obstructions. Any disabled ships would drop out of the line to westward and make no further attempt to enter the bay until all the remaining ships of the squadron had passed. Once the Union ships were in the bay, the smaller gunboats would move against the Confederate gunboats to prevent them from escaping up the bay.[19]

Farragut was concerned about the Confederate torpedoes. Although refugees and deserters had reported that many were watersoaked and probably unreliable, these individuals could provide no information on their location or extent. On several occasions Farragut's flag lieutenant, John C. Watson, conducted night reconnaissances, but he was unable to learn anything.

On 31 July the *Winnebago* arrived at the fleet anchorage at Sand Island. It also brought the welcome news that the *Chickasaw* was close behind. Farragut then dispatched Capt. Thornton Jenkins in the *Richmond* to Pensacola to hurry along the *Tecumseh*. The next day, Granger met with Farragut aboard the *Hartford* and informed him of his intent to land on the west end of Dauphin Island; his men would then work their way toward Fort Gaines at the other end. The joint assault was set for 4 August. The *Chickasaw* then came in from New Orleans. When the *Tecumseh* arrived, Farragut would have eighteen warships, four of them monitors.

On 3 August, as Granger's transports steamed up Mississippi Sound toward Dauphin Island, Farragut met with his captains on board the *Hartford*. He had wanted the flagship to lead the attack, but his captains persuaded him that it would be too exposed. Farragut reluctantly agreed that this honor would go to the *Brooklyn*, commanded by Capt. James Alden and equipped with four bow chaser guns and a torpedo catcher. It was a decision he would have cause to regret.

That same afternoon, Farragut learned that the *Tecumseh* would not arrive in time. A displeased Farragut informed Jenkins, still in Pensacola, that the troops were about to go ashore and that he was to return to the squadron on 4 August, with or without the *Tecumseh*. "I can lose no more days," Farragut wrote.[20]

Late on the afternoon of 3 August, fifteen hundred of Granger's men landed unopposed on the west end of Dauphin Island, and the next day skirmishing began between the two sides there. Embarrassed about the failure of his squadron to attack on schedule, Farragut ordered the *Winnebago* to drive off Confederate ships landing men and supplies at Fort Gaines. The ironclad moved to about one thousand yards of the fort and lobbed twenty-four shots in its direction; Fort Gaines responded with several shots of its own. Neither side materially damaged the other.[21]

Later on 4 August, Farragut met with his captains aboard the *Hartford* for the last time before the attack. Farragut's plan called for the monitors *Tecumseh*, *Manhattan*, *Winnebago*, and *Chickasaw* to be closest to Fort Morgan and mask a second column of larger wooden ships to their left, consisting of the seven larger wooden ships the *Brooklyn*, *Hartford*, *Richmond*, *Lackawanna*, *Monongahela*, *Ossipee*, and *Oneida*. Quantities of heavy chain draped over their unprotected sides served as makeshift armor for the wooden ships. Farragut also employed a tactic similar to that he had used against Port Hudson by ordering the seven smallest wooden ships—four side-wheeler gunboats, two screw gunboats, and a screw steamer—lashed to the port sides of the larger wooden screw steamers to provide an additional layer of protection. These ships were, in order, the *Octorara, Metacomet, Port Royal, Seminole, Kennebec, Itasca,* and *Galena.*

Farragut specified an approach en echelon to starboard in order to provide his ships' bow guns a free field of fire. He planned to take his squadron as close as possible to Fort Morgan, believing that their broadsides would be the ships' best defense. At the same time, supporting ships would lay down suppressive fire on the forts. Lt. Cdr. E. C. Grafton's Gulf Flotilla of six gunboats would shell Fort Morgan from the Gulf, while Lt. Cdr. J. C. P. De Kraft's Mississippi Sound Flotilla of five small gunboats would engage Fort Powell.

At about 4:30 PM the *Richmond* returned from Pensacola. It accompanied the *Tecumseh,* which was under tow by the side-wheeler *Bienville.* At dusk the ships that would make the run into the bay steamed beyond the bar and anchored in line abreast on either side of the *Brooklyn.*

At 3 AM on 5 August 1864, all hands were called to stations. The crews made final preparations and received sandwiches. A proper breakfast would be served after the battle. The ships then formed up in pairs, and at 5:30 AM the *Hartford* hoisted the signal, "Get under way." Soon Farragut's ships were steaming into the bay. The monitors were assigned key roles: the *Tecumseh* and *Manhattan* were to engage the *Tennessee* and prevent it from reaching the vulnerable wooden warships, with the *Winnebago* and *Chickasaw* to lay down suppressive fire against Fort Morgan.

Shortly after 6 AM the first Union ships crossed the bar. About this time the morning mist cleared, revealing large U.S. flags at every peak, staff, and masthead. Conditions were ideal for the attack. A light southwesterly breeze would blow smoke from the Union guns toward the forts, inhibiting the aim of the Confederate gunners. A flood tide also helped compensate for the low steam Farragut had ordered aboard the Union ships. The Confederates, however, would have the advantage of being able to rake the Union ships during their approach.

About 6 AM Buchanan on the *Tennessee* received word that the Union ships had begun crossing the bar, and he ordered his flag captain, Cdr. James D. Johnston, to get the ironclad under way. In short order, Buchanan placed his four ships in line-ahead formation across the channel and adjacent to the torpedo field. The smaller ships were to the west of the flagship. Buchanan hoped to "cross the T" of the Union line, raking the advancing Union ships with the sixteen guns available, most of which were long-range rifled pieces. Buchanan also addressed the crew of the *Tennessee*, exhorting the men to fight hard and in no case to surrender. Meanwhile, the Fort Morgan garrison manned the eighteen guns there.[22]

The *Tecumseh* led the Union column and was well out in front of the other ships. Cdr. Tunis A. M. Craven was unfamiliar with the bay and its shoals, but he had on board pilot John Collins, who knew the waters well. The monitor's guns were loaded with shell. When they were fired, the guns would be recharged with solid shot to meet the *Tennessee*. At 6:47 AM the *Tecumseh* opened fire on Fort Morgan, but General Page thought the range too great and would not authorize return fire until 7:05 AM, with the *Tecumseh* some two thousand yards distant and the remainder of the squadron at nearly three thousand yards. The *Brooklyn* then returned fire, and the engagement became general. One of the most important and certainly the bloodiest of Civil War naval battles had begun.

Peering through the narrow slits of the *Tecumseh*'s pilothouse, Craven could see the *Tennessee* some six hundred yards ahead. The *Manhattan* followed in the *Tecumseh*'s wake, but the *Brooklyn* was gaining on the port quarter. The monitors had the responsibility of engaging the *Tennessee* and keeping it away from the wooden ships, but the *Brooklyn* now threatened to overtake them and enter the bay first.

In the *Brooklyn*, Alden realized the situation. He could not afford to be in advance of the *Chickasaw* and *Winnebago*, which were too far west of Fort Morgan to allow the wooden warships to pass east of the minefield. The *Tennessee* lay in wait on the other side of the torpedo field. Buchanan was ready to ram the first ship to enter the bay and hoped that sinking a large Union ship in the narrow channel between Fort Morgan and the torpedo field might deny the others access to the bay and force them to retire back into the Gulf.

Alden ordered one of the army flagmen brought on board the squadron to signal the flagship: "The Monitors are right ahead. We cannot go on without passing them. What shall we do?" It was hard to get answers back and forth through the smoke, and Lt. John Kinney had to climb some one hundred feet above the deck into the *Hartford*'s crosstrees to see the *Brooklyn* and send the reply, "Go ahead."[23]

By the time this message reached Alden, the *Brooklyn* had already overtaken two of the monitors and was abreast of the *Manhattan*. The

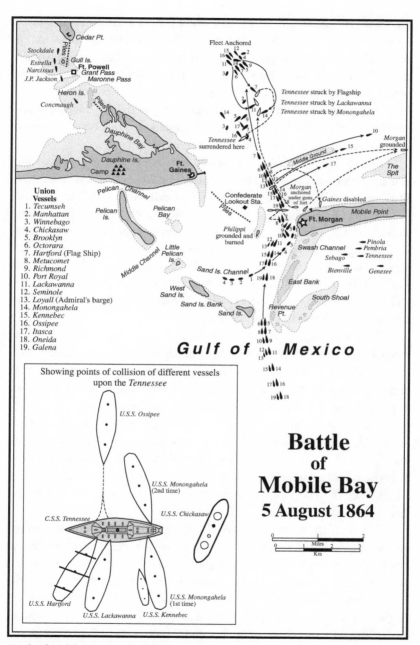

Cedar Pt.
Stockdale
Estrella
Narcissus
J.P. Jackson
Gull Is.
Ft. Powell
Grant Pass
Maronne Pass

Heron Is.
Concmaugh

Dauphine Bay

Dauphine Is.
Camp
Ft. Gaines

Fleet Anchored
15 12
16   2
11   5
3   6   5
7

Tennessee struck by Flagship
Tennessee struck by *Lackawanna*
Tennessee struck by *Monongahela*

14
5   9
3   17
16
Tennessee
surrendered here   4

Pelican Channel

Pelican Is.

Pelican Bay

Confederate
Lookout Sta.

Philippi
grounded and
burned

Middle Ground

10
Morgan
grounded
15
17
The Spit

Morgan
anchored
under guns
of fort
Gaines disabled

Ft. Morgan   Mobile Point

**Union
Vessels**
1. *Tecumseh*
2. *Manhattan*
3. *Winnebago*
4. *Chickasaw*
5. *Brooklyn*
6. *Octorara*
7. *Hartford* (Flag Ship)
8. *Metucomet*
9. *Richmond*
10. *Port Royal*
11. *Lackawanna*
12. *Seminole*
13. *Loyall* (Admiral's barge)
14. *Monongahela*
15. *Kennebec*
16. *Ossipee*
17. *Itasca*
18. *Oneida*
19. *Galena*

Middle Channel

Little
Pelican
Is.

Sand Is. Channel

West
Sand Is.

Sand Is. Bank

Sand Is.

Swash Channel

Pinola
Pembria
Sebago   Tennessee
Bienville   Genesee

East Bank

South Shoal

Revenue
Pt.

Gulf of 12 ̷ 11 *Mexico*
13
15 ̷ 14
17 ̷ 16
19 ̷ 18

Showing points of collision of different vessels
upon the *Tennessee*

U.S.S. Ossipee

U.S.S. Monongahela
(2nd time)

U.S.S. Chickasaw

C.S.S. Tennessee

U.S.S. Hartford

U.S.S. Monongahela
(1st time)

U.S.S. Lackawanna   *U.S.S. Kennebec*

Battle
of
Mobile Bay
5 August 1864

Miles
Km

Battle of Mobile Bay, 5 August 1864

Hartford and *Richmond* were also closing fast. Craven doubted that the *Tecumseh* could pass to the east of the *Red Buoy* and change course in time to be able to engage the *Tennessee* before it could ram the Union wooden ships. The Confederate ironclad, now some two hundred yards ahead, had actually moved a bit to the west in order to be in better position for the very maneuver Craven feared. This situation prompted Craven to order the *Tecumseh* to skirt inside the line of Confederate torpedoes and make directly for the *Tennessee* to engage it at once.

The *Tecumseh* forged ahead, and there was a terrific roar as the monitor struck a mine and rolled immediately to port, its bow down and stern lifted up with the ship's propeller turning madly in the air. The *Tecumseh* sank within four minutes. Craven and pilot Collins both left the pilothouse, meeting at the foot of the ladder to the escape hatch on the turret and struggling in water already up to their chests. "After you, pilot," Craven said. They were the last words Craven was heard to utter, for Collins was the twenty-first and last man free of the ship. He recalled later, "There was nothing after me, for when I reached the top rung of the ladder the vessel seemed to drop from under me."[24]

Craven and ninety-two others perished. Some survivors made it into one of the monitor's boats that had somehow floated free; others were picked up by a cutter sent from one of the sloops, and four men swam to shore where they were taken prisoner. Both sides were so stunned by the explosion that fire slackened for a few moments before resuming.

The *Brooklyn* signaled to the *Hartford*, "Our best monitor has been sunk." Lieutenant Kinney, still in the crosstrees, relayed the message to Farragut. Within minutes Kinney signaled back Farragut's instructions that the monitors were to proceed and the *Brooklyn* would take its place in the line. The *Hartford* was now dangerously close to the *Brooklyn*, and the *Richmond* was not far behind the flagship.

The *Brooklyn* in effect blocked the channel. Farragut, who was lashed in the mizzen shrouds of the *Hartford* to have a vantage point to observe the battle, saw the Union ships behind him slow to a near halt and bunch up. General Page ordered his gun crews to fire as fast as they could at the now-stationary Union ships, and casualties on board the ships mounted as the Confederate shells found their mark. Had it not been for Farragut's order that they run close to the fort and direct a steady fire of grape and shrapnel against it, the Union ships would have been even worse off.

It now appeared that the Confederates might win the battle. Clearly this was its decisive point, and Farragut knew it. When Alden failed to advance, despite three orders from Farragut to go ahead, the admiral took action himself. He knew that if he could only get a number of his ships into the bay, he could control it. There was a major risk from other mines, and Farragut chose to take that with his own ship. Getting the attention of pilot Martin Freeman, Farragut asked if there was sufficient depth of water for the *Hartford* to pass to port of the *Brooklyn*. Freemen replied that there was, and Farragut said, "I will take the lead." Freemen then asked about the torpedoes. Farragut briefly hesitated and then told Freeman to pick his way and enter the bay or blow up. The outcome of the battle now rested in Freeman's hands.[25]

Gathering speed, the *Hartford* passed on the port side of the *Brooklyn*. As the *Hartford* overtook the leading Union ship, Farragut shouted, "What's the trouble?" "Torpedoes," was the reply. "Damn the torpedoes," Farragut said. He then ordered his ship to get up speed, and finally he called to the captain of the gunboat lashed to the side of the *Hartford*, "Go ahead, Jouett, full speed!" Farragut's words have passed into history in shortened form as, "Damn the torpedoes; full speed ahead."[26]

Fortunately for Farragut and the men of the *Hartford*, many of the primer tubes and fuzes in the torpedoes were corroded from long immersion in the salt water. As the *Hartford* pushed past the *Brooklyn* and into the minefield, the men below decks could hear primers going off and mines bumping into the hull beneath them, but no other mines exploded that day. By 7:50 AM the *Hartford* was clear of the minefield and into the bay.

Although the Union ships fired into Fort Morgan as they passed it, the fort gave better than it took, and the last ships in the Union line sustained considerable damage. The *Oneida* was the principal casualty. Its boiler knocked out and rudder cables cut, the ship was dead in the water, but the *Galena*, lashed to its side, was able to move it to safety.

Buchanan, meanwhile, spied Farragut's pennant on the *Hartford* and ordered the *Tennessee* to make for the Union flagship. The Confederate gunboats joined in, raking the *Hartford*. Buchanan's effort to ram was unsuccessful. The *Tennessee* did not have up sufficient speed, and the more nimble *Hartford* easily avoided its charge. As the *Tennessee* passed the Union flagship, both ships fired at each other. Buchanan then attempted to engage the following Union sloops.

As the *Hartford* steamed up the channel, the smaller Confederate gunboats maintained position off its starboard bow, firing into it at close range with devastating effect. Soon, however, the Union flagship brought its own guns to bear and drove them off. Farragut then ordered the *Metacomet* and other smaller ships cut free to attack the Confederate gunboats, which immediately hauled off up the bay.

The *Tennessee*, meanwhile, passed down the column of Union ships. Its lack of maneuverability prevented efforts to ram, but its guns produced both damage and casualties. Farragut wrote later that the Confederate squadron inflicted more casualties than the guns of Fort Morgan. Meanwhile, the smaller Union ships concentrated on the Confederate gunboats. The *Gaines* took several hits below the waterline, and its captain tried to make Fort Morgan. The *Gaines* reached Mobile Point about four hundred yards from Fort Morgan before it sank. The *Selma* continued to fire into the *Hartford* until the *Metacomet*, a double-ended side-wheeler and the fastest of Farragut's gunboats, attacked and drove it into shallow water above Fort Morgan where its crew surrendered. When the *Selma*'s captain, Lt. P. U. Murphy, hauled down its flag, he and six crewmen had been wounded and two officers and six crewmen were dead. Farragut was not pleased, however, that the relatively undamaged *Morgan* managed to reach the fort and take refuge under its guns. That night it escaped up the bay to Mobile.

The *Tennessee*, meanwhile, swept on, unable to ram any of the remaining Federal ships but firing at them and inflicting damage and casualties. Finally, after exchanging fire with the last pair of Union ships, it turned and gained the protection of Fort Morgan. There Buchanan contemplated his next move.

The remaining Union ships were now all safely into the bay and beyond the range of Fort Morgan's guns. At about 8:30 AM Farragut ordered his ships to anchor four miles up the bay. He intended to carry out a quick damage assessment and allow the men their breakfast.

At this time Master's Mate James T. Seaver, captain of the Union support ship *Phillipi* (ex-blockade runner *Elia*), decided to bring his little side-wheeler into Mobile Bay, apparently to share in the glory. Earlier denied permission to accompany the battle line, Seaver disobeyed orders on the excuse that his ship would be able to render assistance to any Union ship that had been disabled. Although Seaver kept to the far side of the channel, about two thousand yards from Fort Morgan, the *Phillipi* soon grounded, whereupon shells from the fort set it on fire and destroyed it. Its crew abandoned the ship in some haste, leaving behind a dead crewman.

The *Tennessee* remained quiescent for a time, its large propeller turning just enough to keep it stationary in the tide. Inspection revealed some damage, but the ironclad was still battleworthy. Although many of his officers and men thought they had satisfied honor and done enough, Buchanan was determined to continue the fight. He assumed that Farragut would soon attack. Rather than have this happen and vowing to "have it out," at 8:50 AM Buchanan ordered the *Tennessee* back into the fray against the entire Union squadron.

The Confederate artillerymen at Fort Morgan cheered the ram on in what seemed to be virtually a suicide mission. The *Tennessee* with 6 guns would face 157 Union guns. Buchanan hoped to inflict what damage he could and then return to Fort Morgan and there ground the *Tennessee* as a stationary battery to assist in repelling attacks on the fort. In any case, he did not want to see a repeat of what had happened to the *Virginia* in the James River, when it had been scuttled without a fight.

The *Tennessee* headed for the larger Federal wooden ships, Union lookouts spotting the movement as soon as it began. At about two miles' range, the *Tennessee* fired a bolt at the Union ships, but it did not hit any of them. Captain Drayton assumed that the ram would head for the bar and attempt to attack the squadron's ships remaining in the Gulf, but Farragut guessed Buchanan's intent and ordered Drayton to ready the crew and get the ship under way. Farragut had Kinney signal to the iron-prowed *Monongahela* and the swifter *Lackawanna* to "run down the ram." Signals were also run up on the flagship ordering all ships in the squadron to join the attack.

Without delaying to hoist in the anchor chain, Cdr. James H. Strong ordered the *Monongahela* to slip its cable and get under way immediately. A few minutes later, Capt. John B. Marchand of the *Lackawanna* also had his ship headed for the ram. Making only six knots, it would take the *Tennessee* about half an hour to reach the Union ships.

Strong and Marchand positioned their ships so as to be able to ram the *Tennessee* on opposite sides. Although Buchanan tried to evade them, both Union warships smashed into the Confederate ironclad at high speed, the *Monongahela* first and the *Lackawanna* about five minutes later.

They did not slow it. In the exchange of fire, the Union shot bounced harmlessly off the ram's sloping sides, and both Union ships were damaged and sustained casualties. The *Tennessee*, meanwhile, continued on course, its target the flagship *Hartford*, some fifteen hundred yards ahead, with Farragut again in the ship's rigging, observing events.

The *Manhattan* took up position between the *Hartford* and the *Tennessee*, but the monitor's slow speed prevented it from being able to ram its adversary. It managed to get off just two shots, neither of which inflicted damage. Leaving the monitor astern, the *Tennessee* closed to within one thousand yards of its target. Accepting the inevitable, Farragut ordered the *Hartford* ahead full steam. At 9:35 AM the two ships struck one another glancing blows on their port sides, each scraping the other. The *Hartford* let loose a broadside at only eight feet, but the shot barely dented the ram's armor. The Confederate ship had only two guns in broadside; one misfired but the other fired a shell that exploded in the *Hartford*'s berth deck, killing five crewmen and wounding eight more. By now the entire Union flotilla surrounded the Confederate flagship, which was still giving more than it was taking.

The collision with the *Hartford* pushed the *Tennessee*'s bow away from its prey, and Commander Johnston decided to circle to build up speed for another ramming attempt. The double-turreted *Chickasaw* followed the *Tennessee*, pounding away at its stern gunport shutter until the end of the battle. At 9:45 AM, the *Manhattan* joined in and at last inflicted serious damage.

A shot from one of the *Manhattan*'s XV-inch Dahlgrens ripped through the *Tennessee*'s side, tearing away five inches of iron and more than two feet of solid wood backing it. This was the sole Union shot during the battle to penetrate. Meanwhile, the *Chickasaw*'s XI-inch Dahlgrens pounded the stern of the Confederate ironclad, cutting its poorly protected tiller chains. This forced the *Tennessee*'s crew to employ tiller tackle, but then the tiller arm was shot away, rendering steering all but impossible. The *Tennessee*'s stack was also knocked down, and other Union shot jammed the after gunport shutter.

The *Hartford* had now carried out a turn, and it made for the Confederate ram. This, however, put the Union flagship on a collision course with the *Lackawanna*, which had also circled in hopes of making another ramming attempt. Neither ship was able to change course before they collided. The *Lackawanna* struck the *Hartford*'s port quarter, cracking open its hull. Fortunately for Farragut it was above the waterline, and the flagship was able to continue the fight.

Aboard the *Tennessee* two crewmen were killed and Buchanan was wounded. The ram was virtually dead in the water, its ammunition was nearly gone, and its bow, stern, and one of the port gunport shutters was jammed shut. Given these conditions, Buchanan, who had been taken below to the cockpit, authorized Johnston to surrender. Johnston ordered the ship's engines stopped and a white handkerchief run up in place of the Confederate battle flag. Cdr. William E. LeRoy's *Ossipee* was bearing down on the *Tennessee* with the intent to ram. LeRoy saw the white flag and ordered engines reversed, but he was unable to avoid striking the ram a hard, glancing blow. LeRoy then identified himself to Johnston, who was standing on the ram's shield.

At 10 AM a boat from the *Ossipee* came alongside, and its party accepted the *Tennessee*'s surrender, carrying Buchanan's sword back to Farragut as the Union admiral had demanded. Lasting three hours, the sea portion of the Battle of Mobile Bay was over. Farragut later describing it as "the most desperate battle I ever fought." The *Richmond Examiner* summed up: "It was a most unequal contest in which our gallant little navy was engaged, and we lost the battle; but our ensign went down in a blaze of glory."[27]

The Battle of Mobile Bay was an important Union victory. It had considerable impact on future naval tactics, and it halted traffic in and out of Mobile Bay, virtually ending Gulf Coast blockade running. It also provided an important psychological boost to Lincoln's reelection campaign.

Following the surrender of the *Tennessee*, Farragut turned his attention to the forts. One of the monitors took up position to the rear of Fort Powell, and that night the Confederates evacuated and blew up that position. This left only Forts Gaines and Morgan. Cut off from assistance, their defeat was inevitable. Gaines surrendered on 8 August.

An old friend of General Page, Farragut sent him a message under flag of truce demanding the unconditional surrender of Fort Morgan in order to avoid unnecessary loss of life. Disappointed, even shocked, that Farragut's ships had been able to get past the fort and into the bay, and angered by the surrender of the other two forts without his permission, Page replied, "I am prepared to sacrifice life, and will only surrender when I have no means of defense."[28]

It took two weeks of bombardment to bring that about. The *Tennessee*, recommissioned as a U.S. Navy ship of the same name on 19 August, participated in the bombardment. Finally, on 23 August Page informed Farragut: "The further sacrifice of life being unnecessary, my sick and wounded suffering and exposed, humanity demands that I ask for terms of capitulation."[29]

The capture of Mobile Bay cost Farragut more casualties than his operations against New Orleans, Port Hudson, and Vicksburg combined: 145 killed and 170 wounded. The Confederates lost 12 killed, 20 wounded, and the crews of the *Tennessee* and *Selma* captured. Farragut's reward came in December. On 22 December Congress created the rank of vice admiral, which Lincoln immediately conferred on him.

Farragut left operations against Mobile itself to the army, and not until March 1865 did it mount an effort against the city. On 12 March the small Union tug *Althea*, a coaler and supply ship, struck a torpedo and went down with two men killed and several injured. It was the first of seven Union ships lost to torpedoes in operations against Mobile in a five-week span, including the river monitor *Osage* sunk on 29 March.

General Canby assembled some forty-five thousand men, with Rear Adm. Henry K. Thatcher having charge of the naval effort. Army–navy cooperation was again excellent. The main land attack moved up the coast, while a simultaneous diversionary effort proceeded by water to a point on the opposite side of the bay to prevent Confederate reinforcements from reaching the city. The navy provided both transport for the troops and carried out resupply.

Beginning on 21 March, Union gunboats supported a landing at Donnelly's Mills on the Fish River in Alabama. Thatcher provided six tin-clads, all the light-draft ships available. With gunboats bombarding Mobile's forts from the water, the land forces worked their way to the main Confederate position at Spanish Fort. A steady Union bombardment forced the Confederates to evacuate that post on 8 April. Batteries Tracy and Huger, up the Blakely River from Spanish Fort, fell three days later. On 12 April Maj. Gen. Dabney Maury's ninety-two hundred Confederate defenders abandoned their defenses and Mobile surrendered.[30]

THE *ALBEMARLE* AND THE NORTH CAROLINA SOUNDS

Following the Battle of Mobile Bay, with the exception of naval units left to operate against Mobile, U.S. Navy attention returned to the East Coast, where the Confederates had constructed several ironclads with a

The Coasts and Sounds of North Carolina

view of engaging and destroying the Union shallow-draft wooden gunboats in the North Carolina sounds. The *Albemarle* and its sister ship *Neuse* were the smallest of Constructor John Porter's coast defense ironclads. The *Neuse* was shelled and damaged in a Union attack on Whitehall in December 1862; towed to Kinston for repairs, it ran aground there in May 1864 and was not gotten free until that fall. It never left the river, being used for defensive purposes until it was scuttled in March 1865 to prevent capture.

The *Albemarle* was a different story; it became one of the most famous Confederate ships of the war. Constructed at Edward's Ferry on the Roanoke River, the *Albemarle* was laid down in April 1863, launched in

July, and commissioned in April 1864. It was 158 feet in length, displaced 376 tons, had 4-inch casemate and 1-inch deck armor, and was driven by two screws from two steam engines capable of 400 horsepower and a speed in excess of four knots. With a crew of 150 men, the ironclad mounted only two 6.4-inch rifled guns. Damaged at launch, it was taken to Halifax, North Carolina, for repairs and completion. The ship's great advantage lay in its shallow draft, which allowed it to operate in the sounds, whereas the deeper-draft Union monitors could not.[31]

The *Albemarle* was ready in time to play a key role in the attack by Brig. Gen. Robert F. Hoke's seven thousand Confederate troops against three thousand troops under Brig. Gen. H. W. Wessells defending the Union base of Plymouth, North Carolina. The Confederates opened their assault on the afternoon of 17 April 1864, with artillery fire against Fort Gray, followed by an unsuccessful infantry attack early the next morning. Fearing an appearance by the *Albemarle*, the Union commander, Lt. Cdr. Charles W. Flusser, had ordered his two principal warships, the gunboats *Miami* and *Southfield*, lashed together for mutual protection and to maximize their firepower. The wooden hulled side-wheeler *Southfield*, commanded by Lt. Charles A. French, was a former Staten Island Ferry mounting one 6.4-inch Parrott rifle and five IX-inch Dahlgrens. Cdr. Richard T. Renshaw's *Miami* was a side-wheeler double-ended gunboat mounting one 6.4-inch Parrott, six IX-inch Dahlgrens, and one 24-pounder boat howitzer.

When the Confederate land attack began, Flusser dispatched the little *Ceres* up the Roanoke to communicate with the tinclad *Whitehead* then on picket duty watching for the *Albemarle*. Confederate batteries ashore opened up the *Ceres*, killing two men and wounding seven, but it made it upriver and returned. Meanwhile, the *Southfield* separated from the *Miami* and moved up the Roanoke to fire over the town of Plymouth, while the *Miami* moved downriver to open fire on Confederate troops attacking Fort Williams. The small Union steamer *Bombshell* took several hits while endeavoring to reach Fort Gray. It turned back, gaining Plymouth wharf before sinking.

By 9:00 PM, thanks in large part to the gunfire support from their ships, the Union troops had driven off the attackers. The *Miami* remained in place below the town to assist against any Confederate flank attack, and at 10:30 PM the *Southfield* returned and anchored nearby. Flusser then ordered the two ships again lashed together with hawsers.

The night before, Confederate Cdr. James W. Cooke had started out with the *Albemarle* down the Roanoke River from Hamilton, but the ram encountered mechanical problems. Repaired, it anchored above Plymouth at 10 PM on 18 April. Although unable to establish contact with Confederates ashore, Cooke sent out a boat to reconnoiter. It returned to the ironclad after midnight, and its crew reported the location of the Union gunboats and shore batteries and provided the welcome news that, because the river was up, the *Albemarle* could pass over the Union obstructions in the river.

At 3:30 AM on 19 April, Cooke weighed and headed for the Union gunboats. The *Whitehead* had provided warning of its approach, and when the *Albemarle* appeared, Flusser turned his two gunboats toward the ram, firing as the distance closed. The *Albemarle* made for the *Southfield*, crashed into it, and tore a great hole in its hull. Reportedly the *Albemarle* came to rest some ten feet inside the gunboat. Cooke ordered engines backed on striking the *Southfield* but could not immediately extricate his ship and was thus unable to reply to firing by the *Miami*, although the Union shot proved ineffective against the sloping, plated sides of the ram. Finally, after about three minutes, the *Albemarle* pulled free as the *Southfield* went down. Many of the seamen on the *Southfield* leapt aboard the *Miami* or took to the ship's boats; others were taken prisoner.

French took command from Flusser, who was the only one on the Union side killed in the engagement (eleven others were wounded in addition to eight prisoners; the *Albemarle* lost only one man, killed by a pistol shot). French withdrew the *Miami* and his other ships from the river to watch the ram from a distance. The *Albemarle* now controlled the water approaches to Plymouth. Its gunfire support and that of a Confederate steamer, the *Cotton Plant*, containing Confederate sharpshooters, enabled the more numerous Confederate attackers to capture Plymouth on 20 April.[32]

Capt. Melancton Smith, commanding Union naval forces in the North Carolina sounds, assembled additional ships below Portsmouth. His squadron consisted of the double-ender gunboats *Mattabesett* (the flagship), *Sassacus*, *Wyalusing*, and *Miami*, the converted ferryboat *Commodore Hull*, and the *Ceres*, *Whitehead*, and *Isaac N. Seymour*.

On the afternoon of 5 May 1864, another engagement occurred at the head of Albemarle Sound off the mouth of the Roanoke River, in consequence of Cooke's plan to convoy the *Cotton Plant* to the Alligator River.

On exiting the Roanoke in the *Albemarle*, which was accompanied by the steamer *Bombshell* (raised and taken into Confederate service as a tender), Cooke discovered six Union gunboats under Lt. Cdr. F. A. Roe in the *Sassacus*. The *Bombshell* surrendered early in the action, and the *Cotton Plant* withdrew back up the Roanoke, but the *Albemarle* continued on alone.

Making between ten and eleven knots, the *Sassacus* rammed the starboard side of the *Albemarle* just abaft the casemate. Simultaneously, the ram fired a bolt that passed completely through the Union ship. Meanwhile, crewmen on the *Sassacus* tried to throw hand grenades down the deck hatch of the ram, and both sides traded rifle fire. Another Confederate bolt then pierced the starboard boiler of the *Sassacus*. Steam filled the Union ship, killing several men and forcing it out of action. The Union side-wheelers *Mattabesett* and *Wyalusing* continued to engage the ram, however. The action continued for three hours until halted by darkness, but the ram was little damaged. The *Albemarle* then withdrew up the Roanoke River, and the Union side-wheelers *Commodore Hull* and *Ceres* took up position at that river's mouth to try to prevent it from reentering the sound.

The *Albemarle* represented a great threat to Union coastal operations and especially the wooden gunboats. Union observers also noted the *Albemarle's* ability to turn quickly, and its superior speed for an ironclad of six to seven knots. They also reported that 6.4-inch rifled projectiles broke up on hitting its armored sides.[33]

During the next five months, Captain Smith sought to find a way to destroy the *Albemarle*, but monitors drew too much water and wooden ships were too vulnerable. A boat raid appeared to be the only option. On 25 May, five volunteers from the *Wyalusing* went up the Roanoke in a boat with two 100-pound torpedoes, hoping to place them against the ram's hull at night. They were discovered by a sentry ashore before they could reach the ram, however. In the ensuing hail of musket fire, all five men escaped, two of them through the swamps.[34]

On 5 July, Rear Adm. Samuel P. Lee, commanding the North Atlantic Blockading Squadron, met with twenty-one-year-old Lt. William B. Cushing and asked him to lead another effort. Cushing proposed an attack by gunboats, which Lee rejected. Cushing then suggested two plans for boat attacks, the first to utilize an inflatable rubber boat launched from the swamps behind Plymouth and the second by two launches fitted with spar torpedoes. Lee approved the second plan but insisted that Cushing travel to Washington and secure final approval from the Navy Department. Welles and Fox thought the plan worth the effort and authorized Cushing to proceed.

In New York City, Cushing purchased two thirty-foot steam launches, arming each with a single twelve pounder Dahlgren howitzer. Each launch had at its bow a fourteen-foot-long spar that could mount a torpedo and be lowered by a windless. Once the torpedo was in position under the *Albemarle*'s hull, a tug on a line would release it, allowing it to float up under the hull of the ship. A second line would activate the firing mechanism. Cushing planned for the first launch to carry out the attack while the second fired canister from its boat howitzer and stood ready to attack should the attempt by the first launch fail.

Acting Ens. Andrew Stockholm commanded one launch and Cushing the other. Both launches experienced engine problems on the trip south by the inland water route, but the engine on Stockholm's *Steam Picket Boat No. 2* quit entirely, and he put ashore in Wicomico Bay, Virginia, where it was discovered. Following a firefight, Stockholm scuttled the launch and surrendered. Although Cushing blamed Stockholm, clearly the lieutenant had erred in allowing the two launches to become separated. *Steam Picket Boat No. 1* arrived safely in the North Carolina sounds on 24 October. Cushing then revealed his plans to the launch crew and asked for volunteers; all seven crewmen joined him.

In early September 1864 Welles named Farragut to replace Admiral Lee in command of the North Atlantic Blockading Squadron, but Farragut had already written to request leave for health reasons, and Welles settled on David D. Porter instead. It was thus Porter who approved Cushing's request that he be allowed to undertake the mission with the one launch only. Cushing set out on his attempt the night of 26 October 1864, but the launch grounded at the mouth of the Roanoke River. The crew managed to free it, but the mishap forced Cushing to postpone his attempt until the next night.

The night of 27 October was ideal: dark and foul. A heavy tarpaulin helped muffle the noise of the launch's steam engine during the approach, and Cushing was able to get close to the Plymouth waterfront where the *Albemarle* was moored. Fourteen men accompanied Cushing, the others being volunteers from the squadron. *Steam Picket Boat No. 1* towed a cutter with two officers and ten men from the *Shamrock* to neutralize the *Southfield*. The Confederates had raised this Union ship and then scuttled it again in the middle of the river about a mile from Portsmouth to serve as a picket location. Escaped slaves provided word that several dozen Confederate soldiers were on board.

The steam launch passed undetected within thirty yards of the *Southfield*. While Cushing was contemplating whether to try to cut out the *Albemarle*, about 3 AM a sentry ashore spotted the launch and gave the alarm. Cushing immediately ordered the cutter cast off to make for the *Southfield*, as the launch got up steam for the run to the *Albemarle*.

The Confederates opened fire on the launch both from the ram and the shore. Pickets ashore touched off a large bonfire to provide illumination, but this also enabled Cushing to spot a protective boom of logs the Confederates had placed in the water around the ram. Cooly ordering the launch about, Cushing then ran it at full speed toward the obstruction while firing canister from the boat howitzer against the Confederates ashore.

Striking the boom at high speed, the launch rode up and over the logs to rest next to the *Albemarle*. As bullets whizzed around him, Cushing somehow managed to lower the spar under the ram. Almost simultaneously, a shot from one of the *Albemarle*'s rifled guns flew over the launch and the torpedo went off, the resulting wash of water swamping the launch.

The explosion of the torpedo tore a gaping six-foot hole in the *Albemarle*, which then settled rapidly. Soon only the superstructure and smokestack were visible. Cushing had ordered his men to save themselves. He sought to escape by swimming downriver. In the process, he encountered one of the launch crewmen struggling in the water but was too weak at that point to save him, and the sailor drowned. In the morning, Cushing managed to secure a skiff on shore. He then rowed it eight miles to Albemarle Sound, where he was picked up by the *Valley City*. Of the fourteen men who had accompanied Cushing in the launch, only one other escaped; two drowned and eleven were captured. All those on the cutter returned, bringing with them four Confederates from the *Southfield*.

Admiral Porter hailed the event, and Union ships fired signal rockets in celebration. The destruction of the *Albemarle* enabled Union forces to retake Plymouth and control the entire Roanoke River area, and it released Union ships there for other blockade duties. Congress subsequently commended Cushing for his bravery and promoted him to lieutenant commander.[35]

Destruction of the Confederate ironclad Albemarle *at Plymouth, North Carolina, 27 October 1864.* NAVAL HISTORICAL CENTER (NH 57267)

ASSAULT ON FORT FISHER

The destruction of the *Albemarle* facilitated Porter's plans to move against Wilmington, North Carolina, the last remaining major Confederate port for blockade runners and a principal overseas supply link for the Army of Northern Virginia. Both General Grant and the navy concurred on the need to close Wilmington. Although Porter was anxious to proceed, it took time for Grant to provide the requisite troops. Finally, in December 1864, Porter assembled the most powerful naval force to that point in U.S. history: sixty-one warships, including five ironclads, mounting a total of 635 guns. Accompanying the warships were two divisions of sixty-five hundred men under Maj. Gen. Benjamin Butler.

The key to an assault on Wilmington was destruction of Fort Fisher. This powerful Confederate works was located on a narrow spit of land at the entrance to the Cape Fear River. If Fisher could be taken, blockade running out of Wilmington would be ended. Fort Fisher was fortified principally on the east facing the sea and on the south facing the river access. The side facing the sea extended nearly three-quarters of a mile, whereas the southern face was about a quarter mile in length. Porter and Butler worked out a plan whereby the troops would come ashore on the beach north of the fort. Porter's ships would then bombard the fort, after which the troops would assault from its north face, supported by naval gunfire.[36]

Confederate Col. William Lamb commanded Fort Fisher's nineteen hundred defenders. His men, who were well protected in a carefully laid-out earthworks with shell-proof chambers, manned forty-five heavy guns as well as numerous smaller pieces. The fort's northern land face was protected by a high palisade of logs, beyond which the Confederates had planted numerous land mines.

Butler suggested that the attackers blow up a ship filled with cannon powder under Fisher's walls, with the hope that the blast would severely damage the fort. Porter agreed and the former blockade runner *Louisiana* was selected and loaded with 150 tons of powder. As a precaution the Union transports were held twenty miles away at Beaufort, while Porter moved his warships to sea about a dozen miles. Although Butler informed Porter that he could not be ready before Christmas Day, Porter was tired of waiting. In his history of the naval war, Porter claims he did not expect much from the explosion of the powder ship. It is doubtful, as one writer claims, that Porter believed the blast would allow him to land sailors and marines and not have to share the glory with the army.[37]

During the night of 23 December Cdr. Alexander C. Rhind of the *Agawam* and fourteen volunteers undertook the dangerous task of positioning the *Louisiana* close to the fort. The men had resolved that, if it appeared they might be boarded, they would blow themselves up with the ship. Following in a blockade runner, Rhind brought the *Louisiana* to what he believed to be about 250 yards off Fort Fisher. The actual distance was probably about 600 yards. The crew anchored the ship bow and stern, set the powder trains to the explosive charges, and escaped in the accompanying steam tug *Wilderness*. The *Louisiana* exploded as planned about 1:50 AM on 24 December, but the blast did no damage to the fort; indeed, Colonel Lamb reported that he thought that a blockade runner had gone aground and been blown up.[38]

At daybreak that day the Union armada got under way. Porter's ships formed in line of battle in front of the Confederate works and about noon commenced a bombardment of some 115 shots a minute. Although most of the Confederate gunners were forced to seek refuge in the bombproofs, some of the heavy guns returned fire. The Union

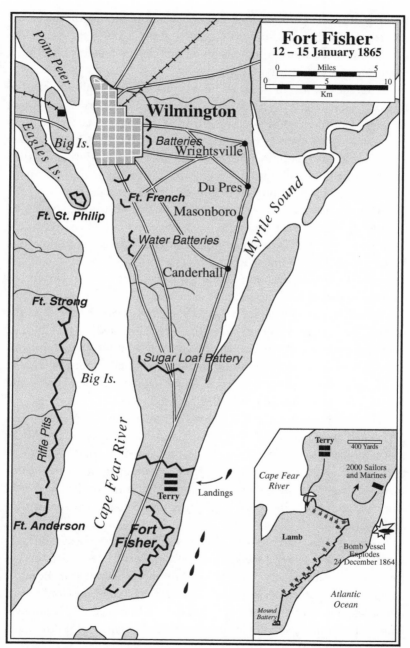

Fort Fisher, 12–15 January 1865

shelling did little damage, and most of the casualties in the fort were caused by the bursting of several rifled guns. Among the ships, the *Mackinaw* took a shot through its boiler and the *Osceola* was hit near its magazine and was only barely kept afloat.

Nonetheless, within about an hour and a half of bombardment, the fort's guns had largely been silenced. Porter then maintained a continuing slow bombardment while awaiting arrival of the transports, which, however, came up too late to effect a landing that day. On Christmas Day Porter resumed the bombardment about 10:30 AM, continuing it while seventeen of his smaller warships covered and assisted with the unopposed landing of two thousand of Butler's troops in boats.

Meanwhile, Porter endeavored to locate a channel through New Inlet in order to bring Fisher under fire from the Cape Fear River. When the *Iosco* and several double-ender gunboats encountered a shallow bar, Porter called on Cushing, who employed several small boats to sound a channel. Heavy Confederate fire that cut one of his boats in two forced Cushing to discontinue the effort.

Late that afternoon some of Butler's men, protected by fire from the ships offshore, worked their way to within several hundred yards of the fort. They reported the fort was virtually undamaged from the naval bombardment. Following a brief demonstration but without attempting an assault, on 27 December Butler concluded that nothing more could be done and simply reembarked his men and sailed back to Fortress Monroe.[39]

Porter was understandably furious at Butler's unilateral action and demanded he be removed from command. Grant agreed. Promising there would be no repeat of the debacle, he assured his friend Porter that the troops would soon return in greater strength under a new commander. Brig. Gen. Alfred H. Terry took over from Butler, who now complained loudly that Fort Fisher was impregnable and demanded an investigation.

Grant ordered Terry to work closely with Porter. Despite the admiral's initial misgivings, the two men got on well and Porter later praised Terry's leadership. Meanwhile, Porter kept his ships in the Wilmington-Beaufort and periodically shelled Fort Fisher in an effort to stymie any Confederate rebuilding. Fox was insistent that the next operation succeed. He wrote to Grant, "The country will not forgive us for another failure at Wilmington, and I have so informed Porter."[40]

The second Union assault on Fort Fisher, on 13 January 1865, was very much a textbook operation. For the attack, Porter assembled fifty-nine warships and Terry commanded eight thousand troops. That same day Terry landed his four divisions north of the fort with entrenching tools and provisions for twelve days. Terry deployed some of his men to build a strong defensive line across the upper neck of the peninsula. They were to keep at bay some six thousand Confederate troops in the Wilmington area under Gen. Braxton Bragg and Maj. Gen. Robert F. Hoke.

On 14 January, as Terry's troops prepared to assault Fisher's northern face, Porter's ships again bombarded the fort's eastern, seaward side. This time Porter assigned each of the bombardment ships a specific target, with it to be shelled until destroyed. He concentrated his most powerful ships against Confederate guns able to fire on the Union troops. These included the *New Ironsides* and the monitors *Saugus, Canonicus, Monadnock,* and *Mahopac.* To increase the effectiveness of their fire, the Union ships anchored less than one thousand yards from their targets.

The bombardment lasted all day, with a few ships continuing to lob shells into the night before they departed. The shelling inflicted some three hundred Confederate casualties. Certainly more effective than the previous efforts, it disabled some of the fort's heavy guns, opened breeches in the defenses, and severed wires used to detonate the land mines. During the day the Confederate twin-screw steamer *Chickamauga* (the former blockade runner *Edith*) fired on the Union troops from the Cape Fear River, but on 15 January Cushing utilized the screw steamer *Monticello* to drive the *Chickamauga* from range.

On the evening of 14 January, Porter and Terry met on board Porter's flagship, the *Malvern.* The two commanders set the timing of the land assault for 3 PM on 15 January. Porter agreed to put ashore some four hundred marines and sixteen hundred sailors for a simultaneous assault against the fort's sea face to the north.

Shortly after 9 AM on 15 January, the Union ships recommenced their bombardment. At about noon, landing detachments drawn from thirty-five ships went ashore just north of the fort to be hastily organized into four divisions, the marines under Capt. L. L. Dawson and the sailors under three commanders, C. H. Cushman, James Parker, and T. O. Selfridge. Cdr. K. R. Breese had overall command. The men had not undergone specialized training and were only lightly armed. The marines had rifles and bayonets, and the sailors were equipped with pistols and cutlasses. This force then worked its way along the shore to the point where the north and east faces of the fort met. The Union attack, which was to have been simultaneous, did not work out that way, as the soldiers, obliged to work their way through woods to their front, were delayed.

The sailors and marines approached along an open beach. Halting at the salient and under heavy fire from the fort, they attempted to charge through gaps in the palisades effected by the naval gunfire. A great many were cut down by Confederate canister and rifle fire, including two of their leaders, Lt. Samuel W. Preston and Lt. Benjamin H. Porter. Ens. Robley D. Evans, later a rear admiral, was wounded four times that day. Some sixty men broke through the palisade, but that was as far as they got. A number of the attackers then retreated in panic, some lying down and pretending to be dead until they could escape that night. In all, about a fifth of the attackers were casualties.

The attack was not in vain, however. The defenders assumed it to be the major Union effort and concentrated their efforts there. Exploiting the opportunity, three Union Army brigades pushed through the palisade and up the parapet on the land face. Many fell to Confederate artillery and rifle fire, but the survivors poured into the works. As they did so, the ships provided gunfire support. Porter ordered the *New Ironsides* and monitors to fire on the traverses held by the Confederates, clearing a number of them. This accurate naval gunfire was of immense assistance to the troops.

The fighting was hand-to-hand and the outcome remained in doubt until early evening, when Terry committed his reserve brigade. At about 9 PM on 15 January, the Confederates surrendered. The attackers had suffered some one thousand casualties, the defenders half that number. Among the Confederate casualties was Colonel Lamb, severely wounded. Subsequently, three dozen Union sailors and marines received the Medal of Honor for the action. Terry was rewarded with advancement to major general of volunteers and brigadier general in the regular army.[41]

Fort Fisher was the most heavily fortified position taken by amphibious assault during the war. With its capture, Union forces then took all the surrounding works, including 139 guns. They then advanced up the Cape Fear River. Wilmington surrendered on 23 February 1865, starving Lee's Army of Northern Virginia of essential supplies. Meanwhile, as Grant continued the siege of Petersburg and sought to destroy Lee, Sherman captured Atlanta before driving east to the sea, cutting a wide swath through Georgia to Savannah. Sherman then turned north through the Carolinas to link up with Grant.

THE WAR ENDS

The war was now nearly over. In January 1865 Confederate commander of the James River Squadron Flag Officer John K. Mitchell, under pressure from Secretary Mallory to take action, launched a precipitous assault down the James River to take Grant's City Point supply base. Mitchell commanded eleven ships, including the three most powerful remaining Confederate ironclads: the *Richmond, Fredericksburg,* and *Virginia II.* Mitchell's hopes were bolstered by the fact that Porter had withdrawn a number of Union warships for the Fort Fisher–Wilmington operation. U.S. Navy Cdr. William A. Parker had in the river only one Union ironclad, the powerful double-turreted monitor *Onondaga* (two XV-inch Dahlgrens and two 8-inch Parrotts), supported by seven wooden gunboats. Parker could, if necessary, call on additional ships from the blockading squadron ninety miles downstream at Hampton Roads. The Confederates had learned that heavy rains had washed out some of the obstructions at Trent's Reach, which had been placed in the river there by the Union side to pen in the Confederate squadron.

On 23 January, on the approach of the Confederate squadron, Parker immediately withdrew his ships downriver. The Confederate effort soon came to an inglorious end, however. That same day both the *Virginia No. 2* and *Richmond* grounded while trying to pass river obstructions and came under fire from powerful Union shore batteries. Two other Confederate ships, the gunboat *Drewry* and torpedo boat *Scorpion,* also grounded. Just after the crew had evacuated it, the *Drewry* blew up when a Union mortar shell penetrated its magazine and exploded. This blast, heard by General Grant at City Point eighteen miles away, killed two men on the *Scorpion* and washed over board four others. That ship then drifted downstream out of control and fell into Union hands.

The next morning, 24 January, Parker returned with the *Onondaga* to Trent's Reach and opened fire on the Confederate ironclads with its XV-inch guns. Both Confederate ships sustained damage and withdrew upriver with the remaining Confederate ships to Chaffin's Bluff as soon as they were refloated. The last clash of the war between ironclads thus ended in a Union victory, although there was sufficient displeasure over what both sides regarded as a lost opportunity, that Parker and Mitchell were each removed from command.[42]

Recognizing the inevitable, and with his own position collapsing, on 2 April Lee abandoned Richmond and Petersburg and attempted to escape westward. This decision forced Confederate Rear Adm. Raphael Semmes, commander of the James River Squadron since 18 February, to scuttle his ships. Early on the morning of 3 April Semmes ordered the three ironclads fired and the five wooden gunboats moved upsteam to Richmond. Semmes described the destruction of the *Virginia II* in these words:

> The spectacle was grand beyond description. Her shell-rooms had been full of loaded shells. The explosion of the magazine threw all these shells, with their fuses lighted, into air. The fuses were of different lengths, and as the shells exploded by twos and threes, and by the dozen, the pyrotechnic effect was very fine. The explosion shook the houses in Richmond, and must have waked the echoes of the night for forty miles around.[43]

At Richmond, the men of the squadron found much of the city in flames, including the school-ship *Patrick Henry*. The crews came ashore and the gunboats were then themselves set on fire and set adrift in the James. The *Beaufort* failed to sink, and the Union took possession of it and the unfinished *Texas*. [44]

Cornered at Appomattox Court House, meanwhile, Lee surrendered on 9 April 1865. Johnston surrendered in North Carolina two weeks later on 26 April. Although some isolated units held out for longer, the Civil War was then for all intents and purposes over, although on the high seas the Confederate raider *Shenandoah* continued to take and burn U.S. merchant ships.

CHAPTER FOURTEEN

Conclusion

―――∿∿―――

In employment of sea power, the Civil War had much in common with the American Revolutionary War, the War of 1812, and the Mexican War. All three of these conflicts saw one side dominant at sea (Britain in the case of the American Revolutionary War and the War of 1812 and the United States in the Mexican War). That side used its naval strength with great effect to impose a blockade on its opponent and then strike at will along the enemy coasts with amphibious operations and riverine incursions. In these wars, as in the Civil War, the weaker side struck back through commerce raiding, attempts to run ships through the blockade, and innovative defensive measures. Of these four contests, the Civil War saw much more expansive use of naval power by the winning side than in any of the previous American wars; the Civil War also saw greater technological innovation by both sides than in the previous three conflicts.

Although often overlooked or trivialized through concentration on a few battles, such as the *Monitor* versus the *Virginia* or the *Alabama* versus the *Kearsarge*, naval operations were extremely important. There can be no question that the U.S. Navy played a critical role in the Union victory. Throughout the long war, Secretary Welles and other Northern strategists kept their focus on the chief strategic goals of the blockade of the Confederate coasts, ending Confederate commerce raiding and assisting the Union Army in securing control of the great Western rivers. To administer his rapidly expanding naval force, Welles created a highly effective managerial system.

The Confederacy, with far inferior resources, nonetheless made a credible showing on the seas and rivers and contributed significantly to the development of naval technology and tactics. As Secretary Mallory summed up after the war:

> I am satisfied that, with the means at our disposal, and in view of the overwhelming force of the enemy at the outset of the struggle, our little navy accomplished so much. Our Navy alone kept that of the U.S. from reaching Richmond by the James River, and from reaching Savannah and Charleston; and yet not ten men in ten thousand of the country know or appreciate these facts.[1]

Both navies were blessed with effective leadership at the top, yet Welles, ably assisted by Fox, generally ran a more efficient effort than that of his Southern counterpart. Although the Union resources were ample for the tasks, the effort was on a vast scale, and difficulties abounded. Effective management was critical. Welles has been criticized for failing to place sufficient assets to hunt down and destroy the Confederate commerce raiders, but there was a limit even to Northern resources, and he was certainly correct in placing primary emphasis on the blockade to deny his opponent one of his most important strategic goals. Union cruiser captains were often the victims of poor luck rather than lack of skills. As was the case in World War I and II, it was much more difficult for commerce raider destroyers to locate the commerce raiders than it was for the latter to find their prey of merchant ships.

A more reasonable criticism of Welles is that both he and Fox suffered from myopia as far as the monitors were concerned. The *New Ironsides* was a much more successful type of ship for the war fought by the Union along the Atlantic coast than were the monitors, especially in assisting with Union Army landings. Meanwhile, senior Union officer leadership was highly effective; among notable commanders were David G. Farragut, Andrew H. Foote, Samuel F. Du Pont, and David D. Porter.

Confederate Secretary of the Navy Stephen Mallory did the most with the assets available to him. His decision to go over to commerce raiders proved to be an effective one given his resources, although it could not win the war. He also was quicker than Welles to embrace new technology at sea, including the ironclad, but once that race was begun there was no way that the South could win it. The South's casemated ironclads, beginning with the *Virginia*, were an inexpensive and effective response, but they continually suffered from inadequate steam-propulsion plants and shortages of iron armor, problems that the industrially handicapped South never could overcome. Mallory never achieved his goal of breaking the blockade with these new ships, but later light-draft coast-defense iron-clads such as the *Albemarle* showed what might have been accomplished. Mallory was less successful than Welles in his selections of senior com-manders and in getting them to fight, but he was also handicapped by too many higher-ranking officers for the slots available and a system that emphasized seniority in command positions. Notable naval officers included Franklin Buchanan and Raphael Semmes. Confederate Cdr. John M. Brooke vied with Union Adm. John A. Dahlgren as the preeminent ordnance designer of the war.

The war saw dramatic battles, from the duels between the *Monitor* and *Virginia* and the *Kearsarge* and *Alabama*, to the destruction of the *Albemarle*, and the bloodiest at Mobile Bay. The war saw plenty of firsts, including the first clash between ironclad ships in history, the first use of a revolving turret in warfare, the first sinking of an active warship by a submersible, and the extensive use of mines. It also produced its share of naval heroes, ranging from Farragut to William Cushing to George Dixon.

Both sides worked out effective strategies for the resources available. In addition to the blockade, Union strategists embraced the major tenets of the Anaconda Plan, that the South could be bisected by its major rivers. The U.S. Navy made that possible, and control of the Mississippi, the Tennessee, the Cumberland, and other rivers greatly inhibited the Confederate movement of supplies. The Union was not as successful early in the war in reducing and securing major Confederate ports—New Orleans being the prominent exception. Mobile, Wilmington, and Charleston fell only near the end. The Union side never did undertake an amphibious operation with the idea of using it as the basis of a major land campaign to the interior. There was ample opportunity for this, with pos-sible war-winning results, especially early in the contest.

The North developed no joint planning mechanism. Nor was there the means to resolve interservice differences. A commander's only recourse was to appeal to the service secretary and, barring resolution there, to have the secretary take the matter to President Lincoln for resolution. In joint oper-ations much depended simply on the men selected to command. Where they coordinated their activities and got on well, much was achieved.

Technological constraints played a role in Union strategic planning. The Committee of Commerce recommended bases that could be easily defended once they were taken—that is, sites poorly accessible to the Confederates from the land. But this very factor of poor land communications made it difficult for the Union to launch major land operations from them to the interior. For the Union to attack a principal port with easy access to the interior by rail lines meant that the Confederacy would also be able to bring up reinforcements quickly. As Du Pont pointed out, there were opportunities early in the war to take the major Confederate cities, but that would have meant large commitments of ground troops, and, once taken, the cities would have to be held. Nonetheless, a drive against Richmond from a North Carolina coastal enclave, coupled with a concurrent one from the north, might have ended the war in a year. Such an operation was imperfectly mounted in the Peninsula Campaign.

The U.S. Navy moved large numbers of troops and supplies by water in a number of campaigns, the most prominent being the slow-to-develop Peninsula Campaign, which, however, lacked an effective ground commander. Other examples of effective army–navy cooperation are the Forts Henry and Donelson Campaign; operations on the Mississippi, especially against Vicksburg; Mobile Bay; and the last stage of operations against Fort Fisher.

Waging primarily a defensive war at sea, the Confederacy did much more than the Union with torpedoes (mines) and submarines. Goaded by Maury, Mallory established a Torpedo Bureau for their development early on. Although primitive in The Civil War, such weapons reached maximum effectiveness in the Russo-Japanese War of 1904–05 and in World Wars I and II.

Of all naval operations of the war, the Union blockade of the Confederate Atlantic and Gulf coasts predominates. It rightly claimed the lion's share of Union naval assets, and although it was never completely effective, it nonetheless starved the Confederacy of foreign arms imports and, more important, machinery, including steam engines, iron products, and other goods essential to the Confederate war effort. The blockade also inhibited the Confederates from getting to Europe the cotton and other exports necessary to pay for those goods. Critical in its success was the decision taken by Washington early in the war to secure bases from which the blockading squadrons could operate. The Union side demonstrated great ability in setting up and maintaining repair and supply facilities as well as the logistics network that went with this. The effort here was a vast one, and it is largely unsung in histories of the war.

As with the army, the Union Navy was tasked with taking the offensive at sea, and the two services conducted a number of joint operations. These ranged from the very successful, such as Fort Henry, the James River in 1862, Vicksburg, and the second attack on Fort Fisher, to failures, such as the Confederate recapture of Galveston and the Red River Expedition. In this regard, both services learned a great deal, with the most important lesson being the need for close army–navy cooperation beginning at the top. Examples of successful army–navy tandems were Grant and Foote at Forts Henry and Donelson, Grant and Porter in the Vicksburg Campaign, Canby and Farragut at Mobile Bay, and Terry and Porter at Fort Fisher. Examples of poor coordination and resultant failure are found in Banks and Porter in the Red River Campaign and Butler and Porter at Fort Fisher. Where there was poor coordination and a clash of personalities, even the best plans could not be salvaged.

Undoubtedly, Union Navy activities shortened the war. Had the conflict been more prolonged, foreign powers might have entered the conflict or at least been inclined to provide additional military assistance to the South. The Civil War reveals the truism that victory in warfare results from all services working together toward a common goal, supported by overwhelming industrial power. Both navies performed well, but the overwhelming advantages enjoyed by the North in industrial might, population, organization, and logistics proved the difference on both land and sea.

After the great tragic chapter of the Civil War, the United States largely disbanded its military establishment. The army went from one million men under arms at Appomattox to only twenty-five thousand by the end of 1866. The navy also languished. The second-largest in the world in 1865, the U.S. Navy was, within a decade and a half, inferior to that of Chile and to every major European power, when its ships and ordnance were also essentially those of the Civil War and it was unable to project naval power to any significant degree. Fortunately for the United States, by 1890 a modern steel navy began to emerge, and it was this force that established the United States as a world military power in 1898.

Notes

INTRODUCTION

1. Nathan Miller, *Sea of Glory: The Continental Navy Fights for Independence,*
   1775–1783 (New York: David McKay, 1974), 260.
2. Ibid., 260–61.
3. On the gunboat program, see Spencer C. Tucker, *The Jeffersonian Gunboat Navy*
   (Columbia, SC: University of South Carolina Press, 1993); and Gene A. Smith,
   "For the Purposes of Defense": The Politics of the Jeffersonian Gunboat Program
   (Newark: University of Delaware Press, 1995).
4. Dudley W. Knox, *History of the U.S. Navy* (New York: G. P. Putnam's Sons, 1936),
   82. Royal Navy figures for the North American station are from *The Weekly*
   Register, II:356 and American State Papers, Naval Affairs, I:248–49. Also see
   Charles O. Paullin, *Paullin's History of Naval Administration, 1775–1911*
   (Annapolis, MD: Naval Institute Press, 1968), l48; Alfred T. Mahan, *Sea Power in*
   Its Relations to the War of 1812 (London: Sampson Low, Marston & Co., 1905), I:
   279–80; II: J. Fenimore Cooper, *The History of the Navy of the United States of*
   America (New York: G. P. Putnam & Co., 1856), 37–40; Howard I. Chapelle, *The*
   History of the American Sailing Navy: The Ships and Their Development (New York:
   W. W. Norton, 1949), 244.
5. Mahan, *Sea Power in Its Relations to the War of 1812,* II:242.
6. Paullin, *Paullin's History of Naval Administration,* 176–77.
7. Paul Silverstone, *The Sailing Navy, 1775–1854* (Annapolis, MD: Naval Institute
   Press, 2001), 23–25.
8. Spencer C. Tucker, "U.S. Navy Steam Sloop *Princeton*," *The American Neptune,*
   XLIX (Spring 1989): 96–113.
9. Spencer C. Tucker, "The Stevens Battery," *The American Neptune,* LI, No. 1 (Winter
   1991): 12–21.
10. The classic study is James Phinney Baxter III, *The Introduction of the Ironclad*
    Warship (Annapolis, MD: Naval Institute Press, 2001; reprint ed. of Harvard
    University Press, 1933).
11. Spencer C. Tucker, "The Explosion of the 'Peacemaker' Aboard Sloop Princeton,"
    New Interpretations in Naval History: Selected Papers from the Eighth Naval History
    Symposium (Annapolis, MD: Naval Institute Press, 1989), 175–89.

CHAPTER 1

1. Annual Report of the Secretary of the Navy, 1865, xiii, 200; Paullin, *Paullin's History of Naval Administration*, 250, 304. Raimondo Luraghi gives a slightly larger figure of 1,338 for June 1861: Raimondo Luraghi, *A History of the Confederate Navy* (Annapolis, MD: Naval Institute Press, 1996), 22. Luraghi cites J. Thomas Scharf, who provides a detailed breakdown of 1,338 naval officers of all ranks and 225 marine officers: Scharf, *History of the Confederate States Navy: From Its Organization to the Surrender of Its Last Vessel* (reprint; New York: Random House, 1996), 32–33.
2. The standard biography of Welles is John Niven, *Gideon Welles: Lincoln's Secretary of the Navy* (New York: Oxford University Press, 1973).
3. U.S. Congress, Exec. Docs., 37th Cong., I Sess., No. I, 96; U.S. Congress, Statutes at Large, XII, 510–12; on the bureaus, see Paullin, *Paullin's History of Naval Administration*, 260–62.
4. Luraghi, *A History of the Confederate Navy*, 22; Michael J. Bennett, *Union Jacks: Yankee Sailors in the Civil War* (Chapel Hill: University of North Carolina Press, 2004), 5.
5. Donald L. Canney, *Lincoln's Navy: The Ships, Men and Organization, 1861–65* (Annapolis, MD: Naval Institute Press, 1998), 140–142; Kenneth E. Thompson Jr., *Civil War Commodores and Admirals: A Biographic Directory* (Portland, ME: The Thompson Group, 2001), xii.
6. Canney, *Lincoln's Navy*, 151.
7. Bennett, *Union Jacks*, 5–6.
8. Ibid., 8, 14–18.
9. Ibid., 8–11.
10. Paul Calore, *Naval Campaigns of the Civil War* (Jefferson, NC: McFarland and Co., 2002), 48.
11. Steven J. Ramold, *Slaves, Sailors, Citizens: African Americans in the Union Navy* (DeKalb: Northern Illinois University Press, 2002), 55. Ramold, Bennett, and Joseph Reidy of Howard University all estimate African-Americans at 15 to 16 percent of U.S. Navy enlisted personnel.
12. Edward A. Miller, *Gullah Statesman: Robert Smalls from Slavery to Congress, 1839–1915* (Columbia: University of South Carolina Press, 1995).
13. Luraghi, *A History of the Confederate Navy*, 22; William N. Still Jr., ed., *The Confederate Navy: The Ships, Men and Organization, 1861–65* (Annapolis, MD: Naval Institute Press, 1997), 22.
14. U.S. War Department, *The War of the Rebellion*, I, 2, Pt. 3:414.
15. Still, *The Confederate Navy*, 30–31.
16. Diary entry for 6 August 1863, Josiah Gorgas, Frank E. Vandiver, ed., *The Civil War Diary of General Josiah Gorgas* (Tuscaloosa: University of Alabama Press, 1947), 58–59; the standard biography of Mallory is Joseph T. Durkin, *Stephen R. Mallory: Confederate Navy Chief* (Chapel Hill: University of North Carolina Press, 1954).
17. Still, *The Confederate Navy*, 24–32.
18. Ibid., 34.
19. Scharf, *History of the Confederate States Navy*, 32–33.

20. William H. Roberts, *Now for the Contest: Coastal & Oceanic Naval Operations in the Civil War* (Lincoln: University of Nebraska Press, 2004), 28–29.
21. Thompson, *Civil War Commodores and Admirals*, 24–26; Calore, *Naval Campaigns of the Civil War*, 55.
22. Still, *The Confederate Navy*, 30.
23. James Lee Conrad, *Rebel Reefers: The Organization and Midshipmen of the Confederate States Naval Academy* (Cambridge, MA: Da Capo Press, 2003); also R. Thomas Campbell, *Academy on the James: The Confederate Naval School* (Shippensburg, PA: Burd Street Press, 1999).
24. Raphael Semmes, *Memoirs of Service Afloat During the War Between the States* (reprint; Secaucus, NJ: The Blue & Grey Press, 1987), 412–13.
25. Frank L. Owsley Jr., *The C.S.S. Florida: Her Building and Operations* (new ed., Tuscaloosa: University of Alabama Press, 1987), 45.
26. Still, *The Confederate Navy*, 134–35; Luraghi, *History of the Confederate Navy*, 308–9.
27. Canney, *Lincoln's Navy*, 118–20; Still, *The Confederate Navy*, 133–34.
28. Dennis J. Ringle, *Life in Lincoln's Navy* (Annapolis, MD: Naval Institute Press, 1998), 26–31.
29. Spencer C. Tucker, *Arming the Fleet: U.S. Navy Ordnance in the Muzzle-Loading Era* (Annapolis, MD: Naval Institute Press, 1989), 44; *Ordnance Instructions for the United States Navy* (Washington, DC: Government Printing Office, 1864), 75.
30. Ringle, *Life in Lincoln's Navy*, 40–45; Canney, *Lincoln's Navy*, 128–29.
31. Ringle, *Life in Lincoln's Navy*, 47.
32. Still, *The Confederate Navy*, 133.
33. John W. Grattan, *Under the Blue Pennant: Or Notes of a Naval Officer, 1863–1865* (ed. Robert J. Schneller; New York: John Wiley & Sons, 1999), 76.
34. Roberts, *Now for the Contest*, 76–77.
35. Ringle, *Life in Lincoln's Navy*, 38.
36. Ibid., 64–65.
37. Ibid., 66.
38. Ibid., 65.
39. Christopher McKee, *A Gentlemanly and Honorable Profession. The Creation of the U.S. Naval Officer Corps, 1794–1815* (Annapolis, MD: Naval Institute Press, 1991), 451–53. For the temperance campaign in the U.S. Navy, see Spencer C. Tucker, *Andrew Foote: Civil War Admiral on Western Waters* (Annapolis, MD: Naval Institute Press, 2000).
40. Bennett, *Union Jacks*, 105.
41. Ibid., 106–8.
42. Tucker, *Andrew Foote*, 200.
43. Stephan F. Blanding, *Recollections of a Sailor Boy on the Cruise of the Gunboat Louisiana* (Providence, RI: E. A. Johnson, 1886), 66; Ringle, *Life in Lincoln's Navy*, 71.
44. Ringle, Life in Lincoln's Navy, 31; Bennett, *Union Jacks*, 25.
45. Bennett, Union Jacks, 25.
46. Charles M. Robinson III, *Shark of the Confederacy: The Story of the CSS* Alabama (Annapolis, MD: Naval Institute Press, 1995), 50–51, 61.
47. Canney, *Lincoln's Navy*, 321.

CHAPTER 2

1. For a discussion of this, see Richard N. Current, "God and the Strongest Battalions," *Why the North Won the Civil War* (David Donald, ed., New York: Collier Books, 1962), 15–32. See also James M. McPherson, *Battle Cry of Freedom: The Civil War Era* (New York: Oxford University Press, 1988), 318.
2. Paullin, *Paullin's History of Naval Administration*, 295–97.
3. Canney, *Lincoln's Navy*, 33–34.
4. Senate Report 37th Cong. 2nd Session, No. 37, 96–101; House Ex. Doc., 40th Cong, 2nd Session, No. 280; Annual Report of the Secretary of the Navy, 1864, xxii–xxiv; Ibid., 1865, xii–xiii; also Paullin, *Paullin's History of Naval Administration*, 280.
5. William H. Roberts, *Now for the Contest: Coastal & Oceanic Naval Operations in the Civil War* (Lincoln: University of Nebraska Press, 2004), 18.
6. David A. Mindell, *War, Technology, and Experience Aboard the USS* Monitor (Baltimore, MD: The Johns Hopkins University Press, 2000), 27.
7. Ibid., 26.
8. Armaments given here do not include Dahlgren boat howitzers, at least one or two of which were usually carried on board ship and could be utilized both on boats and field carriages. Of these, in 1861 the *Merrimack* carried two 12-pounders. Guns were usually designated by bore size for rifles and Dahlgren shell guns, whereas the shot guns were usually identified by weight of projectile, for example a 32-pounder. It must be noted that armaments, even with a particular class of ship, varied widely, depending on the individual ship and the date. Paul H. Silverstone, *Warships of the Civil War Navies* (Annapolis, MD: Naval Institute Press, 1989) is a good source for armaments of individual ships of the war at different periods and is the primary source for the information here.
9. Mindell, *War, Technology, and Experience*, 28.
10. William H. Roberts, *USS New Ironsides in the Civil War* (Annapolis, MD: Naval Institute Press, 1999), 9, 11, 106–11.
11. Roberts, *Now for the Contest*, 81.
12. *Official Records of the Union and Confederate Navies in the War of the Rebellion* [hereinafter cited as *ORN*], Ser. II, 2:69.
13. Robert G. Elliott, *Ironclad of the Roanoke: Gilbert Elliott's Albemarle* (Shippensburg, PA: The White Mane Publishing Co., 1999), 79.
14. Ivan Musicant, *Divided Waters: The Naval History of the Civil War* (New York: HarperCollins, 1995), 69.
15. On the Confederate ironclads and their fate, see William N. Still Jr., *Iron Afloat: The Story of the Confederate Armorclads* (Columbia: University of South Carolina Press, 1985); and Maurice Melton, *The Confederate Ironclads* (Cranbury, NJ: Thomas Yoseloff, 1968).
16. Still, *The Confederate Navy*, 57–58.
17. The standard biography of Dahlgren is Robert J. Schneller Jr., *A Quest for Glory: A Biography of John A. Dahlgren* (Annapolis, MD: Naval Institute Press, 1996). It is, however, weak on his ordnance. On this see Edwin Olmstead, Wayne Stark, and Spencer C. Tucker, *The Big Guns: Civil War Siege, Seacoast and Naval Cannon* (Alexandria Bay, NY: Museum Restoration Service, 1997), 83–110.

18. Spencer C. Tucker, "The Dahlgren Boat Howitzer," *Naval History VI*, No. 3 (Fall 1992), 50–54.

19. Spencer C. Tucker, *Arming the Fleet: U.S. Naval Ordnance in the Muzzle-loading Era* (Annapolis, MD: Naval Institute Press, 1989), 228–32.

20. Larry J. Daniel and Riley W. Gunter, *Confederate Cannon Foundries* (Union City, TN: Pioneer Press, 1977), 80.

21. Olmstead, Stark, and Tucker, *The Big Guns*, 113.

22. On Brooke's life see George M. Brooke Jr., *John M. Brooke: Naval Scientist and Educator* (Charlottesville: University Press of Virginia, 1980); for his role in the *Virginia*, see John Mercer Brooke, "The *Virginia* or *Merrimac*: Her Real Projector," *Southern Historical Society Papers*, XIX (January 1891), 3–34; on the Brooke guns, see Olmstead, Stark, and Tucker, *The Big Guns*, 125–34.

23. *Ordnance Instructions for the United States Navy* (1864), 47–57.

CHAPTER 3

1. John D. Eisenhower, *Agent of Destiny: The Life and Times of Winfield Scott* (New York: The Free Press, 1997), 359–60.

2. Ibid., 361.

3. Gideon Welles, *Diary of Gideon Welles, Secretary of the Navy under Lincoln and Johnson* (3 vols.; Boston, MA: Houghton Mifflin, 1911), I:3–21; John Niven, *Gideon Welles, Lincoln's Secretary of the Navy* (New York: Oxford University Press, 1973), 325–32; also David Dixon Porter, *Incidents and Anecdotes of the Civil War* (New York: D. Appleton and Co., 1985), 13–16.

4. Porter, *Incidents and Anecdotes of the Civil War*, 16–20; Niven, *Welles*, 332–33.

5. Lt. T. A. Roe to Foote, 6 Apr 1861, Foote Papers, New Haven (Connecticut) Colony Historical Society; Niven, *Welles*, 335–36; Welles, *Diary of Gideon Welles*, 24–25; Porter, *Incidents and Anecdotes of the Civil War*, 20–22.

6. Welles to McCauley, to Commo. S. L. Breese, and to Alden, all 11 Apr 1861, *ORN*, Ser. I, 4:275.

7. Isherwood to Welles, 18 Apr 1861, *ORN*, Ser. I, 4:280–81; lost at Norfolk were the *Merrimack* (40 guns); the sailing sloops *Germantown* and *Plymouth* (22 guns); the frigates *United States* (44 guns, the oldest ship in the navy), *Raritan*, and *Columbia*; the brig *Dolphin* (4 guns); and ships of the line *Pennsylvania* (120 guns), *Columbia*, *Delaware*, and *New York* (unfinished). David D. Porter, *Naval History of the Civil War* (reprint; Secaucus, NJ: Castle, 1984), 28–32.

8. Sinclair to Mallory, 22 Apr 1861, *ORN*, Ser. I, 4:306.

9. Paulding to Welles, 23 Apr 1861, Ibid., 389–91.

10. Porter, *Naval History of the Civil War*, 28.

11. Eisenhower, *Agent of Destiny*, 357, 385–87.

12. United States Congress, Executive Document No. I, "Annual Report of the Secretary of the Navy," 37th Cong., 1st Sess., Vol. 3, Ser. 1119, 2 Dec 1861, 3–23.

13. Lynn M. Case and Warren F. Spencer, *The United States and France: Civil War Diplomacy* (Philadelphia: University of Pennsylvania Press, 1970), 17, 39, 52.

14. On this topic, see Norman B. Ferris, *The Trent Affair: A Diplomatic Crisis* (Knoxville: The University of Tennessee Press, 1977).

15. William Morrison Robinson Jr., *The Confederate Privateers* (Columbia: University of South Carolina Press, 1990; reprint of 1928), 13–17.
16. Ibid., 14.
17. *U.S. Senate Document No. 332,* 64th Cong., Sess. 1, serial No. 6952, 19.
18. Robinson, *Confederate Privateers,* 30; Silverstone, *Civil War Navies,* 193–94.
19. Robinson, *Confederate Privateers,* 35–46.
20. *ORN,* Ser. I, 5:692–93, 780; *Trial of the Officers and crew of the privateer* Savannah *on the charge of piracy, in the United States Circuit Court for the Southern District of New York, Hon. Judges Nelson and Shipman, presiding.* Reported by A. F. Wharton, stenographer and corrected by the counsel (New York: Baker & Godwin, 1882); Robinson, *Confederate Privateers,* 49–57, 133–51.
21. Robinson, Confederate Privateers, 59–78.
22. Ward to Welles, 22 Apr 1861, *ORN,* Ser. I, 4:420; Welles to Capt. Samuel Breese, 27 Apr 1861, Ibid., 430.
23. Schneller, *A Quest for Glory,* 186.
24. Lt. H. C. Craven to Cdr. S. C. Rowan, 18 Jun 1861, *ORN,* Ser. I, 4:539–40.

CHAPTER 4
1. Pendergast to Welles, 30 Apr 1861, *ORN,* Ser. II, 4:355.
2. Paullin, *Paullin's History of Naval Administration,* 275.
3. Ibid., 277.
4. Stringham to Welles, 30 May 1861, *ORN,* Ser. I, 5:682.
5. Robert M. Browning Jr., *Success Is All That Was Expected: The South Atlantic Blockading Squadron During the Civil War* (Washington, DC: Brassey's, 2002), 14–15.
6. Canney, *Lincoln's Navy,* 179–80.
7. Stringham to Welles, 2 Sep 1861, *ORN,* Ser. I, 6:120–23; Forrest to Hunter, 28 Aug 1861, Ibid., 719; Barron to S. R. Mallory, 31 Aug 1861, Ibid., 138–40; Browning, *Success Is All That Was Expected,* 13–14.
8. Stringham to Welles, 2 Sep 1861, *ORN,* Ser. I, 6:124.
9. Du Pont to Welles, 6 and 8 Nov 1861, *ORN,* Ser. I, 12:259–63; Acting Lt. John Barnes to Lt. C. R. P. Rodgers, 8 and 9 Nov 1861, Ibid., 270–71; Report of Brig. Gen. Thoms F. Drayton, CSA to Capt. L. D. Walker, 24 Nov 1861, Ibid., 300–307; Browning, *Success Is All That Was Expected,* 34–35.
10. Du Pont to Welles, 11 Nov 1861, *ORN,* Ser. I, 12:263.
11. Du Pont to Welles, 10 Nov 1861, *ORN,* Ser. I, 12:261–64, 266; C. R. P. Rodgers to Du Pont, 10 Nov 1861, Ibid., 267–68; Brig. Gen. Drayton, CSA to Capt. L. D. Walker, 24 Nov 1861, Ibid., 306.
12. Welles to Du Pont, 15 Nov 1861, *ORN,* Ser. I, 12:294; Browning, *Success Is All That Was Expected,* 41.
13. *ORN,* Ser. I, 6:367.
14. Du Pont to Welles, 4 Dec 1861, *ORN,* Ser. I, 12:380–81.
15. Welles to Lincoln, 2 Dec 1861, in Naval History Division, Navy Department, *Civil War Naval Chronology* (Washington, DC: Department of the Navy, 1971), 1–38.
16. Welles to George D. Morgan, 17 Oct 1861, *ORN,* Ser. I, 12:416–17; Welles to Du Pont, 7 Nov 1861, Ibid., 417.

17. Rodgers to Du Pont, 6 Dec 1861, *ORN*, Ser. I, 12:385–86.
18. Cdr. J. S. Missroon to Du Pont, 5 Dec 1861, *ORN*, Ser. I, 12:419–20; Capt. Charles H. Davis to Du Pont, 21 Dec 1861, Ibid., 422–23; Gen. R. E. Lee CSA to Jp. P. Benjamin, 20 Dec 1861, Ibid., 423.
19. C. R. P. Rodgers to Du Pont, 3 Jan 1862, *ORN*, Ser. I, 12:448–50.
20. Stephen R. Wise, *Lifeline of the Confederacy: Blockade Running During the Civil War* (Columbia: University of South Carolina Press, 1988), 66–67.
21. Wise, *Lifeline of the Confederacy*, 71–72.
22. Silverstone, Civil War Navies, 80.
23. Goldsborough to Fox, 30 Jan 1862, Gustavus Vasa Fox, *Confidential Correspondence of Gustavus Vasa Fox, Assistant Secretary of the Navy, 1861–1865* (eds. Robert Means Thompson and Richard Wainwright; 2 vols.; New York: De Vinne Press, 1918), I:234–35.
24. Goldsborough to Welles, 29 Jan 1862, *ORN*, Ser. I, 6:536–37; Robert M. Browning Jr., *From Cape Charles to Cape Fear: The North Atlantic Blockading Squadron During the Civil War* (Tuscaloosa: University of Alabama Press, 1993), 22.
25. Goldsborough to Welles, 18 Feb 1862, *ORN*, Ser. I, 6:552.
26. Browning, *From Cape Charles to Cape Fear*, 23–24.
27. Goldsborough to Welles, 18 Feb 1862, *ORN*, Ser. I, 6:550–55.
28. Lynch to Mallory, 18 Feb 1862, Ibid., 594.
29. Ibid., 594–95.
30. Lynch to Mallory, 18 Feb 1862, Ibid., 594–97.
31. Porter to Goldsborough, 10 Feb 1862, Ibid., 578–79.
32. Goldsborough to Welles, 18 Feb 1862, Ibid., 553–55; Lt. C. W. Flusser to Cdr. Rowan, 16 Feb 1862, Ibid., 564; Midshipman Benjamin Porter to Goldsborough, 10 Feb 1862, Ibid., 579; Browning, *From Cape Charles to Cape Fear*, 26–27.
33. Lynch to Mallory, 18 Feb 1862, *ORN*, Ser. I, 6:596; Rowan to Goldsborough, 11 Feb 1862, Ibid., 600–603; Rowan to Goldsborough, 26 Mar 1862, *ORN*, I, 7:110–12; *Civil War Naval Chronology*, VI:197.
34. Cdr. Samuel Lockwood to Goldsborough, 27 Apr 1862, *ORN*, I, 7:278–79.
35. Wise, *Lifeline of the Confederacy*, 221.
36. David G. Surdam, *Northern Naval Superiority and the Economics of the American Civil War* (Columbia: University of South Carolina Press, 2001), 93.
37. Wise, *Lifeline of the Confederacy*, 50–51.
38. Still, *The Confederate Navy*, 58–61; Jim McNeil, *Masters of the Shoals: Tales of the Cape Fear Pilots Who Ran the Union Blockade* (Cambridge, MA: Da Capo Press, 2003), 47–48.
39. Browning, *Success Is All That Was Expected*, 320–21.
40. Wise, *Lifeline of the Confederacy*, 138–39. Wise has the incorrect date for its capture. Also, Roswell H. Lamson, *Lamson of the Grettysburg: The Civil War Letters of Lieutenant Roswell H. Lamson, U.S. Navy* (eds. James M. McPherson and Patricia R. McPherson; New York: Oxford University Press, 1997), 145–46, 194.
41. Calore, *Naval Campaigns of the Civil War*, 69.
42. Wise, *Lifeline of the Confederacy*, 144–47.
43. McNeil, *Masters of the Shoals*, 46; Lamson, *Lamson of the Gettysburg*, 23.
44. Wise, *Lifeline of the Confederacy*, 110.

45. Ibid., 115.
46. Roberts, *Now for the Contest*, 103.
47. *Annual Report of the Secretary of the Navy* for 1865 in Silverstone, *Civil War Navies*, x.
48. The table is a compilation of various appendices in books by Stephen Wise and Marcus Price in Surdam, *Northern Naval Superiority*, 5.
49. Wise, *Lifeline of the Confederacy*, 226.
50. The blockade's detractors include historians Richard Beringer, Frank Owsley, Raimondo Luraghi, and Stephen Wise. Defenders include Edwin Coddington, Bern Anderson, Stanley Lebergott, David G. Surdam, and Robert M. Browning Jr.
51. Quoted in Surdam, *Northern Naval Superiority*, 3.
52. Surdam, *Northern Naval Superiority*, 5–7, 206–7.

Chapter 5

1. Welles to Rodgers, 16 May 1861, *ORN*, Ser. I, 22:280.
2. Paullin, *Paullin's History of Naval Administration*, 283.
3. Eads to Welles, 29 Apr 1861, *ORN*, Ser. I, 22:278–79; Welles to Cameron and Cameron to McClellan, both 14 May 1861, Ibid., 277, 279; John D. Milligan, *Gunboats Down the Mississippi* (Annapolis, MD: Naval Institute Press, 1965), 3–4.
4. Robert E. Johnson, *Rear Admiral John Rodgers, 1812–1882* (Annapolis, MD: Naval Institute Press, 1967), 156–57; Jay Slagle, *Ironclad Captain: Seth Ledyard Phelps and the U.S. Navy, 1841–1864* (Kent, OH: Kent State University Press, 1996), 113.
5. Phelps to Rodgers, 16 Aug 1861, *ORN*, Ser. I, 23:299.
6. *ORN*, Ser. I, 3:390; Johnson, *Rodgers*, 165–66; Niven, *Welles*, 378; Milligan, *Gunboats Down the Mississippi*, 19.
7. The standard biography of Foote is Tucker, *Andrew Foote*.
8. Ibid., 116–19; Foote to Fox, 5; Mar 1862, Gustavus Fox, *Confidential Correspondence of Gustavus Vasa Fox, Assistant Secretary of the Navy, 1861–1865* (ed. by Robert Means Thompson and Richard Wainwright; 2 vols.; New York: De Vinne Press, 1918), II:39.
9. Edwin C. Bearss, *Hardluck Ironclad: The Sinking and Salvage of the Cairo* (Baton Rouge: Louisiana State University Press, 1966), 27; Porter, *Naval History of the Civil War*, 134–35; Milligan, *Gunboats Down the Mississippi*, 20, 28; Frémont to Foote, 16 Sep 1861, *ORN*, Ser. I, 22:335.
10. Ibid., 22–23.
11. Slagle, *Ironclad Captain*, 124–25; Tucker, *Foote*, 121; William S. McFeely, *Grant, A Biography* (New York: W. W. Norton, 1981), 92.
12. On naval aspects of the battle, see *ORN*, Ser. I, 22:402–28; the definitive account of the battle is Nathaniel Cheairs Hughes Jr., *The Battle of Belmont: Grant Strikes South* (Chapel Hill: University of North Carolina Press, 1991); Ulysses S. Grant, *Memoirs and Selected Letters* (New York: Library of America, 1990), 178–86.
13. Stephen E. Ambrose, "The Union Command System and the Donelson Campaign," *Military Affairs* (Summer 1960), 78–86.
14. Dave Page, *Ships Versus Shore: Civil War Engagements Along Southern Shores and Rivers* (Nashville, TN: Rutledge Hill Press, 1994), 253; Rowena Reed, *Combined Operations in the Civil War* (Annapolis, MD: Naval Institute Press, 1978), 65.

NOTES TO PAGES 120–35 | 375

15. T. Harry Williams, *P. G. T. Beauregard, Napoleon in Gray* (Baton Rouge: Louisiana State University Press, 1995), 116.
16. Milligan, *Gunboats Down the Mississippi*, 32; Henry Walke, "The Gun-boats at Belmont and Fort Henry," *Battles and Leaders of the Civil War* (4 vols.; edited by Robert U. Johnson and Clarence C. Buel; Secaucus, NJ: Castle; reprint of 1883 edition), I:367.
17. Phelps to Foote, 18 Jan 1862, *ORN*, Ser. I, 22:507–8; Tucker, *Foote*, 131–32.
18. Tucker, *Foote*, 132–35.
19. Jesse Taylor, "The Defense of Fort Henry," *Battles and Leaders of the Civil War*, I:370.
20. Slagle, *Ironclad Captain*, 156–62; Taylor, "The Defense of Fort Henry," 369–72; Tucker, *Foote*, 137–45; Spencer C. Tucker, *Unconditional Surrender: The Capture of Forts Henry and Donelson* (Abilene, TX: McWhiney Foundation Press, 2001), 47–60.
21. Foote to Welles, 6 Feb 1862, *ORN*, Ser. I, 22:537.
22. Foote to his wife, 6 Feb 1862, in Slagle, *Ironclad Captain*, 176.
23. Phelps to Foote, 10 Feb 1862, *ORN*, Ser. I, 22:571–74; Slagle, *Ironclad Captain*, 162–73; Silverstone, *Warships of the Civil War Navies*, 156.
24. Tucker, *Foote*, 146–47; Williams, *Beauregard*, 118–19.
25. Foote to Welles, 11 Feb 1862, *ORN*, Ser. I, 22:550.
26. Phelps, *Ironclad Captain*, 176–77; Porter, *The Naval History of the Civil War*, 150.
27. Henry Walke, "The Western Flotilla at Fort Donelson, Island Number Ten, Fort Pillow, and Memphis," *Battles and Leaders of the Civil War*, I:431–32; Grant, *Memoirs*, 201.
28. Tucker, *Foote*, 155–57; Tucker, *Unconditional Surrender*, 61–104.
29. Walke, "The Western Flotilla," 433.
30. Ibid., 434–45; Slagle, *Ironclad Captain*, 179–80.
31. Walke, "The Western Flotilla," 433–34; Foote to Welles, 15 and 17 Feb 1862, *ORN*, Ser. I, 22:585–87.
32. Foote to Welles, 15, 16 Feb 1862, *ORN*, Ser. I, 22:584–86; Walke to Foote, 15 Feb 1862, Ibid., 590–91; Thompson to Foote, 17 Feb 1862, Ibid., 592; Walke, "The Western Flotilla," note, 436.
33. Porter, *The Naval History of the Civil War*, 162.
34. Tucker, *Unconditional Surrender*, 87–104.
35. Ibid., 105–7.
36. Gwin to Foote, 1, 5 Mar 1862, *ORN*, Ser. I, 22:643–47.
37. Charles P. Roland, *Albert Sidney Johnston: Soldier of Three Republics* (Austin: University of Texas Press, 1964), 342.
38. Gwin to Foote, 8 Apr 1862, *ORN*, Ser. I, 22:763.
39. Larry J. Daniel and Lynn N. Bock, *Island No. 10: Struggle for the Mississippi Valley* (Tuscaloosa: The University of Alabama Press, 1996), 35; Walke, "The Western Flotilla," 445.
40. Daniel and Bock, *Island No. 10*, 94–95.
41. Foote to Chief of Bureau of Ordnance Henry A. Wise, 7 and 13 Mar 1862, *ORN*, Ser. I, 22:659–60, 665.
42. A. H. Kelty, etc. to Foote, 9 Feb 1862, Foote Papers, Library of Congress; Foote to Welles, 17 Mar 1862, *ORN*, Ser. I, 22:693; A. M. Pennock to Wise, 20 Feb 1862, Ibid., 620–21.

43. Du Pont to his wife, 12 Apr 1862, *Samuel F. Du Pont, Samuel F. Du Pont: A Selection from His Civil War Letters* (3 vols.; Ithaca, NY: Cornell University Press, 1969), I:423.

44. Foote to Welles, 17 Mar 1862, *ORN*, Ser. I, 22:693–94; Daniel and Bock, *Island No. 10*, 98–99, 101.

45. Daniel and Bock, *Island No. 10*, 86–87; Halleck to Pope, 24 Mar 1862, *ORN*, Ser. I, 22:698.

46. Daniel and Bock, *Island No. 10*, 104–8; 115–16.

47. Foote to Welles, 2 Apr 1862, *ORN*, Ser. I, 22:706–7; Foote to Welles, 4 Apr 1862, Ibid., 709; Walke to Foote, 4 Apr 1862, Ibid., 710; For a vivid description of the *Carondelet*'s run to New Madrid, see Charles B. Boynton, *History of the Navy During the Rebellion* (2 vols.; New York: D. Appleton, 1867–68), I:549–53.

48. Foote to Welles, 7 and 8 Apr 1862, *ORN*, Ser. I, 22:720–21; Slagle, *Ironclad Captain*, 209; Daniel and Bock, *Island No. 10*, 133–36.

49. Daniel and Bock, *Island No. 10*, 144–45; John D. Milligan, comp., *From the Fresh-Water Navy, 1861–64: The Letters of Acting Master's Mate Henry R. Browne and Acting Ensign Symmes E. Browne* (Annapolis, MD: Naval Institute Press, 1970), 57–60.

50. Foote to Welles, 12 and 19 Apr 1862, *ORN*, Ser. I, 23:3–4, 9.

51. Slagle, *Ironclad Captain*, 211.

52. Foote to Welles, 19 and 23 Apr 1862, *ORN*, Ser. I, 23:8–11.

53. Quoted in Bearss, *Hardluck Ironclad*, 53.

54. Foote to Welles, 29 Apr 1862, Huntington Library; Slagle, *Ironclad Captain*, 216; Bearss, *Hardluck Ironclad*, 55–56. For discussion of Foote's health and his departure from the flotilla, see Tucker, *Foote*, 195–96.

55. Davis to Welles, 11 and 12 May (2) 1962, *ORN*, Ser. I, 23:14, 16–17; Montgomery to Beauregard, 12 May 1862, Ibid., 55–57; Walke, "The Western Flotilla," 447–49; Ivan Musicant, *Divided Waters: The Naval History of the Civil War* (New York: HarperCollins, 1995), 212–15; Milligan, *Gunboats Down the Mississippi*, 64–67; Acting Ensign Browne of the *Mound City* to his fiancée, 12 May 1862, in Milligan, *From the Fresh-Water Navy*, 74–77; Julius Henri Browne, *Four Years in Secessia* (Hartford, CT: O. D. Case, 1865; Reprint. Arno Press, 1970); 169–78; Slagle, *Ironclad Captain*, 219–25.

56. Slagle, *Ironclad Captain*, 225, 230, 232.

57. H. Walke to C. Davis, 6 Jun 1862, *ORN*, Ser. I, 23:122–23; C. Ellet to E. M. Stanton, Ibid., 25–26; Slagle, *Ironclad Captain*, 233–40.

58. Davis to Welles, 6 Jun 1862, *ORN*, Ser. I, 23:119–21; Ellet to Stanton, 11 Jun 1862, Ibid., 132–34; Phelps to Foote, 9 Jun 1862, Ibid., 135–36; Browne, *Four Years in Secessia*, 179–91; Musicant, *Divided Waters*, 215–16; Milligan, *Gunboats Down the Mississippi*, 68–77.

59. Davis to Welles, 15 and 16 Jun 1862, *ORN*, Ser. I, 23:164–65; Lt. W. McGunnegle to Davis, 18 Jun 1862, Ibid., 165–67; Davis to Welles, 19 Jun 1862, Ibid., 171–72; Fitch to Brig. Gen. Quinby, Ibid., 173–74.

CHAPTER 6

1. On the resulting Peninsula Campaign, see Stephen W. Sears, *To the Gates of Richmond: The Peninsula Campaign* (New York: Ticknor & Fields, 1992).

2. Ibid., 11.

3. For much useful information on the *Merrimack* and its conversion into the *Virginia*, see John V. Quarstein, *C.S.S. Virginia: Mistress of Hampton Roads* (Appomattox, VA: H. E. Howard, 2000), 1–51.

4. Mallory to Buchanan, 24 Feb 1862, *ORN*, Ser. I, 6:776–77; George M. Brooke Jr., *John M. Brooke: Naval Scientist and Educator* (Charlottesville: University Press of Virginia, 1980), 248–51; William N. Still Jr., *Iron Afloat: The Story of the Confederate Armorclads* (Columbia: University of South Carolina Press, 1985), 19–25.

5. John Mercer Brooke, "The *Virginia* or *Merrimac*: Her Real Projector," *Southern Historical Society Papers*, 19 (January 1891), 31.

6. Brooke, *John M. Brooke*, 250.

7. The standard biography of Buchanan is Craig L. Symonds, *Confederate Admiral: The Life and Wars of Franklin Buchanan* (Annapolis, MD: Naval Institute Press, 1999).

8. Mallory to Buchanan, 2 Mar 1862, *ORN*, Ser. I, 6:779.

9. George M. Brooke Jr., ed. *Ironclads and Big Guns of the Confederacy: The Journal and Letters of John M. Brooke* (Columbia: University of South Carolina Press, 2002), 59.

10. William C. Davis, *Duel Between the First Ironclads* (New York: Doubleday, 1975), 34–35.

11. Mallory to Buchanan, 24 Feb and 7 Mar 1862, *ORN*, Ser. I, 6:777, 780; Buchanan to Mallory, 19 Mar 1862, Buchanan Letterbook, quoted in Davis, *Duel*, 107.

12. Sears, *To the Gates of Richmond*, 12–14.

13. Still, *Iron Afloat*, 24.

14. Quoted in Quarstein, *C.S.S. Virginia*, 74.

15. Ibid., 76.

16. Buchanan to Mallory, 27 Mar 1862, *ORN*, Ser. I, 7:44; Quarstein, *C.S.S. Virginia*, 74–82.

17. John Taylor Wood, "The First Fight of Iron-Clads," *Battles and Leaders of the Civil War*, I:698, 707.

18. On the 8 March 1862 battle, see Buchanan to Mallory, 27 Mar 1862, *ORN*, Ser. I, 7:44–46; Wood, "The First Fight of Iron-Clads," 696–700; Quarstein, *C.S.S. Virginia*, 72–90; and Davis, *Duel*, 78–104.

19. On the *Monitor*'s design and construction, see John Ericsson, "The Building of the 'Monitor,'" *Battles and Leaders of the Civil War*, I:720–44; David A. Mindell, *War, Technology, and Experience Aboard the USS* Monitor (Baltimore, MD: The Johns Hopkins University Press, 2000), 38–50; James Tertius deKay, *Monitor* (New York: Walker and Co., 1997), 7–15; and Davis, *Duel*, 42–53.

20. Mindell, *War*, 31.

21. On the passage south, see Mindell, *War*, 66–69; Davis, *Duel*, 2–3, 58–66, 111; deKay, *Monitor*, 138–49. Welles to Paulding, 6 Mar 1862, *ORN*, Ser. I, 6:682. The excerpt of Keeler's letter is in William Marvel, ed., *The Monitor Chronicles* (New York: Simon & Schuster for the Mariner's Museum, 2000), 25.

22. Wood, "The First Fight of Iron-Clads," 702.

23. Ibid.

24. For official accounts, see Greene to Welles, 12 Mar 1862, *ORN*, Ser. I, 7:25; Buchanan to Mallory, 27 Mar 1862, Ibid., 43–49. An excellent account of conditions in the

Monitor's turret is S. Dana Greene, "In the 'Monitor' Turret," *Battles and Leaders of the Civil War*, I:719–29. General accounts of the battle are in Davis, Duel, 116–37; deKay, *Monitor*, 180–98; and Quarstein, *C.S.S.* Virginia, 102–22.

25. *ORN*, Ser. I, 7:39.
26. Naval History Division, *Civil War Naval Chronology*, II:31; Wood, "The First Fight of the Iron-Clads," 692.
27. McClellan to Goldsborough, 3 and 5 Apr 1862, *ORN*, Ser. I, 7:195–96, 205.
28. Tattnall to Mallory, 12 Apr 1862, *ORN*, Ser. I, 7:223–24.
29. Smith to Goldsborough, 12 May 1862, *ORN*, Ser. I, 7:315–16; Lincoln to Goldsborough, 7 May 1862, Ibid., 326; Rodgers to Goldsborough, 11 May 1862, Ibid., 329; Goldsborough to Lincoln, 9 May, Ibid., 330–31; Goldsborough to Welles, 9 May, Ibid., 331–32.
30. Tattnall to Mallory, 14 May 1862, *ORN*, Ser. I, 7:335–38.
31. Rodgers to Goldsborough, 16 May 1862, *ORN*, Ser. I, 7: 357–58; an excellent summary of the battle is in John M. Coski, *Capital Navy: The Men, Ships and Operations of the James River Squadron* (Campbell, CA: Savas Publishing Co., 1996), 41–52.
32. William Frederick Keeler, *Aboard the U.S.S.* Monitor*: 1862* (edited by Robert W. Daily; Annapolis, MD: Naval Institute Press, 1964), 126–27, 130.
33. McClellan to Goldsborough, 1 Jul 1862, *ORN*, Ser. I, 7:532.
34. Ibid., 532–33; Rodgers to Goldsborough, 1 Jul 1862, Ibid., 533–34.
35. Browning, *From Cape Charles to Cape Fear*, 58.
36. Goldsborough to Welles, 15 Jul 1862, *ORN*, Ser. I, 7:573–74; Welles to Goldsborough, 21 Jul 1862, Ibid., 574.
37. See the account by Seaman George Geer, *The* Monitor *Chronicles*, 235–36.

CHAPTER 7
1. Cdr. Melancthon Smith to McKean, 20 Sep 1861, *ORN*, Ser. I, 16:677–78; Phelps to McKean, 3 Dec 1861, Ibid., 805–6.
2. Pope to McKean, 9 Oct 1861, Ibid., 699–700.
3. Still, *Iron Afloat*, 46–48.
4. Pope to McKean, 13 Oct 1861, *ORN*, Ser. I, 16:703–4.
5. Handy to McKean, 14 Oct 1861, Ibid., 709; Porter, *Naval History of the Civil War*, 91.
6. McKean to Welles, 25 Nov 1861, *ORN*, Ser. I, 16:775–77; Bragg to Adjutant General, 4 Dec 1861, Ibid., 784–85.
7. Porter, *Naval History of the Civil War*, 453–60.
8. James P. Duffy, *Lincoln's Admiral: The Civil War Campaigns of David Farragut* (New York: John Wiley & Sons, 1997), 50–60; Welles to Farragut, 10 Feb 1862, *ORN*, Ser. I, 18:14–15.
9. On Farragut, see Duffy, *Lincoln's Admiral*; and Robert J. Schneller Jr., *Farragut: America's First Admiral* (Washington, DC: Brassey's, 2002).
10. J. P. Benjamin to Lovell, 19 Jan 1862, *ORN*, Ser. I, 17:160–61.
11. Porter, *Naval History of the Civil War*, 178.
12. Bradley S. Osbon and Albert Bigelow Paine, *A Soldier of Fortune: Personal Memoirs of Captain B. S. Osbon* (New York: McClure, Phillips & Co., 1906), 185.

13. Instructions of Cdr. H. H. Bell, 20 Apr 1862, *ORN*, Ser. I, 18:138; Farragut general order, 20 Apr 1862, Ibid., 162–63; Farragut to Welles, 6 May 1862, Ibid., 156.
14. Farragut to Welles, 6 May 1862, Ibid., 155–56; Duffy, *Lincoln's Admiral*, 80.
15. Osbon and Paine, *A Soldier of Fortune*, 188.
16. Porter, *Naval History of the Civil War*, 181, 221.
17. Diary of Lieutenant Roe, *ORN*, Ser. I, 18:769.
18. George Dewey, *Autobiography of George Dewey: Admiral of the Navy* (New York: Scribner, 1913), 63–64.
19. Ibid., 64–65.
20. Osbon and Paine, *A Soldier of Fortune*, 192.
21. Report of Lieutenant Warley, 13 Aug 1862, *ORN*, Ser. I, 18:336–43.
22. *ORN*, Ser. I, 18:306.
23. Dewey, *Autobiography*, 68–69.
24. *ORN*, Ser. I, 18:344.
25. Farragut to Porter, 24 Apr 1862, *ORN*, Ser. I, 18: 142; Farragut to Welles, 25 Apr and 6 May 1862, Ibid., 152–53, 155–59. See also Porter, *Naval History of the Civil War*, 175–245.
26. Porter, *Naval History of the Civil War*, 185–87.
27. Farragut to Craven, 3 and 11 May 1862, *ORN*, Ser. I, 18:465, 485.
28. Palmer to Farragut, 9 May 1862 with correspondence to the mayor of Baton Rouge, Ibid., 473–75.
29. Palmer to Farragut, 13 May 1862, Ibid., 489–90; Farragut to Butler, 22 May 1862, Ibid., 507; Farragut to Fox, 30 May, Ibid., 519–20.
30. Farragut to Welles, 2 Jul 1862, Ibid., 608–11.
31. Farragut to Halleck, 28 Jun 1862, Ibid., 590; Halleck to Farragut, 3 Jun 1862, Ibid., 593.
32. Farragut to Welles, 4 Jul 1862, Ibid., 624.
33. Davis to Welles, 16 Jul 1862, *ORN*, Ser. I, 19:6–7; W. D. Porter to Welles, Farragut to Davis, 15 Jul 1862, Ibid., 7–8; 1 Aug 1862, Ibid., 60.
34. Ellet to Edwin M. Stanton, 23 Jul 1862, Ibid., 46–47; Davis to Welles, 23 Jul 1862, Ibid., 48–49; W. D. Porter to Davis, 22 Jul 1862, Ibid., 50.
35. W. D. Porter to Welles, 1 Aug 1862, Ibid., 60–62.
36. Porter to Welles, 2 April 1863, *ORN*, Ser. I, 24:522–24. On the Marine Brigade, see Chester G. Hearn, *Ellet's Brigade: The Strangest Outfit of All* (Baton Rouge: Louisiana State University Press, 2000).

Chapter 8

1. Michael B. Ballard, *Vicksburg: The Campaign That Opened the Mississippi* (Chapel Hill: University of North Carolina Press, 2004), 24.
2. Maj. Gen. Sherman to Porter, 8 Dec 1862, *ORN*, Ser. I, 23:539–40; Porter, *Naval History of the Civil War*, 284.
3. Porter to Welles, 17 Dec 1862, *ORN*, Ser. I, 23:544–46; Selfridge to Walke, 13 Dec 1862, Ibid., 548–50; Bearss, *Hardluck Ironclad*, 97–101. Efforts to locate the wreck paid off in 1956, and in the early 1960s the remains of the *Cairo*, still largely intact, were raised and removed to the National Battlefield Park at Vicksburg, where they are now displayed. The adjacent *Cairo* Museum houses artifacts recovered from the wreck.

4. Grant, *Memoirs*, 288–90.
5. William Tecumseh Sherman, *Memoirs of William T. Sherman* (New York: Library of America, 1990), 308–17.
6. Porter to Welles, 11 and 13 Jan 1863, *ORN*, Ser. I, 24:107–9; 118–19; Sherman, *Memoirs*, 320–25; Churchill to Lt. Gen. T. H. Holmes, 6 May 1863, Ibid., 128–30; Thomas L. Snead, "The Conquest of Arkansas," *Battles and Leaders of the Civil War*, III: 452–53; Porter, *Naval History of the Civil War*, 289–94.
7. Ulysses S. Grant, *Memoirs and Selected Letters* (New York: Library of America, 1990), 393–94.
8. Porter to Ellet, 1 Feb 1863, *ORN*, Ser. I, 24:218–19; Ellet to Porter, 2 Feb 1863, Ibid., 219–21.
9. Porter to Welles, 5 Feb and 20 Apr 1863, Ibid., 222–23, 572; Ellet to Porter, 5 Feb 1863, Ibid., 223–24; Porter to Ellet, 8 Feb 1863, Ibid., 374; Porter to Brown, 12 Feb 1863, Ibid., 376–77; Brown to Porter, 18 Feb 1863, Ibid., 377–79; Brown to Welles, 28 May 1863, Ibid., 379–81; Brand to Pemberton, 25 Feb 1863, *ORN*, Ser. I, 24:402; Brand to Maj. Gen. Gardner, 26 Feb 1863, Ibid., 408–9; Wirt Adams to Maj. J. J. Reeve, Ibid., 411; *Civil War Naval Chronology*, III, 34.
10. Farragut to Welles, 16 Mar 1863, *ORN*, Ser. I, 19: 665–68; numerous attachments from subordinate commanders, Ibid., 668–95; Farragut to Welles, 19 Mar 1863, Ibid., Ser. I, 20:3.
11. Farragut to Porter, 22 Mar and 27 Mar 1863, *ORN*, Ser. I, 20:12, 33–34; Brig. Gen. Ellet to Walke, 24 Mar 1863, Ibid., 16; Gen. Ellet to Col. Ellet, 24 Mar 1863, Ibid., 17; Col. Ellet to Gen. Ellet, 25 Mar 1863; Ibid., 19–20; Gen. Ellet to Porter, 1 Apr 1863, Ibid., 32.
12. Grant, *Memoirs*, 297–98.
13. Ibid., 298–99.
14. Smith to Porter, 2 Nov 1863, *ORN*, Ser. I, 24:243–49.
15. Porter to Welles, Ibid., 474–78; Grant, *Memoirs*, 299–302; Sherman, *Memoirs*, 329–35.
16. Porter to Welles, 19 Apr 1863, *ORN*, Ser. I, 24:553–54; General Order by Porter of 10 Apr 1863, Ibid., 554–55.
17. Porter to Welles, 29 Apr 1863, Ibid., 610–12; Grant, *Memoirs*, 321.
18. Breeze to Porter, 2 May 1863, Ibid., 589–91.
19. Grant, *Memoirs*, 321.
20. Porter to Welles, 7 and 13 May 1863, Ibid., 645–46.
21. Grant, *Memoirs*, 321–56.
22. Porter to Welles, 20 May, 24 May, 14 Jun, 22 Jul 1863, *ORN*, Ser. I, 25:5–8, 284.
23. Bache to Porter, 27 May 1863, *ORN*, Ser. I, 25:38–39.
24. Grant, *Memoirs*, 357–86.
25. David Herbert Donald, *Lincoln* (London: Jonathan Cape, 1995), 457.

CHAPTER 9

1. The best study of the campaign, although its focus is largely on the land actions, is Stephen R. Wise, *Gate of Hell: Campaign for Charleston Harbor, 1863* (Columbia: University of South Carolina Press, 1994).
2. On the admiral, see Kevin J. Weddle, *Lincoln's Tragic Admiral: The Life of Samuel Francis Du Pont* (Charlottesville: University of Virginia Press, 2005);

Samuel F. Du Pont, *Samuel F. Du Pont: A Selection from His Civil War Letters* (3 vols; Ithaca, NY: Cornell University Press, 1969); Henry A. Du Pont, *Rear Admiral Samuel Francis Du Pont, United States Navy: A Biography* (New York: National Americana Society, 1926).

3. Du Pont to Commo. Bailey, 30 Oct 1862, *ORN*, Ser. I, 13:423.

4. Welles to Du Pont, 6 Jan 1863, Ibid., 503.

5. Du Pont to John Rodgers, 6 Jan 1863, Rogers Collection, cited in Robert Erwin Johnson, *Rear Admiral John Rodgers, 1812–1882* (Annapolis, MD: Naval Institute Press, 1962), 238.

6. Du Pont to Fox, 22 December 1862, Gustavus Fox, *Confidential Correspondence of Gustavus Vasa Fox, Assistant Secretary of the Navy, 1861–1865* (eds. Robert Means Thompson and Richard Wainwright; 2 vols.; New York: De Vinne Press, 1918), I:172; Du Pont to Gustavus Fox, 2 Mar 1863, in Samuel F. Du Pont, *Samuel Francis Du Pont*, II:463.

7. Worden to Du Pont, 27 Jan and 2 Feb (2) 1863, *ORN*, Ser. I, 13:544–55, 626–29, 630–31; *Montauk* log extract, 27 Jan 1863, Ibid., 547. Du Pont to Benjamin Gerhard, 30 Jan 1863, Samuel F. Du Pont, *Samuel Francis Du Pont*, II:394.

8. Du Pont to Welles with enclosures, 3, 9, and 11 Feb 1863, *ORN*, Ser. I, 13:577–83, 601–2; 604–7; Capt. Wiilliam Rodgers Taylor to Du Pont, 31 Jan 1863, Ibid., 587–88; Rear Adm. W. B. Shurbrick to Welles, 12 Mar 1863, Ibid., 614; Beauregard to Gen. S. Cooper, 31 Jan 1863, Ibid., 616; Beauregard to Capt. D. N. Ingraham, 31 Jan 1762, Ibid.

9. Du Pont to Worden, 27 Feb 1863, *ORN*, Ser. I, 13:694; Worden to Du Pont, 28 Feb and 3 March 1863 with enclosures, Ibid., 697–98; 700–704.

10. Du Pont to Welles, 6 Mar 1863 with enclosures, *ORN*, Ser. I, 13:716–20; Johnson, *Rear Admiral John Rodgers*, 238.

11. Johnson, *Rear Admiral John Rodgers*, 239.

12. Rodgers to Du Pont, 29 Oct 1862, *ORN*, Ser. I, 13:421–22; Johnson, *Rear Admiral John Rodgers*, 240–41.

13. Du Pont to Welles, 15 Apr 1863, *ORN*, Ser. I, 14:5–9.

14. Quoted in Weedle, *Lincoln's Tragic Admiral*, 188.

15. Du Pont to Welles, 15 Apr 1863, *ORN*, Ser. I, 14:5–9; Rodgers to Du Pont, 8 and 20 Apr 1863, Ibid., 11–13; 43–45; Johnson, *Rear Admiral John Rodgers*, 244–45.

16. Report of Admiral Du Pont, 8 Apr 1863, *ORN*, Ser. I, 14:3; Du Pont to Major General Hunter, 9 Apr 1863, Ibid., 438; Du Poont to Sophie Du Pont, in Du Pont, *Civil War Letters*, 3:3–5.

17. Du Pont to Welles, 6 Jun 1863, *ORN*, Ser. I, 14:242–43.

18. Du Pont to Welles, 27 May 1863, Ibid., 65–73; Welles to Du Pont, 3 Jun 1863, Ibid., 230.

19. Dahlgren to Welles, 1 and 11 Oct 1862, *ORN*, Ser. I, 13:353–54, 377–78; Welles to Dahlgren, 14 Oct, 1862, Ibid., 389–91; Welles, *Diary*, I:317. Du Pont related in October 1862 that Foote and Wise had approached him about giving up his command to Dahlgren, which Du Pont rejected immediately, as well as the suggestion that Dahlgren become his ordnance officer, replacing Rodgers. Du Pont said he would give him command of an ironclad and that was all. Du Pont told Fox that "Dahlgren is a diseased man on the subject of preferment and position. As I told

Foote, he chose one line in the walks of his profession while Foote and I chose another; he was licking cream while we were eating dirt and living on the *pay* of our *rank.* Now he wants all the honors belonging to the other but without having encountered its joltings—it is a disease and nothing else." Du Pont to Fox, 8 Oct 1862, *Du Pont Letters,* II:243.

20. Tucker, *Andrew Foote;* Robert J. Schneller Jr., *A Quest for Glory: A Biography of Rear Admiral John A. Dahlgren* (Annapolis, MD: Naval Institute Press, 1996), 233–34.
21. Rodgers to Du Pont, 17 Jun 1863, *ORN,* Ser. I, 14:265–66; Ibid., 267–85; Johnson, *Rear Admiral John Rodgers,* 252–56.
22. Dahlgren to Parker, 12 Jul 1863, *ORN,* Ser. I, 14:337.
23. Extract from Dahlgren diary, 10 Jul 1863, Ibid., 325–26; Dahlgren to Welles, 19 Jul 1863, Ibid., 359–60.
24. Dahlgren to Welles, 22 Aug and 2 Sep 1863, Ibid., 470; 531–33; Dahlgren to Gillmore, 24 Aug 1863, Ibid., 506–7; extract from Dahlgren diary, 22 Aug 1863, Ibid., 507–8.
25. Wise, *Gate of Hell,* 169–72.
26. Dahlgren to Welles, 8 Sep 1863, *ORN,* Ser. I, 14:549–50; Lt. Cdr. Edward Simpson to Dahlgren, 10 Sep 1863, Ibid., 556–57.
27. Dahlgren to Welles, 11 Sep 1862, Ibid., 610–11; Browning, *Success Is All That Was Expected,* 254–57.
28. Welles to Dahlgren, 9 Oct 1863, *ORN,* Ser. I, 15:26–27; Browning, *Success Is All That Was Expected,* 266–68.

CHAPTER 10
1. R. B. Bradford, *History of Torpedo Warfare* (Newport, RI: U.S. Torpedo Station, 1882), 3.
2. Nathan Miller, *Sea of Glory: The Continental Navy Fights for Independence, 1775–1783* (New York: David McKay, 1974), 164; Philip K. Lundeberg, *Samuel Colt's Submarine Battery: The Secret and the Enigma* (Washington, DC: Smithsonian Institution Press, 1974), 2–3; Gregory K. Hartman with Scott C. Truver, *Weapons that Wait: Mine Warfare in the U.S. Navy* (Annapolis, MD: Naval Institute Press, 1991), 17–19; Alex Roland, *Underwater Warfare in the Age of Sail* (Bloomington: Indiana University Press, 1978), 83.
3. Wallace S. Hutcheon Jr., *Robert Fulton: Pioneer of Undersea Warfare* (Annapolis, MD: Naval Institute Press, 1981), 62–92. The quote is on page 87.
4. Hartman and Truver, *Weapons that Wait,* 28–29; Roland, *Underwater Warfare in the Age of Sail,* 121.
5. Lundeberg, *Samuel Colt's Submarine Battery,* 3; Hartman and Truver, *Weapons that Wait,* 27–28; Roland, *Underwater Warfare in the Age of Sail,* 129–30.
6. Quoted in Roberts, *Now for the Contest,* 74.
7. Quoted in Ibid., 73.
8. Dahlgen to Welles, 16 Jan 1865, with enclosures, *ORN,* Ser. I, 16:171–80.
9. Fleet Capt. John S. Barnes to Acting Rear Adm. S. P. Lee, 10 May 1864, with enclosures, Ibid., Ser. I, 10:10–15.
10. J. Carlin to Beauregard, 22 Aug 1863, Ibid., Ser. I, 14: 498–99; Silverstone, *Civil War Navies,* 165.

11. Capt. S. C. Rowan to Dahlgren, 6 Oct 1863, *ORN*, Ser. I, 15:12–13; Dahlgren to Fox with enclosures, 7 Oct 1863, Ibid., 14–16; report of First Asst. Engineer J. H. Tomb CSN to Flag Officer J. R. Tucker CSN, 6 Oct 1863, Ibid., 20–21.

12. Dahlgren orders, 3 Dec 1863 and 7 Jan 1864, Ibid., 148, 226.

13. Bradford, *History of Torpedo Warfare*, 46–47; for a list of Union ships destroyed see Milton F. Perry, *Infernal Machines: The Story of Confederate Submarine and Mine Warfare* (Baton Rouge: Louisiana State University Press, 1965), 199–201.

14. John W. Grattan, *Under the Blue Pennant, or Notes of Naval Officer, 1863–1865* (edited by Robert J. Schneller; New York: John Wiley & Sons, 1999), 82.

15. Drew Middleton, *Submarine: The Ultimate Naval Weapon—Its Past, Present & Future* (Chicago: Playboy Press, 1976), 5.

16. Roland, *Underwater Warfare in the Age of Sail*, 69–82; Miller, *Sea of Glory*, 159–64.

17. Hutcheson, *Robert Fulton*, 31–53.

18. Roland, *Underwater Warfare in the Age of Sail*, 121.

19. Lambert, *Steam, Steel, and Shellfire*, 148–49.

20. Dahlgren to Welles, 19 Feb 1864, *ORN*, Ser. I, 15:329–30; also 332–38; Edwin P. Hoyt, *The Voyage of the Hunley* (Short Hills, NJ: Burford Books, 2002); Mark K. Ragan, *Union and Confederate Submarine Warfare in the Civil War* (Mason City, IA: Savas Publishing, 1999), 113–203; Brian Hicks and Schuyler Kroph, *Raising the Hunley: The Remarkable History and Recovery of the Lost Confederate Submarine* (New York: Ballantine Books, 2002).

21. *Civil War Naval Chronology*, VI:296.

22. Ragan, *Union and Submarine Warfare in the Civil War*, 64–73, 97–105, 132–33; *Naval History* (Jun 2005), 66–67.

23. Order of Rear Admiral Dahlgren, 19 Feb 1864, *ORN*, Ser. I, 15:330–31.

24. *Civil War Naval Chronology*, VI:243–44; Roberts, *Now for the Contest*, 134; and unpublished book manuscript by Joseph M. Thatcher.

Chapter 11

1. Robinson, *Confederate Privateers*, 342.

2. James D. Bulloch, *The Secret Service of the Confederate States in Europe, or How the Confederate Cruisers Were Equipped* (New York: Modern Library, 2001), 34.

3. *Civil War Naval Chronology*, I:13.

4. Ibid., 203; Porter, *Naval History of the Civil War*, 602.

5. Spencer C. Tucker, *Raphael Semmes and the* Alabama (Fort Worth, TX: Ryan Place, 1996), 18–22. Also see John M. Taylor, *Semmes: Rebel Raider* (Dulles, VA: Potomac Books, 2004).

6. Welles to Semmes, 18 Apr 1861, *ORN*, Ser. I, 1:613; Silverstone, *Warships of the Civil War Navies*, 214; Raphael Semmes, *Memoirs of Service Afloat, During the War Between the States* (Baltimore, MD: Kelly, Piet & Co., 1869; reprint Secaucus, NJ: The Blue & Grey Press, 1987), 96.

7. Porter, *Naval History of the Civil War*, 605–6.

8. Ibid; Semmes, *Memoirs*, 109–19.

9. Semmes journal, *ORN*, Ser. I, 1:695; Porter, *Naval History of the Civil War*, 606.

10. On the cruise, see Semmes, *Memoirs*, 108–345; Porter, *Naval History of the Civil War*, 606–20. *John M. Kell, Recollections of a Naval Life* (Washington, DC: Neale, 1900), 176.

11. Semmes, *Memoirs*, 344–53.
12. Stern, *The Confederate Navy*, 36.
13. Bulloch, *The Secret Service*, 76–86; Browning, *Success Is All That Was Expected*, 74; Philip Van Doren Stern, *The Confederate Navy: A Pictorial History* (Garden City, NY: Doubleday, 1962), 37–38.
14. The standard work on the *Florida* is Frank L. Owsley Jr., *The C.S.S. Florida: Her Building and Operations* (Tuscaloosa: University of Alabama Press, 1987).
15. Bulloch, *The Secret Service*, 109–15. On Maffitt, see Royce Shingleton, *High Seas Confederate: The Life and Times of John Newland Maffitt* (Columbia: University of South Carolina Press, 1994).
16. Maffitt journal extract, *ORN*, Ser. I, 1:766–67.
17. Ibid.; Shingleton, *High Seas Confederate*, 50–53.
18. Shingleton, *High Seas Confederate*, 53.
19. Commo. R. R. Hitchcock to Rear Admiral Farragut, 16 Jan 1863, *ORN*, Ser. I, 2:27–28; Cdr. George F. Emmons to Farragut, 21 Jan, 12 Mar 1863, Ibid., 28–29, 30–31; Shingleton, *High Seas Confederate*, 54–60.
20. On Reed's exploits, see David W. Shaw, *Sea Wolf of the Confederacy: The Daring Civil War Raids of Naval Lt. Charles W. Read* (New York: Free Press, 2004), and Robert A. Jones, *Confederate Corsair: The Life of Lt. Charles W. "Savez" Read* (Mechanicsburg, PA: Stackpole Books, 2000).
21. Owlsey, *The C.S.S. Florida*, 102–37.
22. Ibid., 137–55.
23. George W. Dalzell, *The Flight from the Flag: The Continuing Effect of the Civil War Upon the American Carrying Trade* (Chapel Hill: University of North Carolina Press, 1940), 129–30; Robinson, *Shark of the Confederacy*, 20; Stern, *The Confederate Navy*, 117.
24. Stern, *The Confederate Navy*, 117; Dalzell, *Flight from the Flag*, 131–36.
25. Robinson, *Shark of the Confederacy*, 28; Arthur Sinclair, *Two Years on the Alabama* (Boston: Lee and Shepard, 1895), 11–12.
26. Dalzell, *Flight from the Flag*, 136–47; Robinson, *Shark of the Confederacy*, 33.
27. Semmes, *Memoirs*, 402–3, 419–20; Sinclair, *Two Years on the Alabama*, 3. Most sources differ on statistics; Silverstone and Dalzell have the *Alabama*'s displacement at 1,050 tons and dimensions as 220 feet in overall length (211 feet, 6 inches on the waterline); Silverstone, *Civil War Navies*, 207; Dalzell, *Flight from the Flag*, 129, 162.
28. Semmes, *Memoirs*, 423–24.
29. Dalzell, *Flight from the Flag*, 154; Owsley, *The C.S.S. Florida*, 102.
30. Semmes, *Memoirs*, 456–78.
31. Ibid., 479–519.
32. Ibid., 519–35.
33. Report of Lieutenant Commander Blake to Welles, 21 Jan 1863, *ORN*, Ser. I, 2:18–20; Semmes, *Memoirs*, 540–50; Porter, *Naval History of the Civil War*, 122.
34. Wilkes to Welles, 11 Dec 1863, *ORN*, Ser. I, 2:567–69; Welles to Wilkes, 15 Dec 1863, Ibid., 568–71; Robinson, *Shark of the Confederacy*, 97–98.
35. Ibid., 94.
36. Semmes, *Memoirs*, 627; Sinclair, *Two Years*, 124–25; Silverstone, *Civil War Navies*, 218.

37. Robinson, *Shark of the Confederacy*, 108–9, 111.
38. Lt. Cdr. D. McDougal to Welles, 9 Dec 1863, *ORN*, Ser. I: 2:560–61; Dalzell, *Flight from the Flag*, 154–56; Robinson, *Shark of the Confederacy*, 115, 120–21.
39. Semmes, Journal, 12 and 24 May 1864, *ORN*, Ser. I, 3:671; Semmes to Barron, 5 Jul 1864, Ibid., 664; Sinclair, *Two Years*, 243.
40. *ORN*, Ser. I, 3:677–81; Civil War Naval Chronology, VI, 192; Robinson, *Shark of the Confederacy*, 194.
41. Semmes to Barron, 14 Jun 1864, *ORN*, Ser. I, 3:651.
42. Dalzell, *Flight from the Flag*, 161.
43. Semmes to Barron, 21 Jun 1864, Ibid., 651.
44. Semmes journal, 15 Jun 1864, *ORN*, Ser. I, 3:677; Semmes to Barron, 21 Jun 1864, Ibid., 651; Semmes, *Memoirs*, pp 759–62; Dalzell, *Flight from the Flag*, 163; Bulloch, *Secret Service of the Confederate States*, 201.
45. Sinclair, *Two Years*, 263.
46. Winslow to Welles, 19 Jun and 30 Jul 1864, *ORN*, Ser. I, 3:59, 79–81; Sinclair, *Two Years*, 258–60; Semmes, *Memoirs*, 757. Also Tucker, *Raphael Semmes and the Alabama*, 80–89; William Marvel, *The Alabama & the Kearsarge: The Sailor's Civil War* (Chapel Hill: The University of North Carolina Press, 1996), 250–58.
47. Stern, *The Confederate Navy*, 194. On 7 November 1984, the French minesweeper *Circé* located the wreckage of the *Alabama* at a depth of slightly less than two hundred feet about six miles off the coast in what is now French territorial waters. Since 1978 the French Navy had been looking specifically for the wreck as a test for sonar operators. See Captain Max Guérout, "The Last Remains of a Legend; The Modern Discovery of the C.S.S. *Alabama*" in *Special Commemorative Naval Issue, CSS Alabama, 1864–1989*, IV, Frank J. Merli, ed. *Journal of Confederate History* (Brentwood, TN: Southern Heritage Press, 1989), 1–14. British preservationist groups want the wreck, if it is raised, to be displayed at Birkenhead where the ship was built and where the British Government has ordered number 4 dockyard preserved as a historical site specifically for that purpose. The U.S. government asserts ownership to the wreck, however, and in 1989 Congress passed the CSS *Alabama* Preservation Act. Cherbourg has also been designated an official Civil War historical site, the first outside the United States. The fight for the *Alabama* continues.
48. Dalzell, *Flight from the Flag*, 160; Bennett, *The Monitor and the Navy Under Steam*, 187.
49. Sinclair, *Two Years*, 281; Porter, *Naval History of the Civil War*, 653–54.
50. Sinclair, *Two Years*, 270; Semmes, *Memoirs*, 759; Dalzell, *Flight from the Flag*, 160; Bennett, *The Monitor and the Navy Under Steam*, 187; Stern, *The Confederate Navy*, 193.
51. Semmes, *Memoirs*, 789–92.
52. Winslow to Welles, 30 Jul 1864, *ORN*, Ser. I, 3:78; Porter, *Naval History of the Civil War*, 653; Bennett, *The Monitor and the Navy Under Steam*, 200–202.
53. Chester G. Hearn, *Gray Raiders of the Sea: How Eight Confederate Warships Destroyed the Union's High Seas Commerce* (Camden, ME: International Marine Publishing, 1992), 129–39.
54. Bulloch, *The Secret Service*, 400–407. There are a number of books on the *Shenandoah*. See James I, Waddell, *C.S.S. Shenandoah: The Memoirs of Lieutenant*

Commanding James I. Waddell (ed. James D. Horan; New York: Crown Publishers, 1960); William C. Whittle Jr., *The Voyage of the CSS* Shenandoah: *A Memorable Cruise* (intro and annotations by D. Alan Harrisa and Anne B. Harris; Tuscaloosa: The University of Albama Press, 2005); Murray Morgan, *Confederate Raider in the South Pacific: The Saga of the C.S.S.* Shenandoah, *1864–65* (Pullman: Washington State University Press, 1995).

55. Bulloch, *The Secret Service*, 407–29.
56. Dalzell, *Flight from the Flag*, 237–62; Bennett, *The* Monitor *and the Navy Under Steam*, 184.
57. Dalzell, *Flight from the Flag*, 231–36.

Chapter 12

1. Grant, *Memoirs*, 636–37.
2. Gary Dillard Joiner, *One Damn Blunder from Beginning to End: The Red River Campaign of 1864* (Wilmington, DE: Scholarly Resources, 2003), 15–18.
3. Grant, *Memoirs*, 484.
4. Joiner, *One Damn Blunder*, 9.
5. Sherman, *Memoirs*, 471; Joiner, *One Damn Blunder*, 37–38.
6. Joiner, *One Damn Blunder*, 38.
7. Ibid., 20–22.
8. Phelps to Porter, 16 March 1861, *ORN*, Ser. I, 26:30–31; Joiner, *One Damn Blunder*, 48–51.
9. Jay Slagle, *Ironclad Captain* 355–57; Joiner, *One Damn Blunder*, 52.
10. U.S. Congress, *Report of the Joint Committee on the Conduct of the War, 1863–1866: The Red River Expedition* (1865. Reprint. Millwood, NY: Krauss Reprint Co., 1977 [hereinafter cited as *JCCW*]), 28; Joiner, *One Damn Blunder*, 54–59.
11. Porter to Hon. S. H. Treat, 24 Mar 1864, *ORN*, Ser. I, 26:35; Joiner, *One Damn Blunder*, 59–62.
12. *JCCW*, 275; Porter to Sherman, 14 Apr 1864, *ORN*, Ser. I, 26:50; Hearn, *Ellet's Brigade*, 223; Joiner, *One Damn Blunder*, 63–68.
13. Richard B. Irwin, "The Red River Campaign" *Battles and Leaders of the Civil War*, Vol. IV:350; Thomas O. Selfridge, "The Navy in the Red River," Ibid., 362–63; Joiner, *One Damn Blunder*, 67–68.
14. Joiner, *One Damn Blunder*, 67–69.
15. Porter to Sherman, 14 Apr 1864, *ORN*, Ser. I, 26:51.
16. Joiner, *One Damn Blunder*, 75–79.
17. Irvin, "The Red River Campaign," 352–57; Joiner, *One Damn Blunder*, 81–120.
18. Selfridge, "The Navy in the Red River," 363–64.
19. Porter to Sherman, 16 Apr 1864, *ORN*, Ser. I, 26:60–62.
20. Porter to Welles, 17 Apr 1864, Ibid., 71.
21. Porter to Welles, 23 Apr 1864, Ibid., 68–69; Slagle, *Ironclad Captain*, 364–73.
22. *Philadelphia North American*, reprinted in the *Jeffersonian Democrat* (Ohio), 17 June 1864, quoted in Slagle, *Ironclad Captain*, 372.
23. Porter to Welles, 28 Apr 1864, *ORN*, Ser. I, 26:74–76; Phelps to Porter, 28 Apr 1864, Ibid., 82–83; J. S. Watson to Porter, 1 May 1864, Ibid., 83–84; John Pearce to Porter, 30 Apr 1864, Ibid., 85.

24. Porter to Welles, 23 Apr 1864, Ibid., 69.

25. Porter to Welles, 28 Apr 1864, Ibid., 92–95; Brig. Gen. T. K. Smith to Porter, 25 Apr 1864, Ibid., 90–91.

26. Porter to Welles, 16 May 1864, *ORN*, Ser. I, 26:130.

27. Ibid., *ORN*, Ser. I, 26:131.

28. Porter to Welles, 16 May 1864, Ibid., 130–32; Irwin, "The Red River Campaign," 258–60; Joiner, *One Damn Blunder*, 137–51, 159–68.

29. Irwin, "The Red River Campaign," 360.

30. Lord to Porter, 8 May 1864, *ORN*, Ser. I, 26:112–14; Selfridge, "The Navy in the Red River," 365.

31. Irwin, "The Red River Campaign," 360; Thomas O. Selfridge, "The Navy in the Red River," *Battles and Leaders of the Civil War*, Vol. 4:366.

32. Joiner, *One Damn Blunder*, 123–35.

33. U.S. Congress, *Report of the Joint Committee on the Conduct of the War, 1863–1866: The Red River Expedition* (1865. Reprint. Millwood, NY: Krauss Reprint Co., 1977).

34. Joiner, *One Damn Blunder*, xix.

CHAPTER 13

1. Renshaw to Farragut, 8 Oct 1862, *ORN*, Ser. I, 19:255–60. On the struggle for Galveston, see Donald S. Frazier, *Cottonclads! The Battle of Galveston and the Defense of the Texas Coast* (Abilene, TX: McWhiney Foundation Press, 1996).

2. Frazier, *Cottonclads!*, 60.

3. Gen. Magruder CSA to Gen. S. Cooper, 26 Feb 1863, *ORN*, Ser. I, 19:470–77; various other Union reports, Ibid., 447–64; Frazier, *Cottonclads!*, 64–88.

4. Frazier, *Cottonclads!*, 105–6.

5. Watkins to Captain E. P. Turner, 23 Jan 1863, *ORN*, Ser. I, 19:564–66.

6. Various reports, Ibid., 20:519–61; Frazier, *Cottonclads!*, 105–12.

7. Various reports, *ORN*, Ser. I, 20:658–700 passim.

8. Parker to Rear Adm. S. P. Lee, 9 Jan 1863, Ibid., 8:409–10.

9. Candby to Maj. Gen. Halleck, 18 Jun 1864, Ibid., 21:339; Jack Friend, *West Wind, Flood Tide: The Battle of Mobile Bay* (Annapolis, MD: Naval Institute Press, 2004), 37–39. On the battle of Mobile Bay, see also Chester G. Hearn, *Mobile Bay and the Mobile Campaign: The Last Great Battles of the Civil War* (Jefferson, NC: McFarland & Company, 1993).

10. J. Thomas Scharf, *History of the Confederate States Navy* (reprint; New York: Gramercy Books, 996), 552–53.

11. Ibid., 556.

12. Still, *Iron Afloat*, 187–94; Friend, *West Wind, Flood Tide*, 41–42.

13. Report of Col. Albert G. Myer, 7 Jul 1864, *ORN*, Ser. I, 21:361; Silverstone, *Civil War Navies*, 155–56, 165, 178.

14. Farragut to Welles, 7 and 28 Feb, 1 Mar 1864, *ORN*, Ser. I, 27:90, 97–98; Chester G. Hearn, *Mobile Bay and the Mobile Campaign: The Last Great Battles of the Civil War* (Jefferson, NC: McFarland & Company, 1993), 49.

15. Craig Symonds, *Confederate Admiral: The Life and Wars of Franklin Buchanan* (Annapolis, MD: Naval Institute Press, 1999), 204–7.

16. Friend, *West Wind, Flood Tide*, 54–55.

17. Ibid., 63–64.
18. General Order No. 10, 12 Jul 1864, *ORN*, Ser. I, 21:397–98; Canby to Farragut, 26 and 29 Jul 1864, Ibid., 388, 390.
19. General Order No. 11, 29 Jul 1864, Ibid., 398.
20. Farragut to Capt. T. A. Jenkins, 3 Aug 1864, Ibid., 403.
21. Farragut to Cdr. T. H. Stevens, 4 Aug 1864, Ibid.
22. Craig L. Symonds, *Confederate Admiral: The Life and Wars of Franklin Buchanan* (Annapolis, MD: Naval Institute Press, 1999), 208–9.
23. Alden to Farragut, 5 Aug 1864, *ORN*, Ser. I, 21:508.
24. Quoted in Loyall Farragut, *The Life of David Glasgow Farragut, Fleet Admiral of the U.S. Navy* (New York: D. Appleton and Co., 1879), 425.
25. Friend, *West Wing, Flood Tide*, 186–87.
26. James P. Duffy, *Lincoln's Admiral: The Civil War Campaigns of David Farragut* (New York: John Wiley, 1997), 247–48.
27. Farragut's account of the battle with enclosures is in Farragut to Welles, 12 Aug 1864, *ORN*, Ser. I, 21:415–24; Charles L. Lewis, *David Glasgow Farragut: Our First Admiral*, (2 vols; Annapolis, MD: Naval Institute Press, 1943), II:280; Quote in Edward A. Pollard, *The Lost Cause: A New History of the War of the Confederates* (New York: E. B. Treat, 1866), 547. Other accounts are in Friend, *West Wind, Flood Tide*, 161–227; Symonds, *Confederate Admiral*, 208–19.
28. Page to Farragut, 9 Aug 1864, *ORN*, Ser. I, 21:563.
29. Page to Farragut, 23 Aug 1864, Ibid., 537.
30. See John C. Waugh, *Last Stand at Mobile* (Abilene, TX: McWhiney Foundation Press, 2001); see also Hearn, *Mobile Bay and the Mobile Campaign*, 146–211.
31. Robert G. Elliott, *Ironclad of the Roanoke: Gilbert Elliott's Albemarle* (Shippensburg, PA: White Mane Publishing Co., 1999), 164; Silverstone, *Civil War Navies*, 155.
32. French to Rear Adm. S. P. Lee, 21 Apr 1864, *ORN*, Ser. I, 9:641–42; Wessells to Maj. Gen. John J. Peck, 18 Aug 1864, Ibid., 652–56; Cooke to Mallory, 23 Apr 1864, 656–58.
33. Roe to Captain M. Smith, 6 May 1864, Ibid., 738–40; Cooke to Cdr. R. F. Pinkney, CS Navy, 7 May 1864, Ibid., 770–71.
34. Elliott, *Ironclad of the Roanoke*, 224–25.
35. For many reports and a drawing of the steam launch, see *ORN*, Ser. I, 10:616–24; a short readable biography of Cushing is Robert J. Schneller Jr., *Cushing: Civil War SEAL* (Washington, DC: Brassey's, 2004). The destruction of the *Albemarle* is on 75–85.
36. On the Fort Fisher campaign, see Charles M. Robinson III, *Hurricane of Fire: The Union Assault on Fort Fisher* (Annapolis, MD: Naval Institute Press, 1998); and Richard B. McCaslin, *The Last Stronghold: The Campaign for Fort Fisher* (Abilene, TX: McWhiney Foundation Press, 2003).
37. Porter, *Naval History of the Civil War*, 692; Robinson, *Hurricane of Fire*, 112, 118.
38. Rhind to Porter, 23 Dec 1864, *ORN*, Ser. I, 11:225–27, subsequent investigation and reports are in Ibid., 230–45; also Porter to Welles, 13 Feb 1865, Ibid., 420–21; Robinson, *The Last Stronghold*, 118–20.
39. Porter to Welles, 26, 27, and 29 Dec 1864, *ORN*, Ser. I, 11:254–60, 261–65.

40. Porter to Welles, 20 Jan 1865, Ibid., 444–45; Fox to Grant, 4 Jan 1865, Ibid., 409; Robinson, *The Last Stronghold*, 143–49.
41. Porter to Welles, 14, 15, 17 Jan 1865, *ORN*, Ser. I, 11:432–42; Robinson, *The Last Stronghold*, 150–90.
42. William A. Parker to Welles, 26 Jan 1865, *ORN*, Ser. I, 11:644–45; Mallory to Mitchell, 21 Jan 1865, Ibid., 803; Coski, *Capital Navy*, 196–209.
43. Semmes, *Memoirs of Service Afloat*, 812.
44. Ibid., Coski, *Capital Navy*, 220–22.

CHAPTER 14
1. John M. Coski, *The Confederate Navy* (Richmond, VA: Museum of the Confederacy, 2005), 5.

Glossary

Abaft: Further aft than. Toward or at the stern.

Abeam: On a line at right angles to a ship's keel.

Aft: Near, toward, or at the stern of the ship. The opposite of forward and fore.

Amidships/Midships: The center part of the ship. This is both between the fore and aft sections and between the port and starboard sides.

Astern: Behind a ship.

Athwart: At right angles to a point; across.

Aweigh: Said of an anchor immediately when it is broken out of the ground, as in anchor's aweigh.

Ballast: Additional weight placed low in the hull to improve stability and to enable a ship to carry more sail.

Bark: Sailing ship of three or more masts, all of which are square-rigged save for the after mast, which is fore-and-aft rigged.

Barkantine: Sailing ship of three masts, square rigged on the foremast with the main and mizzenmasts carrying fore-and-aft sails.

Battery: A group of guns. All the guns on one side of the ship.

Beam: The breadth of a ship, measured at the widest point. The waterline beam is the measurement of the breadth of the ship at the point where the hull touches the waterline.

Bearing: The horizontal direction of one terrestrial point from another.

Berth: The location where a ship is secured in port; a place to sit or sleep on a ship.

Bolt: Elongated solid shot designed to be fired by a rifled gun in order to penetrate armor.

Bow: The front end of a ship.

Bow Chaser: Cannon mounted on the fore part of the ship, used in pursuit of an enemy ship.

Breech: The back end of a cannon.

Breeching: Stout rope attached to the breech end of a gun to limit its recoil on board ship.

Bridge: The main control point of a ship.

Bulkheads: Partitions dividing a ship into watertight compartments.

Bulwark: The side of a ship above the upper deck.

Canister: Ammunition for a gun that consisted of a light, sheet-metal case containing many musket balls or scrap iron that broke apart on firing and was used for antipersonnel fire at close ranges, much like a shotgun.

Cannonade: Application of artillery to naval warfare; a ship's effort to attack an object.

Carronade: Short, light muzzle-loading gun designed to fire a large shell at low velocity.

Casemate: Armored enclosure on a ship behind which the main battery guns were located.

Close Hauled: When a ship has the wind before its beam or is sailing as close to the wind as possible.

Cockpit: Compartment within a ship where a surgeon attended to battle casualties.

Columbiad: Ambiguous term for a large, relatively short-barreled cannon designed to project shell and principally employed in fortresses and coastal defense.

Conn: To direct the helmsman as to the movements of the helm.

Crow's Nest: Lookout tower at or near the masthead.

Draft: Vertical distance from the lowest point of keel to the waterline; the depth of water at which a ship floats.

Enfilade: Gunfire directed from a flanking position along the length of the enemy battle line rather than from its front.

Fathom: Unit of measurement equal to six feet.

Fire Raft: Name applied to a boat, usually a flat boat, filled with combustibles or explosive materials to be set on fire and set adrift to float in the direction of enemy ships with the aim of destroying them.

Flag Captain: Captain of a vessel serving as the flagship for a fleet commander.

Flag Officer: Naval officer above the rank of captain, entitled to display a personal flag. Equivalent to general officer in the army.

Flagship: The ship that carries the flag officer of a squadron or fleet and carries his flag.

Fore: Toward or near the bow.

Forecastle: The part of the upper deck of a ship forward of the foremast.

Frigate: Fast, medium-sized, three-masted warship, usually mounting between thirty and fifty guns.

General Quarters: Call to man battle stations in preparation for action.

Gig: A light, long ship's boat.

Glassis: A slope running downward from a fortification.

Grape Shot: Cluster of balls, usually nine, around a center spindle in a canvas bag tied down with rope that resembled a bunch of grapes in appearance; employed against personnel and enemy boats.

Grapplings: Instruments with iron claws used to secure an enemy ship so that one's own crew might board it.

Gunboat: Small warship of shallow draft, designed primarily for use on rivers.

Gun Deck: The main deck of a frigate immediately below the spar deck, supporting the principal guns of the ship.

Gunner: A warrant officer whose duties are to take charge of artillery and ammunition of the ship and to train the crew in the use of its guns.

Gunport Lids: Outside covers or lids to protect the gunports from weather.

Hawser: A large rope used to tow, moor, or otherwise secure a ship.

Heading: Direction in which a ship's head is pointing; its course.

Heel: To list to one side as a result of wind pressure or shift in weight.

Hogging: Distortion in a ship's hull wherein it tends to arch up amidships, making the bow and stern lower and adversely affecting performance; the opposite of sagging.

Holystone: A soft sandstone used to scrub a ship's deck.

Hot Shot: Solid shot that was heated in a furnace for the purpose of setting an enemy ship on fire.

Hulk: An unrigged hull usually stripped of gear, rigging, engines, etc., and condemned as unseaworthy; hulks were frequently utilized as floating depots in a harbor or roadstead.

Hull: Actual body of a ship, excluding the superstructure, rigging, masts, and rudder.

Hulled: Shot in the hull, normally fired at point-blank range, not necessarily in modern warfare.

In Irons: Condition whereby, through lack of wind, a sailing ship is unable to move while heading into the wind and attempting to tack; also a term used to describe a shackled prisoner.

In Ordinary: A ship laid up in reserve.

Ironclad: Ship protected by iron plating.

Keel: Backbone of a ship. The lowest timber or steel plate running fore and aft along the centerline of the hull.

Knot: Unit of speed at sea, equal to one nautical mile per hour.

Laid Up: A sailing ship in reserve, without masts or rigging.

Larboard: Antiquated term for left side of a ship when facing toward the bow; officially replaced in the U.S. Navy by "port" in 1846 to avoid confusion with "starboard."

Lee: The direction toward which the wind blows.

Leeward: Downwind, away from the winds.

Letters of Marque: Government license or permit sanctioning the attack by privately owned ships on the ships of an enemy power.

Liberty: Authorized absence from duty.

Lock: The device used to explode a firearm or cannon.

Magazine: Area deep in a ship where ammunition is stored.

Main Battery: Ship's battery made up of its largest guns.

Match: Chemically treated wick or cord used to set off firearms or powder.

Midships: See *amidships*.

Monitor: Warship with low freeboard and a revolving gun turret.

Mortar: Short weapon, usually fixed on its mount at forty-five degrees elevation, used for plunging fire to project shell at very high angles over obstacles.

Mortar Boat: Vessel carrying a mortar.

Nautical Mile: Unit of measurement at sea, equal to 6,076 feet.

Parapet: Wall used to screen troops from frontal enemy fire.

Picket: Individual or ship so positioned to warn of the approach of an enemy.

Pilot: A qualified navigator authorized to pilot or direct incoming/outgoing ships in a particular pilotage area.

Pilothouse: A forward deck house used for navigating a ship.

Pivot Gun: Large gun usually mounted on the centerline of a ship on a rotating carriage and capable of extensive traverse.

Port: As a direction, it is the left hand side of the ship when facing forward.

Prize: Ship taken by force and later sold.

Quarterdeck: Part of the deck that is designated for both official and ceremonial functions. It is also where crew members board the ship by gangways.

Rake: To fire projectiles the length of an enemy's ship from its bow or stern.

Ram: Ship with a metal projection at its bow, usually below the waterline, used to attack and sink an opposing ship.

Rate: Class of warship determined by the number of its guns (in sailing warships generally from first rate of one hundred guns or more to sixth rate of thirty-two guns); the level of a sailor's rating.

Rating: Grade below the rank of officer.

Razee: Ship that has had one or more decks removed.

Receiving Ship: Older ship stripped of its guns and used to receive new recruits or seamen awaiting reassignment.

Reefer: Lower deck colloquialism for midshipman.

Rifled Gun: Gun with spiral grooves or rifling in its barrel that imparts spin to a projectile along its longer axis, yielding greatly improved range and accuracy.

Rigging: Ropes, chains, and other gear used to support and position the masts and sails of a ship.

River Gunboat: Small warship carrying one or more guns, with a broad underwater body and a shallow draft. Formerly used in inland waters.

Round Shot: A ball of iron the size of which is expressed by its weight or the diameter of its gun's bore.

Rudder: Device for steering a ship, usually fitted at the stern.

Schooner: Sailing ship with two or more masts, fore-and-aft rigged.

Scuttling: The intentional letting of water into a ship's hull in order to sink the ship.

Sheer: To turn aside sharply, swerve.

Shoal: Shallow water formed by a sandbar or rising ground and dangerous to navigation by deep-draft ships.

Side-wheeler: Steamboat driven by two paddle wheels amidships, one on each side.

Sloop-of-war: Fore-and-aft rigged sailing ship with its guns on the open, spar deck only.

Snag Boat: Powerful steamboat used to remove obstructions from the water.

Sound: Narrow passage of water between land masses; to find the water's depth by measuring the distance from the keel to the water's bottom.

Spar Deck: Top deck of a ship, exposed to the weather.

Squadron: Detachment of ships on an expedition commanded by a flag officer.

Starboard: The right-hand side of the ship when facing forward.

Stern: The aft end of the ship.

Superstructure: The part of a ship above the main deck.

Tender: Small ship or boat traveling in concert with a larger ship and used to transport men and supplies to it.

Tinclad: Light-draft gunboats used in riverine operations, usually protected by iron armor less than an inch thick.

Torpedo: Nineteenth-century term for mine.

Trunnions: Two knobs or arms that project from opposite sides of the barrel of an artillery piece that support it in its carriage or mounting.

Van: The foremost division of any naval armament, or the part that leads way into battle or advances first in the order of sailing.

Watch: Period of time in which the nautical day is divided, usually in four-hour intervals.

Weather Decks: Decks open to the wind and sea.

Selective Bibliography

Anderson, Bern. *By Sea and by River: The Naval History of the Civil War*. New York: Knopf, 1962.

Ballard, Michael B. *Vicksburg: The Campaign that Opened the Mississippi*. Chapel Hill: University of North Carolina Press, 2004.

Baxter, James Phinney III. *The Introduction of the Ironclad Warship*. Annapolis, MD: Naval Institute Press, 2001. [Reprint of Harvard University Press, 1933 ed.]

Bearss, Edwin C. *Hardluck Ironclad: The Sinking and Salvage of the Cairo*. Baton Rouge: Louisiana State University Press, 1966.

Bell, John. *Confederate Seadog: John Taylor Wood in War and Exile*. Jefferson, NC: McFarland, 2002.

Bennett, Frank M. *The Monitor and the Navy Under Steam*. Boston: Houghton Mifflin, 1900.

Boynton, Charles B. *History of the Navy During the Rebellion*. 2 vols. New York: D. Appleton, 1867–68.

Brooke, George M. Jr., ed. *John M. Brooke: Naval Scientist and Educator*. Charlottesville: University Press of Virginia, 1980.

———. *Ironclads and Big Guns of the Confederacy: The Journal and Letters of John M. Brooke*. Columbia: University of South Carolina Press, 2003.

Browne, Julius Henri. *Four Years in Secessia*. Hartford, CT: O. D. Case, 1865; Reprint. Arno Press, 1970.

Browning, Michael J. *Union Jacks: Yankee Sailors in the Civil War*. Chapel Hill: University of North Carolina Press, 2004.

Browning, Robert M. Jr. *From Cape Charles to Cape Fear: The North Atlantic Blockading Squadron During the Civil War*. Tuscaloosa: University of Alabama Press, 1993.

———. *Success Is All That Was Expected: The South Atlantic Blockading Squadron During the Civil War*. Dulles, VA: Brassey's, 2002.

Bulloch, James Dunwody. *The Secret Service of the Confederate States in Europe, or How the Confederate Cruisers Were Equipped*. New York: Modern Library, 2001.

Campbell, R. Thomas. *Academy on the James: The Confederate Naval School*. Shippensburg, PA: Burd Street Press, 1999.

———. *Fire & Thunder: Exploits of the Confederate States Navy*. Shippensburg, PA: Burd Street Press, 1997.

———. *Southern Service on Land and Sea: The Wartime Journal of Robert Watson, CSA/CSN*. Knoxville: University of Tennessee Press, 2002.

Canney, Donald L. *Lincoln's Navy: The Ships, Men and Organization, 1861–65*. Annapolis, MD: Naval Institute Press, 1997.

———. *The Old Steam Navy: Frigates, Sloops, and Gunboats, 1815–1885*. Annapolis, MD: Naval Institute Press, 1990.

———. *The Old Steam Navy: Ironclads, 1842–1885*. Annapolis, MD: Naval Institute Press, 1993.

Conrad, James Lee. *Rebel Reefers: The Organization and Midshipmen of the Confederate States Naval Academy*. Cambridge, MA: Da Capo Press, 2003.

Cook, Adrian. *The Alabama Claims: American Politics and Anglo-American Relations, 1865–1872*. Ithaca, NY: Cornell University Press, 1975.

Coombe, Jack D. *Gunfire Around the Gulf: The Last Major Naval Campaigns of the Civil War*. New York: Bantam Books, 1999.

———. *Thunder Along the Mississippi: The River Battles that Split the Confederacy*. New York: Sarpedon, 1996.

Coski, John M. *Capital Navy: The Men, Ships and Operations of the James River Squadron*. Campbell, CA: Savas Publishing, 1996.

Dalzell, George W. *The Flight from the Flag: The Continuing Effect of the Civil War upon the American Carrying Trade*. Chapel Hill: University of North Carolina Press, 1940.

Daniel, Larry J., and Lynn N. Bock. *Island No. 10: Struggle for the Mississippi Valley*. Tuscaloosa: University of Alabama Press, 1996.

Davis, Charles H. Jr. *Life of Charles Henry Davis, Rear Admiral, 1807–77*. Boston: Houghton Mifflin, 1899.

Davis, William C. *Duel Between the First Ironclads*. Garden City, NY: Doubleday, 1975.

deKay, James Tertius. *Monitor*. New York: Walker, 1997.

Duffy, James. P. *Lincoln's Admiral: The Civil War Campaigns of David Farragut*. New York: John Wiley, 1997.

Du Pont, Henry A. *Rear Admiral Samuel Francis Du Pont, United States Navy: A Biography*. New York: National Americana Society, 1926.

Du Pont, Samuel F. *Samuel F. Du Pont: A Selection from His Civil War Letters*. 3 vols. Ithaca, NY: Cornell University Press, 1969.

Elliott, Robert G. *Ironclad of the Roanoke: Gilbert Elliott's Albermarle*. Shippensburg, PA: White Mane Books, 1999.

Ferris, Norman B. *The Trent Affair: A Diplomatic Crisis*. Knoxville: University of Tennessee Press, 1977.

Fox, Gustavus. *Confidential Correspondence of Gustavus Vasa Fox, Assistant Secretary of the Navy, 1861–1865*. Eds. Robert Means Thompson and Richard Wainwright. New York: De Vinne Press, 1918.

Friend, Jack. *West Wind, Flood Tide: The Battle of Mobile Bay*. Annapolis, MD: Naval Institute Press, 2004.

Gosnell, Harper Allen. *Guns on the Western Waters*. Baton Rouge: Louisiana State University Press, 1949.

Grattan, John W. *Under the Blue Pennant, or Notes of a Naval Officer, 1863–1865*. Ed. Robert J. Schneller Jr. New York: John Wiley, 1999.

Greene, Jack, and Alessandro Massignani. *Ironclads at War: The Origins and Development of the Armored Warship, 1864–1891*. Conshohocken, PA: Combined Publishing, 1998.

Hackemer, Kurt. *The U.S. Navy and the Origins of the Military-Industrial Complex, 1847–1883*. Annapolis, MD: Naval Institute Press, 2001.

Hearn, Chester G. *Admiral David Dixon Porter: The Civil War Years*. Annapolis, MD: Naval Institute Press, 1996.

———. *Ellet's Brigade: The Strangest Outfit of All*. Baton Rouge: Louisiana State University Press, 2000.

———. *Gray Raiders of the Sea: How Eight Confederate Warships Destroyed the Union's High Seas Commerce*. Camden, MN: International Marine Publishing, 1992.

———. *Mobile Bay and the Mobile Campaign: The Last Great Battles of the Civil War*. Jefferson, NC: McFarland & Company, 1993.

Hicks, Brian, and Schyler Kropf. *Raising the Hunley: The Remarkable History and Recovery of the Lost Confederate Submarine*. New York: Ballantine Books, 2002.

Hoehling, A. A. *Damn the Torpedoes! Naval Incidents of the Civil War*. New York: Gramercy Books, 1999.

Horn, Stanley F. *Gallant Rebel: The Fabulous Cruise of the C.S.S. Shenandoah*. New Brunswick, NJ: Rutgers University Press, 1947.

Hoyt, Edwin P. *The Voyage of the Hunley*. Short Hills, NJ: Burford Books, 2002.

Hughes, Nathaniel Cheairs Jr. *The Battle of Belmont. Grant Strikes South*. Chapel Hill: The University of North Carolina Press, 1991.

Johnson, Ludwell H. *Red River Campaign: Politics and Cotton in the Civil War*. Kent, OH: Kent State University Press, 1993.

Johnson, Robert Erwin. *Rear Admiral John Rodgers, 1812–1882*. Annapolis, MD: U.S. Naval Institute Press, 1967.

Joiner, Gary Dillard. *One Damn Blunder from Beginning to End: The Red River Campaign of 1864*. Wilmington, DE: Scholarly Resources, 2003.

Jones, Howard. *Union in Peril: The Crisis over British Intervention in the Civil War*. Lincoln: University of Nebraska Press, 1992.

Jones, Robert A. *Confederate Corsair: The Life of Lt. Charles W. "Savez" Read*. Mechanicsburg, PA: Stackpole Books, 2000.

Jones, Virgil Carrington. *The Civil War at Sea: Vol. One: The Blockaders*. New York: Holt, Rinehart, Winston, 1960.

Keeler, William Frederick. *Aboard the U.S.S. Monitor: 1862*. Edited by Robert W. Daly. Annapolis, MD: Naval Institute Press, 1964.

Kell, John McIntosh. *Recollections of a Naval Life*. Washington, DC: Neale, 1900.

Lamson, Roswell H. *Lamson of the Gettysburg: The Civil War Letters of Lieutenant Roswell H. Lamson, U.S. Navy*. Eds. James M. McPherson and Patricia R. McPherson. New York: Oxford University Press, 1997.

Lewis, Charles Lee. *Admiral Franklin Buchanan*. Baltimore, MD: Norman, Remington, 1929.

———. *David Glasgow Farragut: Admiral in the Making*. Annapolis, MD: Naval Institute Press, 1941.

Luraghi, Raimondo. *A History of the Confederate Navy*. Tr. Paolo D. Coletta. Annapolis, MD: Naval Institute Press, 1996.

Macartney, Clarence Edward. *Mr. Lincoln's Admirals*. New York: Funk & Wagnalls, 1956.

Marvel, William. *The* Alabama *and the* Kearsarge: *The Sailor's Civil War*. Chapel Hill: University of North Carolina Press, 1996.

McCaslin, Richard B. *The Last Stronghold: The Campaign for Fort Fisher*. Abilene, TX: McWhiney Foundation Press, McMurry University, 2003.

McNeil, Jim. *Masters of the Shoals: Tales of the Cape Fear Pilots Who Ran the Union Blockade*. Cambridge, MA: Da Capo Press, 2003.

Melton, Maurice. *The Confederate Ironclads.* New York: Thomas Yoseloff, 1968.

Merli, Frank J. *Great Britain and the Confederate Navy, 1861–1865.* Bloomington: Indiana University Press, 1970.

Merrill, James M. *Battle Flags South: The Story of the Civil War Navies on the Western Waters.* Rutherford, NJ: Fairleigh Dickinson University Press, 1970.

———. *DuPont, the Making of an Admiral.* New York: Dodd, Mead, 1986.

Milligan, John D. *Gunboats Down the Mississippi.* Annapolis, MD: Naval Institute Press, 1965.

———., comp. *From the Fresh-Water Navy, 1861–64: The Letters of Acting Master's Mate Henry R. Browne and Acting Ensign Symmes E. Browne.* Annapolis, MD: Naval Institute Press, 1970.

Mindell, David A. *War, Technology, and Experience Aboard the USS* Monitor. Baltimore, MD: Johns Hopkins University Press, 2000.

Morgan, Murray. *Dixie Raider: The Saga of the C.S.S.* Shenandoah. New York: Dutton, 1948.

Musicant, Ivan. *Divided Waters: The Naval History of the Civil War.* New York: HarperCollins, 1995.

Niven, John. *Gideon Welles, Lincoln's Secretary of the Navy.* New York: Oxford University Press, 1973.

Owsley, Frank L. Jr. *The C.S.S.* Florida: *Her Building and Operations.* Tuscaloosa: University of Alabama Press, 1965.

Page, Dave. *Ships Versus Shore: Civil War Engagements along Southern Shores and Rivers.* Nashille, TN: Rutledge Hill Press, 1994.

Paullin, Charles Oscar. *Paullin's History of Naval Administration, 1775–1911.* Annapolis, MD: Naval Institute Press, 1968.

Perry, Milton F. *Infernal Machines: The Story of Confederate Submarine and Mine Warfare.* Baton Rouge: Louisiana State University Press, 1965.

Porter, David Dixon. *Incidents and Anecdotes of the Civil War.* New York: D. Appleton, 1985.

———. *Naval History of the Civil War.* New York: Sherman, 1886.

Quarstein, John V. *C.S.S.* Virginia: *Mistress of Hampton Roads.* Appomattox, VA: H. E. Howard, 2000.

Ragan, Mark K. *Union and Confederate Submarine Warfare in the Civil War.* Mason City, IA: Savas Publishing, 1999.

Ramold, Steven J. *Slaves, Sailors, Citizens: African Americans in the Union Navy.* DeKalb: Northern Illinois University Press, 2002.

Reed, Rowena. *Combined Operations in the Civil War.* Annapolis, MD: Naval Institute Press, 1978.

Ringle, Dennis J. *Life in Mr. Lincoln's Navy.* Annapolis, MD: Naval Institute Press, 1998.

Roberts, Walter A. *Semmes of the* Alabama. New York: Bobbs-Merrill, 1938.

Roberts, William H. *Civil War Ironclads: The U.S. Navy and Industrial Mobilization.* Baltimore, MD: Johns Hopkins University Press, 2002.

———. *New Ironsides in the Civil War.* Annapolis, MD: Naval Institute Press, 1999.

Robinson, Charles M. III. *Hurricane of Fire: The Union Assault on Fort Fisher.* Annapolis, MD: Naval Institute Press, 1998.

——. *Shark of the Confederacy: The Story of the CSS* Alabama. Annapolis, MD: Naval Institute Press, 1995.

Robinson, William M. Jr. *The Confederate Privateers*. Columbia: University of South Carolina Press, 1980. [Reprint of New Haven, CT: Yale University Press, 1928.]

Scharf, J. Thomas. *History of the Confederate States Navy*. New York: Random House, 1996. [Reprint.]

Schneller, Robert J. Jr. *A Quest for Glory: A Biography of Rear Admiral John A. Dahlgren*. Annapolis, MD: Naval Institute Press, 1996.

——. *Cushing: Civil War SEAL*. Washington, DC: Brassey's, 2004.

——. *Farragut: America's First Admiral*. Washington, DC: Brassey's, 2002.

Semmes, Raphael. *Memoirs of Service Afloat: During the War Between the States*. Secaucus, NJ: Blue & Grey Press, 1987. [Reprint of Baltimore, MD: Kelly, Piet, 1869.]

Shaw, David W. *Sea Wolf of the Confederacy: The Daring Civil War Raids of Naval Lt. Charles W. Read*. New York: Free Press, 2004.

Shea, William L., and Terrence J. Winschel. *Vicksburg Is the Key: The Struggle for the Mississippi River*. Lincoln: University of Nebraska Press, 2003.

Shingleton, Royce. *High Seas Confederate: The Life and Times of John Newland Maffitt*. Columbia: University of South Carolina Press, 1994.

Silverstone, Paul H. *Warships of the Civil War Navies*. Annapolis, MD: Naval Institute Press, 1989.

Sinclair, Arthur. *Two Years on the* Alabama. Boston: Lee and Shepard, 1895.

Slagle, Jay. *Ironclad Captain: Seth Ledyard Phelps and the U.S. Navy, 1841–1864*. Kent, OH, and London: Kent State University Press, 1996.

Smith, Gene A. *Iron and Heavy Guns: Duel Between the* Monitor *and* Merrimac. Abilene, TX: McWhiney Foundation Press, 1996.

Soley, James Russell. *The Blockade and the Cruisers*. New York: Charles Scribner's Sons, 1983.

Stern, Philip Van Doren. *The Confederate Navy: A Pictorial History*. Garden City, NY: Doubleday, 1962.

Still, William N. Jr. *Confederate Shipbuilding*. Columbia: University of South Carolina Press, 1987.

——. *Iron Afloat: The Story of the Confederate Armorclads*. Columbia: University of South Carolina Press, 1985.

——, ed. *The Confederate Navy: The Ships, Men and Organization, 1861–65*. Annapolis, MD: Naval Institute Press, 1997.

Summersell, Charles G. *CSS* Alabama: *Builder, Captain, and Plans*. Tuscaloosa: University of Alabama Press, 1985.

——. *The Cruise of C.S.S.* Sumter. Tuscaloosa, AL: Confederate Publishing, 1965.

Surdam, David G. *Northern Naval Superiority and the Economics of the American Civil War*. Colombia: University of South Carolina Press, 2001.

Symonds, Craig L. *Confederate Admiral: The Life and Wars of Franklin Buchanan*. Annapolis, MD: Naval Institute Press, 1999.

Taylor, John M. *Confederate Raider: Raphael Semmes of the* Alabama. Washington, DC: Brassey's, 1984.

———. *Semmes: Rebel Raider*. Dulles, VA: Potomac Books, 2004.

Tucker, Spencer C. *A Short History of the Civil War at Sea*. Wilmington, DE: Scholarly Resources, 2002.

———. *Andrew Foote: Civil War Admiral on Western Waters*. Annapolis, MD: Naval Institute Press, 2000.

———. *Arming the Fleet: U.S. Navy Ordnance in the Muzzle-Loading Era*. Annapolis, MD: Naval Institute Press, 1989.

———. *Raphael Seemmes and the* Alabama. Abilene, TX: McWhiney Foundation Press, 1996.

———. *Unconditional Surrender: The Capture of Forts Henry and Donelson*. Abilene, TX: McWhiney Foundation Press, McMurry University, 2001.

Underwood, Rodman L. *Waters of Discord: The Union Blockade of Texas During the Civil War*. Jefferson, NC: McFarland, 2003.

U.S. Congress. *Report of the Joint Committee on the Conduct of the War, 1863–1866: The Red River Expedition*. 1865. Reprint. Millwood, NY: Krauss Reprint Co., 1977.

U.S. Navy Department. *Official Records of the Union and Confederate Navies in the War of the Rebellion*. 30 vols. Washington, DC: Government Printing Office, 1896–1922.

U.S. Navy Department, Naval History Division. *Civil War Naval Chronology, 1861– 1865*. Washington, DC: Government Printing Office, 1971.

———. Riverine Warfare. *The U.S. Navy's Operations on Inland Waters*. Revised edition. Washington, DC: Government Printing Office, 1969.

Walke, Henry. *Naval Scenes and Reminiscences of the Civil War in the United States*. New York: F. R. Reed, 1877.

Watson, William. *The Civil War Adventures of a Blockade Runner*. Intro. J. Barton Arnold III. College Station: Texas A&M Press, 2001.

Waugh, John C. *Last Stand at Mobile*. Abilene, TX: McWhiney Foundation Press, McMurry University, 2001.

Weddle, Kevin J. *Lincoln's Tragic Admiral: The Life of Samuel Francis Du Pont*. Charlottesville: University of Virginia Press, 2005.

Welles, Gideon. *Diary of Gideon Welles, Secretary of the Navy Under Lincoln and Johnson*, 3 vols. Boston: Houghton Mifflin, 1911.

Wells, Tom H. *The Confederate Navy: A Study in Organization*. Tuscalooosa: University of Alabama Press, 1971.

Whittle, William C. Jr. *The Voyage of the CSS* Shenandoah: *A Memorable Cruise*. Introduction and annotations by D. Alan Harris and Anne B. Harris. Tuscaloosa: University of Alabama Press, 2005.

Wilkes, Charles. *Autobiography of Rear Admiral Charles Wilkes, U.S. Navy 1798–1877*. Eds. William James Morgan et al. Washington, DC: Department of the Navy, 1978.

Wise, Stephen R. *Gate of Hell: Campaign for Charleston Harbor, 1863*. Columbia: University of South Carolina Press, 1994.

———. *Lifeline of the Confederacy. Blockade Running During the Civil War*. Columbia: University of South Carolina Press, 1988.

Index

About the Author

SPENCER C. TUCKER retired from teaching in 2003. He was a professor at Texas Christian University for thirty years, and in the last six years he held the John Biggs Chair in Military History at the Virginia Military Institute. Dr. Tucker is the author or editor of twenty-six books on military and naval history. His books treating the naval Civil War include *Arming the Fleet: U.S. Navy Ordnance in the Muzzle-loading Era, Raphael Semmes and the* Alabama, *The Big Guns: Civil War Siege, Seacoast and Naval Cannon* (with Edwin Olmstead and Wayne Stark), *Andrew Hull Foote: Civil War Admiral on Western Waters, "Unconditional Surrender": The Capture of Forts Henry and Donelson, February 1862,* and *A Short History of the Civil War at Sea.* His most recent book, published by the Naval Institute Press, is *Stephen Decatur: A Life Most Bold and Daring,* which won the Theodore and Franklin D. Roosevelt Naval History Prize for 2004. Dr. Tucker and his wife, Beverly, live in Lexington, Virginia.

The Naval Institute Press is the book-publishing arm of the U.S. Naval Institute, a private, nonprofit, membership society for sea service professionals and others who share an interest in naval and maritime affairs. Established in 1873 at the U.S. Naval Academy in Annapolis, Maryland, where its offices remain today, the Naval Institute has members worldwide.

Members of the Naval Institute support the education programs of the society and receive the influential monthly magazine *Proceedings* and discounts on fine nautical prints and on ship and aircraft photos. They also have access to the transcripts of the Institute's Oral History Program and get discounted admission to any of the Institute-sponsored seminars offered around the country. Discounts are also available to the colorful bimonthly magazine *Naval History*.

The Naval Institute's book-publishing program, begun in 1898 with basic guides to naval practices, has broadened its scope to include books of more general interest. Now the Naval Institute Press publishes about seventy titles each year, ranging from how-to books on boating and navigation to battle histories, biographies, ship and aircraft guides, and novels. Institute members receive significant discounts on the Press's more than eight hundred books in print.

Full-time students are eligible for special half-price membership rates. Life memberships are also available.

For more information about Naval Institute Press books that are currently available, visit www.usni.org/press/books. To learn about joining the U.S. Naval Institute, please write to:

Customer Service
U.S. Naval Institute
291 Wood Road
Annapolis, MD 21402-5034
Telephone: (800) 233-8764
Fax: (410) 571-1703
Web address: www.navalinstitute.org

CPSIA information can be obtained
at www.ICGtesting.com
Printed in the USA
BVHW030322180123
656425BV00029B/56